STUDIES OF THE AMERICAS

edited by

Maxine Molyneux

Institute for the Study of the Americas
University of London
School of Advanced Study

Titles in this series are multidisciplinary studies of aspects of the societies of the hemisphere, particularly in the areas of politics, economics, history, anthropology, sociology, and the environment. The series covers a comparative perspective across the Americas, including Canada and the Caribbean as well as the United States and Latin America.

Titles in this series published by Palgrave Macmillan:

Cuba's Military 1990–2005: Revolutionary Soldiers during Counter-Revolutionary Times
 By Hal Klepak

The Judicialization of Politics in Latin America
 Edited by Rachel Sieder, Line Schjolden, and Alan Angell

Latin America: A New Interpretation
 By Laurence Whitehead

Appropriation as Practice: Art and Identity in Argentina
 By Arnd Schneider

America and Enlightenment Constitutionalism
 Edited by Gary L. McDowell and Johnathan O'Neill

Vargas and Brazil: New Perspectives
 Edited by Jens R. Hentschke

When Was Latin America Modern?
 Edited by Nicola Miller and Stephen Hart

Debating Cuban Exceptionalism
 Edited by Bert Hoffman and Laurence Whitehead

Caribbean Land and Development Revisited
 Edited by Jean Besson and Janet Momsen

Cultures of the Lusophone Black Atlantic
 Edited by Nancy Priscilla Naro, Roger Sansi-Roca, and David H. Treece

Democratization, Development, and Legality: Chile, 1831–1973
 By Julio Faundez

The Hispanic World and American Intellectual Life, 1820–1880
 By Iván Jaksic'

The Role of Mexico's Plural *in Latin American Literary and Political Culture: From Tlatelolco to the "Philanthropic Ogre"*
 By John King

Faith and Impiety in Revolutionary Mexico
 Edited by Matthew Butler

Reinventing Modernity in Latin America: Intellectuals Imagine the Future, 1900–1930
 By Nicola Miller

The Republican Party and Immigration Politics: From Proposition 187 to George W. Bush
 By Andrew Wroe

The Political Economy of Hemispheric Integration: Responding to Globalization in the Americas
 Edited by Diego Sánchez-Ancochea and Kenneth C. Shadlen

Ronald Reagan and the 1980s: Perceptions, Policies, Legacies
    Edited by Cheryl Hudson and Gareth Davies
Wellbeing and Development in Peru: Local and Universal Views Confronted
    Edited by James Copestake
The Federal Nation: Perspectives on American Federalism
    Edited by Iwan W. Morgan and Philip J. Davies
Base Colonies in the Western Hemisphere, 1940–1967
    By Steven High
Beyond Neoliberalism in Latin America? Societies and Politics at the Crossroads
    Edited by John Burdick, Philip Oxhorn, and Kenneth M. Roberts
Visual Synergies in Fiction and Documentary Film from Latin America
    Edited by Miriam Haddu and Joanna Page
Cuban Medical Internationalism: Origins, Evolution, and Goals
    By John M. Kirk and H. Michael Erisman
Governance after Neoliberalism in Latin America
    Edited by Jean Grugel and Pía Riggirozzi
Modern Poetics and Hemispheric American Cultural Studies
    By Justin Read
Youth Violence in Latin America: Gangs and Juvenile Justice in Perspective
    Edited by Gareth A. Jones and Dennis Rodgers
The Origins of Mercosur
    By Gian Luca Gardini
Belize's Independence & Decolonization in Latin America: Guatemala, Britain, and the UN
    By Assad Shoman
Post-Colonial Trinidad: An Ethnographic Journal
    By Colin Clarke and Gillian Clarke
The Nitrate King: A Biography of "Colonel" John Thomas North
    By William Edmundson
Negotiating the Free Trade Area of the Americas
    By Zuleika Arashiro

Negotiating the Free Trade Area of the Americas

Zuleika Arashiro

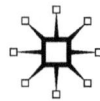

NEGOTIATING THE FREE TRADE AREA OF THE AMERICAS
Copyright © Zuleika Arashiro, 2011.
Softcover reprint of the hardcover 1st edition 2011 978-0-230-11279-7
All rights reserved.

First published in 2011 by
PALGRAVE MACMILLAN®
in the United States—a division of St. Martin's Press LLC,
175 Fifth Avenue, New York, NY 10010.

Where this book is distributed in the UK, Europe and the rest of the world, this is by Palgrave Macmillan, a division of Macmillan Publishers Limited, registered in England, company number 785998, of Houndmills, Basingstoke, Hampshire RG21 6XS.

Palgrave Macmillan is the global academic imprint of the above companies and has companies and representatives throughout the world.

Palgrave® and Macmillan® are registered trademarks in the United States, the United Kingdom, Europe and other countries.

ISBN 978-1-349-29473-2   ISBN 978-0-230-11905-5 (eBook)
DOI 10.1057/9780230119055

Library of Congress Cataloging-in-Publication Data is available from the Library of Congress.

A catalogue record of the book is available from the British Library.

Design by Newgen Imaging Systems (P) Ltd., Chennai, India.

First edition: May 2011

To my parents, Hiroko and Jorge, my tree.

But the examination of the object is not an isolated act; it takes place in a context which is coloured by values and collective-unconscious, volitional impulses.

(Karl Mannheim, *Ideology and Utopia*, 1936)

Contents

List of Tables and Figure	viii
List of Abbreviations	ix
Acknowledgments	xi
Map of the Americas	xii

Part I   Analytical Framework

Introduction	3
Chapter 1	
Trade Cooperation as a Policy Idea	11

Part II   The FTAA Negotiations

Chapter 2	
The FTAA Negotiations	23

Part III   Background

Chapter 3	
Economic Paradigms and Trade Regionalism in Latin America	51
Chapter 4	
Lessons from Economic Cooperation in the Americas	65

Part IV   Case Studies

Chapter 5	
U.S. Foreign Trade Policy: Leadership in a Constrained System	79
Chapter 6	
Brazilian Foreign Trade Policy: Instrument for an Autonomous Nation	109

Part V   Conclusion

Conclusion	143
Appendices	151
Notes	171
References	235
Index	267

Tables and Figure

Tables

2.1	Bilateral trade flow between the United States and selected countries, 1992 (%)	25
2.2	Structure of exports by integration group, 2002 and 2009 (% distribution)	29
3.1	Price variation of selected commodities (index 1985=100)	58
5.1	U.S. Free Trade Agreements, through July 2010	105

Figure

1.1	Analytical framework	19

Abbreviations

AFL-CIO	American Federation of Labor and Congress of Industrial Organizations
APEC	Asia Pacific Economic Cooperation
BRIC	Brazil, Russia, India, and China
CAMEX	Câmara de Comércio Exterior
CACM	Central American Common Market
CARICOM	Caribbean Community
CEB	Coalizão Empresarial Brasileira
CEPAL/ECLAC	Comisión Económica para América Latina y el Caribe/Economic Commission for Latin America and the Caribbean
CNBB	Confederação Nacional dos Bispos do Brasil
CNI	Confederação Nacional das Indústrias
CUSFTA	Canada–U.S. Free Trade Agreement
CUT	Central Única dos Trabalhadores
EAI	Enterprise for the Americas Initiative
EU	European Union
FTAA	Free Trade Area of the Americas
GATT	General Agreement on Tariffs and Trade
GSP	General System of Preferences
IDB	Inter-American Development Bank
IMF	International Monetary Fund
ISI	Import Substitution Industrialization
ALADI/LAIA	Asociación Latinoamericana de Integración/Latin American Integration Association
LAFTA	Latin American Free Trade Area
MDB	Movimento Democrático Brasileiro
MERCOSUR	Southern Common Market
NAFTA	North American Free Trade Agreement
PMDB	Partido do Movimento Democrático Brasileiro
PSDB	Partido da Social Democracia Brasileira
PRI	Partido Revolucionario Institucional
PT	Partido dos Trabalhadores
OAS	Organization of American States
SAFTA	South American Free Trade Area

SENALCA	Secretaria Nacional de Coordenação dos Assuntos Relacionados à Alca
REBRIP	Rede Brasileira pela Integração dos Povos
TPA	Trade Promotion Authority
UNASUL	Union of South American Nations
UNCTAD	United Nations Trade and Development Conference
USTR	Office of United States Trade Representative
WTO	World Trade Organization

Acknowledgments

I owe this book to my family in Brazil. Your patience and ability to trust are the best evidence of how beliefs influence behavior.

My initial encounter with the FTAA happened a decade ago, during my time at the Center for Latin American Studies, at Georgetown University. I am grateful to all the academics and friends with whom I shared the passion for *nuestra Latinoamerica*. Robin King, Marisol Reyes, Naomi Moniz, and Arturo Valenzuela, all contributed to the foundations of this work.

A certain distance from events helps us achieve clarity. I am particularly in debt to Barry Carr, Nick Bisley, and John Minns for their continuous academic support in Australia. I also thank Maxwell Cameron, Richard Feinberg, and Anthony Jarvis for their comments on my doctoral dissertation. To all those friends who have patiently supported me throughout these years of immersion in research, I extend my gratitude. I especially wish to thank Russell L. Marks, Sophie Mav, Vanessa Nakamura, Vantier Lima, and Italo Paiva. In your unique ways, you kept me grounded in the world beyond politics.

This project would not have been accomplished without the funding received through the Australian Government's Endeavour International Postgraduate Research Scholarship, and the La Trobe University Postgraduate Research Scholarship.

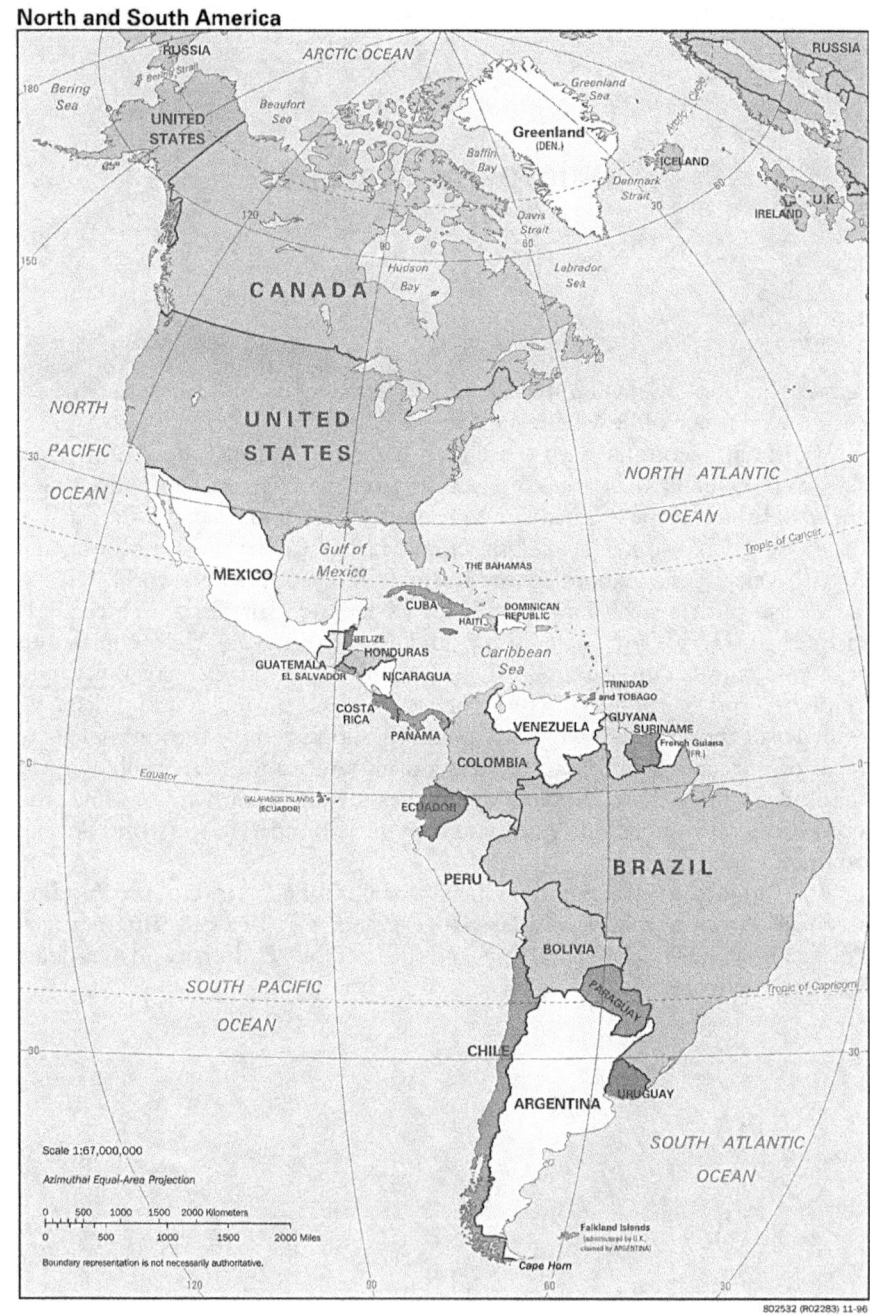

Map of the Americas

Part I

Analytical Framework

Introduction

In December 1994, representatives of thirty-four states in the Americas[1] gathered in Miami for the First Summit of the Americas. On the occasion they announced their commitment to work toward the formation of a Free Trade Area of the Americas (FTAA). For the first time in the history of inter-American relations, the ideal of economic cooperation was grounded in a reality that signaled hemispheric convergence toward market economy and electoral democracy. By late 2003, when the FTAA negotiations stagnated, that convergence was not as clear. Almost a decade after the launching of the FTAA idea, the negotiation process was paralyzed and was followed by fragmented trade agreements that defied the initial attempt of hemisphere-wide cooperation.

This book looks at the failed attempt to form a Western Hemisphere free trade area—the FTAA—which, if consolidated, would have created the world's largest economic bloc. It examines the reasons why the two main players in the negotiations, Brazil and the United States, decided to paralyze the negotiation process a decade after the FTAA idea was raised.

The failure of the negotiations is attributed to the fact that the FTAA, conceived as an *inter-American policy idea* that required cooperation among thirty-four countries, was incompatible with the predominant views of U.S. and Brazilian decision makers as to how they could and should conduct their countries' foreign trade policy in the Western Hemisphere. In the end, for both the United States and Brazil, the strategy of trade bilateralism prevailed over the idea of a hemisphere-wide trade agreement, and neither country provided the leadership required to transform the FTAA idea into an actual policy.

After working with policy research to the FTAA negotiations, I was surprised at the resistance shown by many in the FTAA "expert community" against the idea that politics would play a determining role in the negotiations. Their passionate defense of the viability of the initiative gradually evidenced that beneath highly technical discussions, the essential division between defenders and critics of the project ultimately resided in their different beliefs with regard to the space that states should allow for noneconomic considerations when formulating their foreign trade policies.

My decision to analyze the FTAA as a policy idea was also influenced by the realization that an assessment focused exclusively on material interests was insufficient to explain two aspects of the paralysis of the negotiations. First, a purely material assessment could not account for the specific choice of abandoning the negotiations when other alternatives were still available, such as a slow but diplomatic continuation of the process in parallel with the then alive multilateral negotiations of the World Trade Organization's Doha Round (WTO Doha Round). In fact, the diplomatic solution was the alternative Brazil and other members of the Southern Common Market (Mercosur) followed in their trade negotiations with the European Union. Second, a material incentives analysis could not explain the timing of the decision, that is, why it occurred in 2003, and not before.

Moreover, in an academic field dominated by models inspired by and designed to explain the foreign policy of Western democracies, a significant incentive for this book was the possibility of examining material and ideational components influencing foreign trade policymaking in a developing country.[2] The case of Brazil challenges systemic explanations about the foreign policy of developing countries, in which inferences about the structure of international distribution of power often lead to a disregard for the space for agency in these countries.

Contrary to approaches that simplify the political dynamic within developing countries and minimize the nuances in power relations, this book shows that even within the constraints of the international environment, governments are still capable of pursuing particular notions of development. It is because national governments hold different views of the international role of their country that international relations continue to be characterized by diversity and unpredictability. As the experience of coalitions of developing countries on matters of public health and intellectual property rights in the WTO Doha Round demonstrated, developing states can use nonconventional sources of power, such as ethical principles, to confront the material and knowledge predominance of developed states.[3] The repeated deadlock in the negotiations in agriculture is also revealing of how particular views of power and capability lead states to undertake differentiated levels of risk.

This book offers the first detailed reconstruction of the FTAA as a policy idea. It relies on historical narrative as its main base of analysis, embedding foreign trade policies and institutions into the national settings in which they are shaped. The literature on the new trade regionalism, of which the FTAA initiative was a manifestation, is still weak in empirical studies on how the decision to move toward such agreements first takes place within states. The detailed examination of a case of failure in trade negotiations provides us with the opportunity to revise assumptions about state motivations and to place greater emphasis on the process that lies at the center of international negotiations.

Although this book explores the foreign trade policy of Brazil and the United States only, the foreign trade policies of individual Latin American countries in relation to the United States remain a rich field for further comparative analysis, which scholarly value goes beyond Latin America. The various bilateral trade agreements involving Latin American countries indicate that how individual states perceive a particular set of variables as a stimulus or constraint will vary according to material considerations and to the beliefs of decision makers, and that such variations are determinant for their decision to cooperate, even if through asymmetrical arrangements.

The New Trade Regionalism

Since the mid-1980s, the number of regional trade agreements has increased at an impressive pace. While between 1948 and 1994, only 44 trade agreements had been notified to the General Agreement on Tariffs and Trade (GATT), by December 2008, the number of notifications had risen to 421 agreements.[4]

This rapid increase in the number of regional trade agreements has challenged the multilateral trading system from many angles. It has evolved in parallel to the first years of the institutional development of the WTO, showing that at the same time that states were expressing a commitment to an intergovernmental organization, they were adopting individual solutions to face a highly competitive international environment. The proliferation of trade agreements exemplifies the permanent tension between collective compromises and the individual interests of a diverse group of member states, within multilateral systems. As argued by Barton et al., the trade regime "authoritative gap"—most recently exposed in the Doha Round crisis—has derived from its inability to keep pace with the "changing interests and power of its members."[5]

The GATT recognizes this tension between the ideal of shared international norms to promote a free trade system and the need to accommodate the various interests of individual states. Similar to what occurs in other multilateral institutions, in the GATT/WTO system, the approval of shared rules has depended heavily on the incorporation of flexible mechanisms that accommodate the interests of the various parties. This flexibility was particularly important in the post–Second World War period, in which embedded liberalism predominated.[6] Despite its efforts to regulate exceptions, the system has been unable to contain the proliferation of trade agreements. The free trade agreements notified to the WTO have not been regarded as violating Article XXIV of the GATT, even though very few would fit neatly into the category of free trade area or custom union covering substantially all trade.[7]

The main triggers for the current wave of trade regionalism can be located in the core areas of the world. The economic recession of the 1970s had raised the costs for individual states, and particularly for the United States, of continuing to defend the primacy of multilateralism as a support mechanism for a liberal economic order. In that context, the difficulties in advancing U.S. trade priorities through the GATT system, the economic rise of Japan, and the European Community's announcement of its intention to create a Single European Market only increased U.S. fears of erosion of its hegemonic position. With the Canada-U.S. free trade agreement (CUSFTA, 1988) and the North American Free Trade Agreement (NAFTA, 1992) the United States signaled that, like other economic powers, it was willing to look for alternatives outside the multilateral system as a mechanism to cope with increasing international competition.

In contrast to the experiences of the 1950s and the 1960s, the latest wave of trade regionalism has evolved in a period of intense economic liberalization.[8] In many cases, autonomous trade liberalization reforms have preceded the move toward regional trade agreements,[9] and the regional space has been described as a platform for better insertion in the international economy. The instrumental use of regional trade liberalization to build competitiveness has been particularly prominent in trade initiatives involving developing countries that had once tried inward-looking forms of regionalism, such as those in Latin America and in Southeast Asia.[10]

The new trade regionalism has been also characterized by an expansion of the scope of the agreements. The introduction of behind-the-border issues into the new generation of trade agreements has brought to the trade sphere a series of issues previously addressed as matters of domestic policy. In fact the regulatory power hidden under the label "trade agreements" shows they have acquired an instrumental value beyond trade liberalization.[11] As they expand into policy areas previously under states' autonomous regulation, agreements now carry the potential to be used as a mechanism for the international standardization of market-based rules.[12] In this context, the term "trade," used either to characterize the agreements or the dimension of regionalism, has become insufficient to fully reflect all regulatory policies now affected by trade agreements, such as those related to public services and access to medicine.

Economists were the first to point out the risks involved that the proliferation of regional trade arrangements represents,[13] but governments do not seem impressed by those warnings. The multiplication of regional agreements has become so intense that by 2007 the WTO had moved beyond the stumbling bloc versus stepping stone debate to search for practical ways to deal with the actual implications of the phenomenon.[14]

The resurgence of trade regionalism has stimulated an expanding literature in the field of international political economy. From the examination of new free trade agreements to investigation of the deepening and widening of the integration process in Europe, regions have been rediscovered as a locus for rethinking the social and political strategies needed to deal with the new conditions created by globalization.

Before moving into a discussion of how the phenomenon has been explained, a conceptual clarification is useful. In a broad sense the term "regionalism" can be used to simply describe regionally coordinated actions, including those led by nonstate actors.[15] Even in its specific use in association with trade, the boundaries between regional and multilateral dimensions are not easy to grasp.[16] The WTO, for instance, applies the term "regionalism" to describe the "actions by governments to liberalize or facilitate trade on a regional basis, sometimes through free-trade areas or customs unions."[17] At the same time, it uses "regional trade agreement" and "preferential trade agreement" as interchangeable expressions, thus including under the regional category bilateral trade agreements between countries located in different geographical regions.

I use the term "trade regionalism" in contrast to "trade regionalization" specifically to refer to state-led actions oriented toward trade coordination on a regional basis. While trade regionalization describes a process of geographical restructuring of production that may develop regardless of state decisions,[18] regionalism necessarily requires negotiation among states.

Globalization is often cited as the major driving force behind states' pursuit of the new trade agreements.[19] The changes in global production and allocation of foreign direct investment constitute the background against which individual states now operate.[20] The liberalization of the developing economies and the growing economic relevance of technology and services have imposed new challenges for states' participation in the international economy. Under the umbrella of global market forces, the motives most commonly cited in the literature to explain the current trade regionalist wave include[21]

a. use of regional spaces to enlarge markets;
b. use of regional coalitions to increase bargaining power in multilateral negotiations;
c. domino effect, triggered by the fear of being left behind;
d. the ability to lock in neoliberal reforms in developing countries;
e. use of regional pacts as a hedge against protectionist backlashes;
f. the standardization of rules in areas such as investment and services;
g. for developed countries, the possibility of pushing regional rules for trade in goods and services that are stricter than those at the WTO level;
h. for developing countries, the expectation of becoming more attractive as a foreign investment destination and to benefit from technology transfer through North-South associations; and
i. expectations of gains deriving from the dynamic effects trade integration generates on the local economies.

It would appear then, in view of the structural transformations brought about by globalization, that the new regionalism is more a consequence of the new patterns of international trade and investment than a choice made by national governments.[22] This is important as it highlights the fact that, despite the optimistic views that claim that governments are responding to the stimulus of global markets by *choosing* to strengthen the liberal economic framework, it is plausible that some governments perceive these conditions as pressures and are reacting out of fear.

Schirm's analysis of the new regionalism exemplifies the difficulties in objectively distinguishing constraints from stimulus. According to his first hypothesis, if global markets contribute to the crisis of the inward-looking model, strengthen transnational interest groups, and weaken the regulatory government instruments, "then a simultaneous preference for liberal global competitiveness-enhancing policies will be stimulated." In those terms, regional cooperation will be a viable solution if it provides governments with a means to implement market-oriented reforms in a domestically acceptable way, giving them "a better chance of staying in power as a result of enhanced economic performance." However, in Schirm's case studies, it is apparent that the perception of *chance* and *choice* varies substantially depending on whether an individual government perceives the global forces as a stimulus or as a further constraint.[23]

Perceptions and interpretations of international conditions are relevant to understanding why states continue to have different reactions and strategies. Regionalism in Asia and the Pacific, for instance, has followed a very different pace and institutional logic from the regionalism observed in the Americas.[24] East Asia has shown higher propensity for state-led initiatives for the institutionalization of regional mechanisms for economic cooperation.[25] In the case of the Asia-Pacific Economic Cooperation (APEC) forum, coordination is complicated by the gathering of Eastern and Western states with different ambitions and levels of development,[26] and by the parallel multiplication of trade arrangements within Asia, which have created competing associations that challenge the initial idea of building a nondiscriminatory regionalism.[27]

What I propose is that as scholars we should be intellectually more "curious" about the actual weight of economic incentives in the decision of states to commit to trade agreements. Trade simulation models cannot offer exact predictions,[28] and policymakers ultimately act according to their interpretation of the gains and risks in an uncertain environment. As the two cases analyzed in this book show, bilateral free trade agreements of uncertain economic benefit have been viewed as valuable political bargaining tools.[29] Without denying the importance of the economic interests behind the new trade regionalism, I argue that political reasoning must be taken into consideration in understanding why states promote trade regionalism.

In this regard, studies aligned with the critical perspective in international political economy offer a more substantial basis for examining the new trade regionalism. The critical approach recognizes globalization as the driving force behind the new regionalism,[30] but it emphasizes the historicity of processes as central to political economy analysis. Rather than taking an existing order as given, it questions how a particular order has been constructed, and how states and nonstate actors can eventually transform such an order.[31] Within the dynamic process of globalization, the critical perspective recognizes that region-based actions[32] can be directed not only to adjustment but also to contestation of the prevailing liberal economic order.[33]

The emphasis on the potential for contestation is particularly prominent in the New Regionalism Approach (NRA),[34] which provides a multidisciplinary perspective on regionalism. However, its normative description of the new regionalism as a form of political reaction against the logic of the markets[35] renders the NRA less able to explain trade agreements in which states in the South actively pursue trade integration with the North.[36]

Gamble and Payne's World Order Approach offers a less enthusiastic view of the new regionalism.[37] They contextualize the new regionalist projects in the post-hegemonic world order, in which power is distributed around three main cores—North America, Western Europe, and East Asia—with none of them in the position of world hegemon.[38] The new regional projects they focus on are those led by the core states. These projects evolve within a neoliberal framework, are said to "originate in discussions and negotiations within the policy-making elites in the core states,"[39] and are conceived instrumentally as part of a strategy to guarantee that the core states remain in control of the new world order. The incentives for the peripheral states to join are presumably related to their hope of improvement in their economic and social conditions, through a gradual, even if unequal, convergence upward.

However, various regional trade initiatives involving North and South do not fit easily into the idea of contestation of the liberal economic order, nor can they be interpreted simply as an automatic accommodation to policy decisions made by the elites in core states. Should the "new" trade regional projects, in which developing states decide to enforce the market-based system, be disregarded? How can cases in which governments in the South perceive trade integration with the North as advantageous be evaluated?

Trade Regionalism and Policy Analysis

As the brief review above has shown, an encompassing explanatory framework for the new trade regionalism is yet to be developed. The political, social, and cultural diversity of specific regional projects partly explain the difficulties with generalizations. However, considering the worldwide dimension of the new trade regionalism, the identification of shared characteristics can benefit from empirical studies.[40] Case-based analyses can serve, first, to explore the domestic processes through which the idea of a regional trade agreement comes to be seen as an adequate policy solution for a particular state, and second, to examine how from that initial stimulus, states succeed in negotiating an agreement.

Examining the state from within can assist in a more accurate assessment of the motives and interests that move governments toward trade regionalism. Finally, studies of the rise of trade regionalism in developing contexts can contribute to challenging the predominance of systemic analyses of decision-making in developing countries,[41] effectively engaging with the developing world as an empirically and theoretically meaningful category.[42]

It is in this space that this book is placed. It looks at the reasons for the low level of political support shown by Brazilian and U.S. decision-making elites for transforming the FTAA idea into an actual inter-American policy. Given their respective views on and strategies for relating to the Americas, a hemisphere-wide free trade agreement was not a priority. Domestic perceptions varied in each country and were never sufficiently convergent to provide the political support necessary for the FTAA trade initiative to be concluded successfully. More broadly, the FTAA story reveals the difficulties in predicting the outcomes of trade negotiations, and the importance of looking at ideas and beliefs within states in order to explain negotiation results.

This book is divided into five parts. Part I includes this introduction and chapter 1, which presents the approach adopted in the book. Part II, comprising chapter 2 only, provides a narrative of the FTAA project from its launching in 1994 to 2004, highlighting the incentives and difficulties the parties faced throughout the negotiations. Part III includes chapters 3 and 4. Chapter 3 looks at the shift in economic paradigms predominant in Latin America. More specifically, it examines how the economic crisis of the 1980s provided the space for the political rise of a new group of policy makers whose ideology made the idea of economic integration with the United States more acceptable. At a time when another international financial crisis has opened an opportunity for rethinking paradigms, revising the economic history of the region can be an illuminating exercise. Chapter 4 shows how, in view of the history of inter-American economic relations, the willingness of various Latin American governments to embark on cooperative initiatives with the United States was a surprise. Part IV addresses the individual cases of the United States (chapter 5) and Brazil (chapter 6). After describing the institutional framework for foreign trade policymaking in each country, the central ideas that influenced their trade policies are discussed. I then move to an analysis of the national contexts in which foreign trade policy was formulated from the 1990s onward, examining how the different views and responses of policymakers affected the FTAA. Finally, Part V presents the conclusions.

Chapter 1

Trade Cooperation as a Policy Idea

For some reason, the role of individuals and ideas in policy making arouses little interest among political scientists.
—Hugh Heclo[1]

1.1. International Cooperation from Within

Although the scholarship on the role of ideas in policymaking has expanded over the past twenty years, this development has not reached studies on the political economy of trade negotiations. In the academic field of International Relations, despite the growing space occupied by constructivists,[2] neorealism and neoliberal institutionalism continue to be the dominant frameworks for analyzing international trade negotiations.

A central assumption of this book is that ideas matter to the outcomes of international negotiations. Negotiations are intrinsically characterized by uncertainty and a margin for subjective assessment by the involved parties with regard to the possible outcomes of an agreement.[3] Decision makers with different perceptions and interpretations of events that occur during negotiations are likely to manifest different preference rankings that will consequently affect the negotiation outcomes.[4] While they take into account pure material incentives, they do so through an interpretive process that evolves throughout the negotiations and affects their very definition of what the national interests are. In this process, ideas are not only relevant because they can instruct decision makers on how to maximize revealed interests, but they are also constitutive of the interpretive process through which such interests are defined.

When trade regionalism is conceived as a state-driven project, analysis of how states succeed in building cooperation becomes fundamental. According to Keohane's classic definition, cooperation can be defined as a situation in which "actors adjust their behavior to the actual or anticipated preferences of others, through a process of policy coordination."[5] Under this definition, the core requirement for cooperation is the existence of *mutual adjustments*, with no value judgment implied.[6] The fact that the more powerful actor may push for a highly asymmetrical level of concessions does not invalidate cooperation as long as all states adopt some level of policy adjustment.

Neorealism and neoliberal institutionalism provide two mainstream approaches to examine cooperation. For neorealists, cooperation is a difficult and fragile endeavor, since the primary interests of states are security and independence in an anarchical system. In pursuing their goals, states acting rationally are not only concerned with the risks of betrayal by others, but they also worry about preserving their relative capabilities.[7]

Neoliberal institutionalists hold a less pessimistic view of cooperation. They claim that in a world of increasing interdependence and linked problems, states find themselves dependent upon one another at different levels.[8] It is worth mentioning that for Keohane and Nye, it is reciprocal costs, rather than reciprocal benefits, what characterizes the interdependence condition. Considering that mutual benefits are not required and the distribution of costs can be highly asymmetrical, it is easy to see why cooperation does not flow automatically from a condition of interdependence.[9]

Both perspectives take the existing structure of power in the international system as a given and from that structure assess the interests that will guide the actions of different states. They recognize the anarchical nature of the system as a force-limiting cooperation, and assume that states will behave as rational, self-interested actors, whose actions will be driven by the ambition to maximize their gains.[10]

Challenging the mainstream, the critical perspective sees the structure of power as a central problem. It highlights the constraints that asymmetrical power structures impose on less powerful states, and it deals with agency not only in the restricted sense of actions within the limits of a given order but also as a source for effecting change.[11] To date, however, the critical perspective has not accumulated a body of empirical studies explaining what leads less powerful states to move voluntarily toward cooperation with more powerful states. Here further analyses of policymaking in developing states, informed by Cox's work on hegemony,[12] could provide interesting cases to look at the ideological dimension of power and its influence on state actions.[13]

In the specific case of cooperation in the new trade regionalism, most studies are based on the argument that states cooperate regionally as a means to increase their integration to the liberal economic order. Implicit in this explanation is the presumption that the values of the actors are not profoundly in opposition to the existing order, since if that was the case, their enthusiasm with an open kind of regionalism would be contradictory. But a brief reference to cases of trade cooperation shows the limitation of this assumption.

In the Americas, while neoliberal institutionalist arguments could be applied to justify the behavior of many Latin American governments that have pursued the consolidation of asymmetrical interdependence with the United States, they would fail to explain why some states, such as Venezuela, Ecuador, Bolivia, and Brazil, have resisted. The behavior of these states would seem to fit better into a neorealist explanation, with its emphasis on relative gains. But neorealists would have difficulty explaining the decisions of states such as Chile which, despite being relatively less dependent on trade with the United States, have signed an agreement that increased U.S. relative power.

As the history of the European integration demonstrates, what emerges at a given time as the revealed interest of a state is the outcome of a complex process of interest-building in which the battles of ideas and power, both domestically and internationally, play a significant role. This is particularly evident in contexts of uncertainty such as those characterizing trade negotiations, in which actors are guided by perceptions, and "beliefs, not realities,"[14] orient actions. Since the process of reasoning depends on the reading of signs emitted by other parties in negotiation, elements such as values, beliefs, and memory of previous interactions will affect the assessment of risk.[15]

These observations are not simply part of an academic discussion about the parsimony of explanations. The recognition of the elements influencing the construction of interests is important even to the rational choice approach, since it can affect how rational actors perceive the likely outcome of a game as a manifestation of either cooperation or coercion.[16] Thus from the viewpoint of decision makers, the acceptance of a policy adjustment granted under conditions of extreme pressure, which in theory could characterize cooperation, may be interpreted as such a coercive action that will be considered worse than defection from negotiations.

The neat separation of interests from values and beliefs of the parties is a daunting task with unclear explanatory value. While in short-term interactions, it may still be possible to isolate and presume immediate interests, in more prolonged processes of cooperation, the accuracy of such presumptions decreases. However, values and beliefs, often disregarded in analyses of short-term interactions, provide a more stable basis for explaining the behavior of decision makers.

1.2. Decision Makers and Rationality

Despite the predominance of systemic analyses of international relations until the 1980s, concern with domestic-level analysis in studies of international politics is not recent. In a seminal contribution published in 1954, Snyder, Bruck, and Sapin proposed a framework for the study of international politics that placed decision makers at the center of the stage:

> *State action is the action taken by those acting in the name of the state.* Hence, the state is its decision-makers... It is also one of our basic choices to take as our prime analytical objective the re-creation of the "world" of the decision makers as *they* view it.[17]

Detailed studies of the national processes of foreign policymaking have since then contributed to the recognition of human action as a fundamental variable in the international politics.[18] With the end of the cold war bipolar logic and the growing relevance of nontraditional security issues, the scholarship moved from disputes over whether domestic-based factors are relevant to understanding how states act internationally, to enquiries into how and when they matter.[19]

With regard to international negotiations, Putnam's two-level game framework has been widely applied. It places decision makers as pivotal actors in a double process of negotiating with domestic forces and simultaneously coordinating the international moves of the state they represent.[20] Putnam's work was mainly informed by the observation of experiences of Western democracies, although it did not exclude the possibility of application to other regimes.[21] Subsequently, scholars applied his framework in a broad range of negotiations, including negotiations between North and South.[22] These studies offered a more refined analysis of variations in countries in which the concentration of power in the executive, and the absence or weakness of formal channels for social mobilization, make the assumptions of a functioning pluralist system inadequate. In such systems, in contrast to the more constrained environment of pluralist democracies, decision makers may enjoy greater margin "to follow their own political preferences,"[23] making their role in negotiations even more relevant.

Attempts to model the dynamic interaction between domestic and international levels in international negotiations have helped to demystify the image of a unitary state acting according to a clear, unitary national interest. Nevertheless, they tend to present two main limitations. First, they rest predominantly on a mainstream view of international relations, in which the asymmetrical structure of power is not critically challenged.[24] Second, they are usually informed by a view of rational behavior according to which individuals aggregated in categories such as labor, business, government officials, and politicians, are presumed to have relatively stable interests, defined in an egoistic manner. However, if rational behavior is interpreted as synonymous with self-interested behavior, it is unclear why individual interests can be so easily aggregated for analytical purposes.[25] Inevitably, this aggregation of human behavior can only occur because there is recognition of the effects of social interaction on the formation of interests.[26] It is also paradoxical that while this view of rationality emphasizes choice, the human cognitive process is instrumentally reduced to the selection of options within the limits of a given structure.[27]

Criticism of the concept of rationality based on the *homo economicus*[28] does not imply a denial of rational behavior. A dismissal of the assumption of rationality could lead to an equally elusive presumption of irrational behavior on the part of decision makers. What is emphasized here is the need to reintroduce notions of rationality beyond the instrumental concept referred to above so that actions which, in addition to material interests, derive from a consideration of shared norms, values, and culture—that is, actions that reveal the recognition of *the other*—can enter the terrain of rationality.[29]

The need to move away from a restricted definition of rational behavior emerges from the very nature of the subject matter under analysis, as well as from epistemological concerns. Since there is always uncertainty in international negotiations, actors behaving rationally will still interpret situations and rely on their perception of interests.[30] Decision makers will act according to what they believe will be the impact of a chosen path, not on an accurate knowledge of the consequences of all choices. Here, it is worth remembering that even if preferences are set, decision makers still must choose among different possible strategies.[31] This uncertainty is even more explicit in contemporary trade negotiations, in which the inclusion of regulatory issues whose impact cannot be properly anticipated creates a complex scenario that requires continuous risk evaluation.

Moreover, when individuals make decisions, they are not hermetically isolated from the historical, political, and social contexts in which they exist. If one acknowledges such contextualization of human action, then decisions informed by concerns beyond self-interest cannot be dismissed.

It is at this point that the relevance of nonmaterial variables becomes apparent. Since decision makers are social beings, embedded in social and political systems and acting in specific moments of history, the picture of risks and costs they will form when assessing the possibility of cooperation is likely to be affected by elements such as memories of previous interactions with the parties, compatibility of specific options with their belief systems and with their social networks, personal experiences, and emotions, among other factors.[32]

The idea that individual perceptions can affect the outcomes of a negotiation has already gained supporters in the discipline of economics. Denzau and North's shared mental model originated from the recognition that under conditions of uncertainty, mental models and ideologies would influence the individual process of making choices. They define *mental models* as "the internal representations that individual cognitive systems create to interpret the environment,"[33] whereas *ideologies* consist of "the shared framework of mental models that groups of individuals possess that provide both an interpretation of the environment and a prescription as to how that environment should be structured."[34] In the construction of these shared models, institutions, as "the external (to the mind) mechanisms individuals create to structure and order their environment,"[35] function as external constraints.

The greatest contribution of the shared mental model was to reinsert ideas and beliefs as analytically relevant to debates in the discipline of economics.[36] But it is worth observing that the shared mental model does not move away from the assumption of self-interest as reflecting the purest form of rational choice. It refers to ideology and institutions to explain how these can lead to the adoption of mental models that limit the capacity of individuals to choose what is in their best self-interest.[37] The model, therefore, flows from a specific vision of human nature, in which egoistic behavior is a definitional element of rational choice.

This book assumes that decision makers act rationally. However, rationality is understood as the result of human interaction in various social systems, in a mutually influential process in which consideration of shared values and beliefs is constitutive of the process of individual reasoning.

1.3. The Role of Ideas in Policymaking

The analytical framework applied here draws from studies on the role of ideas in policymaking. Despite the divisions between disciplines, there is a rich possibility of communication between policy studies and the International Relations literature. International negotiations can be seen as "policymaking by another means,"[38] as they are related to a broad policy process that takes place within states and requires the development of multiple bureaucratic relations. For researchers interested in how and why certain policy decisions emerge from within states, observing policymakers, their ideas, and their behavior, becomes a methodological imperative.[39]

During the past two decades, the study of ideas as explanatory variables has regained importance among political scientists. These studies initially covered economic policies,[40] capturing the fascination of scholars with the power with which the economic rationalist ideology emerged in the late 1970s and was disseminated internationally throughout the 1980s. The consequences of that ideology, evidenced in the international financial crisis that erupted in 2008, offered a recent example of how ideas and beliefs heavily influence policymaking and policy decisions.

Institutionalist analyses[41] have been criticized for using ideas as a residual category, applied to address the limitations of the main categories utilized in institutionalist approaches, but not as an explanatory variable per se.[42] In Goldstein's analysis of the impact of ideas on U.S. trade policy, the kinds of ideas emphasized are those that function as "road maps," guiding individuals from a set of given interests toward their realization through particular policy choices.[43] For historical institutionalists,[44] institutions are the predominant variable to which ideas are subjected. Institutions can create "innovation boundaries"[45] in policymaking that are reproduced and consolidated, and are expressed through patterns that restrict the space for innovation.

Since "ideas do not float freely"[46] their ability to influence policies will depend on being carried forward by politically influential individuals. While such individuals may be part of a state institution formally in charge of policymaking, this is not a precondition. Indeed, policy networks that are influential in the legitimization of knowledge and interpretation of policies are frequently made up of nongovernment members such as intellectuals and technical experts, in both domestic-based networks[47] and transnational ones.[48] What is required is that they be able to influence the decision makers and political leaders, who ultimately hold the capacity to mobilize the institutional apparatus to act toward the implementation of a policy idea.[49]

The case studies contained in this book focus on bureaucratic elites, based on the assumption that if an idea has gained sufficient appreciation to inform foreign trade policy, it will be necessarily revealed at the decision-making level. In other words, it will be observable in the content of the policies promoted by decision makers at the government level.

There is also a methodological emphasis on agency rather than structure. Although it is acknowledged that institutions can filter ideas and influence the degree to which individuals supporting an innovation will be able to carry it forward, institutional analysis tends to amplify the perception of continuity in policy ideas. In order to explain how, given a stable institutional framework, variations in policy ideas occur, it is necessary to look beyond institutional constraints. The introduction of new policy ideas and their transformation into policy can only occur because individuals retain the intellectual capacity to reinterpret and redefine norms,[50] thus not only being affected by but also affecting institutions. If, as Polanyi defined, "institutions are embodiments of human meaning and purpose,"[51] then they can be reshaped in different periods and contexts through the battle over ideas and beliefs.

A factor often mentioned as triggering policy innovation is the coming of a crisis. Crises open windows for policy change to be considered by delegitimizing the old solutions and adding to the pressure for innovation.[52] It is important to note that the term "innovation" refers to the adoption of ideas that were previously not dominant in a particular policy setting, but which become politically influential.[53] In that sense, those ideas might have existed for a long time, but what characterizes innovation is their political empowerment through the policymaking process.

Sikkink's interpretive-institutional approach was a key influence in this book. According to Sikkink's approach, although institutions are fundamental to the implementation and consolidation phases of new policy models, at the stage at which a new policy idea is adopted, the key determinant for it success is its embrace by top-level policymakers.[54]

As other studies on policy ideas have shown, in the selection stage, the quality of a policy idea, that is, whether it is technically appropriate to a policy, seems to be less relevant than whether that idea is harmonious with the predominant, central beliefs of a particular policy circle.[55] Policy networks are exposed to risks of bias that may exclude alternative sources of knowledge even when their members imagine themselves to be acting on a purely technical basis.[56] As the 2008 financial crisis demonstrated, good ideas may be excluded from policy circles for decades, while bad ideas advanced by powerful individuals often find their way into policies.

1.4. Ideas and Interests in Policymaking

Studies centered on the value of the ideas and beliefs of decision makers always face the challenge of providing sufficient indication that the ideational aspect, rather than pure material incentives, effectively influenced policies. Despite this methodological difficulty, this book is developed on the premise that ideas and material interests are mutually constituted,[57] and that the intensity with which negotiators perceive a particular material incentive as a sufficient stimulus is affected by their views and beliefs.

I use a historical approach in order to observe the degree of consistency between rhetoric and action in the foreign trade policy of the United States and Brazil. A lengthy historical perspective is important to show that some of the ideas and visions that influenced the 2003 Brazilian-U.S. FTAA decision were not novel in their respective national settings. Instead, they had been available in the policy systems of both countries well before the FTAA process, and provided decision makers with the lens through which they could evaluate their broad interests in a hemispheric trade area. Historical narratives are also valuable for discerning gradual changes in views and variations in ideology even within stable institutional settings, providing a base for observation that would not be available through an exclusive focus on the short period of negotiations.

The selection of the cases of the United States and Brazil is justified by their relevance to the FTAA negotiations. Despite the downfall and increasing Chinese competition, the United States is still the predominant economy in the Americas. In 2008 it accounted for approximately 66 percent of the region's gross domestic product (GDP), and is a key market and investor for most Latin American and Caribbean countries. Alternatively, Brazil is the most important market that could be open to the United States through the FTAA. In 2008, with NAFTA countries excluded, Brazil alone accounted for 44.5 percent of the GDP in the Western Hemisphere.[58] In addition to generating the strongest resistance the United States faced during negotiations, Brazil was responsible for proposing the fragmentation of the negotiations in late 2003. As cochairs of the FTAA, both countries showed little commitment to realizing the idea of a hemispheric trade agreement.

In observing the developments in foreign trade policy in these two national settings, I acknowledge that institutions affect the degree to which ideas can influence particular policy groups, but institutions are not addressed as causal variables in and of themselves. Since the focus is on the effective adoption of an idea, the advocacy of politically influential individuals can often be more relevant than institutional constraints.

For those interested in comparative politics, the United States and Brazil provide an interesting case for comparative foreign policymaking. In the U.S. pluralist trade system, interest groups use a variety of formal channels to try to influence foreign trade policymaking. Moreover, the Executive's autonomy is constrained by the need to obtain congressional authorization to negotiate trade concessions. In Brazil, trade negotiations are a prerogative of the Executive while Congress exercises only a veto power a posteriori. However, the organizational structure of the agency in charge of foreign policy tends to create innovation "boundaries" to new ideas.[59] Still, in each country, the political rise of individuals with different ideological orientations led to central changes in the perceptions and actions regarding the FTAA negotiations.

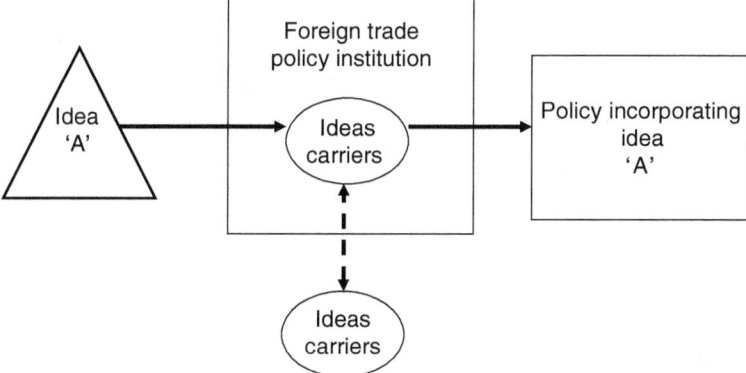

Figure 1.1 Analytical framework

This book benefited from a small set of twenty-five interviews with participants in the FTAA process, conducted in Brazil and in the United States during 2006. The individuals were selected on the basis of their knowledge of and participation in the FTAA negotiations, as trade advisers in international institutions, representatives of interest groups or government positions, as well as their accessibility for interview during the period in which the field research was conducted. Interviewees were also classified according to their activities and actions during the FTAA negotiations.[60] Overall, I avoided identification unless previous authorization had been given and the information conveyed was not considered sensitive.

Due to the semistructured nature of the interviews, participants were also invited to answer a questionnaire that allowed me to address a small but valuable set of specific questions. Fourteen of the twenty-five interviewees answered the questionnaire, and the results are presented in Appendix A. Although the interviews and questionnaires are not sufficiently representative for the development of inferences, they constitute a rich source of original data on the participants' views and interpretations of the FTAA.

A final observation, related to the treatment of Brazilian sources, is necessary. Until the late 1980s, the literature on Brazilian foreign policymaking and diplomacy was predominantly written by diplomats. While these materials offer a rich contribution to the historiography of Brazilian diplomacy, they are deficient in critical analysis of government decisions. As one Brazilian scholar comments, students of Brazil's foreign policy have operated in an environment where official documents suffer from restricted access,[61] and "testimonies by direct observers are rare or deliberately self-censored."[62] In this book, the diplomatic production is treated predominantly as primary source, representative of individual views of reality. Considering that the focus is on ideas and beliefs that have oriented choices in foreign trade policy, those contributions proved to be of central importance.

Part II
The FTAA Negotiations

Chapter 2

The FTAA Negotiations

For about a decade, from 1994 until 2004, the FTAA project mobilized human and financial resources throughout the Americas as countries prepared the ground for negotiations. Still, those efforts were insufficient to overcome the lack of political commitment by the cochairs of the negotiations, the United States and Brazil, to transform the project into reality.[1]

This chapter reconstructs the history of the FTAA negotiations. It begins with a brief assessment of the economic incentives for the various negotiating parties, grouped in subregional blocs, to show that the degree of trade dependence varied considerably among Latin American and Caribbean countries, and that the level of engagement of individual states in the initiative did not directly correspond to their relative dependence on the U.S. market. This chapter also captures signals emitted by the United States and Brazil, and that reveal how they perceived the FTAA relevance in their respective foreign trade policies.

The section "The Genesis of the FTAA" explores the genesis of the FTAA as it developed from an idea into an official project announced during the First Summit of the Americas in December 1994. The preparatory phase, from 1995 to the official launch of negotiations in April 1998, is described in the section "The Preparatory Phase (1995–1998)." The section "The Negotiations Phase (1998–2003)" addresses the negotiation phase, with emphasis on the tensions that emerged particularly from 2002 onwards. In the final section, a general evaluation of the FTAA negotiation is conducted from the perspective of international cooperation.

Setting the Stage for Negotiations

In June 1990, a few days after officially announcing the beginning of trade negotiations with Mexico,[2] President George H.W. Bush launched the Enterprise for the Americas Initiative (EAI), an inter-American policy project focused on the pillars of trade liberalization, investment, and debt restructuring. In trade the EAI suggested that, although the priority continued to be the Uruguay Round of multilateral negotiations, the United States would be willing to negotiate with subregional blocs in the Americas that were already implementing trade liberalization reforms. As Latin American countries were at different stages of liberalization, a transition mechanism was proposed, following the model of trade and investment framework agreements already signed with Mexico and Bolivia.[3]

As President Bush's assistant for economic and domestic policy, Roger Porter affirmed, "there [was] no intention to create a Hemispheric trading bloc," and although individual negotiations of free trade agreements were possible, "the Bush administration's vision [was] of a region where countries trade freely among themselves and with the United States."[4] The linguistic choice of the term hemispherewide trade liberalization, rather than trade integration, was indicative that a single agreement simultaneously subscribed to by all countries in the hemisphere was not envisioned at that time.

As an inter-American policy idea, the EAI was less innovative than the Bush administration claimed. It essentially reintroduced an emphasis on private capital and entrepreneurship as engines for economic growth in Latin America, an old recipe that had already been prescribed in the post–Second World War period.[5] As on that occasion, the EAI's "trade, not aid" formula functioned as a convenient solution for the U.S. administration: it gave international creditors and the United States a mechanism to protect their economic interests in the region through the promotion of free market rules, at the same time that it avoided budget disputes and justified a reduction in traditional aid assistance.

With the EAI stimulus, some Latin American and Caribbean states accelerated trade liberalization and integration with regional partners willing to do so. The agreements varied from low-scope preferential arrangements within the Latin American Integration Association (ALADI), to free trade agreements and customs unions.[6] By the early 1990s most Latin American countries had already begun unilateral trade liberalization, and tariff elimination was not their only goal. In a region previously known for its protectionist policies, the new trade regionalism helped to signal commitment to trade openness to the international community. The consolidation of free market rules was also envisioned as a means for reshaping national institutions and "locking in" market-based reforms. Regional agreements, framed by the notion of open regionalism, were seen as providing countries with an incentive to resume economic growth, generating dynamic effects that would contribute to increasing their competitiveness and attracting foreign investors.[7]

Still, the risks of trade diversion were high. Unlike APEC's orientation toward trade facilitation, regional trade agreements in Latin America created a complex overlapping of rules at borders, which increased transaction costs and led to frequent complaints from exporters. More importantly, the belief in the potential of trade agreements to attract foreign investment did not take into account that the simultaneous conversion of economies of similar profile to the same regulatory parameters could eliminate the differential effect that such a conversion could generate.[8]

Another difficulty was that regionalism involving only Latin American countries was not necessarily harmonious with a regionalism that included the United States. While "centripetal forces" stimulated intrabloc cooperation in Latin America, arrangements involving the United States were subject to "centrifugal forces" that favored fragmentation of action, and the pursuit of individual bargains with the United States,[9] rather than collective action.

As shown in Table 2.1, the United States continued to be the key trading partner for many Latin American and Caribbean countries in 1992. For many states in the region, import-substitution industrialization had not succeeded in altering the position of the United States as their main trading partner. In contrast, from the U.S. perspective, Latin America and the Caribbean, with the exclusion of Mexico, accounted for an extremely small

Table 2.1 Bilateral trade flow between the United States and selected countries, 1992 (%)

	Share of exports going to the Unites States	Share of U.S. imports	Share of imports coming from the U.S.	Share of U.S. exports
Mexico	76.4	5.9	69.4	10
MERCOSUR				
Argentina	8.3	0.2	22.4	0.8
Brazil	19.6	1.3	25.4	1.3
Uruguay	12.5	0		
Andean Community				
Colombia	38.9	0.5	43.3	0.8
Ecuador	43.4	0.3	35.7	0.2
Peru	20.0	0.1	26.8	0.3
Venezuela	50.3	1.4	44.4	1.3
CACM				
Costa Rica	54.6	0.2	51.9	0.3
El Salvador	57.1	0.1	42.1	0.2
Guatemala	55.0	0.2	44.8	0.3
Honduras	60.0	0.1	57.1	0.1
Caricom				
Jamaica	42.9	0.1	55.6	0.2
Trinidad and Tobago	47.4	0.2		
Others				
Chile	16.8	0.3	19.6	0.5
Dominican Republic	66.7	0.1	40.7	0.3
Panama	40.0	0	40.0	0.2

Source: Original data from IMF. Based on Raymond J. Ahearn and Alfred Reifman, *U.S. Interest in Western Hemisphere Free Trade*, U.S. Congressional Research Service Report, November 12, 1993 (Washington, DC: US Library of Congress/CRS, 1993), 20–21.

share of its total trade. This structural asymmetry in trade relations meant that in the case of an agreement with the United States, Latin Americans would be expected to offer more concessions.[10]

NAFTA

For the United States, Canada, and Mexico, NAFTA was by far the most important economic arrangement in the Americas. In 1992, NAFTA members accounted together for $6.5 trillion out of a total hemispheric gross domestic product of approximately $7.5 trillion. The reference to the FTAA as the largest economic bloc in the world somehow exaggerated what would be, in fact, added through a hemispheric agreement, if NAFTA's contribution was discounted. Although broader liberalization would give the United States preferential access to Latin American and Caribbean markets, the relatively low-economic weight of the other countries involved made a weak case for a special focus on the Americas.[11]

As a foreign policy idea, however, free trade in the hemisphere had some appeal. The risk of a world divided into competing regional powers made U.S. consolidation of its power in the Western Hemisphere more pressing. As Jaguaribe observed, in the early 1990s, both the United States and Latin America found themselves "being rejected by Europe, albeit for different reasons and different ways," and such a "double rejection" could facilitate inter-American cooperation.[12]

The neofunctionalist premise that economic integration could favor cooperation in high politics was invoked to promote trade as a means of achieving collaboration in areas of primary concern to the United States, such as drug trafficking, terrorism, and immigration.[13] As a report to the U.S. Congress indicated, despite the limited significance of trade south of Mexico, "habits of economic cooperation could spill over to make the peaceful resolution of regional disputes easier."[14] Moreover, trade cooperation could provide the United States with the opportunity to push for free market democracies.

The use of trade as a carrot in U.S. foreign policy is an old practice in inter-American relations, as well as the attempt to promote rules that protected private sector interests. But less explored in political economy analyses of the FTAA is how the U.S. foreign policy on Latin America and the Caribbean in the early 1990s indicated the reappearance of an old U.S. vision in which economic and political freedoms formed the basis for a shared destiny in the New World. As President George H.W. Bush stated in his announcement of the EAI:

> we trace our origins, our shared history, to the time of Columbus' voyage and the courageous quest for the advancement of man. Today the bonds of our common heritage are strengthened by the love of freedom and a common commitment to democracy.[15]

Tussie and Labaqui argue that a U.S.-led system in which economic and political freedoms prevail has been for decades the essence of "the universal projection of the American dream."[16] That support for democracy has been frequently overlooked on behalf of material priorities, does not mean that prodemocratic beliefs have not existed in U.S. policy makers' conceptions of their country's role in the world.[17] Although it is yet to be seen whether idealism by itself is able to sustain foreign policy. As an inspiration for hemispheric trade integration, the ideal of the consolidation of free market democracies created a stronger ideological motivation that a pure economic rationale was unable to generate.

Canada and Mexico, the other NAFTA parties, entered the FTAA debate from different positions. For Canada, hemisphere-wide integration could contain the expansion to the rest of the Americas of the hub-and-spoke system initiated with NAFTA. The FTAA offered Canada the possibility of counterbalancing U.S. dominance and the potential to play the role of a middle power in the hemisphere. Economically, Canada could gain by expanding its access to Latin American markets in which its trade remained weak. For Mexico, however, an extension of NAFTA represented an erosion of its recently acquired and heavily pursued privileges with the United States. The fact that Mexicans avoided the formation of a trinational team of negotiators to deal with the potential enlargement of NAFTA[18] was a clear indication that it perceived that its interests could be best served bilaterally with the United States. With these divergent incentives, Canada and Mexico exemplified how the United States continued to exercise a centrifugal force even after NAFTA has come into effect.

The Central American Common Market

For the members of the Central American Common Market (CACM), NAFTA imposed a harder new economic reality. As other subregional blocs, CACM was still recovering from the economic debacle of the 1980s. Intra-regional trade had fallen from 22 percent in 1980 to 13 percent in 1990. CACM members' long economic dependence on the United States, as both market and investor meant that access to the U.S. market was vital to their economic recovery. NAFTA directly threatened the bloc, eroding the unilateral trade preferences that the United States had granted to countries in Central America and the Caribbean through the Caribbean Basin Initiative (CBI).[19] CACM members, with their high economic structural dependence on the United States were pressured to move toward a "dwarf regionalism,"[20] driven by the need to avoid worsening already fragile positions in the global economy.

The Caribbean Community

The position of the Caribbean Community (CARICOM) was in many ways comparable to that of the CACM. Formed by a group of small economies, CARICOM faced the dilemma of improving intra-bloc coordination in order to become more effective in international negotiations, while the lack of complementarities and asymmetries among the economies of its members limited further cooperation.

Like most small economies, the economic development of CARICOM members has been heavily shaped by external variables. Their colonial past meant that most members had more developed cultural, political, and economic relations with Great Britain than with Latin America. Relations with Central and South America, which according to a Caribbean analyst, remained "terra incognita,"[21] have just begun to be recognized as relevant to CARICOM's international bargaining power. Despite political independence, its economic structure remained dependent on foreign assistance, particularly from the United States. CARICOM was also a beneficiary of the CBI unilateral preference program.[22] NAFTA had eroded the value of that preferential access, and in some sectors, such as textiles, guaranteed Mexico even better access. That explained why CARICOM, like CACM, fought so strenuously for NAFTA-parity conditions for market access.[23]

The Southern Common Market

The Southern Common Market (Mercosur) was officially created a few months after the announcement of the EAI, upon the signing of the Treaty of Asunción by Argentina, Brazil, Paraguay, and Uruguay in March 1991.[24] However, the gestation of the bloc preceded the U.S. initiative. The origins of Mercosur can be traced back to the process of redefinition of bilateral relations between Brazil and Argentina, from one of competition and animosity to one of cooperation. In 1986, with the military out of power in both countries, the new civilian regimes took a historic step by agreeing to a program for integration and economic cooperation. Though cooperation in the economic sphere was like a path to survival in a highly competitive international environment,[25] the high level of commitment of both countries demonstrated the political value of the initiative. Later, Uruguay and Paraguay, whose relationships with Brazil and Argentina had been historically punctuated by resistance to attempts at domination by the other sides,[26] joined the initiative.

As shown in Table 2.2., of all subregional blocs, Mercosur has been the least dependent on the North American market. While the United States maintained its position as the region's preeminent individual trading partner, as a bloc, the European Union constituted Mercosur's most significant source of trade. In principle, this relative independence enabled Mercosur's members to adopt a stronger negotiating position with the United States.

Despite its relatively lower trade dependence from the United States, individual members held different foreign policy ideas from the beginning.[27] The deep asymmetry within the bloc, which favors Brazil and Argentina, and the difficulties of developing institutional supranational mechanisms to address this imbalance, have placed Mercosur closer to the asymmetrical conditions observed in the FTAA than those existing within the European Union. In 1992, Brazil accounted for 80 percent of the bloc's population,

Table 2.2 Structure of exports by integration group, 2002 and 2009 (% distribution)

Export Region	Destination											
	Mercosur		Andean Community		ALADI		CACM		NAFTA		Hemisphere	
	2002	2009	2002	2009	2002	2009	2002	2009	2002	2009	2002	2009
Mercosur	11	15	4	4	25	26	1	0	29	12	51	39
Andean Community	3	5	12	7	18	23	2	2	47	34	69	62
ALADI (a)	4	8	4	3	12	16	1	1	63	45	74	63
CACM	0	0	1	1	3	6	23	24	52	44	79	76
NAFTA	1	2	1	1	11	14	1	1	57	48	62	56
Hemisphere	2	4	2	2	13	15	1	1	54	43	61	54

Notes:
(a) Cuba is not included.
(b) Data for 2009 is provisional.
Source: Original data from Inter-American Development Bank.

72 percent of its territory, and 75 percent of its gross domestic product.[28] If NAFTA members were excluded, Brazil would alone account for almost half of the GDP in the hemisphere.

In the initial years of Mercosur, Brazil and Argentina held remarkably different views of how to approach trade negotiations with the United States and NAFTA. Brazil insisted that the bloc should act as a single actor and that it should first achieve internal coherence through the consolidation of a common external tariff. On the other hand, Argentina initially placed less emphasis on the common external tariff, while attempting to retain its margin for individual negotiations over accession to NAFTA. Consistent with the reorientation of Argentine foreign policy under Carlos Menem (1989–99) toward greater alignment with the United States,[29] the Argentinean government expressed its willingness to enter into a trade agreement with the United States until late 1994, despite its commitments to Mercosur.

Brazil was the only country that maintained a more gradualist approach to the idea of a hemispheric free trade area since the announcement of the EAI. Despite the fact that Brazil had already initiated unilateral trade liberalization, compared with other Latin American countries, market-based reforms in the country had not advanced, and economic instability would remain a challenge until 1994. For Brazil, an agreement that used NAFTA as a model would restrict policy autonomy in the new areas that the agreement covered, such as investment, intellectual property, and services, and would require intense domestic political negotiations with domestic groups likely to lose.[30]

Yet Brazil was also expected to gain from a hemispheric free trade area. In contrast to most Latin American exports, Brazilian diversified exports include a mix of highly competitive agricultural commodities, manufactures, and high-technology goods. Brazil's economic base and lower trade dependence on the United States allowed it to negotiate under less pressure. With a large economy and sharing borders with almost every other South American country, it was the strongest candidate to become a production base on the subcontinent. Since South America is a major importer of Brazilian manufactured goods, a hub-and-spoke system centered on the United States from which Brazil was excluded could negatively affect the competitiveness of Brazilian exports to the region. Despite those incentives, Brazil was not a vocal proponent of a hemispheric trade area. Indeed, a few months before the FTAA launching, it attempted to push for a parallel project, calling for the formation of a South American Free Trade Area (SAFTA).[31]

The Andean Community

Members of the Andean Community[32] were at an intermediary level of trade dependence on the United States. As CACM and CARICOM, they struggled to coordinate commitments to deepen intra-bloc integration, harmonize competing economic incentives, and deal with the political instability of some of members.[33] Colombia deserves special mention as it was among the Latin American countries that most celebrated the EAI. Referring to the Colombian government's enthusiasm, one scholar commented, "all that is lacking is a verification of miracles that would elevate [the EAI] to the status of sainthood. In the case of Colombia, this syndrome has been particularly notable."[34] When the EAI was announced, Colombia responded promptly by signing a bilateral trade and investment framework agreement with the United States. At the same time, Colombia, Venezuela, and Mexico signed a free trade agreement—the Group of Three—in order to facilitate future accession to NAFTA.

For the United States, trade relations, however important, were not the central issue linking the Andean countries. By 1990, the Andean region had become more important to U.S. foreign policy because of the war on drugs; trade initiatives could be used as a means to guarantee cooperation in operations to combat drug trafficking.[35]

Chile

Chile stands out as a case of a country in which free trade agreements have been highly valued in the state strategy to face the challenges of economic globalization.[36] Under General Augusto Pinochet, tariffs were drastically reduced from an average of 105 percent in 1976 to 10 percent by 1979. Though the economic crisis inaugurated in 1982 led to a temporary tariff rise, by 1991 the average linear tariff was 11 percent. Trade liberalization initiated under General Pinochet was accompanied by an emphasis on export promotion. Export performance improved and Chile diversified its trading partners, but at the cost of deindustrialization. While in the 1960s, most of the Chilean exports went to the United States (29 percent) and Europe (52 percent), by the 1980s their participation had decreased to approximately 21 percent and 38 percent, respectively, while Latin America and other parts of the world became more relevant as destinations.[37]

Chilean trade policy maintained its outward orientation under successive administrations of the center–left wing coalition *Concertación*, which remained in power from 1989 to 2010. This continuity was favored by the arrival in power of many Chilean intellectuals who, having gone through what Grugel calls a "shock of intellectual *realism*," came to agree on the need to work within domestic and international structural constraints.[38] As the major part of the costs of trade liberalization had already been paid in previous years, the *Concertación* faced the choice of either attempting to stall liberalization or using what had been carried out to make Chile a front runner in open regionalism. Trade agreements became an instrument to allow Chile to gain access to other markets, through collecting some benefits from the unilateral liberalization effected by General Pinochet's regime. But together with the economic rationale, the civilian government also saw in trade agreements an opportunity to reinsert Chile into the international arena as a democratic state. As a Chilean former trade adviser described, "it was not just a matter of reestablishing diplomatic relations with a number of countries, but also of strengthening bilateral relations through a whole set of different policies. And one of those policies was trade."[39] Chile's willingness to become NAFTA's "fourth amigo" was, therefore, part of a foreign policy strategy that was open to, but not exclusively focused on, the United States.[40]

The Genesis of the FTAA

When Bill Clinton was elected U.S. president in 1992, for the first time in the history of inter-American relations there was a high degree of regional convergence around the U.S.-promoted model of free market democracies.[41] While the triggering forces of that process of convergence can be located in the worldwide ideological crisis that followed the fall of the socialist regimes in Latin America, this process was accelerated by the depth of the economic crisis, and pragmatism became a brand pursued by many policy makers.

Pragmatic politics reinforced the idea of conciliation and opened the door to a more flexible approach to relations with the United States. This reconceptualization was particularly important at a time when the United States was redefining the nature and extent of its external actions in a unipolar world system. For President Clinton politics and economics were interwoven with foreign policymaking. Markets were supportive of democracy and the advancement of both was seen as vital in protecting U.S. national security and economic interests.[42] As he declared during the Haiti crisis in 1994, "[Democracies are] more likely to create free markets and economic opportunity, and to become strong, reliable trading partners."[43]

By the twenty-first century and, particularly after September 11, 2001, the cynicism with which democracy promotion has been met has contributed to a reading of democracy in U.S. foreign policy as predominantly rhetorical. It would be simplistic, however, to reduce the political changes of the late 1980s and early 1990s in Latin America to such an interpretation. Participants in the initial phase of the FTAA interviewed for this book demonstrated a genuine enthusiasm with the possibilities for cooperation open by the specific conjuncture of the early 1990s.[44]

But while Latin American governments were finally more open to the idea of another attempt at inter-American cooperation, the relative lack of U.S. strategic interests in the region signified that Latin America risked being categorized as a low–foreign policy priority. It was in this U.S. process of redefining its role in the world that the idea of a hemispheric trade area was reintroduced. During the election campaign, a memorandum advising candidate Clinton on the U.S. foreign policy directions to Latin America raised the possibility of opening up NAFTA to the rest of the Americas. Once Clinton was elected, the administration began the process of foreign policy review. However, because of "disagreements over a few remaining issues, and the lack of urgency felt by key senior officials," it would take almost two years for the new guidelines to become part of the official Presidential Decision Directive 28.[45]

In late 1993, following the approval of NAFTA, Vice-President Al Gore was due to visit Mexico to celebrate the agreement. According to Richard Feinberg, then special assistant to the president and senior director of Inter-American Affairs at the National Security Council, Al Gore noted that his speech lacked substance. It was at that moment that Feinberg proposed the idea of a hemispheric summit, which Gore warmly supported.[46]

On December 1, 1993, Gore visited Mexico and invited all democracies in the Americas to meet for a summit in which they could "codify" their "shared principles" and form a "Western Hemisphere community of democracies." A few days later, Clinton announced that he would instruct the office of the U.S. Trade Representative (USTR) to examine the possibility of extending free trade beyond Mexico.[47] The call for the summit aimed to indicate to Latin Americans that the United States recognized regional affairs as more than just bilateral relations with Mexico. However, the content to be addressed by the summit was still to be defined and in the year following the announcement, the challenge of building an agenda acceptable for all parties became evident.

For the Clinton administration, democracy was a guiding principle in its relationships with governments in the hemisphere. In defining the U.S. goals in the hemisphere, Clinton commented:

> Now, we [the United States] are the home of democracy. We are the home of expanded trade. We are the country that, of all the great democracies of the world, has the most racial and ethnic and cultural and religious diversity. And we must make these nations feel that we are their true friend and partners.[48]

Chile actively supported the inclusion of democracy on the summit agenda and Mercosur became the first bloc in the Americas to include democracy as a requirement for membership. For some governments, the democracy "conditionality" was not ideal, but awareness of the domestic political game that Clinton had to play led them to accept the inclusion of a less tractable issue as part of the trade-off for obtaining benefits in other areas.[49]

The inclusion of trade on the summit agenda was particularly contentious in the United States. Ambassador Charles Gillespie Jr., U.S. coordinator of the summit process, observed that the inclusion of trade on the agenda caused such a division within the administration that a final decision over the issue could only be made a few days before the summit.[50] The NAFTA experience had exposed the domestic tensions over labor and environmental issues in trade relations with a less developed country. Moreover, the USTR had to concentrate its efforts on the successful ratification of the recently signed Uruguay Round agreements. Early intra-bureaucratic discussions of the issue revealed that, if free trade were to be negotiated, then the option of accession to NAFTA over bilateral trade pacts was preferred.[51] Strikingly absent from the U.S. debate was any notion of a single, hemispheric trade pact. Indeed, Presidential Decision Directive 28, signed a few months before the Summit of the Americas, supported the use of trade expansion and agreements on intellectual property and investment as means of ensuring U.S. security interests, but it did not recommend a hemisphere-wide free trade agreement as a policy.[52]

The lack of a clear vision around a hemispheric free trade area seems apparent in the model adopted to discuss the issue during the summit preparations. While participants confirmed that general preparations were made through a collaborative process, with participation of representatives from all countries in the various working groups,[53] the United States adopted a unilateral approach with respect to trade, with centralized meetings organized with individual countries and subregional blocs. It also signaled a preference for a gradual extension of NAFTA through bilateral negotiations, rather than a single enterprise.

In fact, pressures to include trade in the summit came from other countries. Vocal promoters of the free trade component included Chile, Canada, Colombia, and Argentina. In November 1994, just a couple of weeks before the summit, the United States circulated its draft for the Summit's Declaration of Principles and Plan of Action, in which it finally raised the idea of building a free trade area in the Americas. Without much detail on the actual architecture of the proposal, the U.S. document projected ministerial meetings, the development of a trade database, and the assessment of the current stage of existing subregional arrangements, with the assistance of the Organization of American States (OAS), IDB, and the UN Economic Commission for Latin America and the Caribbean (ECLAC). The United States also indicated its intention to use the Trade and Investment Councils set up during the Bush administration, as channels through which trade and investment issues could be addressed. Finally, the proposal mentioned the need for improvement of labor and environmental conditions.[54]

In contrast with the U.S. draft, the Rio Group proposal,[55] drafted by thirteen Latin American countries, decoupled labor and environmental issues from trade. It emphasized implementing WTO-based directives and demonstrated the need to address tariff peaks and unfair trade practices. Moreover, Brazil, then chair of the Rio Group, insisted that hemispheric free trade should proceed through the deepening of subregional arrangements and, contrary to Argentina, rejected the proposal of setting a deadline for the formation of the hemispheric trade area.[56]

In December, 1994, the heads of state of thirty-four countries in the Western Hemisphere met in Miami for the First Summit of the Americas[57] to inaugurate a new phase in inter-American relations.[58] The Summit's Declaration of Principles (Appendix B) highlighted the commitment of participants to "democracy, free trade and sustainable development in the Americas," excluding Cuba from participation. Its Plan of Action covered twenty-three topics, from poverty reduction and community participation to democracy and free markets.[59] While the variety of issues reflected the more democratic process that preceded the summit, the excessive number of policy items was symptomatic of the fact that, in practice, priorities had not been defined.

It is possible to detect similarities between the Miami Summit and past attempts at regional cooperation, as it will be discussed in chapter 4. Although more than a century had passed since the First International Conference of American States in 1890, the Miami Summit was also inspired by a vision of cooperation and stability in which political goals were linked to economic interests. Moreover, as in the Alliance for Progress of the 1960s, social and economic objectives were combined, regardless of the tensions that would derive from trying to pursue both objectives simultaneously.

The Free Trade Area of the Americas was the ninth topic of the Plan of Action, under the section "Promoting prosperity through economic integration and free trade." The plan recommended an assessment of trade agreements within the existing trade and investment councils, directed the OAS Special Committee on Trade, IDB, and ECLAC to work toward an inventory of existing trade arrangements and rules, and fixed dates for two ministerial meetings to follow up on the FTAA process.

In order to satisfy the United States, provisions related to labor and environment protection were included. Contrary to Brazil's aspiration, 2005 was set as the deadline by which countries aimed to achieve the hemispheric free trade area, with significant progress in negotiations expected by the end of the century. But, both Brazil and the United States gained time with the absence of detail concerning the path to be adopted for the formation of the free trade area. For Brazil, this meant the possibility of continuing to insist on a gradual integration, starting from subregional blocs and without centralization by the United States. For the United States, vagueness relieved the pressure for free trade actions with Latin Americans in the short run.

The fast-track authority, essential to diminish uncertainty in trade negotiations, had expired, and it would not be until mid-1997 that Clinton would seriously pursue its renewal. Chile, which had already been invited in 1994 to become the "fourth amigo" in NAFTA, would have to wait another decade for an agreement.

The Preparatory Phase (1995–1998)

Once the FTAA initiative was announced, intensive preparations for negotiations began. Beginning in 1995, government officials and trade specialists from international organizations and private institutions met regularly to prepare the foundations for negotiations.[60] Government teams had to decode the meaning of the complex task on which they had embarked. From the Miami Summit in 1994 to the Santiago Summit in 1998, efforts were mainly concentrated on creating a knowledge base of what the FTAA would address.

Asymmetry of technical knowledge and financial resources between developed and developing countries are well known in the multilateral trading system,[61] but they were also noticeable in the FTAA process. In the mid-1990s, many countries had just opened up their economies and national bureaucracies were at different learning stages as how to operate in an open economy scenario. They not only lacked accumulated negotiating experience in trade issues but were also called upon to deal simultaneously with multilateral, regional, and bilateral trade negotiations. In addition to the various negotiation fronts, negotiators were exposed to a new set of issues that were unfamiliar even to the old members of the General Agreement on Tariffs and Trade /World Trade Organization (GATT/WTO) system. Services and intellectual property were examples of issues that had become part of the multilateral trading system during the Uruguay Round, after intense pressure from OECD countries. Most developing countries were unaware of the real implications of the new regulation framework.[62] Moreover, under the constraints imposed by tight fiscal budgets, financial resources allocated to participating in trade negotiations were scarce.

With NAFTA taken as the baseline measure for what the United States expected from a future agreement, governments were preparing for a negotiation agenda that would require countries to achieve at least a NAFTA-like, WTO-plus commitment, in order to attract the United States. Although the agreement was officially described as having to be *consistent* with the WTO commitments, in practice, the parties were aware that the attraction of a regional trade agreement for the United States would rest precisely on the possibility of extracting concessions from developing countries that were hardly, or only slowly, achieved through the WTO consensus-based system. In this regard, the FTAA was a project to transform the regulatory functions of the states involved, directing state power to reshape and lock in domestic rules favorable to an open market system.

The United States started the process with ambitious demands. Its initial proposal pushed for early commitments in market access in services, sanitary and phytosanitary measures, competition policy, and labor and environment standards; defended a WTO-plus scenario; and required the elimination of a products exception list from existing trade agreements. But lacking fast-track authority, the Clinton administration was unable to put forward any substantial offer.

Most Latin American and Caribbean countries rejected an acceleration of the WTO commitments, and the inclusion of labor and environmental rights at the center of the negotiations. In early June, a revised U.S. draft for the ministerial declaration was distributed. The new draft replaced the idea of WTO-plus with its notion of consistency with the WTO rules, recognized the need for differential treatment according to the level of economic development and reduced the number of working groups initially suggested. Most importantly, by affirming that the FTAA should represent "a single undertaking comprising mutual rights and obligations," for the first time the United States recognized the possibility of working toward a single, hemispheric agreement.[63] Since the Clinton administration had formerly signaled a preference for accession to NAFTA of individual countries or subregional blocs, the acceptance of a collective endeavor with thirty-four parties negotiating simultaneously was a significant concession. The shift partly reflected the administration's openness to a more participatory FTAA process. However, on a more pragmatic level, the option for negotiating a single hemispheric agreement implied a prolonged process that diminished the pressure on the U.S. administration for immediately acting on trade initiatives with Latin American countries.

The first trade ministerial meeting took place in Denver in June 1995. The ministers responsible for trade reinforced the commitment to complete negotiations by 2005, and agreed to build on existing bilateral and subregional trade agreements to construct a balanced FTAA, consistent with WTO rules. The ministerial declaration also recognized that the agreement should represent a "single undertaking."[64] The initial U.S. push for countries to consider joining international conventions on intellectual property was excluded from the final declaration. On the structure of the negotiations, the parties agreed to immediately set up working groups on market access; customs procedures and rules of origin; investment; standards and technical barriers to trade; sanitary and phytosanitary measures; subsidies, antidumping, and countervailing duties; and smaller economies, which should start assessing the status of all parties in regard to those issue areas. The establishment of U.S.-promoted working groups on government procurement, intellectual property rights, services, and competition policy, was delayed.[65]

The final declaration reflected the position of most Latin American countries and was particularly beneficial to Brazil, which defended a slower process.[66] Nevertheless, as technical work advanced in the working groups,[67] pressure to move ahead toward actual negotiations increased. Although most countries continued to oppose the U.S. idea of stronger environmental and labor linkages to the FTAA, there was an increasing acceptance of the need to achieve concrete advances on selected issues. By that stage, the division of positions between the negotiating parties started to become more explicit. While Canada, Chile, Colombia, and Costa Rica actively pursued advances in the process, Brazil opposed the idea of setting a date to effectively launch negotiations. The small economies, and CARICOM members in particular, struggled to ensure that differential treatment mechanisms would be developed to address their special needs. The climate of rivalry worsened when Mercosur proposed the formation of a committee with representatives of the subregional blocs to coordinate the working groups. If implemented, the idea would ultimately neutralize the individual weight of the parties, reducing the voice of the smaller countries.[68]

In March 1996, the second trade ministerial meeting took place in Cartagena. From the viewpoint of hemispheric cooperation, the Cartagena meeting revealed a style of dialogue between Brazil and the United States that would emerge at other moments of the FTAA negotiations. Before reaching Colombia, USTR Mickey Kantor met with the Brazilian minister of foreign affairs, Luiz Felipe Lampréia. When they arrived in Cartagena, the United States announced that it would support Brazil's candidature to host the next trade ministerial meeting, rather than Costa Rica. During the meeting, Brazil and the United States worked bilaterally on a proposal for the trade-related environmental language to be adopted in the ministerial declaration, a behavior that generated discontent among other participants.[69] Agreement between the two countries was equally evident in issues related to deadlines for future achievements. There was no decision on when to launch negotiations and the parties simply reaffirmed that "concrete progress" in the FTAA negotiations should be achieved by the end of the century.[70]

As governments approached the third trade ministerial meeting, consensus on the launching of negotiations by 1998 was achieved, but countries disagreed on a negotiation framework. A month before the meeting, the United States, Chile, and Canada were defending simultaneous negotiations of all issue areas. Canada even suggested 2003 as a date for concluding negotiations, in order to give governments time to ratify the deal before it entered into force by 2005. At the other extreme was Mercosur: The Southern Cone bloc proposed a three-tiered negotiation process, starting with business facilitation measures in 1998, moving toward issue areas such as subsidies and customs procedures between 2001 and 2002, and reserving market access and government procurement for a later stage, to begin in 2003.[71]

The third trade ministerial meeting took place in Belo Horizonte, Brazil, in May 1997. Despite the recommendation that negotiations be launched in 1998, governments continued to disagree on how they should be conducted. But the most important issue arising out of the Belo Horizonte meeting was the active participation of the nongovernmental sector. Business, organized labor, and civil society organizations from all over the continent entered into the FTAA debate. Business groups, gathered in the Americas Business Forum, had been holding parallel meetings to the trade ministerial meetings since 1995. Organized labor had its first opportunity to effectively act as a united voice in the FTAA process, drafting a joint declaration demanding participation and protection of workers' rights in the FTAA.[72] It was also in Belo Horizonte that the Hemispheric Social Alliance, a movement of nongovernmental organizations and groups opposing the FTAA, was formed.[73]

During the fourth ministerial meeting, which took place in March 1998 in San José, Costa Rica, trade ministers recommended that their governments officially launch the FTAA negotiations during the Second Summit of the Americas. They reaffirmed that the agreement should constitute a single undertaking, consistent with WTO rules, and that bilateral and subregional schemes could coexist so long as they addressed issues not already covered by the FTAA or which transcended its provisions. The various areas of negotiations would be covered through nine negotiation groups, namely: (1) market access; (2) investment; (3) services; (4) government procurement; (5) dispute settlement; (6) agriculture; (7) intellectual property rights; (8) subsidies, antidumping, and countervailing duties; and (9) competition policy. Brazil, which had not chaired any of the working groups until that stage, assumed the negotiating group on antidumping and countervailing duties. For the first time in trade negotiations, a joint public–private sector committee of experts in electronic commerce was created. Additionally, the parties established a Consultative Group on Smaller Economies and a Committee of Government Representatives on the Participation of Civil Society.[74] In recognition of the importance of Brazil and the United States to the successful conclusion of negotiations, these countries were selected to cochair the final stage of the process,[75] in an exception to the standard procedure of having of a chairman and a vice-chairman.

During the preparatory stage of the FTAA, the negotiating parties went through an impressive learning experience. Having committed to the FTAA, officials had first to understand the national regulatory regimes in place for the issues that would be open to negotiation. Technical asymmetry was profound, and it could be noted not only in the traditional North–South axis, but also within Latin America and the Caribbean.[76] While Chile, Brazil, Costa Rica, and Mexico were commonly mentioned as having well-prepared negotiation teams, some countries faced persistent financial and personnel constraints, including the impossibility of maintaining a national negotiating team exclusively devoted to the FTAA. In some cases, the same government officials were required simultaneously to oversee subregional, FTAA, and WTO negotiations. Furthermore, the accumulation of technical knowledge was frequently affected by electoral cycles and subsequent cabinet reshuffles.

Although addressing technical asymmetry was fundamental to building a more balanced negotiation process, the technical gap does not appear to have been the main reason for the slow advance in the FTAA process. Rather, lack of political leadership seemed to be the main problem. The Clinton administration, facing its own domestic political difficulties over the free trade agenda, helped to legitimize Brazil's claim that the subregional blocs should be given time to consolidate and only gradually expand toward a hemispheric project, despite unease among negotiators from other countries who were willing to accelerate the FTAA process. As the Second Summit of the Americas approached, the parties willing to move the FTAA forward faced the task of attracting the two main players to the process. With the United States and Brazil indicating ambiguity about their political commitment to the negotiations, some Latin American officials even questioned whether it was appropriate for them to maintain their high level of engagement.[77]

The Negotiations Phase (1998–2003)

From 1990 to 1996, Latin American total exports grew 73 percent while the region's imports rose 127 percent. Even with the recovery effect from the decline of the 1980s discounted, intraregional trade flows improved.[78] Attention to FTAA, therefore, did not exclude the development of trade initiatives in other directions. Most Latin American and Caribbean governments were pursuing different kinds of regional arrangements, which scope depended on the profile of the partners involved. Chile and Canada signed a free trade agreement in 1996. Mercosur played with the SAFTA idea. It signed trade agreements with Chile and Bolivia, giving them the status of associate members to the bloc, and initiated conversations with the Andean Community and Mexico. Outside of Latin America, Mercosur signed a framework cooperation agreement with the European Union in 1995. This proliferation of trade agreements created a complex web of trade regulatory regimes in the region that risked undermining their expected trade gains. But in the absence of greater political commitment from the United States and Brazil, achieving agreement over rules would remain a challenge.

For the United States, between 1990 and 1997, exports to Latin America, excluding Mexico, had grown at an annual rate of about 13 percent, showing a better performance than its exports to Europe (5 percent) and Asia (9 percent). Foreign direct investment in the region, attracted by privatizations, also expanded. Yet, Latin America continued to represent a small share of United States total trade. This condition, combined with a domestic climate unfavorable to NAFTA-like agreements, led some U.S. scholars to alert that the FTAA could become another victim of a U.S. "attention deficit disorder."[79]

In April 1998, the Second Summit of the Americas was held in Santiago de Chile.[80] Without the fast-track authority, the Clinton administration's ability to make commitments was curtailed. Faced with the restrictions imposed by the U.S. domestic politics, the negotiating parties hoped that the decision to launch negotiations would increase the political relevance of the FTAA in the United States.

In 1999, a new event diminished the prospects for the FTAA. With many developing countries still struggling to incorporate the commitments of the Uruguay Round, developed countries pushed for a new multilateral round of negotiations. A simultaneous multilateral round created immediate coordination problems and competing interests that threatened to decrease even further the interest of the United States and Brazil in a hemispheric-level accord. The payoffs for both countries were greater in multilateral trade negotiations. For the United States, concessions in antidumping and agricultural subsidies that were politically sensitive but of central interest to Brazil, were likely to be reserved for the WTO, as bargaining tools for exchanges with the EU and Japan. For Brazil, the opening of politically divisive areas such as manufacturing and services sectors, and negotiations over intellectual property rules, should be ideally reserved for the WTO, where it expected higher gains from agricultural liberalization.

Furthermore, allocation of human and financial resources was a limiting factor. While this aspect was evident for the small economies, according to Deputy U.S. Trade Representative, Richard Fisher, even the USTR, "a grossly underfinanced and overburdened agency," was not immune from restrictions.[81] When the Seattle WTO Ministerial Meeting of 1999 turned out to be a complete fiasco, the dispute for resource allocation diminished. However, the Seattle debacle exposed the strength of the anti–free trade movement and indicated that raising support for the FTAA, within and outside the United States, would be a long battle.

As the 2000 U.S. presidential elections approached, and President Clinton focused on obtaining permanent normal trade relations with China, the FTAA process remained on hold. Meanwhile, Brazil continued to advance its project of leadership in South America. In 2000, following Brazil's invitation, government officials from twelve South American nations met for the First South American Summit since independence. As they inaugurated the South American summit process, they reaffirmed their commitment to democracy, trade integration, and infrastructure as the priority areas for cooperation.[82]

The Impact of the George W. Bush Administration

When George W. Bush took power in 2001, many trade negotiators and pro-FTAA forces were relieved. After the failure of the Democrats to push for free trade with Latin America, the pro-FTAA groups were betting on the ability of a Republican administration, supported by a Republican Congress, to advance the free trade agenda. President Bush's initial statements helped to feed their hopes. His last speech in the 2000 campaign, entitled "Century of the Americas," was delivered in Miami, a symbolic site for the Latino and Latin American community. In his speech, Bush criticized the Clinton administration for conducting weak policy toward Latin America, based on "summits without substance, and reaction instead of action":

> Those who ignore Latin America do not fully understand America itself. And those who ignore our hemisphere do not fully understand American interests.... Should I become president, I will look South, not as an afterthought, but as a fundamental commitment of my presidency.[83]

In trade, Bush committed to secure fast-track authority. He maintained that "one-size-fits-all negotiations [were] not always the answer," and that a more flexible approach should be adopted. He also singled out the economic importance of Brazil and the need to have its weight properly reflected in bilateral relations. The preelectoral commitments gained more credibility when, in the first months of Bush's administration, a series of presidential-level meetings with Latin American states established a contrasting record with that prevailing in the Clinton years.

In April 2001, at the Buenos Aires sixth trade ministerial meeting, a first draft of the FTAA agreement was presented and a new committee on institutional issues was created to coordinate the architecture of the agreement. In a surprising decision in the socially insulated field of trade negotiations, governments responded to the petition of more than three hundred nongovernmental organizations calling for the publicity of the FTAA documents,[84] by agreeing to publish the drafts of the FTAA agreement through the FTAA official website, in the four languages spoken in the hemisphere. They also stressed the need to improve dialogue with civil society and to disseminate civil society submissions to the negotiation groups.[85] A few days later, during the Third Summit of the Americas in Quebec City, the parties reaffirmed the decision to reach an agreement by January 2005. Beyond trade, they agreed to adopt a democracy clause to guide the summit's process.[86] The United States, repeating the formula of free market and democracy as the axis for inter-American relations, launched "the century of the Americas."[87]

Nevertheless, the enthusiasm of the pro-FTAA forces for the new Republican administration would not last more than a couple of months. The events of September 11, 2001, redefined U.S. priorities; Latin America and the Caribbean had insufficient military and economic power to contribute to the U.S. war against terrorism, and hence lacked the qualities to be seen as a strategically ally of the United States.[88]

The Bush administration obtained fast-track authority—renamed trade promotion authority—but the terms attached to the authorization greatly constrained the administration's margin for maneuver. In addition to requiring the inclusion of labor and environmental protection goals in trade agreements, it reduced the executive's capacity to negotiate U.S. import sensitive agricultural products and trade remedy laws, subjecting negotiations for those products to prior congressional consultation.[89] As side payments for congressional support, the administration agreed to impose temporary safeguards in order to protect the steel industry and enacted a new farm bill that raised subsidies to agriculture.

In addition to the unfavorable domestic political conditions in the post–September 11 attack, negotiations were further affected by the appointment of Robert Zoellick as U.S. trade representative. Zoellick argued that a Republican administration should avoid using international agreements and institutions as "forms of political therapy." Multilateralism should be used as a tool, not required for all issues all the time. In trade, the United States should approach countries either individually or in groups, moving forward with those willing to cooperate.⁹⁰ This strategy, which became known as "competitive liberalization," was first advanced by Treasury Secretary James Baker, whom Zoellick served as deputy assistant secretary and counselor. Commenting on CUSFTA in 1988, Baker argued that the creation of a "market liberalization club" through bilateral and plurilateral trade agreements could pressure other countries to either open their markets or face the risk of being left behind. As he declared, "we will do it with them [other nations] or without them. The choice is theirs."⁹¹

It was in this changing political scenario that the FTAA negotiations occurred. Recommendations on the methods and modalities for negotiations were submitted in April 2002, and a schedule for exchange of offers was defined. Offers on agricultural and nonagricultural products, services, investment, and government procurement were to be submitted between December 2002 and February 2003. Between February and June 2003, the parties should work on improving the offers, so that from July 2003, they could concentrate on the exchange of revised offers in the negotiations.⁹²

Although Latin American and Caribbean governments disliked U.S. unilateralism, most countries did not react by shifting to an anti-U.S. attitude. Only Venezuelan president Hugo Chavez engaged in vocal anti-U.S. rhetoric but this exception did not represent a real threat to the FTAA negotiations. It was Brazil's reaction to the new conditions imposed by the United States that ultimately led to the negotiations paralysis.

The FTAA Crisis

In 2002, the Bush administration undermined the possibility of a balanced outcome by unilaterally removing agricultural subsidies and antidumping rules—issues in which Brazil was a *demandeur*⁹³—from the negotiation table. On the other hand, the United States pushed for WTO-plus commitments in areas such as intellectual property and investment, increasing even further the sense of asymmetry. Throughout the negotiations, Brazil had insisted on balanced negotiations,⁹⁴ and Brazilian negotiators made clear that an "FTAA lite," which removed all the substantive issues of interest to Brazil and demanded WTO-plus rules, would not be of interest to the country.

Despite its critical tone, Brazil remained engaged in the negotiations. As the then Brazilian minister of foreign affairs, Celso Lafer, said, "I don't believe...that one should look at the FTAA as an exercise condemned to an insolvable confrontation."⁹⁵ Moreover, when in May 2002, a visiting Canadian delegation speculated about a potential bilateral agreement between Canada and Mercosur, Lafer reaffirmed the commitment to the hemispheric project.⁹⁶

This attitude of critical engagement changed with the election of a new president in Brazil. In late 2002, Luiz Inácio Lula da Silva, from the Workers' Party, was elected president of Brazil, after a campaign in which his party had strongly criticized the FTAA. In a context in which Brazil's interest in the process was already very limited, the U.S.initial offers, presented in February 2003, came as a shock to the negotiators. In an unexpected move criticized by most trade specialists following the process, the United States designed differentiated offers of market access for each subregional bloc, with the less substantial offer being made to Mercosur.[97]

From that moment on, the negotiations were in serious crisis. Brazilian negotiators openly defended a bilateral negotiation or a Mercosur-U.S. deal (the 4+1 format).[98] They played down the importance of the FTAA to the country's economy and highlighted the relevance of the ongoing negotiations with the European Union and at the Doha Round. Although the United States did not advance on the 4+1 format of negotiations that Brazil desired, neither did it adopt an aggressive tone with Brazil. Instead, U.S. trade representative Zoellick publicly defended the use of "pragmatic ideas"[99] to advance the FTAA.

In June 2003, trade representatives from fourteen of the thirty-four negotiating parties met in the United States. Brazil, insisting on coordination of its multilateral, regional and interregional (Mercosur-EU) agendas, demanded that sensitive issues be excluded from the FTAA. It maintained that if the United States could transfer agricultural subsidies and trade remedy laws to the WTO, then other countries too could reserve to the WTO the discussion on rules such as those related to intellectual property and investment. In essence, Brazil demanded that in order to maintain balance in the negotiations, both U.S. and Brazilian interests should be preserved. Brazilian diplomats proposed a three-track approach to the negotiations, in which countries would be allowed to negotiate market access bilaterally or plurilaterally, and rules on nonsensitive areas, such as provisions on business facilitation, would be negotiated on a hemispheric basis. However, systemic issues, such as rules on antidumping, services, intellectual property, government procurement, investment, and agricultural subsidies, would be reserved for negotiations at the WTO Doha Round.[100]

This proposal, which was informally referred to by negotiators as "FTAA lite,"[101] met strong resistance.[102] The transfer of systemic issues to the WTO became more problematic when, in September 2003, the Cancún WTO ministerial meeting failed.[103] While Brazil celebrated its diplomatic victory in leading the formation of the coalition of developing countries (the G20),[104] the Cancún crisis indicated the difficulties that the United States would face in achieving short term advances at the multilateral level.[105]

The sense of a looming crisis was becoming evident. A few days before the preparatory meeting scheduled for October 2003 in Port-of-Spain, Zoellick's assistant, Chris Padilla, complained about what he considered Brazil's ultranationalist behavior.[106] In Port-of-Spain, Venezuela continued to oppose the FTAA, and the CARICOM maintained caution, but fourteen countries rejected Brazil's three-track approach. Even within Mercosur, divergence increased. Differences within the bloc had already been exposed early in 2003, when its members presented individual offers in the areas of investment, services, and government procurement, rather than acting as a bloc.

In Port-of-Spain, Uruguay submitted a separate document that contained its own view of the FTAA, and Paraguay showed discontent. Only Argentina, whose acute economic crisis was consuming all its political attention, clearly favored Brazil.

A few days before the Miami ministerial meeting, Brazil and the United States drafted a declaration in which their agreement on how to accommodate their interests was presented for consideration by the other negotiating parties. The bilateral solution envisioned the possibility of differentiated levels of commitments on various issues, and as a result, it dismantled the single undertaking principle that had guided the FTAA process since 1995. Although the draft disappointed other parties to the negotiations,[107] the Brazil-U.S. decision became the basis of the Miami trade ministerial declaration (Appendix C):

> Taking into account and acknowledging existing mandates, Ministers recognize that countries may assume different levels of commitments. We will seek to develop a common and balanced set of rights and obligations applicable to all countries. In addition, negotiations should allow for countries that so choose, within the FTAA, to agree to additional obligations and benefits. One possible course of action would be for these countries to conduct plurilateral negotiations within the FTAA to define the obligations in the respective individual areas.[108]

In an indication that the fragmentation of the negotiations did not adversely affect its ambitions, the United States offered the possibility of bilateral trade agreements. Already during the Miami ministerial meeting, the USTR announced its intention to extend bilateral free trade initiatives from Central America to South America, through negotiations with Colombia and Peru.[109] Uruguay also joined the momentum, announcing with the United States that they would start negotiations for a bilateral investment treaty. These agreements ruined any attempt to contain the development of a hub-and-spoke system in the Americas, and allowed the United States to play freely in highly asymmetrical bilateral negotiations. At the same time, the diplomatic solution freed Brazil from any obligation to the FTAA.

In the following months, negotiators from several countries sent letters to the cochairs hoping for clarifications on how to make the vague Miami idea concrete. There were, however, no signs of progress from the cochairs. When negotiators met again in Puebla, in February 2004, the stagnation was clear. Chile, Mexico, and Canada, all already bound by free trade agreements with the United States, voiced their criticisms and alerted that Brazil would not become a free rider in the negotiations.[110] By the end of the Puebla meeting, indecision prevailed. The proposed framework envisioned two levels of negotiations. The first level comprised a common set of obligations agreed by all parties, while the second involved a voluntary movement toward bilateral and plurilateral deals with varying degrees of commitment that would bind only the parties interested in those arrangements.[111]

While the framework adopted in Puebla was a diplomatic solution convenient for both Brazil and the United States, in practice it represented the collapse of the idea of a hemispheric free trade agreement. Brazil did not organize the trade ministerial meeting of 2004. The project for a hemisphere-wide free trade area, which a decade before had represented the hope for a new form of inter-American cooperation, was abandoned by its main negotiating parties.[112]

When representatives of thirty-four states in the Americas met in 2005 for the Fourth Summit of the Americas in Mar del Plata, the climate of tension differed considerably from the optimistic atmosphere of the early 1990s. By 2005, the electoral victory of center-left and left-wing parties in many countries in the region was revealing of strong popular discontent with the policies guided by the Washington Consensus. Although many presidents associated with this rise of the left maintained the economic orthodoxy of the 1990s,[113] in regard to the FTAA negotiations, divisions among Latin Americans became more pronounced. Hugo Chávez addressed thousands of protestors at a rally during the summit, claiming that the occasion should mark the death of the FTAA. Mexico, faced with the resistance of Mercosur—mainly, from Brazil and Argentina—to advances on the free trade issue, suggested the resumption of negotiations without the Southern Cone bloc.[114] Outside the official meetings, massive anti-FTAA and anti-Bush demonstrations gave strength to those governments that opposed the resumption of the project, which was becoming even less appealing to the United States.[115]

At the Fifth Summit of the Americas in 2009, the political configuration in the United States had changed once again. With the arrival of Democrat Barack Obama, there was a sense that cooperation—or a less unilateral approach—was possible in U.S.–Latin American relations. Obama's measures to improve relations with Cuba were a significant change in relation to decades of unsuccessful U.S. foreign policies toward that country. But the optimism during the Fifth Summit was built around issues of security and sustainable development. Free trade, and the FTAA in particular, disappeared from the list of priorities.[116]

Lack of Leadership an d Cooperation Crisis

For a decade, governments in the Western Hemisphere participated in a collective initiative which, if successful, would have led to the largest trading bloc in the world. Despite the fact that the various parties involved in the process supported the FTAA moving forward, it was the bilateral negotiations between the two main players Brazil and the United States that ultimately defined the outcome of the negotiations.

As a cooperative initiative, the FTAA failed, exposing the difficulties of constructing a regional initiative in the continent, when the option of bilateralism is perceived by most countries as an attractive way to gain privileges from the United States. In this regard, Brazil's behavior as cochair of the process was no different. Since for both Brazil and the United States, fragmentation of the FTAA suited their respective foreign policy strategies, it would be possible to claim that the outcome was not a complete failure from the individual perspective of these two governments. But despite optimistic predictions,[117] in the case of the United States, the competitive liberalization strategy might have created the opposite of what was intended, that is, piecemeal agreements that increase the inefficiencies in the multilateral trading system.

Interpreted through the lens of U.S.–Latin American relations, it appears that U.S. interests in engaging in the FTAA were less clear than in former attempts at economic cooperation. In the 1990s, there was no evident regional crisis affecting U.S. interests and pushing the United States to engage in the process. In trade and investment, unilateral reforms in different countries in Latin America already favored the economic interests of the United States and the business sector. Though Latin America represented an expanding market for U.S. exports, its place in total U.S. trade, apart from Mexico, was minimal. While NAFTA was strongly supported by interest groups, the FTAA never managed to mobilize a similar level of support.[118] Ironically, in 2002, only Brazil (14th) and Venezuela (20th), two forces of resistance to the FTAA, ranked among the top twenty U.S. trade partners.[119] Moreover, from a U.S. foreign policy perspective, critical issues such as drug trafficking and immigration were more efficiently addressed unilaterally. In bilateral relations, the asymmetry of bargaining power reduced negotiations to a "take it or leave it" process, with the United States mainly defining the terms for an agreement. This tension was obvious in the FTAA, where the idea of hemispheric trade integration through the gradual accession of individual countries and subregional blocs to NAFTA was present from the project's beginning.

As the various bilateral free trade agreements that have been signed between the United States and Latin Americans demonstrate, a low level of U.S. commitment does not impede cooperation. The free trade agreements signed with Mexico, Chile, Colombia, Peru, and Central America, challenged predictions that a hegemonic U.S. project in trade would be strongly opposed in Latin America.[120] As a bidirectional process, cooperation can still occur if the party negotiating with the United States perceives the gains of an agreement or the costs of being left behind as sufficiently high to overshadow concerns about asymmetry.[121] This situation has characterized U.S. negotiations of free trade agreements not only with Latin American countries but also with developed countries such as Canada and Australia.

It is here that the role of Brazil in blocking the FTAA negotiations was decisive. In Brazil's foreign policy, preservation of autonomy and less asymmetrical relations with developed countries are essential components of its self-conceived role in the international system. In this vision, Brazilian foreign policy makers have consistently insisted on a balanced relationship with the United States, one that recognizes the distinct power of Brazil on the continent. For the Brazilian foreign policymaking elite, a successful bilateral negotiation with the United States, which occurred through the prevalence of Brazil's idea of fragmenting the FTAA, was an indication of the country's position as a special player, one that could refuse to be treated as "just another" Latin American country.

Since the early 1990s, prospective economic benefits had been insufficient to mobilize fully the domestic political resources necessary for sustained leadership in the FTAA. Although governments in both the United States and Brazil shifted to a moderate position of accepting a thirty-four party agreement during the 1990s, in the end, the preference for bilateralism prevailed.

Part III

Background

Chapter 3

Economic Paradigms and Trade Regionalism in Latin America

Between the first attempt at trade integration in the Americas, which took place during the First International Conference of American States (1889–1890), and the proposal for the formation of a hemispheric free trade area announced by the Bush administration in 1990, one hundred years have passed. Over a century, the idea of regional trade cooperation has ebbed in scope and political relevance in inter-American relations without ever being completely eliminated.

This book examines how decision makers within states perceived a set of domestic and international variables as motivations or constraints, and how such assessments formed the basis for particular courses of actions. In the case of the FTAA project, perceptions are particularly relevant to understanding the impressive "change in attitude"[1] among Latin American states concerning their economic dependence from the United States.

Until the late 1980s, U.S. relations with various Latin American countries had been dominated by frustrated initiatives for economic cooperation, and tension over the great asymmetry of power. But in 1990, when President George H.W. Bush announced the U.S. intention of forming a free trade area from Alaska to Tierra del Fuego, he found in Latin America a responsive audience. As Uruguay's president commented: "When, after years of our complaining of neglect, the most important man in the world offers his hand, then I think we should grab it—and the arm and the elbow and the shoulder, too."[2]

While studies of the FTAA process usually emphasize trade and investment indicators in order to detect the motivations for the initiative, this chapter focuses on the economic history of Latin America. It traces the change in economic paradigm in the region from a "development" concept that relied on the state as a central actor, to a paradigm according to which state intervention in the economy should be reduced, giving way to market rules as the guiding force of the economy. An examination of the shifts in economic paradigms enables us to locate the ideas and beliefs that allowed specific notions of trade regionalism to gain policy influence in particular historical contexts.[3] Following this orientation, the FTAA is placed in the context of the rise of a new group of decision makers, ideologically aligned with the neoliberal paradigm, and who gave the project its political advocacy basis.The section "A Latin American Path to Development" describes the emergence of *structuralism* in Latin America, examining how the regional trade initiatives of the 1960s reflected the predominant economic paradigm of that period. The section "The Empowerment of Neoliberal Ideas" deals with the rise of neoliberalism in the region that followed the crisis of the previous paradigm. It explores the external and domestic conditions that contributed to the political empowerment of a new profile of policymakers in various Latin American countries and looks at how their views influenced the direction of economic reforms and expectations prevailing by 1990. The section "From Latin American to Hemispheric Integration" addresses the new open trade regionalism in Latin America, and how it reflected political and ideological conditions favorable to a rapprochement with the United States. The final section concludes with discussions about how the change in economic paradigms contributed to the development of political support for the idea of hemispheric trade integration in the early 1990s.

A Latin American Path to Development

By the time the Enterprise for the Americas Initiative (EAI) was launched in 1990, trade regionalism in Latin America was already moving away from protectionism. In contrast to the old regionalism of the 1960s, the new wave of regional trade integration was outward-oriented, directed to improving the competitiveness of the countries in the region and to reinforcing rather than blocking multilateral liberalization.[4] It appeared that after decades of attempts to develop from within, Latin America was finally reconverted to liberal economic principles, becoming the ideal laboratory for Washington Consensus–based experiments.[5]

Inspired by the depth and fast pace that characterized the shift in economic thinking in the region, studies of the economic history of Latin America gained new impetus.[6] In comparison with previous accounts, in which structural explanations predominated and human agency was left unexamined,[7] recent scholarship has placed more emphasis on institutions and ideas in economic policymaking.

In Latin America, liberal economic ideas have circulated since political independence.[8] Though not all policies could be accurately characterized as liberal,[9] until the Great Depression, state intervention in the economy was not consistently practiced and the existing structure basically relied on static comparative advantages. Despite the achievement of political independence in the early nineteenth century, most Latin American states maintained a peripheral position in the international economy, characterized by dependence on the exports of primary goods and imports of manufactured products.

A distinguishing variable that has heavily influenced the economic development of the region is its geographic proximity to the United States. For many countries in the world, relationships with the United States can be imagined before they turn into reality. For Latin America, this is not an option. The degree of U.S. influence has varied between countries and time periods, but overall, the rise of the United States as a world power in the last century configured a structure of extreme power asymmetry in the hemisphere that does not find an equivalent in other areas in the world in the same period. By 1920, the United States had already passed Britain as the top Latin America's trade partner, accounting for approximately half of the region's exports and imports.[10]

While during the first decades of the twentieth century, Latin America could rely on a more liberal economic system dependent on export of primary products, the First World War and the Great Depression imposed very different conditions. The reduction in international demand for primary goods, fluctuation in commodity prices, and difficulties in importing manufactured goods increased pressures for state action.[11] Nevertheless, it would be only from the early 1940s onwards that defense of state intervention in the economy would become broadly diffused. By then, Keynesianism and successive world economic crises had helped to transform the idea of government intervention in the economy into an acceptable policy across the world.[12] Although the phenomenon was not peculiar to Latin America, it acquired a specific value in the region, as the state planning of industrialization became part of political projects of the construction of economic identities.[13] State intervention was also pushed by the contraction in the availability of loans from traditional sources. With the United States concentrating on the reconstruction of Western Europe and Japan, Latin Americans' pleas for funds were ignored.

The postwar context and U.S. neglect created a crisis that stimulated governments and intellectuals throughout Latin America to search for ways to address the region's economic challenges. In this task, they were aided by the creation of an institution that would host new ideas. In 1948, the United Nations Economic Commission for Latin America (CEPAL) was established.[14] Although the creation of CEPAL was part of a larger UN initiative in the post–Second World War period to set up regional development commissions, unlike its sister institutions in other regions of the world,[15] it became a unique institutional umbrella under which a regional model of economic development emerged and was disseminated throughout Latin America and beyond.[16]

Within CEPAL, a Latin American version of structuralism took shape. *Cepalinos* rejected the idea of universal economic rules to guide development and argued instead that economic development required an analysis of the structural specificities at both national and regional levels. Since structuralism considered that social actors create and reproduce structures, the neoclassical model of universal rules in an atomized society ruled by the forces of the market had little intellectual resonance.[17]

The claim for specificity in economic analysis was not uncommon in the 1940s. In an article published in 1947, economist Jacob Viner had warned about the risk of pushing for an international standardization of trade rules, noting that as "no economic principle has universal appeal," international regulation could not "reasonably be expected to be tidier than the patterns with which we are familiar in the field of domestic legislation."[18]

Raúl Prebisch became the best-known contributor to structuralism.[19] He became CEPAL's executive secretary in 1949 and remained in the institution until 1964, when he was appointed general secretary of the United Nations Trade and Development Conference (UNCTAD). Originally a neoclassical economist, Prebisch later observed that the reality of the international economic system led him to reconsider his initial position.[20] Based on his observation of the deterioration of terms of trade, Prebisch argued that in order to change the peripheral economic position of Latin American economies, characterized by their dependence on the export of primary goods and import of manufactured goods,[21] it was necessary to foster the production of higher value-added goods. Originally, protectionism was envisioned as a temporary mechanism that would allow industrialization to develop. Economic development also required that attention be paid to exports. While the initial concept was to foster exports of the new manufactures in addition to primary commodities, in practice export policies received less attention.[22] Despite warnings about the risk of a superficial modernization funded by foreign capital,[23] the scarcity of domestic resources to finance the industrial expansion and the need to import capital goods led to continuous dependence on external investment and loans.[24]

Beginning in 1960, Latin Americans moved to establish subregional integration initiatives whose logic was subsumed to the ISI framework. Although these initiatives were inspired by the European experience, the motivations for integration in Latin America differed considerably from the European case. While the Second World War had given Western Europeans an abnormal incentive to cooperate, Latin Americans lacked such a strong geopolitical incentive. In the experiments with trade regionalism that were initiated in Latin America and the Caribbean, trade integration was conceived mainly as a tool to achieve economies of scale and to make industrialization viable, contributing to the reduction of economic dependence on the core economies.

In his comments on the challenges for the formation of a Latin American common market, Prebisch recalled that since independence in the nineteenth century, declarations of goodwill among Latin American governments had been insufficient to move economic relations in the region beyond a basic level of economic complementarity. In order to avoid the mistakes of the past, he suggested that countries would have to be convinced that "only by means of their increasing close integration—in the setting of a common market—will they be able to implement their own individual development programmes."[25]

Intraregional cooperation was a logical solution within the framework of ISI-based development. With the exception of Mexico, Brazil, and Argentina, economies in the region were too small to sustain industrialization within the limits of their own borders. Integration of the national economies would generate economies of scale and optimize production structures. Furthermore, regional trade integration could help countries to achieve reciprocal liberalization while still retaining control over the level of openness.[26]

The first group to move toward integration was made up of Central American countries: Costa Rica, El Salvador, Guatemala, Honduras, and Nicaragua. Intergovernmental negotiations began in 1951. A series of bilateral preferential trade agreements were signed, and later compiled into a single preferential system in 1958. In 1960, El Salvador, Guatemala, and Honduras signed the General Treaty for Central American Integration— Nicaragua and Costa Rica joined later—giving birth to the Central American Common Market (CACM).

Countries in South America and Mexico also considered the formation of a free trade area. In 1960, Argentina, Brazil, Chile, and Uruguay signed the Treaty of Montevideo, which laid the foundation for the Latin American Free Trade Area (LAFTA). Other South American countries joined gradually and by 1968, LAFTA membership included all Spanish-speaking countries in South America, as well as Brazil and Mexico.[27]

The smaller economies within LAFTA soon realized the problems posed by the economic asymmetries between them and the dominant economies of Argentina, Brazil, and Mexico. In 1969, Bolivia, Chile, Colombia, Ecuador, and Peru signed the Andean Pact, with Venezuela joining the group in 1973. The Andean Pact was broader in scope and institutionally more sophisticated than LAFTA. It envisioned the formation of a customs union, and coordination in industrial and investment policies, regional funding mechanisms, and cooperation in labor, cultural, and social policies. Together, its members expected to improve their positions within LAFTA.[28]

The English-speaking territories in the Caribbean Basin also moved toward the formation of a subregional economic bloc. The Caribbean Free Trade Agreement was signed in 1968, and in 1973 the Caribbean Community (CARICOM) was formed,[29] with plans for the formation of a common market. Similar to the Andean Group, the Caribbean countries aimed for a level of integration that went beyond trade, including coordination in social and foreign policies.[30] But, since economic spaces do not necessarily coincide with borders,[31] various governments struggled to harmonize notions of national identity with a strategy of economic survival that required the capacity to imagine a borderless economy.

The Crisis of the Developmentalist Paradigm

By the 1970s, the developmentalist policies oriented by structuralism were under heavy criticism.[32] Countries reached the decade more dependent on foreign capital. From the import of intermediate and capital goods, to the expansion of transnational corporations and foreign loans, the import substitution industrialization model had fostered "dependent development."[33]

The resulting economic situation was augmented by problems in the political sphere. The development vision promoted by most structuralists was not designed to oppose capitalism, but attempted to find development solutions within it. This orientation began to be challenged by the events of the 1960s and 1970s, when various countries experienced an escalation in social unrest. Industrialists and an urban, "modern," professional middle class united to support military coups throughout the Southern Cone so that modernization could proceed, even at the cost of high social repression.[34]

By then, the *cepalinos* were reviewing their own position. The economic ideas that had been so powerful in the 1950s were now dismissed by both the left and the right. Whereas Marxists saw developmentalist ideas as a byproduct of capitalism, unable to generate the ruptures required for structural transformation, for conservatives the model had failed precisely because of an excessive reliance on the state's ability to manage the economy.[35] The most significant failure, however, was the fact that economic growth seemed unable to reduce inequality.[36] The entrenched nature of inequality in Latin America raised the uncomfortable but persistent question of who had gained under the dominant model.

Even in semiperipheral Mexico and Brazil, where a more complex industrial base was possible, transnational corporations won out of the alliances with local elites and states, which were the basis of associated-dependent development.[37] Protectionism, initially seen as a mechanism for fostering development, became an end in itself, and rent-seeking behavior by industrialists, regardless of the origin of the capital, was widespread.

With regard to trade integration, though results were substantially below expectations, intraregional trade diversification increased. By 1975, approximately half of the intraregional trade was made up of manufactured products, in sharp contrast to the pattern of extraregional exports, which continued to be dominated by primary goods.[38] Still the United States remained the most important trade partner and source of investment for many Latin American countries. While intraregional trade in manufactured goods diminished the importance of the United States as a provider of those goods, its share in Latin American imports of primary products actually increased.[39]

The performance of the subregional associations was also severely limited by political differences. In 1976, under General Augusto Pinochet, Chile left the Andean Pact.[40] In the CACM, political polarization in Central America and U.S. interventionism deepened the cleavages among members from the late 1970s onwards. Within LAFTA, resistance to greater institutional commitment, particularly on the part of Argentina, Brazil, and Mexico, led to stagnation.[41] Without mechanisms to address the asymmetries among the economies in the region, regional integration tended to deepen regional unbalances,[42] with the countries with a larger industrial base expanding their intraregional exports of manufactured goods. By 1980, LAFTA was substituted by a more modest venture—the Latin American Integration Association (LAIA or ALADI, in Spanish)—which attempted to deal with the conflict of individual interests by adopting a minimalist approach to liberalization, based on preferential trade agreements signed on a bilateral basis.[43]

During the 1970s, the crisis of the developmentalist paradigm that had dominated in the previous decades prompted a search for policy alternatives. Advocates of market-based reforms seized the opportunity to condemn the notion of state-led industrialization, erroneously portrayed as equivalent to ISI industrialization.[44] The fact that in the successful experiences of the new industrialized countries in East Asia, states played a central role in the economy, received little attention. The shift to another economic paradigm in Latin America had begun.

Structuralism entered economic history as an original contribution, developed in and inspired by the reality of a peripheral region in the world.[45] The debate about the external vulnerability of countries highly dependent on commodity exports, and the need to reduce the technological gap between center and periphery, continues. A less passionate reexamination of structuralist ideas has become possible now that the weaknesses of the neoliberal paradigm were revealed in practice.[46] In a reaction to the economic crisis initiated in late 2008, the World Bank emphasized the differentiated impact of particular kinds of export dependence and how drastic shifts in commodity prices exposed countries, especially the poorer, to higher economic and social instability.[47]

Nevertheless, until the late 1990s, the hegemony of the neoliberal paradigm meant signals of deficiency in the new model and alternatives were often disregarded.[48] Those defending reform policies that resembled the developmentalist paradigm lost political influence.[49] The next section revisits that shift in paradigm in view of a changing international context, and the empowerment of a new group of policymakers.

The Empowerment of Neoliberal Ideas

In the 1980s, Latin American countries had to manage a deep financial crisis under unfavorable external conditions. Like in the post–Second World War period, a changing international environment increased the pressure for innovative economic policies that aimed to repair the failures of the previous economic model. In the global reorganization of capital that began in the 1970s,[50] trade, particularly of an intraindustry kind, expanded in connection with the transnational corporations' reorganization of production. The rise of the East Asian economies further challenged the prevailing Latin American strategy of development. In both regions, state-led developmentalist projects had been implemented during the 1960s and 1970s.[51] Business and the state formed corporatist alliances and transnational corporations were central in the implementation of industrial policies. But, while Latin American developmentalism had focused on import substitution, Asian

Table 3.1 Price variation of selected commodities (index 1985=100)

	1980	1981	1982	1983	1984	1985	1986	1987	1988	1989	1990
Coffee	115	93	95	91	95	100	141	79	87	69	62
Copper	153	123	104	112	97	100	97	126	183	201	188
Tin	139	117	106	108	102	100	62	57	60	72	52
Oil	132	126	116	105	105	100	51	66	52	64	82

Source: UNCTAD Handbook of Statistics Online.

developmentalism had been outward-oriented. With Japanese foreign direct investment, developmentalism in East Asia was geared toward the building of a competitive production structure, based on the export of high technology, low labor-cost manufactured products.[52]

If the contrast in performance with East Asia was already disturbing, the fact that Latin American financial dependence on foreign loans had risen in the 1970s furthered the sense of economic failure. By the end of the decade, the cost of the borrowing-for-growth policies was apparent. The steep rise in interest rates increased Latin American foreign debt to unmanageable proportions. Mexico, whose debt accounted for about 44 percent of the capital of the U.S. nine largest financial institutions,[53] declared a moratorium in 1982.

Following Mexico's debacle, almost every Latin American country was affected by the reduced credit and uncontrolled rise in interest rates. The size of international loans allocated to Latin America gives a good indication of why the region became the focus of much concern in international financial centers. By 1982, accumulated loans disbursed to the region by eighteen leading financial institutions reached US$ 70 billion, and for most of these banks, the ratio of loans to equity in the region surpassed 100 percent.[54]

Improving export performance was fundamental, but Latin Americans faced two adverse external constraints. First, there was a steep fall in the world prices of commodities, which remained the most relevant items in the extraregional exports (Table 3.1). Although Latin American exports increased in volume, actual revenues from exports by 1985 remained at the levels of 1981.[55]

Second, multilateral financial institutions pressured Latin Americans to liberalize their trade at a time when industrially developed countries maintained strong protectionist mechanisms in place. A 1986 study using data on nontariff barriers revealed that those types of barriers were particularly damaging for the exports of products in which developing countries tended to specialize, such as agriculture and mineral resources,[56] and were higher for the exports of the subgroup of highly indebted countries.[57]

In handling the debt crisis, the International Monetary Fund (IMF) used conditionalities to push debtors to adopt structural adjustment programs[58] considered necessary to bring creditors to the debt restructuring negotiation table. While the push by the IMF and international banks heavily influenced the adoption of neoliberal policies in Latin America, the prescribed reforms differed in pace, order, and depth. Chile, for instance, initiated its orthodox experiment in the mid-1970s, before the shift observed in the United Kingdom and the United States.[59] Argentina, Brazil, and Peru, in contrast, insisted on heterodox plans well into the late 1980s, despite extremely high rates of inflation and pressures from international creditors. Comparative studies of stabilization programs confirm that despite the transnational character of the neoliberal project,[60] the degree to which the Washington Consensus package was embraced and implemented in each national setting depended on domestic political and social characteristics,[61] including the level of receptivity by national policy elites to the new ideology.[62]

During this period, the role of economists in the transformation of the neoliberal paradigm into actual policies became more pronounced.[63] It was through politically influential carriers that the new economic ideas gained power and ultimately led to a change in perception of the value of a closer economic alliance with the United States.

From the 1970s onwards, interaction between academics from Latin America and the United States expanded, mainly through the inflow of Latin American scholars to U.S. universities and research institutions.[64] For Latin American economists, a doctoral degree obtained in the United States began to be seen informally as a prerequisite for a high-level government position.[65] At a time when governments had to endure complex economic negotiations with the United States and international financial institutions, the experience acquired in the United States became particularly valuable. Discussions of structural adjustments required a new set of skills for policymakers, which included not only technical capacity but also the ability to network with external creditors. Economists trained in the United States gradually came to occupy decision-making positions throughout Latin America.[66]

Advocates of market-based reforms were pleased with this new generation of policymakers. Some scholars even applied a new term—"technopols"—to underline the combination of technical expertise and political skills that characterized the rising generation of policy makers in Latin America.[67] Expertise, according to their definition, was measured by the degree to which the policy maker's ideas fit "normal international professional standards,"[68] which essentially meant the commitment to the free market democracy ideal. Despite the variety of perspectives in the discipline of economics, a manual for the technopols prescribed that the path to the "general good" would be paved if this new group of decision makers managed to pursue the objectives set out by "traditional normative economic analysis."[69] The synchronicity among the new generation of policymakers was not simply a case of an "epistemic community"[70] sharing a similar perspective on economic issues. The strength of the policymaking teams was frequently enhanced by personal bonds of trust and loyalty[71] which, following the personalist tradition in Latin America, often meant coherence of action and bureaucratic insulation.

The debt crisis of the 1980s functioned as a catalyst for economic reforms, creating an opportunity for change in economic policy ideas. By 1990, most Latin American governments had to some degree converged toward a paradigm of economic development that focused on export-led economic growth and trade liberalization as central means for improving international competitiveness. It was within this conjuncture of external constraints and a change in ideas about how to conduct the economy, that a new version of trade regionalism gained support.

Open Regionalism as a New Policy Solution

In 1991, almost a decade after the beginning of the debt crisis, all Latin American countries with the exception of Chile and Colombia had a GDP per capita below that registered in 1980. Throughout the 1980s, per capita output growth in the region registered a decline of about 0.6 percent per year.[72] The economic recession, combined with diminishing investment in public services such as health and education, aggravated poverty and inequality. Unemployment also soared, and overall, real wages were lower than at the beginning of the 1980s. In 1991, average real wages had declined to 76.2 percent in Argentina, 87.8 percent in Brazil, and 41.8 percent in Peru in comparison to the levels registered in 1980. Very few countries showed some improvement (109.9 percent in Chile and 115.3 percent in Colombia).[73]

The legacy of the 1980s was not merely a fiscal crisis. More deeply, the "lost decade" reflected an environment of prolonged chaos that fractured the social fabric and worsened already deficient social and economic conditions for the majority of Latin Americans. The political battle for solutions to the crisis was fundamentally a dispute between contrasting views on how to balance social and economic considerations.

Although most analysts agreed on the need to open Latin American trade, the timing and mode of liberalization were debatable. At a time when countries needed to improve their balance of payments, it was unclear whether unilateral trade liberalization simultaneously with the unification of exchange rates was a wise policy. As one economist suggested, the inclusion of free trade policy in structural adjustment reforms might have been more a matter of convenience for the multilateral financial institutions than a prescription based on sound technical analysis.[74]

Regardless of the technical dissent,[75] most Latin American governments implemented trade liberalization programs.[76] A region that had closed itself off to foreign competition now liberalized through the politically costly path of unilateral liberalization.[77] When individual cases of trade reforms are examined, it appears that beyond the pressures from multilateral financial institutions, ideological convergence assisted in tipping the balance toward trade liberalization. In the case of Mexico, Babb argues that a combination of "coercive" and "expert isomorphism" went on the trade agenda, with international institutions operating in synchronicity with like-minded free traders in the Salinas administration.[78]

It was at this point that ideas for a new regionalism started to take shape. As with the regionalism of the 1960s, the new trade regionalism in Latin America was also influenced by external factors. The formation of the European Single Market, the U.S. move toward bilateral alternatives, and the participation of Latin American countries in the Uruguay Round of multilateral trade negotiations (1986–1993) increased the external pressure on already overloaded national policy agendas.

In the new context in which the idea of trade regionalism reemerged, Latin Americans had to take into account a more complex set of conditions associated with the globalization process.[79] Reciprocal tariff reductions were important, but considering that most countries had already conducted or were in the process of implementing trade reforms unilaterally, the new wave of regionalism was not aimed at tariff elimination only.

If extraregional factors contributed to a discussion of regionalism that rejected the inward-looking model, the deficiencies of the old regionalism of the 1960s and 1970s further delegitimized it. In addition to political difficulties of cooperation, during the debt crisis the subregional blocs were unable to provide a protection against external shocks. Intra-LAFTA exports as a percentage of the total exports of members decreased from 13.7 percent in 1980 to 9.1 percent in 1984.[80] Throughout Latin America and the Caribbean, countries were forced to recognize that integration was a complex process characterized by interruptions and slowdowns, and whose sustainability required continuous political commitment.

The initiatives of the 1990s were built upon the idea of an "open regionalism." Participation would be nonexclusive and countries remained free to pursue other associations and trade strategies. The new open regionalism reflected a belief that in view of the interdependence that characterized many of the economies in the region, the strengthening of subregional blocs could generate more attractive conditions for foreign investors and improve the competitiveness of the countries involved.[81] Interestingly, one of the most supportive voices in the new trade regionalism was CEPAL. Its definition of open regionalism accurately reflected the move away from the vision of trade regionalism as a regionally grounded developmental solution:

> a process of growing economic interdependence at the regional level, promoted both by preferential integration agreements and by other policies in a context of liberalization and deregulation, geared toward enhancing the competitiveness of the countries of the region and, in so far as possible, constituting the building blocks for a more open and transparent international economy.[82]

Although the Latin American open regionalism broke with the past vision of inward-looking economic development, it differed from the Asia-Pacific notion of open regionalism. The APEC-fomented open regionalism, at least in the early days of the initiative, envisioned a more informal system of intergovernmental coordination for nondiscriminatory trade liberalization.[83] In the Latin American version, the regional space continued to matter. In addition to the fact that for most countries trade was heavily concentrated in the region, many identified in the regional level an intermediary space in which they could acquire experience with market rules and gradually build competitiveness, while an association with the United States offered the advantage of privileged market access that necessarily discriminated against outsiders.

The importance of ideological beliefs in this shift to open regionalism in Latin America[84] is clear when one takes into account the persistent disagreement between specialists on the benefits of multiple regional trade initiatives.[85] Nowhere was this mix of technical expertise and belief more evident than in the NAFTA negotiations. As discussed in chapter 4, in the case of NAFTA, Mexico redefined its traditional notion of sovereignty to see in modernization through "subordinate integration"[86] an option that had been politically unthinkable a decade earlier.

NAFTA accelerated the reorganization of the subregional trading blocs. In 1989, the Andean Group redesigned the bloc's orientation toward an open model of integration. Its members began the liberalization of services, committed to the formation of a free trade area by 1993, and to the adoption of a common external tariff by 1995.[87] In June 1990, CACM resumed talks to improve coordination in trade, investment, industry, and macroeconomics. It also discussed the possibility of Panama's membership. In 1991, its members signed the Protocol of Tegucigalpa in an attempt to improve institutional coordination and to promote the principles of economic cooperation and democracy.[88] CARICOM members agreed to work toward the formation of a single market and economy, covering free flow of goods, services, capital, and skilled labor. Finally, in March 1991, Argentina, Brazil, Paraguay, and Uruguay launched Mercosur.

Throughout Latin America and the Caribbean, governments were showing willingness to move toward regional trade cooperation. Intergovernmental conversations were also facilitated by the political transformations of that period. By the end of the 1980s, most Latin American countries had undergone a double conversion to electoral democracy and free markets, which together were seen as the least damaging formulae for political and economic stability. It was this new political and ideological base that led to a change in the perception of how to conduct relations with the United States.

From Latin American to Hemispheric Integration

In June 1990, U.S. president Bush announced the Enterprise for the Americas Initiative (EAI). The announcement was made in a context of uncertainty about the future of inter-American relations. With the end of the cold war, U.S. foreign policy priorities were reassessed, and it was unclear what position Latin America would occupy. From the U.S. perspective, with the debt crisis under control and most countries converging toward the U.S. model of market democracy, there was no sense of a crisis requiring immediate action.[89] At the same time Latin American governments feared that in the absence of a crisis, the U.S. foreign policy would return to benign neglect of the region. In the search for new guidelines in inter-American relations, the idea of hemispheric economic cooperation was received as good news.

But even though the post–cold war international conditions pressured Latin American states to rethink their strategies of insertion into the international system, those conditions in themselves do not fully explain the particular choice of deepening economic association with the United States. This is especially the case when the choice is contrasted with previously influential ideas about development, which attempted to diminish the economic predominance of the United States over Latin America. In less than a decade, the region that had originated a school of thought grounded in its reality, was eagerly pursuing a new form of open regionalism aimed at adjusting it to international competition.

In many countries, national policymaking elites were increasingly convinced of the need to adopt market economy practices and political pragmatism. This shared ideology altered their perceptions of how to engage with the United States, from a previous attitude of suspicion to one that assumed the possibilities of advantages in an asymmetrical association. It was this change in perception on the part of various Latin American governments that made the idea of a free trade area with the United States an appealing policy alternative.

While growing international economic competition may have eroded U.S. power on a world scale, in the Americas of the early 1990s the United States had strengthened its hegemonic position in both material and ideological terms.[90] But the convergence of policies in the hemisphere was not a product of direct coercive action. The fragility of the previous national developmentalist model in addressing the problem of social and economic exclusion reinforced the perception of crisis in the paradigm that opened up the space for new economic policy ideas. Political violence, ideological struggles, and the authoritarian experience in several states gave way to electoral democracy guided by new leaders committed to pragmatic politics.

Throughout the 1990s, problems associated with excessive reliance on market forces and a disregard for structural limitations in the most unequal region in the world, were exposed.[91] The social costs of the top-down reforms and their resulting democratic deficit[92] prompted a broader public debate on the legitimacy of those reforms. Groups negatively affected by economic liberalization began to mobilize across Latin America and elections became a channel for citizens to express discontent. Latin America may have shifted economic paradigms, but it continued to be affected by the syndrome of trends in policymaking. Hirschman's warning that excessive reliance on economic paradigms could limit the region's ability to adequately address its reality, remained painfully valid.[93]

Chapter 4

Lessons from Economic Cooperation in the Americas

The previous chapter examined how the shift in economic paradigms in Latin America created a mindset among policymakers that facilitated rapprochement with the United States. But even though those conditions provided initial support for the hemispheric free trade area idea, its successful implementation still depended on the politics of negotiations.

As discussed in chapter 1, international negotiations are always characterized by a degree of uncertainty. Their development depends on the extent to which each party is willing to compromise; this in turn depends on how each side perceives the strategies and objectives of others.[1] In this subjective process, negotiators have to *read* signals emitted by each party in order to assess potential risks and benefits in an interpretive exercise that is affected by, among other factors, their values and beliefs.[2]

Here three initiatives of economic cooperation in the Americas are reviewed to illustrate how each party's perception of each other affected the outcomes of those cooperation attempts. The section "Inter-American Economic Cooperation before 1990" revisits two cases of failure, namely, the First International Conference of American States (1889–1890) and the Alliance for Progress (1961), and it shows how lack of trust and conflicting assessments of the value of the initiatives led to frustrating results. The section "Good North American Neighbors" examines the successful case of cooperation in the North American trade integration, starting with the negotiations of the Canada-U.S. free trade agreement (CUSFTA, 1988), then moving on to the North American Free Trade Agreement (NAFTA, 1992), signed by Canada, Mexico, and the United States. In these agreements, the change in the predominant policy views on how to relate to the United States, initially by Canada and later by Mexico, meant that an idea that had been previously rejected turned to be considered not only viable but highly desirable. Although these agreements were not hemispherewide, they are reviewed here as they provide rich insights into the dynamic of trade negotiations with the United States. NAFTA, in particular, deserves detailed analysis. In addition to having being transformed into a blueprint for the U.S. model of bilateral free trade agreements, NAFTA stands out as the first North-South free trade agreement resulting from cooperation under extremely asymmetrical conditions, between states whose relations had been characterized by a history of mistrust and dispute. The chapter concludes with an assessment of the contributions of these three initiatives to understanding the dynamics of economic cooperation in the Americas.

Inter-American Economic Cooperation before 1990

In comparison with other regions in the world, states in the Americas have become, over more than a century, more familiar with the idea of regionally based actions and norms to cope with international challenges. The inter-American system, despite its fragilities,[3] survived and experienced a revival in areas such as democracy and human rights in the 1990s.[4] Overall, the imagined construct of the Americas as a region has retained appeal in inter-American relations.[5] Equally resilient, however, has been the discrepancy in views about the meaning and value of a hemispherewide regionalism. From the Bolivarian dream to a U.S.-centered version of pan-Americanism, the notion that nations in the Americas share common ground that allows them to be imagined as part of one single region has inspired cooperation initiatives for two centuries. But until the late 1980s, the Latin American version of economic cooperation, reflected in the initiatives of the old regionalism, aimed to assist countries to contain U.S. hegemonic aspirations on the continent.

On the opposite side, the U.S. version of pan-Americanism[6] was based on the idea that the New World of the Americas would realize its manifest destiny through the convergence of Latin America toward the U.S. model of liberal democracy and market economy. Within the United States, the executive has frequently referred to the inter-American ideal in attempts to win domestic support for engaging with the Americas. On the rhetorical level, emphasis on the supremacy of U.S. values has served as the moral legitimizing factor behind which the United States could justify its interventions in Latin America and the Caribbean.[7] Still the notion that the country should pay attention to Latin America has remained controversial, and presidential grand visions of engagement have been constantly challenged within the United States. In the nineteenth century, in contrast to the belief that convergence was possible, supporters of the "no benefit doctrine"[8] highlighted the incompatibility of the U.S. system with those existing in Latin American countries. As one of the masters of the Monroe Doctrine, Secretary of State John Quincy Adams, declared:

> I had little expectation of any beneficial result to this country from any future connection with them [Latin Americans], political or commercial. We should derive no improvement to our own institutions by any communion with theirs.[9]

In the almost two centuries since the Monroe Doctrine was announced, U.S. foreign policy to Latin America has remained locked in what has been described as a "whirlpool," with the usual neglect giving way to interventionist reactions whenever a crisis in the region is perceived as threatening U.S. interests.[10] Sponsors of a more cooperative pattern of engagement with Latin America have persistently fought domestic battles for greater U.S. commitment to cooperation with the region.

The First International Conference of American States (1889–1890), which for the first time brought to the fore the idea of inter-American cooperation for trade integration, exemplifies this situation. For many years, Secretary of State James G. Blaine had insisted on hosting an inter-American conference. In Blaine's vision, Latin America's trade "annexation"[11] to the United States offered an efficient mechanism for promoting the latter's economic interests and a peaceful environment in the hemisphere. Arguing against those in the United States who saw the initiative as an unnecessary source of conflict with Europe, Blaine maintained that it would be humiliating for the United States to opt for inaction based on fear of the European reaction.[12] However, the proposal remained dormant until the late 1880s and it was only when an economic recession pushed politicians to look for market expansion that the idea gained political support.[13]

The First International Conference of American States took place in Washington, DC between October 1889 and April 1890. Although several Latin American leaders were suspicious of U.S. motives, the conference attracted representatives of seventeen countries. Its central issues were the definition of an inter-American dispute settlement mechanism and the improvement of trade relations. The trade agenda, which was strikingly similar to the FTAA agenda, included (i) the formation of a customs union and standardization of customs procedures; (ii) uniform systems of measures and weights; (iii) improvement of port communications; and (iv) use of a common silver coin for commercial transactions in the hemisphere. Intellectual property rules were also to be addressed.[14]

The U.S. Congress, demonstrating complete disregard for the conference, approved in December 1889 a rise in import tariffs that negatively affected Latin American exports and aggravated suspicions of U.S. intentions. Faced with reduced political space to discuss the formation of a hemispheric customs union, the U.S. administration moved to sign bilateral reciprocal trade agreements.[15] The only lasting outcome of the conference was the establishment of the Commercial Bureau of the American Republics, the seed of what later became the Organization of American States (OAS).

In the decades following the conference, the main features of U.S. foreign policy toward Latin America were intervention and unilateralism. Latin Americans' lack of trust in the United States was reduced temporarily in the early 1930s, when Franklin D. Roosevelt's Good Neighbor policy promoted the principle of nonintervention in the hemisphere.[16] But as efforts to reconstruct Western Europe and Japan came to dominate U.S. policy in the postwar period, Latin America was relegated to status quo condition.

As with the mobilization of political support for the First Inter-American Conference, a crisis was required to redirect U.S. policy attention to the region. Although signs of discontent with the United States were emerging in several Latin American countries, the Cuban revolution made clear the risks to U.S. security in its own neighborhood. As a response, in 1961 President John Kennedy announced the Alliance for Progress. Through the alliance, the Kennedy administration reversed the previous U.S. dogma of prescribing private capital to fix economic problems in Latin America and instead allocated public funds for a peaceful, capitalist-based revolution in Latin America. The United States would cooperate to promote economic development in the hemisphere and support economic and social reforms seen as conducive to achieving modernization in the region.

Inspired by an earlier proposal of Brazil's president Juscelino Kubitschek[17] to assist the economic development of Latin America, the alliance was adjusted to mirror U.S. ideology and priorities during the cold war. Among its designers was economist Walt Rostow, a leading scholar in the development of modernization theory who served as Kennedy's national security adviser and chief of policy planning at the State Department.[18] The alliance was a test for modernization theory and it reflected the belief that the United States could shape Third World societies to foster, within the boundaries of capitalism, economic development, and political modernization as antidotes to communist ideas.[19]

However, a decade after its launch, enthusiasm for the initiative had vanished. Hirschman's observation that "unlike the Russians, we [the United States] do not have much experience in promoting social change abroad"[20] captured the risks of failure. The belief of the alliance's crafters that local societies could be reengineered to resemble the U.S. model, and the fact that containment of social upheaval was more important than development, led to another frustrated initiative for economic cooperation in the Americas.[21]

Good North American Neighbors

When one takes into consideration the mutual suspicion and legacy of frustration in attempts of U.S.-Latin American economic cooperation throughout much of the twentieth century, it seems surprising that by 1990 the U.S. proposal to deepen trade relations with Latin America was warmly supported by many Latin American political leaders. In order to understand this change, the idea of trade cooperation has to be placed in the context of the reconceptualization of national strategies to integrate the world economy, in which ideological convergence created new potential for cooperation. The most representative cases of such transformation were the agreements for trade integration in North America.

CUSFTA

During his presidential campaign in 1979, Ronald Reagan advanced his clear vision of a North American trade alliance:

> A developing closeness among Canada, Mexico and the United States—a North American accord—would permit achievement of that potential in each

country beyond that which I believe any of them—strong as they are—could accomplish in the absence of such cooperation.... We will also put to rest any doubts of those cynical enough to believe that the United States would seek to dominate any relationship among our three countries, or foolish enough to think that the governments and peoples of Canada and Mexico would ever permit such domination to occur.[22]

But in the late 1970s, despite Canada and Mexico's strong economic dependence on the United States, neither country seemed willing to abandon its fears of U.S. dominance. Yet, in a space of a few years, this situation was reversed. In 1989, the Canada-U.S. free trade agreement (CUSFTA) came into force. Although Canada's relations with the United States had not been characterized by the same level of tension as existed in relations between the United States and various Latin American countries, issues related to Canadian national identity have favored for decades a cautionary attitude toward the United States. Although the idea of free trade with the United States had been postulated at different times for more than a century, it had never gained sufficient political support in Canada. By the mid-1980s, however, Canada unexpectedly changed its attitude and began to actively pursuing a free trade agreement with the United States.[23]

The negotiations with Canada reveal that even a developed country with a longer history of cooperation with the United States, is not immune from the effects of deep power asymmetry. Partly due to its colonial history and geographic isolation from Latin America, Canada has never achieved a level of interaction with the region comparable with that reached by the United States. Yet, the dominant position that the latter occupies in the hemisphere has placed Canada in a peripheral situation in the Americas, in many ways similar to those of Latin American countries. Its special position as main trading partner of the United States was still insufficient to guarantee a smooth negotiation, and Canada had to strongly mobilize political capital and resources in order to reach a bilateral free trade agreement.

In the early 1980s, mired in an acute economic recession and constantly hit by U.S. abusive utilization of trade remedy laws, Canadian policymakers began considering the alternatives for economic recovery. In this search for new ways to put Canada in a better economic position, the idea of a bilateral free trade agreement began to gain support.[24]

In September 1985, Prime Minister Brian Mulroney announced Canada's intention to pursue a trade agreement with the United States. Though Mulroney had dismissed free trade during the electoral campaign, once in power he made trade integration with the United States a top priority and a personal goal.[25] Canada had strong economic motives for pursuing such a trade pact. Economic integration between the two countries had been developing for decades and these countries were each other's main trading partners. In 1984, total trade of goods between Canada and the United States reached $155 billion. Canada accounted for 22 percent of U.S. exports—more than twice the share of its second top partner, Japan—and 20 percent of its imports. On the Canadian side, the United States alone accounted for

76 percent of the country's exports and 72 percent of its imports.[26] Sectoral liberalization agreements were already in place, but with growing world competition, Canada was facing increasing pressure for stable market access and production coordination with its main trading partner.[27]

Bipartisan political support played a central role in making the case for an agreement. In 1985, before the announcement of the intention to negotiate with the United States, the bipartisan Royal Commission on the Economic Union and Development Prospects for Canada (the Macdonald Commission) released a report that spelled out the case for free trade with the United States. The Head of the Commission was Liberal Donald Macdonald, a former minister for Energy known for his nationalist policy stances. Macdonald's shift to support for trade liberalization—a change also observed among other prominent figures of the Liberal party— strengthened the sense of internal political consensus forming around the idea of a free trade agreement with the United States.[28]

From the perspective of the United States, the economic benefits of an agreement with Canada were not as clear. Canada's population and gross national product represented only one-tenth of that of their U.S. counterpart, and trade relations were already quite open by the time that the idea of a bilateral deal was raised. The fact that, unlike Canada, the United States did not allocate much resource to developing prospective economic evaluations of a potential agreement indicates that the value of CUSFTA to the United States was not as high as it was to Canada.[29]

Nevertheless, Canada was a partner with the ideal profile to test the new U. S. strategy of bilateral trade agreements. Unlike Mexico, it was a developed country that did not raise concerns among the American public or labor unions. For the United States, a trade agreement with its northern neighbor was a low-risk endeavor. Evolving in parallel to the Uruguay Round of multilateral trade negotiations, CUSFTA could be framed according to U.S. ambitions in order to show to other nations what it could achieve bilaterally.[30] Moreover, at a time when the United States feared rising competition from Japan and Europe, CUSFTA could assist in the consolidation of U.S. economic influence in North America.

Despite the importance of bilateral U.S.-Canada relationships, CUSFTA negotiations exposed how even a special partner would have to cope with the constraints of the U.S. domestic political system. While Canada appointed experienced senior official Simon Reisman as chief negotiator and conducted extensive studies on the potential effects of an agreement, the U.S. Trade Representative team, headed by Peter Murphy, included the modest number of two full-time assistants, equipped with only a few evaluations of the implications of an agreement for the U.S. economy.[31]

In promoting the agreement, Canadians had to lobby intensively in the U.S. capital to ensure that the fast-track authorization to negotiate would be granted. Once the U.S. Congress granted the authority, the battle was transferred to the negotiations. Canadian negotiators had to advance their case both to the U.S. executive and Congress, including facilitating the flow of information.[32] Still, by 1987, Canadian efforts were insufficient to win U.S. concessions on subsidies and rules on antidumping and countervailing duties. Only when total failure of the negotiations became imminent did the U.S. system gear itself toward a resolution, and President Reagan assigned Treasury Secretary James Baker to resolve the crisis. According to the Canadian ambassador to the United States at the time of the negotiations, Allan Gotlieb, Baker's close relationship with the president and his authority within the U.S. administration were crucial to overcoming the stalemate.[33] The fact that the bureaucratic fragmentation required a politically powerful individual to overcome obstacles to the agreement illustrates how in the U.S. trade policymaking system, actual decision making power may often be located outside the formal institution in charge of trade negotiations.

CUSFTA came into force on January 1, 1989. In addition to market access to goods, it included chapters on government procurement, investment, and services, at a time when these issues had not been incorporated into the GATT system. In the sensitive areas of agriculture and textiles, liberalization was modest. Canada celebrated the creation of a dispute settlement mechanism on antidumping and countervailing duties, and the inclusion of a clause requiring the review of each country's legislation of those matters. These mechanisms, Canada hoped, would help diminish the discriminatory, unilateral actions of the United States against Canada's competitive exports.[34]

NAFTA

Only a few months after CUSFTA came into force, Canada had to confront an uncomfortable reality. The initiative that had consumed so much of the Conservative Party's political capital now risked being eroded by another special partner of the United States, Mexico. Though Canada joined NAFTA negotiations, it did so in a defensive manner, primarily to avoid exclusion and the possibility of the consolidation of a hub-and-spoke system of integration in North America.[35] The core of the negotiation process was located in the bilateral relations between Mexico and the United States.

As with Canada, Mexico's trade dependence on the United States was already a reality before the free trade agreement was signed. In 1990, the United States accounted for about 65 percent of Mexican imports and 70 percent of the country's exports.[36] A large part of this trade flow derived from the production originated in the *maquiladora* program. In place since 1965, the program promoted intensive production sharing in the border area of Mexico and the United States. In the 1980s, when severe economic crisis eroded real wages in Mexico, foreign companies eagerly expanded use of the program. Low labor costs were a major incentive. In 1988, wages in *maquiladoras* were at an average hourly rate of $0.98, compared with $1.99 in non-*maquiladora* national industries, and $13.85 paid in manufacturing in the United States. Between 1980 and 1991, the number of *maquiladoras* increased from 620 to 1,925 plants, and the number of employees rose from 119,546 to 467,454.[37]

By 1990, Mexico was emerging from a decade of economic crisis. Following the declaration of a moratorium in 1982, the country adopted a strict stabilization program that was not only recessionary but also failed to produce the dynamic effects that the multilateral financial institutions and Mexican policymakers had hoped for. In 1986, with the support of the World Bank, Mexico joined the GATT and initiated a trade liberalization program that would set the foundations for NAFTA.[38]

Although the country desperately needed foreign investment, there was no significant new inflow. After a frustrated attempt to attract European and Japanese investors at the World Economic Forum of 1990, the Mexican government decided to consider other alternatives. Among the policy options considered was the idea of a free trade agreement with the United States. The administration of President Carlos Salinas de Gortari (1988–1994) predicted that due to Mexico's special position in U.S. foreign policy, bilateralism could work to Mexico's benefit.[39]

From the perspective of the U.S. administration, a trade pact with Mexico offered economic and political benefits. Access to a lower-cost labor force was crucial at a time of decreasing U.S. competitiveness. Mexican oil reserves were a special attraction, and the possibility of gaining privileged access to a sector still under state control increased the economic incentives. Moreover, the agreement would facilitate U.S. economic preponderance over North America, forming a regional bloc that could compete with Europe and Asia. Equally relevant was the signal effect that NAFTA could have on other members of the multilateral trading system. Evolving simultaneously with the Uruguay Round of multilateral negotiations, NAFTA indicated that even with developing countries, the United States could succeed in bilateral trade deals that went beyond the disciplines of the GATT, covering new areas such as services, investment, intellectual property, and government procurement.

From the angle of policy ideas and beliefs adopted in this book, the most impressive feature of NAFTA was the Mexican government's reversal of a position of resistance to U.S. economic dominance to an acceptance of asymmetrical interdependence in the bilateral economic relations. Since the U.S.-led territorial invasions of Mexico in the nineteenth century, the definition of Mexican sovereignty had been linked to containing U.S. hegemonic ambitions. At no previous moment in the economic relations of the two countries did intergovernmental cooperation seem to be have been achieved so easily. Such a shift in the conception of the basis for and advantages of bilateral relations needs to be understood in the context of the empowerment of a new group of policymakers in Mexico during the Salinas administration. With Salinas' new technocrats, the idea of redefining the country's international image as an open, competitive economy became the most powerful vision in the Mexican state.[40] According to this vision, a free trade agreement with the United States provided an opportunity to legally lock in neoliberal reforms through the internalization of rules that would reshape Mexican institutions according to a regulatory framework that favored the consolidation of a market economy. In that regard, the Mexican attitude reinforced the hegemonic power of the United States, with acceptance of asymmetrical interdependence revealing a complex process of material pressures and ideological convergence.[41]

NAFTA was signed on December 17, 1992, comprising a complex framework of rules that bound, for the first time, North and South into a GATT-plus system. Its content showed to the world that the United States could obtain, outside the multilateral system, more concessions on trade rules, at the same time that it maintained its protectionist interests. Rather than a tripartite deal, NAFTA emerged as a result of bilateral negotiations that could not overcome the initial risk of a U.S.-centered trade system.

The agreement consolidated the dispute settlement mechanism for antidumping and countervailing duties, but the requirement for a review of the U.S. legislation that had been prescribed in CUSFTA was removed. Adding to Canada's disappointment, the new definition and the rules of origin applicable to apparel products actually increased the level of U.S. protection against Canadian exports.[42] In agriculture, the three countries guaranteed longer phase-out periods for their sensitive products. For both Canada and the United States, the protectionist rationale dictated the application of a long phase-out period affecting the inflow of competitive Mexican exports of fresh fruits and vegetables. Moreover, neither Mexico nor Canada succeeded in winning concessions from the United States with regard to its agricultural subsidies policies. NAFTA adopted full reciprocity, which disregarded the deep economic and political power asymmetries among the parties,[43] with the pattern of exchange of concessions following predictions of cooperation theory that the more trade-dependent party would be more willing to make greater concessions.[44]

The complex regulations embedded in NAFTA were crafted over a relatively short period of fourteen months of negotiations and were not supported by comprehensive estimates of their impact on the various new matters they covered, such as intellectual property and services. This knowledge gap was particularly evident in Mexico which, having joined the GATT system only in 1986, had not accumulated experience in trade negotiations. Because of the agreement's regulatory impact on national policies, the question of institutional capacity building and pace of reforms should have been considered. Nevertheless, once the Mexican decision makers came to see NAFTA as a good option for the country,[45] the learning process was guided specifically toward the goal of reaching an agreement with the United States.

In pushing for the agreement, NAFTA promoters minimized the importance of examining the assumptions behind particular economic models.[46] Specific characteristics of the Mexican economic structure, such as the dual existence of capitalist and noncapitalist features, and oligopolistic tendencies, were not carefully addressed.[47] While some U.S. think tanks, with financial assistance from the Mexican government, worked to disseminate within the United States a more positive view of Mexican reforms and the agreement,[48] the pro-NAFTA studies were used to sustain the idea that there was a technical consensus. Less optimistic economic evaluations were dismissed by government officials and international trade experts as nonscientific.[49] As an analyst of the process well captured, the battle for NAFTA raised the question of "how much faith" one could have in economic estimates.[50]

While the elitist, bureaucratic-insulated model that characterized the making of the agreement had a democratic deficit, there were some positive effects of the NAFTA process that went beyond the control of the elites in each participating country. NAFTA favored an increase in cross-border contacts among other social groups, with the emergence of new strategies for coalition building. Most notable for their impact on the negotiations were the coalitions formed around labor and the environment. Unfortunately, in the case of labor unions, relations among organizations tended to reproduce the power asymmetry found at the level of state relations, with Mexican labor conditions targeted as "the problem" to be fixed.[51] Canadian and U.S. activists disregarded the fact that labor legislation in Mexico was in many ways more advanced than U.S. legislation.[52] The inability to understand "the other," together with the inflexibility of the American Federation of Labor and Congress of Industrial Organizations (AFL-CIO) and the corporatist dynamics between organized labor and the Mexican state, contributed to weaker cooperation among labor groups than that observed among environmental groups.[53]

Learning from the Past

In view of the legacy of the two cases of failure revisited at the beginning of this chapter, NAFTA represented a clear rupture with the previous pattern. This appears more intriguing when one remembers that this agreement involved two countries that had been, to differing degrees, fearful of U.S. dominance. The contrast of the three experiences shows that in the cooperation for North American integration, the change in perception among the parties, with a shared understanding that they could gain from a formal economic alliance, was the main distinguishing feature.

In the three cases examined here, the idea of linking countries in the hemisphere for the purpose of economic cooperation was not new. Nonetheless, its incorporation into policy depended on a set of variables. First, all initiatives were preceded by a crisis that functioned as a catalyst for politicians and decision makers to rethink existing policies. In the First International Conference of American States, Blaine's idea only echoed in the U.S. Congress when the U.S. economy faced a downturn and there was a need for market expansion. In the Alliance for Progress, the shock caused by the Cuban revolution in 1959 put enormous pressure on the policymaking system. In CUSFTA and then NAFTA, economic concerns and the need to engage in an increasingly competitive international economy created the conditions in which new policy ideas could be considered. Second, the idea of economic cooperation could only gain policy prominence through its embrace by the decision-making elites of the countries involved. At least at the initial stage, the support of top-level members of the administration—and often from presidents—was fundamental.

Once the idea was put on the policy agenda, the challenge was to guarantee its implementation. It was at this stage that the perceptions of the parties—of the value of the initiative in which they were involved—was most significant. In the First International Conference of American States, the U.S. congressional decision to raise import tariffs indicated a lack of internal consensus over whether the United States should take Latin American interests into account. More broadly, it exposed the difficulties of building an inter-American policy in the context of a relationship dominated by suspicion on the part of the less powerful parties, and U.S. doubts about the value of cooperation. The Alliance for Progress, as a long-term project launched and financially supported by the United States, did not require the process of negotiation common in agreements. However, the initiative demonstrates how ideology affected the U.S. view of Latin America. Particular beliefs about social, economic, and political dynamics led to a policy that fed the perception among many Latin American countries that the United States would only engage with the region if its interests were threatened, and even then, would impose its own views of how relations should be conducted.

In the North American cooperation, decision-making elites in Canada, the United States, and Mexico came, for different reasons, to share the view that they could benefit from entering into a formal free trade agreement with each other. But, as seen above, in the CUSFTA and NAFTA negotiations, the United States continued to put pressure on the less powerful parties to accept its preferences. What distinguished NAFTA was the change in the mindset of the less powerful parties. Decision makers shifted from seeing the risks deriving from their highly asymmetrical relation of interdependence with the United States, to highlighting the possibilities of gains. For the governments of Canada and Mexico, old fears of dominance and dependence gave way to the belief that though asymmetrical, interdependence provided an opportunity to guarantee their individual interests in a changing international context.[54] Without this shift in how decision-making elites in Canada and Mexico perceived the value of their bilateral relations with the United States, the idea of a free trade area in North America would continue to lack political support. In the minds of decision makers who imagined a trade agreement with the United States, an opportunity for a privileged partnership—NAFTA—became a prize to be eagerly pursued.

For other Latin Americans, NAFTA was symbolic of the challenges to be faced in adjusting to a new international economic scenario. Intellectually, Mexico's acceptance of an asymmetrical association intensified the debate about the wisdom of closed economies, and the need to reconsider the basis of relations with the United States. In practice, NAFTA set a precedent for the kind of free trade agreements that the United States was pursuing. It was against this background that the FTAA project was initiated.

Part IV

Case Studies

Chapter 5

U.S. Foreign Trade Policy: Leadership in a Constrained System

Part III addressed how convergence of policy making elites toward market democracies provided an ideological base for the development of a hemispheric free trade area. However, while this convergence facilitated preliminary dialogues, the successful implementation of the idea still depended on the sustained political commitment of all parties involved, particularly of the United States and Brazil. This chapter shifts the focus from the international to the domestic level to explore why in the United States the FTAA idea did not attract sufficient political support to transform it into an effective policy.

From Bretton Woods to the late 1970s, the United States exhibited strong commitment to multilateralism as the basis for the construction and maintenance of an international liberal economic order. Given the primacy of the principle of nondiscrimination in the multilateralist paradigm,[1] the U.S. proposal of regional trade agreements was surprising. While the U.S.-Israel trade agreement, CUSFTA and NAFTA had signaled the United States' diminishing faith in the multilateral trade path, the consideration of a hemispherewide free trade area exposed even further the crisis of trade multilateralism.

However, in the selection of potential partners, U.S. foreign trade policymakers did not view the FTAA as an essential goal. From the U.S. perspective, trade incentives for actively pursuing a hemispheric trade area were not strong. If regions were to be selected, East Asia was a more desirable trade partner. Although the United States had specific geopolitical and security interests in the Americas, these could be served bilaterally.

In this chapter, the history of U.S. trade politics is revisited through the changing social and political contexts of the twentieth century. A lengthy historical background is critical to capture both the resilience of certain views and the onset of gradual changes. While consensus over pure free trade has never been reached in the United States, broad support for "freer" trade, and the recognition of the need for selective protection and compensatory mechanisms, was the formula that prevailed for most of the twentieth century.

The chapter is divided into six sections. The section "U.S. Foreign Trade Policy System" describes the U.S. trade policymaking system. The section " The Alliance of Congress and the Executive around Freer Trade" provides an overview of the evolution of the U.S. trade policy system from the early 1900s through the Reagan administration. The section "The Revival of a Centenary Idea" focuses on the administration of George H.W. Bush (1989–1993), highlighting how political leadership enabled the advance of two trade policies involving Latin America, namely, NAFTA and the Enterprise for the Americas Initiative (EAI). The section "The Clinton Years" covers the Clinton period (1993–1997, 1997–2001), showing how in a domestic context of high polarization over free trade and over NAFTA in particular, low political leadership in the FTAA imposed a slow pace for the negotiations. The section "George W. Bush and a Grand Unilateral Vision" deals with the first administration of George W. Bush (2001–2004). It discusses how the ideological shift to unilateralism greatly reduced the scope for balanced negotiations in the FTAA at the same time as it increased the perception, within the Bush administration, of gains to be obtained through bilateral agreements. The final section "Conclusion" contrasts the FTAA idea with the dominant views held by the U.S. foreign trade policy elite, identifying how differences in those views contributed to the low priority given to the project.

U.S. Foreign Trade Policy System

The U.S. Constitution attributes to Congress the task of regulating foreign trade. Although, the president remains responsible for the conduct of foreign affairs, commitments affecting U.S. tariff levels and trade legislation are one of the legislature's competencies. However, since 1934, the limiting effect of this system on the executive's autonomy to define foreign trade policy has been reduced through congressional delegation of authority.

Trade negotiations are coordinated by the Office of the United States Trade Representative.[2] Although the USTR is the principal body in charge of coordinating and implementing U.S. trade policy, policy formulation occurs through a deliberative interagency process.

At the bottom tier, senior officials of various agencies congregate in the Trade Policy Staff Committee. In the development of its technical functions, the TPSC is supported by dozens of subcommittees, involving staff from different government agencies. It is here that most routine work related to specific trade negotiations is conducted, such as by the subcommittees for the FTAA, CAFTA, or the General System of Preferences (GSP) subcommittee. The Trade Policy Review Group, at the second tier, manages issues of higher complexity or sensitivity that cannot be properly dealt with at the bottom tier.

At the apex of the trade policymaking system is the National Economic Council, established by Clinton. Although the USTR is officially the agency in charge of coordination; since the late 1980s, successive presidents have maneuvered to increase their control over decision making. Thus, in the George H.W. Bush administration, final decisions were made by the Economic Policy Council. With President Clinton, a similar role was attributed to his newly created National Economic Council.[3] In Congress, the House Ways and Means Committee and the Senate Finance Committee have been the traditional channels for trade policy coordination. Since the congressional reforms of the mid-1970s, however, power within Congress has become more decentralized, with a consequent multiplication of the bodies that now influence the debate on trade.[4]

The USTR continues to be an active participant in decision making, but it competes with other politically influential voices, both external and internal to the bureaucracy. The nature of its mandate means that the USTR benefits from direct access to trade negotiations and having privileged access to information in relation to other domestic actors. However, USTR's double accountability to the president and to the Congress, combined with budget limitations, ensures that the office cannot act independently of other bureaucratic agencies or the legislature. In the FTAA, nineteen federal agencies were involved, including the departments of Labor, Defense, and the Environmental Protection Agency. Even if congressional and social pressures are left aside, the interbureaucratic process is sufficiently complex to limit USTR's capacity to control the whole process and the nature of decisions.

Inserted in this web of executive, Congress and social forces, the USTR has come to perform a role not envisioned when the position was created in 1962. At that time, the trade representative was expected to be an envoy of U.S. trade interests who could perform his duties with fewer political distractions than would be the case within the State Department. In practice, the USTR has acted as a free trade advocate and broker between different economic interests within the United States. As Michael Mastanduno describes it, "[l]ike the NSC, USTR is a player as well as a coordinator, with its own set of institutional interests."[5] This combination of advocacy and mediatory functions helps to explain why most presidents have opted to appoint, as trade representatives, professionals with negotiating abilities, even if they lack expertise in trade.

From an institutional analysis perspective, the more decentralized structure of the U.S. trade system reflects its political system and the principle of constrained government. The mechanisms of checks and balances reveal the emphasis on bureaucrats as agents, in charge of the execution of goals predefined through political disputes between various groups in society. Nevertheless, there is much room for the adoption and implementation of goals set by bureaucrats.[6] The risk that bureaucrats might transgress their ideal function as executors has been long recognized,[7] and the politicization of the bureaucracy is now a common phenomenon.[8] The overlapping of functions of politicians and bureaucrats has been described as forming a "hybrid image," in which both politicians and bureaucrats define goals, mediate interests, and formulate policies, with only execution being exclusively performed by bureaucrats.[9]

In the U.S. bureaucratic structure, a high degree of politicization in the administration is enabled by the flexible system of appointments to the civil service.[10] Presidents are allowed to reshuffle the top echelons of executive agencies, and new appointees enjoy wide scope to form their own team.[11] Decision making can be more easily concentrated among groups personally formed by the president and who are more likely to share his or her views and values. This means that in practice presidents retain more coordination power on policies than the bureaucratic model would predict.[12] Krasner argues that interbureaucratic disputes and coordination difficulties are more likely to occur when there is lack of presidential attention to an issue. In contrast, a president personally committed to a project—a condition that, according to Krasner, is usually determined by the president's values—is likely to succeed in overcoming interbureaucratic struggles.[13]

The institutional design described above indicates that the U.S. foreign trade policymaking system should not be analyzed separately from identification of the actors within the state who are central to a particular policy area. In trade negotiations, this implies a look beyond the USTR.

The Alliance of Congress and the Executive around Freer Trade

Since the early days of the American republic, tariffs have been a central political issue. The first law enacted in 1789 had tariffs as its subject matter. Political relevance was linked to economic importance. By the late eighteenth century, tariff revenues accounted for approximately 90 percent of the federal income[14] and variations in tariff levels had a direct impact on the fiscal budget. The dilemma that policymakers now face in many least developed countries, regarding the fiscal impact of tariff cuts, was a well-known problem for the young United States. From the mid-nineteenth century until the 1930s, tariffs were a central issue for political clashes. However, unlike the modern alignment, the protectionist flag was carried by Republicans, while the Democratic Party defended trade openness.[15]

It was only with the Great Depression that the protectionist trade system began to be severely challenged. But on the eve of the crisis, Congress still tried other alternatives to trade liberalization. In 1930, the Smoot-Hawley Tariff Act was enacted and generated a steep rise in tariffs that only contributed to deteriorating conditions for American producers.[16] In the post Smoot-Hawley's period, world trade fell from $35 billion to $12 billion.[17]

The signals that the United States was moving toward a liberal trade order came only a few years later during Roosevelt's administration.[18] Roosevelt's appointment of a well-known free trader as Secretary of State, Cordell Hull, inaugurated a new phase in U.S. trade policy. In 1934, Congress approved the Reciprocal Trade Agreements Act (RTAA) that authorized the president to negotiate tariff reductions of up to 50 percent for an initial period of three years. Following the enactment of the RTAA, the government signed bilateral reciprocal trade agreements and in Latin America, Cuba and Brazil became the first countries to join the bilateral wave pushed by Hull.[19]

The most remarkable feature of the RTAA was the introduction of the delegation mechanism. Most studies describe the delegation as the product of a rational decision by congressional representatives in order to overcome the perils of congressional log-rolling in trade,[20] and as a way to release politicians from the pressure of interest groups. This argument rests on the assumption that trade liberalization was desired by both the executive and the Congress. However, the voting for the RTAA challenges the idea of consensus. While Democrats overwhelmingly supported the Act—96 percent in the House and 93 percent in Senate—Republicans roundly rejected it with 98 percent of "no" votes in the House of Representatives and 85 percent in the Senate.[21]

Moreover, while the idea of freer trade had gained ground in relation to manufactured goods, such approval was not extended to the agricultural sector. Goldstein points out that the disjuncture of the U.S. trade policies in sectoral terms was driven by different beliefs about which strategy should be pursued in manufacturing and agriculture. While the "twin ideas of reciprocity and most-favored-nation (MFN) status" guided the policies in the manufacturing sector, agriculture policies were oriented by the idea of "parity" which relied on government intervention in price setting.[22]

Broader support to open trade was only achieved when the specific conditions of the postwar period created international and domestic receptive environments. Following the economic chaos created by two world wars and the Great Depression, several countries began to see the advantages of establishing international mechanisms to assist in the building of a stable international economic system. It was with this in mind that the Bretton Woods institutions were created. Important, however, was the fact that the political support for the creation of the World Bank and IMF was not extended to trade. Disagreements over the priority that should be given to trade in relation to other national priorities such as employment, and tensions between commitment to multilateral rules and preservation of autonomy in trade policies, contributed to the demise of the attempt to create an International Trade Organization.[23] The GATT was signed in 1947, but rather than strictly following the free trade doctrine, it promoted gradual and selective trade liberalization that accommodated national social and political conditions.

In the post–Second World War period, the U.S. position as the world's strongest economic power meant that it could lead the establishment of an international liberal order from which it would benefit politically and economically. In this context, the triangle of state, business, and organized labor found a common basis for cooperation.[24] Favorable international conditions also affected societal preferences more broadly and while Democratic constituencies continued to support free trade, Republican constituencies gradually shifted to a more liberal position on trade.

Nevertheless, the risk of a protectionist backlash was never fully eliminated and as international competition increased, a gradual distancing in views between different social groups and the foreign trade policymaking elite occurred. By the early 1960s, discontent with the free trade option was already noticeable. As Oscar Gass, former adviser to Treasury Secretary Henry Morgenthau, stated in 1962, "trade liberalization [has] become a Holy Cause. Decent people are prepared to lie for it."[25] The rise of the European Common Market and a growing deficit in the U.S. balance of payments put in doubt the benefits of trade liberalization.[26] Democrats, whose support from blue collar workers had increased,[27] were faced with a constituency increasingly uncomfortable with the consequences of free trade.

At the policymaking level, however, protectionism was not defended as an alternative. President Kennedy continued to rely on multilateralism as a mechanism to curtail domestic protectionist forces. It was in this context that the idea of a new GATT round of trade negotiations gained political momentum. At the same time that it served to mobilize proliberalization groups, multilateral trade negotiations were seen as helping to strengthen the U.S.–Western Europe alliance.

The GATT Kennedy Round took place between 1964 and 1967. By the end of it, tariffs for manufactured products had been successfully reduced to an average of 9 percent, but agriculture continued to be protected.[28] In addition to illustrating the difficulties in negotiating agricultural liberalization, the Kennedy Round also exposed conflicts within the U.S. trade system. During negotiations, U.S. representatives made concessions on nontariff barriers that were not explicitly covered by the legislation authorizing them to negotiate tariffs. They agreed with the establishment of an international antidumping code and made concessions regarding the American Selling Price System.[29] The Congress, however, refused to remove the American Selling Price System, and authorized the U.S. Tariff Commission to disregard the international antidumping provisions whenever they conflicted with domestic regulations.[30]

By the early 1970s, social discontent with free trade had intensified. The defense of "fair trade," rather than "free trade," was frequent. Even the AFL-CIO abandoned its postwar support to freer trade. As its Research Department director Nat Goldfinger argued, in a world of managed economies and increasing international competition from multinational corporations, it was of "questionable wisdom for U.S. government officials to base public policy pronouncements on 18th and 19th century theories of free competition and comparative advantage."[31]

Although social pressure led to changes in government rhetoric, through emphasis on "fair competition around the world,"[32] in practice the foreign trade policymaking elite continued to push for a liberal economic order. Under President Nixon, multilateralism was once again used as a mechanism to contain protectionist forces, through the initiation of Tokyo Round of GATT negotiations (1973–1979).

At the domestic level, Congress and the executive mastered a creative solution to deal with protectionist pressures. Through the fast-track authority mechanism, the president should notify Congress of his intentions to enter into agreements involving nontariff barriers at least ninety days in advance. Once the implementing legislation was submitted, Congress had sixty days to make a decision. If approval was granted, Congress' power was restricted to a veto over the totality of the agreement, but no partial modifications were allowed.[33] The special trade representative, who until then answered only to the president, was made accountable to both the president and the Congress. Selected congressional representatives were to be allowed in the U.S. negotiations delegation, and a system of consultation with the Ways and Means and Finance Committees was put in place. In addition, the 1974 Trade Act provided a formal channel for the participation of interest groups through the system of private sector advisory committees.[34]

These modifications led to a trilateral system in U.S. trade policymaking. The executive, through the special trade representative, commanded trade negotiations, but its power was restrained. Through the private sector advisory committees, interest groups guaranteed that they could influence trade policy. Congress retained oversight and veto powers, and the Ways and Means Committee and Finance Committee guaranteed their power over the draft of the fast-track implementing legislation.

Despite these adjustments, tensions between domestic groups over free trade increased. The post-1934 bipartisan alliance between Congress and the executive that had been crafted under the exceptionally favorable conditions for U.S. economic expansion that characterized the postwar period, started to show signs of fragility. In the short period between 1982 and 1987, the U.S. trade deficit rose steeply from $36.5 billion to $159.6 billion.[35] Moreover, the United States moved from being an international creditor to a heavy debtor, with $111 billion in net liabilities by 1985.[36]

In order to move on with trade liberalization, policymakers had to offer more compensatory measures. The 1984 Trade Act facilitated the application of trade remedy laws, which peaked between 1980 and 1994. During that period, 718 antidumping cases were proposed. U.S. industries soon realized that antidumping legislation provided an easy alternative, benefited by "lower injury threshold, no presidential power to overturn an affirmative decision and (until the Uruguay Round changes) indefinite duration for any import relief imposed."[37] The 1984 Act also broke up with the nonreciprocal nature of preferences conceded under the U.S. General System of Preferences. Products could now be removed from the list of beneficiaries once they reached a certain level of competitiveness. A presidential waiver could be granted, however, if the relevant country offered the U.S. market access and protection of intellectual property rights.[38]

But perhaps the most important component of the 1984 Trade Act was the official recognition of bilateral trade negotiations as an alternative path in U.S. foreign trade policy system. From the postwar period until the early 1980s, the faith of the policymaking elites in multilateralism had guaranteed its predominance over other alternatives.[39] However, by the 1980s, social and political actors were challenging this premise.

Ronald Reagan's strong ideological commitment to free markets created the expectation that free trade would be firmly promoted. Instead, there was an increasing recourse to unilateral measures in order to "punish" international competitors. Ideas such as "equivalence" of concessions, which were common before 1934, returned to the trade debate. As various social sectors started to promote the notion of "unfairness" of free trade, politicians had to find ways to adapt to the new conditions.[40]

In a context of increasing uncertainty about its ability to remain the world's hegemonic economic power and after a frustrated attempt to launch a new multilateral trade round in 1982, the United States announced that it would be willing to go for bilateral GATT-plus arrangements. In 1985, the U.S.-Israel trade agreement was signed,[41] showing U.S. disposition to abandoning its commitment to nondiscrimination in trade. A new GATT round was finally launched in 1985, but the faith of U.S. decision makers in multilateralism had diminished.[42] Soon the United States would move toward bilateral trade negotiations with Canada.

The U.S. departure from multilateralism in trade is one of the best examples of how ideas and interests are mutually constituted and validated in policymaking. Uncertainty about the future and domestic constraints undermined the belief that Americans were gaining from a multilateral liberal trading system. The idea of "fairness" in trade, which in the nineteenth and early twentieth centuries had been associated with reciprocity and equivalence in concessions, was expanded to include concerns over workers' rights and environmental protection. Moreover, Reagan's faith in the uniqueness of the United States[43] and the use of coercion to advance U.S. interests, was demonstrated in foreign trade through the growing view that unilateralism was a convenient alternative for the United States.[44] The use of unilateral practices to instruct other nations in how to behave and to punish those that did not comply with the U.S. interpretation of trade rules, exposed the administration's belief that, while free trade should be promoted internationally, there were alternatives to multilateralism that could suit U.S. ambitions.

By the late 1980s, challenging the predictions of economists in the 1970s, the U.S. trade system had not suffered a debacle. Nonetheless, the abusive use of trade remedy measures and agricultural subsidies, and the growth in nontariff barriers, created a less than free trade system.[45] By the end of the Reagan administration, the fracture of social consensus for freer trade had not only begun to affect the behavior of political parties but had also assisted the U.S. departure from multilateralism as an ideal and practice.

The Revival of a Centenary Idea

When George H.W. Bush came to power in 1989, uncertainty about how power would be distributed in a post–cold war world was high. In the economic arena, the formation of the European Single Market and the rise of East Asian economies fed speculations of a world divided into competing economic blocs formed around the Americas, Europe, and East Asia. For the United States, if the world were to be divided into economic blocs, it had to guarantee its power within its traditional zone of influence, Latin America and the Caribbean. However, in the post–cold war period, U.S.

foreign policy for Latin America lacked a grand driving force, either ideological or material.

U.S. trade with the region, which had declined during the first years of the debt crisis, was recovering. The level of U.S. foreign direct investment was also stable, but excluding Mexico, the share of Latin America and the Caribbean in U.S. total exports declined from 10.7 percent in 1980 to 6.6 percent in 1989.[46] Although there were economic incentives to push for closer inter-American economic relations, the recovery of the Latin American and Caribbean economies made the definition of a specific economic policy for the region less urgent. Even taking into account the potential for the expansion of U.S. exports due to the regional economic recovery, evaluations indicated that prioritizing Latin America at the expense of other regions, did not make economic sense for the United States.[47]

In trade, apart from NAFTA, the motivation for a U.S. plan encompassing the entire region was unclear. Market access to the region had already improved. Most Latin American and Caribbean countries had implemented unilateral trade liberalization as part of their structural adjustments. This policy, combined with the reduction of trade barriers expected as a result of the Uruguay Round, offered the United States a chance to deepen free trade with Latin America without the need to engage in additional trade negotiations.

Notwithstanding these modest economic motivations, the Bush Sr. administration paid unusual attention to the region. The negotiations over NAFTA, the announcement of the EAI, the Andean Trade Preference Act (ATPA), and presidential visits throughout the hemisphere, were remarkable for a region that was able to attract U.S. foreign policy attention only when a crisis was perceived as negatively affecting U.S. interests. In the early 1990s this was not the case. For the first time, Latin American governments were aligned with the U.S. agenda of free markets and electoral democracy.

Ironically, it would be upon George H.W. Bush, who was vice-president during the Reagan years of ideological war against Central America, to give a new stimulus to inter-American relations. The fact that the policies of his administration, such as the EAI, helped to consolidate U.S. influence over the hemisphere was not surprising in U.S.–Latin American relations. What was striking, however, was the level of presidential attention given to a region that remained marginal to the international struggles for world power.

The Bush Sr. administration began with a negative score in inter-American relations. It invaded Panama in December 1989 in a unilateral decision rejected by most Latin American governments and thatbrought back memories of U.S. interventionism in the region. But the faulty start was rapidly reversed. Only a few months after the Panama invasion, Bush announced the EAI and signaled economic integration as the new base for inter-American cooperation, a move that several Latin American presidents actively supported. Bush found a receptive audience for his proposal among the new generation of pragmatic civilians elected in Latin America.

NAFTA became the most emblematic representation of this new dynamic in inter-American affairs. NAFTA's political rise in the United States is seen as an example of how the support for the idea from politically influential individuals determined its success.[48] When Salinas de Gortari proposed the negotiation of a free trade agreement with the United States, the idea was well received at the top echelons of the Bush Sr. administration. The proposal of a free trade agreement with Mexico was particularly appealing to the U.S. president, whose long-developed relations with Mexico included personal investments in the country's oil sector.[49] Bush and State Secretary James Baker actively supported the initiative, and beyond the administration circles, the proposal was warmly embraced by influential politicians, such as Democratic Senator and Chairman of the Finance Committee, Lloyd Bentsen. Common to all three personalities was their origin in Texas, the leading U.S. state in exports to Mexico.[50]

In addition to economic relations, Texas, like California, experienced large inflows of Mexican migrants, which contributed to a greater relevance of Mexico-related issues. NAFTA, therefore, benefited from the engagement of U.S. political leaders who had an above-average interest in Mexico. As one interviewee described it, "there was sensibility on the part of these Texan policymakers. Salinas may have pushed it but there was receptivity with George Bush and others who thought it was a good idea."[51]

With the president and other politically influential individuals convinced that an agreement should be pursued, preparations began. Mexican officials met with USTR Carla Hills, State Secretary Baker, and Commerce Secretary Robert Mosbacher to coordinate the negotiation process. The USTR, constrained by budget and staff limitations, was concerned with the problems of coordination that could arise from the simultaneous involvement in the Uruguay Round and another trade negotiation.[52] Moreover, the USTR planned to concentrate efforts on gaining congressional approval for the eventual Uruguay Round agreements, and NAFTA would divert attention. But when the Uruguay Round negotiations stagnated in 1990, the USTR redirected its focus to NAFTA.

In order to proceed with negotiations, President Bush had to ensure congressional renewal of the fast-track authority, due to expire on May 31, 1991. From mid-1990 onwards, top government officials from Mexico and the United States cooperated to sell NAFTA in the United States. The strategy included organizing ministerial-level meetings, and seminars with scholars and government staff. Nevertheless, contrary to the commonly disseminated idea that the business sector was actively engaged in defending the agreement, opposition groups, particularly organized labor and environmentalists, mobilized before the business sector did. In fact, by March 1991, the Chair of the House Ways and Means Committee, Dan Rostenkowski, was calling on the business sector to intensify its lobbying activities if it wanted to see NAFTA move ahead.[53] The anti-NAFTA forces in the United States were articulate and politically vocal, and without political commitment from powerful individuals in the U.S. and Mexican political systems, NAFTA negotiations would have faced a high risk of failure.

A few days after Mexico and the United States officially communicated that they would begin negotiations, Bush announced the EAI, which included the idea of a hemispheric trade area running from Alaska to Tierra del Fuego. A hundred years after its first appearance at the First Conference of American States, trade integration was back to U.S. foreign policy plans for Latin America.

The last trade initiative of the Bush Sr. administration came in December 1991, when the United States promulgated the Andean Trade Preference Act. The act created unilateral tariff reduction for selected imports from Bolivia, Colombia, Ecuador, and Peru, with the objective of promoting an alternative to drug-related crop production.

While the motives for Bush's trade policies on Latin America can be debated, it is hard to imagine that the region would have attracted that level of attention were it not for the president's personal interest. From a simple interest-based viewpoint, Europe, Asia, and the Middle East deserved priority. Raymont argues that Bush's personal relationships with many Latin American leaders, built during his long political career, created more interest in and knowledge about Latin America.[54] On several occasions, he worked to reinforce his own view of how inter-American relations should be strengthened, with NAFTA being the best known case.

The Clinton Years

Democrat William Jefferson Clinton was elected president in late 1992 after a campaign in which domestic issues, and particularly proposals for economic recovery and improvements to the middle class, were the priority. Unlike George H.W. Bush, Clinton did not raise foreign policy as a major campaign issue.

Rhetorically, Clinton distanced himself from ideological classifications and emphasized that it was time to focus on action rather than the "idle rhetoric of 'left' and 'right' and 'liberal' and 'conservative' "[55] that had dominated U.S. politics. In 1992, Clinton and the vice-presidential candidate Al Gore, published the outline of their plan for a new administration. After more than a decade of Republican policies that had protected the rich, they claimed, a Clinton-Gore administration would be committed to a new covenant that, without rejecting free markets, would orient economic policies to "put people first."[56] Job generation and workers training appeared as concerns in several sections of the program. In agriculture, the document highlighted the importance of removing barriers to U.S. exports, but there was no mention of the term "free trade." The plan explicitly mentioned support for free and *fair* trade, and to free trade agreements that respected labor and environmental standards. Limitations on free trade were also evident in the document's treatment of multilateral trade agreements, which would be supported as long as they did not alter U.S. standards and regulatory frameworks on health, environment, and safety measures. The plan also included a proposal for a stronger Super 301, the legislation used to punish competitors for practices the United States considered damaging to its exports.[57] Through the influence of Gore, environmental protection gained prominence and was conceptually crafted as a national security issue. As he explained:

> I believe there is a fundamental link between our current relationship to the earth and the attitudes that stand in the way of human progress... we must face the truth. The task of saving the earth's environment must and will become the central organizing principle of the post-Cold War world.[58]

Once in power, Clinton's economic policies generated criticism from both the left and the more conservative sections of the Democratic Party,[59] which were revealing of the difficulties of classifying his economic ideas in terms of a traditional ideological divide. But at least in his first term there were signals of a shift from an unqualified celebration of free markets, to a position in which the government, though still supportive of open markets, saw itself playing a more active role in improving the conditions under which U.S. firms and workers could compete internationally.

Clinton committed most of his first year to guaranteeing the approval of his economic recovery plan,[60] and selected a mixed profile of staff members to top cabinet positions. While Alan Greenspan (Federal Reserve), Thomas McLarty (Chief of Staff), Lloyd Bentsen (Treasury), and Lawrence Summers (Undersecretary of Treasury for International Affairs), were not controversial appointments, less orthodox choices were made for other agencies.[61] Laura D'Andrea Tyson, a Berkeley economist and an academic who had just published a polemical book suggesting the virtues of managed trade in high technology industries,[62] was appointed Chair of the Council of Economic Advisers. As Secretary of Labor, Clinton appointed Harvard professor and personal friend, Robert Reich, whose book *The Work of Nations* emphasized the accentuation of inequalities produced by globalization and the need for public policies to assist workers. To head the USTR, Clinton chose Mickey Kantor, an attorney who had worked with both Hillary Clinton and the president, and had chaired their presidential campaign. Kantor had professional credentials as an experienced advocate, but like most previous U.S. trade representatives, had little expertise in trade. Jeffrey E. Garten, a former economic and planning advisor in both Republican and Democratic administrations, was appointed Undersecretary of Commerce for International Trade. In his 1992 book, Garten had argued that in a world in which the United States faced strong competition from Germany and Japan, it was acceptable and strategically advisable for the country to adopt aggressive strategies and if necessary, managed trade policies, in order to ensure a strong national economy and the preservation of its power in the world.[63]

Negative reactions to this initial team were not long in coming. While the left complained about Clinton's conservatism and acceptance of free markets,[64] those of a more orthodox economic orientation complained about the president's dubious commitment to free trade. Some of the trade actions adopted by the administration reinforced the perception that the aggressive trade policy referred to in the outline of the new administration's plan would lead to a rise in the familiar U.S. practice of unilaterally punishing its competitors. Early in 1993, the Clinton administration accused the European Community of protecting its market against U.S. products through a "Buy-Europe" policy, despite the fact that the United States also had its own "Buy American" policy.[65] It also made use of antidumping measures to protect its steel industry.

At the beginning of 1994, despite Clinton's celebration of multilateralism in the just concluded Uruguay Round, the United States again attempted to utilize unilateralism in order to pressure Japan to establish numerical targets for import growth in selected sectors. One critic commented that "Mr. Clinton and his senior advisers [were] behaving like economic delinquents."[66] More sophisticated, but equally harsh, were the comments from economists who vehemently rejected the Clinton administration's excessive attention to fixing competitiveness problems.[67] Clinton would soon demonstrate his willingness to promote trade liberalization, but the profile of his cabinet in his first year and the mixed signals it sent out, indicated a degree of doubt in pure free trade that had been unknown under the previous Republican administration.

The inauguration of an economy-driven administration, after a campaign in which foreign policy had not been prominent, prompted criticisms that Clinton lacked a foreign-policy vision. Those rejecting this claim argued that he did have a view of the kind of foreign policy the United States should pursue, but that this view was quite distinct from cold war ideological visions. First, "geo-economics" became central. A good performance at home was seen as necessary to guarantee U.S. competitiveness and ability to retain its power abroad, and both domestic and foreign policies had to be coordinated coherently.[68]

Second, the more cautious approach to grand foreign policy strategies may have derived from a government misinterpretation that public attention to domestic issues in the post–cold war era meant a lack of interest in foreign policy. Apparently, George H.W. Bush's overemphasis on uncertainty in world affairs had negatively affected his campaign, promoting the notion that he had his priorities wrong at a moment when Americans were aspiring for innovative domestic policies that would recast the terms of public debates.[69] For Clinton, known for carefully considering polls before moving on new policies, foreign policy ranked lower than the domestic policies that mobilized public attention.[70] But as opinion polls indicated later, both policymakers and Congress may have confused the public rejection of the U.S. role as "world policeman" with a desire for disengagement from foreign affairs. Polls actually suggested that the American public still supported U.S. participation in international affairs, particularly when constructed multilaterally.[71]

Finally, the sense of incoherence and indecision may have also emerged due to Clinton's personality. Often characterized as an intelligent, articulate, and even charismatic president,[72] his management style was described as a mix of ad hoc consultations with experts inside and outside the government, which did not follow the traditional limits defined by bureaucratic organization.[73]

While poor performance during the crises of Somalia, Haiti, and Bosnia provided ammunition to the critics of his foreign policies,[74] there were also cases of success, in which the key difference was the level of personal commitment of the president. Thus, in 1994 Clinton managed to overcome strong domestic opposition and signed the U.S.-Russia Highly Enriched Uranium Purchase Agreement, which led to the elimination of 40 percent of Russia's weapons-grade uranium.[75] But in his first year, his most challenging test in foreign trade policy—and one that he met successfully—was to obtain approval for NAFTA in Congress.

The NAFTA Battle

NAFTA was signed in 1992, in the last month of the Bush administration, but the battle over the agreement continued beyond the 1990s. In the 2008 U.S. presidential campaign, NAFTA reappeared as a politically sensitive topic. Democrat Barack Obama fiercely criticized the deal and even came to suggest that a revision of NAFTA's commitments was necessary.

It would fall upon Bill Clinton the challenge of obtaining the agreement's ratification. In his presidential campaign, Clinton announced that he would support NAFTA as long as labor and environmental provisions were incorporated. By making these explicit links, Clinton distanced his rhetoric from the Republican defense of free trade as a value in itself and moved toward the validation of fair trade as the goal of U.S. trade policymaking.[76]

Once in power, Clinton demanded the negotiation of side-agreements on labor and the environment before NAFTA could be submitted for congressional ratification. In the meantime, social polarization over NAFTA increased. While outside the United States, critics of the agreement denounced asymmetries as harmful to Mexico, within the United States, it was Mexico that was depicted as the main problem in NAFTA.[77] Organized labor denounced the erosion of labor conditions and the risk of rising unemployment. Environmental organizations pointed out the dangers of environmental degradation, focusing primarily on Mexico as potential violator. Although both movements shared suspicions about Mexico's standards and institutions, they differed in strategy. Organized labor, and particularly the AFL-CIO, launched a strong anti-NAFTA campaign in the United States with little room for negotiation. Environmental groups, whose strategy of action was less attached to old parameters of intermediation through the state, adopted a more flexible approach that facilitated conversations with the U.S. government. Moreover, environmental groups found more space to build alliances with like-minded groups in Mexico and to deal with the Mexican government, in a new issue area that was not so heavily constrained by the corporatist system that guided government and organized labor relations in that country.[78]

In the end, the environmental side-agreement turned out to be more satisfactory to the environmental nongovernmental organizations than the labor side-agreement was for the Northern-based organized labor groups. Unlike the labor agreement, the environmental agreement envisioned a trinational public advisory committee to discuss the agreement's implementation and related matters. In the labor case, power remained with autonomous national committees. Mexico swallowed the trade sanctions pill, but succeeded in avoiding international rules affecting its system of industrial relations.[79] In an indication that the side-agreements were not considered effective constraints, a Mexican negotiator commented they were a "bit of a joke," permeated by complex legal mechanisms that resulted in "lots of public discourse, nothing more."[80]

The side-agreements were signed in September 1993 and in November NAFTA passed the House (234 favorable votes against 200 opposing it) and the Senate (61 against 38), with votes distributed along partisan lines.[81] But when NAFTA entered into force on January 1, 1994, rather than celebration, the Zapatista rebellion erupted in Chiapas. This tension between the interests of the rich and the poor in Mexico contrasted markedly with the cooperative environment that had characterized the relations of government elites in the United States and in Mexico during the agreement's negotiations.

The NAFTA episode also revealed how the domestic politics of the most powerful player could be determinant in international negotiations. The dynamics of the U.S. political system pushed Canada and Mexico to accept resumption of negotiations and extension of the agreement's scope as the only way to diminish the risk of nonratification. Moreover, the behavior of the U.S. administration in the ratification process revealed its domestic struggle to balance priorities. Since the agreement was expected to enter into force by January 1994, the political timing of the ratification was crucial. Yet, well into the middle of 1993, Clinton's attention was directed to approval of his new economic recovery plan. When NAFTA came up on the presidential agenda, disagreements within the administration abounded.[82]

Clinton finally decided to push for ratification. The side-agreements on labor and the environment were negotiated in a short space of a few weeks and the administration launched an intense campaign to obtain NAFTA's ratification. A couple of days before the voting, Vice-president Gore participated in a televised debate with former presidential candidate and anti-NAFTA advocate, Ross Perot, in which he successfully demolished Perot's anti-NAFTA manifesto.[83] With victory in the debate and Clinton's personal engagement in advocating for ratification NAFTA was submitted to the vote.[84]

NAFTA's approval represented Clinton's first victory in foreign affairs,[85] and together with the successful conclusion of the Uruguay Round negotiations in December of the same year, gave the administration a satisfactory score in foreign trade policy. Nevertheless, for Latin Americans, the lessons of the approval process were not a reason for optimism. The high mobilization of anti-NAFTA forces in the United States and the political tensions surrounding the ratification gave the agreement the status of the most controversial trade agreement in U.S. trade history. It was clear that the politicization was not related to Canada, but to the inclusion of the Southern neighbor. As a former member of the State Department's NAFTA task force recalls, "when NAFTA became an issue in the United States, it was not really about the agreement in itself.... It was more an emotional response to Mexico."[86]

The controversy developed despite the fact that the Mexican government had accepted the extremely unbalanced terms the United States had proffered, had partly given up its regulatory power and gained little immediate market access for its competitive agricultural products. As public debates over NAFTA in the United States indicated, there was much distrust of Mexico's ability to implement fully what had been agreed on paper.[87] In a great extent, the overselling of NAFTA, including by trade experts, grew out of the desperation of pro-NAFTA advocates to promote the agreement in a domestic social context of extreme polarization.

The NAFTA battle is revealing of a more complex scenario than the one usually portrayed by the interest groups model. Proagreement lobbying by interest groups was insufficient, and groups had to rely on the advocacy of top-level cabinet members who worked to convince the president and congressional leaders of the importance of the agreement. In fact, by 1993 it was Treasury Secretary Bentsen who was urging the business sector "to get up on the Hill and carry your part of it,"[88] in order to ensure that NAFTA would pass. Rather than acting as mere "agents" for interest groups, these politically influential individuals actively defended their own visions and agendas.

Immediately after the NAFTA victory, Clinton used the momentum to approach Asian countries. This choice was congruent with economic evaluations that showed Asia as both a top "strong neighbor" and "good customer" of the United States, ranked higher than Latin America as a regional partner.[89] Clinton attended the APEC Summit in the United States where he emphasized liberalization of trade and investment among APEC members. While his personal attention was devoted to APEC, Gore celebrated NAFTA's victory with Mexicans and took the opportunity to announce the invitation for the Summit of the Americas.

In November 1994, Clinton participated in the APEC Summit in Indonesia, where APEC leaders committed to the liberalization of trade and investment by 2010, and 2020 for the less developed members. It was only after the APEC Summit that Latin Americans got their share of promises. In December of the same year, during the Summit of the Americas in Miami, the FTAA proposal was officially announced.

Still, reality again overshadowed the excitement that surrounded the Summit's preparation and the event itself. In December 1994, a few days after Clinton praised NAFTA at the Summit, Mexico went into a new financial crisis.[90] Although Clinton personally led the efforts to assemble an assistance package for Mexico, the bailout faced impressive opposition in the United States. When Clinton's proposal for a $40 billion loan guarantee to Mexican debt was put to Congress, fierce rejection led even the Republican leaders who had initially supported the assistance to step back. Clinton organized an international assistance package for Mexico but due to strong congressional resistance, this was reduced to $20 billion, with resources from the executive-managed Exchange Stabilization Fund being used.

Whether affected by the Mexican crisis or not, the already unstable support for the free trade agreement with Mexico declined in the United States. Public opinion polls conducted in 1994 and 1996 revealed an erosion of support for NAFTA regardless of party affiliation. Negative perception of the agreement rose from 37 percent to 41 percent among those identified as Democrats; from 34 to 53 percent among independents; and from 33 to 48 percent among Republicans.[91] Although dissatisfaction among Democrats was expected, there was a surprisingly high increase in negative perception among those identified as independents and Republicans. In Congress, a similar disenchantment was observed. As Pastor and Fernandez de Castro commented, "If anything, Congress seems more insulting toward Mexico and more demanding in a public way than it was before."[92]

As Clinton prepared to run for a second presidential term, the combined ideas of free trade and Latin America remained a high-risk, low-benefit combination. Chile, invited to join NAFTA at the Summit of Miami in 1994, would remain on the waiting list.[93]

The Denial of Fast-Track Authority

The U.S. Trade System under Stress

The fast-track authority expired in 1994. Considering that since its inception in 1974 Congress had never denied authority to the president, renewal was not expected to pose a significant problem for the administration. But by the 1990s, labor and environmental concerns had finally made their way on to the congressional trade agenda. The idea of fair trade had achieved high political visibility and was transformed into a focus for party divide.[94]

In mid-1994, an initial attempt to renew the fast-track authority was made, but it did not reach the formal voting stage. USTR Kantor's emphasis on the inclusion of labor and the environment in the legislation's draft triggered resistance from Republicans, who rejected the incorporation of those issues as an integral part of trade discussions. As tensions remained, Congress and the president decided to separate the fast-track authority issue from the legislation approving the Uruguay Round agreements. The decision proved wise. The Uruguay Round agreements were successfully approved in November 1994 with broad bipartisan support, and Clinton could celebrate another victory in trade.

In November 1994, the Democrats were hit by a historical defeat in the congressional elections. For the first time since Truman's administration, the American political system was controlled by a Democratic president and a Republican majority in both houses of Congress. The profile of the 104th Congress posed a further challenge to the administration. Most of the newcomers lacked the political experience of former generations and had run campaigns centered on rejection of the traditional political game between the White House and Congress. Foreign policy was scarcely addressed during the campaign and when it was discussed, it was essentially to emphasize domestic issues such as job creation.[95]

Following the election results, Democrats were removed from the chairmanship of the committees in charge of trade. Without the leadership in the committees, they experienced reduced financial support from business and their dependence on the votes of their labor constituency increased. Despite these constraints, if one recalls that Democratic and Republican presidents alike had found ways to push free trade ahead, the configuration of political forces by 1995 was not necessarily an impediment to freer trade. Following Kennedy's lessons, Clinton could have pleased labor with compensatory mechanisms. Moreover, could not the Republican Congress be convinced that the provisions on a labor side-agreement would be sufficiently flexible? These possibilities were open and, as at other moments of the U.S. trade history, their realization depended on presidential leadership. However, it was exactly this condition that was unclear.

As mentioned earlier, the content of Clinton's economic plan and the profile of his cabinet signaled that his economic views were not as orthodox as those of the Republicans. An interest-based analysis could maintain that the president's attitude conformed to his pursuit of votes. But an explanation that only focuses on electoral motives disregards the fact that the Clinton administration had, since the beginning, supported the consideration of environmental and labor issues in the context of a debate about *fair trade*, rather than proclaim the virtues of pure free trade.

The administration's view was revealed in the roles played by the president and the USTR in the renewal of the fast-track authority. Kantor's insistence on linking labor and environmental issues to the fast-track legislation made him a unique trade representative. The USTR had previously been on the side of free traders; now, the institution was headed by an advocate of fair trade. As one critic complained, there was a "lack of high official leadership to move free trade ahead. Both Kantor and Clinton do not show convincingly that they believe in an open economy."[96]

Ambiguities in the trade agenda were not unusual. When Clinton was reelected in 1996, conditions were ideal for pursuing the renewal of the fast-track authority. There was broad support within the administration and in the Republican-chaired trade committees to proceed on the issue. An early submission of the bill could avoid the debates over the mandatory NAFTA report, due to Congress in late 1997. Yet, resistance to fast-track renewal came from the presidency. When Clinton finally decided to advance a fast-track proposal in September 1997, the timing was not good. A critical report of the first three years of NAFTA was released and showed that the U.S. trade balance with Mexico had been reversed from a surplus of $1.7 billion in 1993 to a deficit of $16.2 billion in 1996.[97]

Clinton personally worked to gather Democratic support, but was unsuccessful. Supported by Republican House Speaker, Newt Gingrich, he decided to hold back. In July 1998, Gingrich brought the issue back to congressional debates, but it was the bad timing for the Democrats—Congressional elections were coming soon. As the fast-track implementing legislation was put to the vote in September 1998, it was defeated, including by massive opposition from the president's own party.[98] Since the creation of the fast-track authority in 1974, it was the first time that the U.S. Congress had denied a president this authorization.

NAFTA also exposed the complex social developments that had accompanied the increase in the Latino population in the United States. Lack of unity among that group had been visible during NAFTA's passage when ethnicity was far from constituting a sufficient base to mobilize support. Only nine out of seventeen Latino Congress representatives voted in favor of NAFTA. Because Latinos were more likely to be found in blue collar or lower qualification jobs in the United States, they were associated with the groups negatively affected by job transfers to Mexico.[99] While from the outside, one could imagine that Latinos in the United States and Latin Americans shared similar goals, in reality NAFTA's extension down south was a divisive issue among ethnically connected groups.[100]

About a year later, and after surviving the political distress of the impeachment process, Clinton faced another challenge. The debacle of the Seattle WTO Ministerial Meeting in late 1999 restrained even further the scope for maneuver in trade.[101] While developing countries saw in Clinton's emphasis on environment and labor clauses potential for new protectionist mechanisms, U.S. critics of the government included dissatisfied civil society groups that condemned further liberalization. Analysts later highlighted lack of preparation for the event, and presidential miscalculation of the degree of opposition to the free trade agenda.[102] Overall, the Seattle protests served to increase the political sensitivity of economic globalization, particularly free trade.

But despite the lack of fast track and the failure of the Seattle WTO Ministerial Meeting, Clinton still committed to trade initiatives that he considered to be of high political value. In 2000, he signed a free trade agreement with Jordan, as a reward for being a strategic partner in U.S. foreign policy on the Middle East. Clinton also fought for and obtained permanent normal trade relations status—American jargon for the most-favored nation treatment—with China.[103] Finally, in the final moments of his administration, trade negotiations with Singapore and Chile were initiated.

By the end of his second term, Clinton's economic and trade policies continue to divide experts. The approval of NAFTA and success of the Uruguay Round agreements, the revitalization of APEC, and the approval of permanent normal trade relations status for China were interpreted as continued U.S. commitment to the promotion of open trade. For the more left-wing members of the Democratic Party, this was a negative feature that put the president too close to Republican free market advocates. For them, Clinton's insistence on fair trade, the linkage of labor and environmental issues to trade agreements, his support for regional and bilateral trade initiatives, and his lack of leadership in Seattle, revealed his inability to defend the free trade cause.[104]

With trade initiatives judged purely on their economic merits, critics on both sides disregarded the context of trade within broader foreign policy goals defined by the administration. NAFTA, APEC, and China represented opportunities to use trade to promote U.S. national security interests with the countries involved in those initiatives. They were consistent with the foreign trade policy priorities that Clinton had defined in his first State of the Union address following his reelection. In addition to traditional relations with Europe, the president emphasized the need to build cooperation with the East, and particularly, to engage in dialogues with China "for the sake of our [American] interests and our ideals." U.S. exports to expanding markets such as Asia and Latin America were to be promoted, but not for economic reasons only. As Clinton explained, "by expanding trade, we can advance the cause of freedom and democracy around the world."[105]

Clinton's performance in foreign policy shifted from a more idealist position toward a realism based on traditional security and trade with the most promising markets.[106] While one might debate the extent to which his initial steps in foreign policy derived from idealism or lack of interest, by the end of his second mandate, U.S. foreign policy continued to rely on the old modernization assumption according to which economic and democratic advances were described as linked and mutually beneficial.

Implications for Latin America and the Caribbean

In his first State of the Union address after reelection, Clinton referred to the link between democracy and free markets, stating, "there is no better example of this truth than Latin America where democracy and open markets are on the march together."[107] The irony was that while the voluntary adoption of those policies had transformed the region into "an example" in the 1990s, at the same time, it had diminished its ability to attract the attention of the U.S. policymaking system.

In the financial years of 1994 and 1995, U.S. aid to Latin America and the Caribbean declined by approximately 50 percent, the largest reduction among all third world regions.[108] In the absence of strong political advocates at the level of the presidency and senior decision making, U.S. foreign policy was conducted by the middle ranking bureaucracy, suffering from the common constraints that prevailed under the lack of political leadership.[109] Clinton did not visit Latin America during his first term, and Secretary of State, Warren Christopher, traveled to South America only late in 1996, after seventeen visits to Syria. In 2000, neither the president nor Secretary of State Madeleine Albright joined Latin American leaders in the historical ceremony that accompanied the transfer of the Panama Canal.[110]

Lacking a guiding vision from the top level of the administration, foreign policy on Latin America was fragmented. Trade, drugs, and immigration were addressed by different bureaucratic agencies with little coordination. Contradictory signals abounded. In the fight against narco-trafficking, the certification of countries and the heavily militarized Plan Colombia only showed that U.S. foreign policymakers continue to see unilateralism and interventionism as effective alternatives to dealing with countries in the region.

In relation to the FTAA, given that it was a long-term project unlikely to be finalized under Clinton's presidency, it is hard to argue that the level of attention should have been higher. But in several instances, the low interest shown by the high ranks of the administration became evident. The fast-track authority was not pursued as a priority. Chile, invited to become the "fourth amigo" during the Miami Summit in 1994, remained on hold until the very end of the Clinton administration. Although Chile indicated willingness to start negotiations with the UnitedStates without fast-track authority, following the anti–free trade demonstrations in Seattle, the U.S. administration decided to wait.[111] Negotiations finally began at the end of Clinton's second term. But as a State Department staff member recognized, "we were shamed into renewing the talks because of Chile's indignant reaction to the sudden free trade negotiations with Singapore and Jordan."[112] Finally, in the FTAA the U.S. business sector did not organize a strong lobby for the agreement, and in the U.S. media, the FTAA never became a topic of great public interest.

Policy was fragmented not only over issues but also over subregions.[113] For Brazil, this turned out to be an advantage. Brazil was on the list of the ten emerging markets identified by the administration as targets for strengthening trade and investment relations.[114] Security issues also highlighted Brazil's position in U.S. foreign policy. Located at the heart of South America, Brazil has become a corridor in the transnational drug traffic routes. Monitoring of the area served the interests of both countries.[115] As U.S. Assistant Secretary for Inter-American Affairs, Alexander Watson maintained, when disagreements occurred between Brazil and the United States, they were more about tactics than strategy, more about "means rather than ends."[116]

Furthermore, presidential synchronicity contributed to a sense of cooperation in bilateral relations. In late 1997, Clinton visited Brazil as part of his first presidential tour through South America. Brazil's president Cardoso noted the "excellent relations between the two of us, which I think makes it obvious to everyone that there is a friendship that join these two Presidents and that we share a great many interests."[117] Clinton, on the other hand, stressed that as "the largest economies and the most diverse populations in the hemisphere," Brazil and the United States had a leading role in the promotion of democracy and free markets in the Americas. Moreover, contrary to the opinion often expressed by mid-level officials in the U.S. foreign trade bureaucracy, Clinton explicitly supported Mercosur:

> I support MERCOSUR...We believe that we can create a free-trade area of the Americas consistent with MERCOSUR and the leadership and role of

Brazil and the other members in it. And so to me, this [either support FTAA or MERCOSUR] is a false choice.[118]

As seen in chapter 2, on decisive occasions in the FTAA negotiations, the day-to-day clashes between negotiators of Brazil and the United States vanished at high-level meetings. The U.S. acceptance of Brazil's model of building the FTAA from existing subregional blocs, the joint drafting of the environmental language incorporated in the 1996 Cartagena declaration, and support for Brazil's candidature to host a ministerial meeting in 1997, all signaled that during the Clinton administration, compromise, rather than tensions, prevailed between the leaders of the two countries.

George W. Bush and a Grand Unilateral Vision

When George W. Bush took power in 2001, free traders in Latin America felt relief. They hoped that a Republican administration, backed by a Republican Congress, would be better able to contain pressures from labor and environmental groups, and advance the free trade agenda in the Americas. President Bush's first State of the Union address met those expectations. As he reminded Americans, "[f]reedom is exported every day, as we ship goods and products that improve the lives of millions of people." In order to ensure U.S. capacity to continue promoting "freedom" in the world through free trade agreements, the president asked Congress to give him "the strong hand of Presidential trade promotion authority and to do so quickly."[119]

Another sign of the importance of the trade agenda to the new president was the appointment of Robert Zoellick as U.S. Trade Representative. An attorney renowned for his negotiation abilities and experience in economic policymaking, Zoellick had a respected record with Republican administrations. After serving in the Treasury Department under Reagan, he joined the George H.W. Bush administration as undersecretary of state for Economic and Agricultural Affairs, also acting as adviser to State Secretary James Baker. Known as one of the administration's masterminds in economic issues, Zoellick framed the foreign economic policy dimension of the plans circulating at the end of the Bush Sr. administration, and which focused on the definition of a new U.S. role in the post–cold war order. In his view, U.S. foreign economic policy should be tailored to maximize the linkage between economic and geopolitical strategies. In addition to strengthening relations with Western Europe and Japan, the United States should expand its trade alliances throughout Latin America, East Asia, and Eastern Europe. In a preview of what would later become his competitive liberalization strategy under George W. Bush, Zoellick argued that "America's message should be that it wants to reduce barriers to trade and investment with all, but will proceed with those countries that are willing."[120]

During the 2000 presidential campaign, Zoellick returned to the public sphere. In an article published in *Foreign Affairs*, he described the five elements that should constitute the core of a Republican foreign policy agenda.

First, the United States should stop being ashamed of its power and instead apply it to serve its national interests. As he declared, the United States "should not be paralyzed by intellectual penchants for moral relativism." Second, the country should foster coalitions with partners willing to take on their share of responsibility. Third, Zoellick rejected an inflexible commitment to multilateralism, describing "international agreements and institutions as means to achieve ends," and noting that "every issue need not be dealt with multilaterally." The fourth principle referred to U.S. engagement in promoting a technological revolution. Last, the United States should be reminded that there still exists "evil in the world—people who hate America and the ideas for which it stands...People driven by enmity or by a need to dominate will not respond to reason or goodwill."[121] On trade, Zoellick defended an explicit competitive liberalization strategy. The rationale for that strategy had been advanced already in the late 1980s, when James Baker warmly defended bilateral and plurilateral trade deals as tools to pressure other countries to open their markets.[122] In line with the project Zoellick had helped to promote a decade before, he argued that the United States should promote trade links with all willing regions or individual countries, as a way to advance trade liberalization and to increase pressure on the multilateral system, using regionalism "to break the logjam."[123]

In contrast to the Democrats, Republican foreign policy was unlikely to be accused of lack of vision. But for those who believed in multilateralism as a base for the new world order, the Bush administration would bring little comfort. Even before the attacks of September 11, 2001, the top cabinet appointments revealed the empowerment of neoconservatives. Vice-president Dick Cheney, Secretary of Defense Donald Rumsfeld, and U.S. Deputy Secretary of Defense Paul Wolfowitz had been intellectual sources for the neoconservative project advocated through the think tank "Project for the New American Century," founded in 1997.[124] The "moral clarity" guiding the new strategy meant that the defeatist discourse they associated with the Clinton administration should be replaced by a foreign policy that praised U.S. values and pushed for their dissemination, multilaterally if possible, but unilaterally if convenient or necessary.[125]

The crisis created by the attacks of September 11 provided an opportunity for the design of policies guided by the new ideology.[126] The U.S. foreign policies that followed the attacks, both conceptually and in action, revealed such a fusion of material interests and moral crusade that it was hard to ignore the influence of the decision makers' beliefs and ideology. No one symbolized this combination of motivations better than the U.S. president.

Bush constantly referred to clarity of purpose and strong resolution as praiseworthy characteristics. The ability to show results and command of situations was important not only to satisfying the aspirations of the American people, but also affected U.S. credibility worldwide. As he explained in his famous statement, "it's very important for them [world leaders] to come in this Oval Office...and me look them in the eye and say, 'You're either with us or you're against us.'"[127] In regard to unilateralism, a shift in rhetoric and practice occurred. Although unilateralism had frequently appeared in U.S. foreign policy, under the new administration the unilateral option was disentangled from moral debates to become vocally advocated. As the president himself declared with a certain disdain, accusations of unilateralism, which he found "amusing," were usually a product of "resentment."[128]

While Bush's declarations could be interpreted as rhetorical tools to justify policies driven primarily by material considerations, his often religious language and references to a moral mission and to a war where humanitarian aid would not be disregarded seem to reflect a genuine belief in the strange logic of using preemptive war to promote a peaceful, free world.[129] In his own words:

> There is a value system that cannot be compromised—God-given values.... What's very important as we articulate foreign policy through our diplomacy and military action, is that it never look like we are creating—we are the author of these values.... It leads to a larger question of your view about God.[130]

Bush's Foreign Trade Policy

It was within this new vision of how the United States could and should conduct its foreign relations that foreign trade policy, and by extension, the FTAA, were addressed. As the head of the USTR, Zoellick had an opportunity to bring into the trade area the kind of Republican foreign policy that he had envisioned for more than a decade.

A few weeks after the September 11 attacks, on November 9, 2001, the WTO members met in Doha for the Fourth Ministerial Conference. With the postattack climate favoring international solidarity with the United States, the launching of a new round of multilateral trade negotiations was promoted as a symbolic act that would demonstrate a multilateral rejection of those who attacked the principles of economic freedom. As Zoellick recalled on that occasion, "trade is about more than economic efficiency, it reflects and encourages a system of values."[131] Only two years after the Seattle debacle, free trade returned to the multilateral agenda, instrumentally linked to U.S. foreign policy priority of combating terrorism.[132]

In order to be able to move ahead in the trade liberalization front, the Bush administration soon initiated the process of requesting the trade promotion authority (TPA), the politically correct denomination given to the old fast-track authority. Congressional debates on the TPA began in the second half of 2001 and were characterized by the expected clashes between Democrats and Republicans over labor and environmental clauses. But on December 6, 2001, the draft legislation was approved by a margin of one vote (215–214), with only twenty-one votes in favor from the Democrats.

In March 2002, President Bush authorized a rise in import tariffs to satisfy the U.S. steel industry, in violation of WTO rules.[133] The rise in tariffs harmed U.S. credibility with regard to its actual commitment to a new multilateral round of trade negotiations[134] and negatively impacted its relations with competitive steel exporters. Brazil, a major steel producer and exporter, was among the countries severely affected by the measures. As a critical report prepared by the Brazilian Embassy in Washington pointed out, contrasting the five months preceding the imposition of the safeguard measures and the equivalent period following the rise in tariffs, the volume of Brazilian steel exports to the United States declined 41 percent.[135]

Restrictions to free trade also increased with the new Farm Security and Rural Investment Act (the "Farm Bill"), signed in May 2002. At a time when a new multilateral round of trade negotiations had been launched and the FTAA negotiations were approaching the stage of exchange of offers, the U.S. government approved a bill that increased the level of agricultural subsidies.[136] Finally, for the U.S. textile industry, a new arrangement required that "U.S. knit and woven fabrics [undergo] all dyeing, finishing, and printing procedures in the United States"[137] so that the products could qualify for the tariff reductions under the Caribbean and Andean unilateral trade preferences.

The 2002 Trade Act,[138] which incorporated the TPA, once again exposed the political power of protectionist groups within the United States. Following a traditional solution adopted by previous administrations, the act expanded the adjustment assistance to workers. The TPA was granted for an initial period of two years, but under several conditionalities. In addition to the inclusion of environmental and workers' rights as core issues for discussion in trade negotiations, the act subjected negotiations of sensitive agricultural products to prior consultations with Congress. In an attempt to tighten congressional control over the negotiations, a congressional oversight group on trade was established. Furthermore, in regard to trade remedy laws, the act restricted the margin for concessions, stating that the U.S. objective in trade negotiations should be to avoid agreements that restricted its ability "to enforce rigorously its trade laws, including antidumping, countervailing duty, and safeguards laws." Promulgated after September 11, the trade act also incorporated provisions linking trade to the war against terror. It defined cooperation in the fight against terrorism as an eligibility criterion in unilateral trade preferences programs.

Equally relevant for the FTAA negotiations was the set of conditions attached to the unilateral trade programs benefiting the Andean, Central American, and Caribbean Basin countries.[139] Among the eligibility criteria, the act included protection of workers and intellectual property rights, cooperation in the war on drugs, and a commitment to the FTAA negotiations or "another free trade agreement." Moreover, the beneficiaries of such programs were expected to negotiate a reciprocal free trade agreement with the United States, either through the FTAA or bilaterally, ideally before the expiration of the unilateral preferential market access.

Once the trade system managed to accommodate domestic groups, the USTR was free to advance with the strategy of pursuing free trade agreements with those willing to do so in parallel with the Doha Round. In

October 2002, the United States announced the "Enterprise for ASEAN Initiative,"[140] targeting trade agreements with ASEAN members committed to free market reforms. In February 2003, the "Middle East Free Trade Initiative" was launched. Despite a nomenclature that reminded George H.W. Bush's EAI and its use of trade and investment framework agreements as a platform for free trade agreements, in the Bush strategy Latin America was not privileged. The strategy now covered all parts of the world, linking regions and individual countries to the U.S. market in a clear indication that the new administration was not willing to wait for the prolonged, consensus-based negotiations that characterize the WTO negotiations. While back in 1990, the George H.W. Bush administration had preferred negotiations with subregional blocs, under George W. Bush, fragmentation into smaller negotiating units was promoted.

Consonant with Zoellick's unilateral approach, the agreements were built upon a U.S.-designed template. Labor and environment became necessary parts of trade agreements, and U.S. agricultural subsidies, together with its ambiguous antidumping legislation, were in practice kept out of regional or bilateral negotiations.[141] If any alteration in these areas were to be made, it would be at the multilateral level. The asymmetry in the bilateral negotiations was often intensified by the fact that most partners were not very relevant to the United States from a trade viewpoint, whereas the United States constituted a key market for many of the countries joining the agreements.

The multiplication of trade rules generated by this worldwide hub-and-spoke system, defied economic efficiency parameters and threatened the credibility of an already shaken multilateral trading system.[142] For the new administration, however, the possibility of unilaterally linking economic and geopolitical goals added high political value to the new pacts. As the USTR stated in its report to Congress:

> America's trade agenda needs to be aligned securely *with the values of our society*. Trade promotes freedom by supporting the development of the private sector, encouraging the rule of law, spurring economic liberty, and increasing freedom of choice. Trade also serves our security interests in the campaign against terrorism by helping to tackle the global challenges of poverty and privation. Poverty does not cause terrorism, but *there is little doubt that poor, fragmented societies can become havens in which terrorists can thrive.*[143] (author's emphasis)

The use of trade as a carrot or compensation mechanism became more prominent after September 11, 2001. Along the dividing line of "with or against" the United States, the Bush administration used diplomatic instruments to punish those voting against the invasion of Iraq. Mexico and Chile, both holding temporary seats at the UN Security Council at the time of the voting, denied support for the invasion. The U.S. reaction was to show they could be ignored. President Bush refused to answer calls from Mexican president Vicente Fox. Chile which like Singapore had just signed a free trade

Table 5.1   U.S. Free Trade Agreements, through July 2010

FTA	Countries	Year of Signature
Americas		
NAFTA	Canada and Mexico	1992
U.S.-Chile	Chile	2003
CAFTA-DR	Costa Rica, El Salvador, Guatemala, Honduras, Nicaragua, and Dominican Republic	2004
U.S.-Colombia	Colombia	2006 *
U.S.-Peru	Peru	2007
U.S.-Panama	Panama	2007 *
Middle East		
U.S.-Israel	Israel	1985
U.S.-Jordan	Jordan	2000
U.S.-Morocco	Morocco	2004
U.S.-Bahrain	Bahrain	2004
U.S.-Oman	Oman	2005
Asia and the Pacific		
U.S.-Singapore	Singapore	2003
U.S.-Australia	Australia	2004
KORUS	Republic of Korea	2007 *

Note: (*) Agreements pending congressional ratification.
Source: United States Trade Representative.

agreement with the United States, got a modest commemorative ceremony, while the coalition-supportive Singapore was hosted in the White House.[144] Later in 2004, it would be the time for New Zealand to be excluded while U.S. ally Australia was compensated with a trade pact.

Implications for Latin America and the Caribbean

Any assessment of U.S. foreign policy during the first term of the Bush administration must recognize the events of September 11 as a watershed. For Latin America and the Caribbean, their most immediate effect was to dampen the initial spark of presidential attention to the region that was shown at the beginning of Bush's presidency.

Under the new U.S. foreign policy vision based on unilateralism, and in the middle of the war against terrorism, Latin America and the Caribbean had little to offer as a region. Although its second-tier position in U.S. foreign policy was maintained by virtue of problems such as transnational drug trafficking, most issues of great importance to the United States continued to be dealt with through bilateral relations. With regard to the FTAA, if the post–September 11 conditions did not contribute to making it a higher priority in the U.S. foreign trade agenda then the restrictions attached to the TPA deteriorated even further the conditions for negotiations. With the removal in practice of agricultural subsidies and trade remedy provisions from the FTAA negotiating table, the United States violated the FTAA collective agenda established in 1998. Somehow, enthusiastic Latin American free traders had downplayed the fact that despite Republicans' higher support to free trade, the agricultural sector was an exception.[145]

The position of Latin America was further deteriorated by the sensitivity that trade pacts with the region generated in the U.S. Congress. The U.S. free trade agreement with Central America and Dominican Republic (CAFTA-DR), passed the House of Representatives by two votes (217–215), after a long battle that required individual-base deals between the administration and congressional representatives.[146] Fears of immigration and job losses, intensified by the close geographic location, fed antagonism. More importantly, tensions in the United States over free trade with Latin America showed that in the U.S. imaginary, negative views associated with the region continue to affect the chances for cooperation.

The U.S. unilateral reduction of the scope of the FTAA negotiations, and the rise in agricultural subsidies through the 2002 Farm Bill, were particularly problematic for Brazil, the other cochair of the FTAA negotiations. The United States was Brazil's main individual trading partner. In 2002, Brazil's trade with NAFTA countries accounted for 28 percent of the country's total trade, which placed NAFTA for the first time in a higher position than Europe (22 percent). After the devaluation of the Brazilian currency in early 1999, imports from the United States decreased and Brazilian exports increased, finally leading to a surplus in Brazil's favor. But Brazil's competitive strengths resided precisely in the sectors in which U.S. protectionism was stronger. Brazil estimated that about 60 percent of the country's export products to the United States were affected, to differing degrees, by some kind of U.S. trade barrier. The list of U.S. sensitive agricultural products subject to prior congressional negotiation included key Brazilian export products such as sugar, meat, and tobacco. Tariff peaks and tariff quotas were particularly harmful to Brazil's exports.[147] Moreover, Brazil's competitive steel sector, which positioned the country as the ninth world largest producer in 2009,[148] was frequently affected by safeguard measures and antidumping investigations in the United States.

Since the beginning of the FTAA negotiations, Brazil had emphasized the need for balanced concessions that would require U.S. concessions on agriculture and antidumping. By 2002, the possibility of balanced negotiations seemed unlikely. With the Brazilian government already facing difficulties in finding a creative path for negotiations, the growing domestic opposition to the FTAA during the Brazilian presidential campaign of 2002 only increased the political costs associated with the project.

But despite Brazil's discontent, Zoellick's personal enthusiasm for his competitive liberalization strategy continued to generate new trade initiatives. In January 2002 he announced that negotiations for a free trade agreement with Central American countries could start. After Brazil's Workers Party presidential candidate Lula referred to the FTAA as a project for the "annexation" of

Brazil, Zoellick commented that if Brazil was not interested in the hemispheric free trade area, then it could choose "another direction...Antarctica."[149]

When the FTAA entered into the phase of exchanging offers in early 2003, Lula had been elected the new president of Brazil. The USTR was ready to move on with those willing to subscribe to its model but had little intention of making concessions in the areas relevant to Brazil. However, Brazil faced an unbalanced negotiation at a time when a new president, elected by a center-left coalition critical of the FTAA, had just come to power. The distance between the Brazilian and U.S. positions would only increase.

By the beginning of the twenty-first century, balanced forms of cooperation between the United States and Latin America were still a largely unrealized expectation. The predominant belief in U.S. policymaking circles, which saw U.S. political and economic models as exportable values to be promoted in any context, limited the potential for a new perspective in inter-American affairs. As one scholar argued, those assumptions have become so dominant in the United States that a rejection of the advancement of free market democracies and combating narco-trafficking would be as radical as "being against God, motherhood, and apple pie—assuming we [Americans] still believe in these latter items."[150]

Conclusion

Over more than a century, the U.S. trade policy system was adjusted to changing contexts. The economic crisis of the early 1930s exposed the failure of the prevailing defensive mechanisms in trade and allowed new ideas to be proposed. The multilateral solution that gained policy legitimacy in the post–Second World War period was powerful not only because it enabled international economic coordination but also because it was advocated by the most powerful state. Yet the U.S. vision of a liberal-oriented order was not based on doctrinaire economic liberalism, but on "embedded liberalism."[151]

The gradual recovery of Europe and later Japan, recessionary cycles in the United States, and increasing international competition from the 1970s onwards, created new conditions to which multilateralism was less able to respond.[152] By the 1980s, new trade policy solutions were necessary and the response came through the U.S. abandonment of the principle of nondiscrimination in trade relations. Under Reagan, the belief in multilateralism, which for decades had allowed the executive and Congress to master institutions and restrain protectionist forces, was shaken. U.S. trade policymakers continued to promote international trade liberalization, but the view that the Untied States should unilaterally pressure others to act according to its trade priorities was now perceived as legitimate and, on many occasions, better suited to the country's needs than the multilateral path. This tension between the two ideas, already clear under Reagan, continued and with George W. Bush, was resolved in favor of unilateralism.

It was in this environment of changes in policy views on how to best protect U.S. interests in a highly competitive international economy that the idea of a hemispheric free trade area was reintroduced. But since its inception in the EAI, the method imagined by the United States for constructing such an area relied on bilateral negotiations with the subregional blocs rather than on hemispherewide negotiations. In this regard, it reproduced the U.S. practice of unilaterally approaching relations with countries in Latin America. The idea of a collective process of negotiations was not the first option, and though accepted as the base of the FTAA during the Clinton administration, low presidential and senior-level engagement limited advances in the project. When George W. Bush came to power in 2001, there was hope that with a president who, like his father, had demonstrated interest in Latin America, the FTAA would move up the list of U.S. foreign trade policy priorities. But following the events of September 11, that initial presidential attention disappeared. For the new policy making elite, with its firm belief in unilateralism, the idea of a collective process of negotiation, as embodied in the FTAA process, lacked appeal. Consequently, U.S. decision makers found the Brazilian proposal to fragment the negotiation process a convenient solution that allowed the United States to move on freely with bilateral free trade agreements without carrying the burden of first suggesting the fragmentation.

Two final lessons can be drawn here. First, the different ways in which each U.S. administration dealt with trade relations with Latin America show that material incentives were not the only consideration. Since the Bush Sr. administration, material incentives to engage economically with the region have remained reasonably stable. However, the level of presidential attention that both Bush Sr. and Bush Jr. had initially given to Latin America was not shared by Clinton. However, Clinton's acceptance of collective decision making in the FTAA was an innovation. While this inclination may have reflected the low priority of the FTAA, it could also indicate a more multilateral approach in international affairs. Second, the successful incorporation of ideas into policies, such as the EAI and NAFTA, depended substantially from continuous advocacy by the forces that support such initiatives. Once leadership was present, institutional constraints could be overcome.

The failure of the FTAA can be explained as the result of the mismatch between the image of a collective enterprise (gathering thirty-four negotiating parties) and the dominant view among U.S. foreign trade policy decision makers that the region was not sufficiently relevant to the United States to warrant specific attention. If engagement were required then it should take place through bilateral mechanisms. In the history of inter-American relations, the FTAA became another victim of the whirlpool pattern,[153] with fragile commitment during the Clinton administration losing ground, under President George W. Bush, to a strong but unilateral view of how to conduct negotiations.

Chapter 6

Brazilian Foreign Trade Policy: Instrument for an Autonomous Nation

> *No country escapes its destiny and fortunately or unfortunately, Brazil is condemned to greatness...Mediocre and petty solutions do not serve or interest Brazil....We either accept our destiny as a great, free, generous country, without resentments or prejudices, or we run the risk of remaining at the margin of History, as a people and as nationality.*
>
> Ambassador João Augusto de Araújo Castro, 1972[1]

As mentioned in the Introduction, systemic explanations of the foreign policies of developing countries predominate. Recent efforts to create theoretical frameworks for the study of foreign policymaking in developing contexts deserve praise,[2] but ultimately, their explanatory power can only be assessed in combination with detailed case studies.

In this regard, Brazil is an interesting case that reveals the weight of domestic variables in the definition of the country's foreign policy, including in regard to foreign trade. In the battle between systemic international constraints and national ambitions, for more than a century ideas and ideology have been central in guiding Brazilian foreign policymakers in their definition and defense of Brazil's aspired place in the world.[3]

While profound social and economic disparities justify the classification of Brazil as a developing country, some of its features have increasingly contributed to its characterization as a middle power. Geographically the fifth largest country in the world, it accounts for half of South America's territory, sharing borders with all states in the subcontinent with the exception of Chile and Ecuador. With a multiethnic population of approximately 190 million people, and abundance of natural and energy resources, in 2010 Brazil ranked as the eighth largest economy in the world. Brazilian elites have historically referred to these characteristics to justify why Brazil is entitled to occupy a middle-power position in the international system.[4] As Ambassador Nabuco stated in 1908, "Brazil has always been conscious of its size and has been governed by a prophetic sentiment with regard to its future."[5] It is within this national-elite psyche that foreign trade policy has evolved. As one of the several dimensions through which national projects have been revealed internationally,[6] Brazilian foreign trade policy too has reflected broader foreign policy visions that need to be understood through a historical analysis of their rise, meaning, and resilience.

With a few exceptions,[7] analyses of Brazilian interests in the FTAA focused on assessing the country's economic profile either to claim that Brazil should have been more active or to justify the country's low commitment to the project.[8] Given the prospective nature of economic studies of the FTAA, unavoidable in the context of uncertain outcomes in which they were formulated, differences were expected. But in addition to divergence in recommendations, Brazilian studies of the potential impact of the FTAA to the country lacked a detailed evaluation of trade-offs that would have to cover the implications of regulatory changes for sectors such as services, investment, and government procurement.

The understanding of Brazil's strategies during the FTAA negotiations requires moving beyond the identification of material incentives to investigate the reasons that led decision makers to see fragmentation as more desirable than other alternatives. Brazil's rationale for the FTAA is better understood as deriving from decision makers' efforts to construct Brazil's international identity as a middle power, which in turn required the preservation of its margin of autonomy in the international system in order to implement its own vision of how to achieve economic development.

In Brazil the idea that trade relations with Latin America could be conducted with Brazil as the leader was not new. The belief in Brazil's uniqueness in Latin America, and particularly in the country's capacity to lead in South America, has influenced its foreign policy for decades.[9] In the Lula administration, inaugurated in 2003, this notion has gained a more practical dimension, through Brazil's financial support for infrastructure integration in the subcontinent[10] and participation in cooperative initiatives such as the signature in 2008 of a treaty for the constitution of the Union of South American Nations (*União de Nações Sul-Americanas*—UNASUL) together with other Mercosur members, the Andean Community, Venezuela, Guyana, and Suriname. The FTAA, as a project through which Brazil's regional economic dominance would be put at risk, was perceived since its early stages as a potential threat to Brazil's regional ambitions. The FTAA idea was from the beginning associated with risk, and over a decade, lacked advocates who could effectively transform it into a political priority within the Brazilian political system.

Following the framework adopted in the U.S. case study, this chapter uses historical narrative to capture the ideas that have influenced foreign trade policy in Brazil. Unlike in the U.S. system, in Brazil the agency in charge of coordinating foreign trade negotiations plays a central role in policy formulation and in the creation and dissemination of a particular vision of Brazil's national identity. Therefore, in this chapter, the period prior to the FTAA negotiations is examined in more detail in order to show

how specific ideas have persistently influenced the Brazilian foreign policymaking system.

This chapter is organized into six sections. The section "Brazilian Foreign (Trade) Policy System" describes the institutional framework for foreign trade policymaking in Brazil. The section "Development and Autonomy of a Middle Power"reviews the main paradigms that have shaped Brazilian foreign policy, showing how a set of ideas and norms have been constructed and adjusted to serve the national developmentalist project. The section "Years of Transition (1980–1994)" explores the changing domestic and international conditions of the 1980s and how they created pressures for renewal in foreign policy. In the section "The Cardoso Years. Competitiveness in an International Economic Liberal Order," the Cardoso administration (1995–1998; 1999–2002) is examined, with a focus on how a change in views of Brazil's international participation affected foreign policy, in particular the FTAA negotiations. The section "Lula's Foreign Policy and the National Developmentalist Inspiration" moves on to the first Lula administration (2003–2006), showing how the FTAA conflicted with the views and interests of a new group of decision makers. In that new context, U.S. unilateralism further eroded support for the project and transformed its defeat into a political victory. The final section brings the conclusion.

Brazilian Foreign (Trade) Policy System

The Brazilian Constitution grants to the president the prerogative to sign treaties, conventions, and international acts. The Ministry of Foreign Affairs is in charge of foreign policy formulation, including international trade negotiations.[11] Although Congress retains the power to ratify international treaties and acts, its prior authorization for the negotiation of an international trade agreement is not required.

The Ministry of Development, Industry and Foreign Trade deals with most regulatory issues and day-to-day operations related to trade, but international trade negotiations are conducted by the Ministry of Foreign Affairs. From 1990, the opening of the Brazilian economy added complexity to foreign trade policymaking and favored the mobilization of new interest groups. In an attempt to improve policy coordination, the interministerial Chamber of Foreign Trade (*Câmara de Comércio Exterior*—CAMEX) was set up in 1995. Though CAMEX was envisioned as an interbureaucratic space for improving foreign trade policy coordination,[12] its effectiveness as a forum for the domestic conciliation of positions has been questioned. During the FTAA national debates, CAMEX proved unable to guarantee transparency of information and to contain interministerial conflicts.

Despite growing pressures for change, trade negotiations remain under the Ministry of Foreign Affairs, usually referred as "Itamaraty." This institutional design contributes to the subordination of trade negotiations to the logic of diplomatic action. Formal and stable institutional channels for societal participation in foreign trade policy are weak and existing practices are still heavily reliant on personal networks. Until the early 2000s, Congress had shown little knowledge or interest in foreign trade negotiations and it was only with the politicization of the FTAA that that attitude changed.

Like in the United States, the institutional design in Brazil reflects particular views of state and society relations. In contrast with systems with a liberal orientation, Brazilian institutions have embodied notions of state authority and elitism that only began to change from the mid-1980s in the postmilitary period. The reliance on the state as a central actor in national life, including in the economy, characterized business and labor relations with the Brazilian state until the 1990s and gave corporatism a solid base.

The lack of legal means for lobbying does not mean interest groups are alienated from the state. Clientelism and manipulation of the bureaucratic structure have guaranteed access to the state by powerful groups,[13] and it was only from the late 1990s that reforms have favored a structure less distant from the Weberian notion of rational bureaucracy. Bureaucratic insulation has been part of the country's "political grammar"[14] and has been often justified as a strategy to contain the negative effects of the politicization of state agencies.[15]

It is within the dynamic relationships between state and society that the role of Itamaraty has to be examined. Throughout the twentieth century, Itamaraty's performance led to its identification as one of the "efficiency islands" ("ilhas de eficiência")[16] within the state, which not only was able to perform well in its field but also provided qualified staff to other sectors of the state bureaucracy.[17] This image has been reinforced by the fact that the excellence of the Brazilian diplomatic body is recognized domestically[18] and internationally.[19]

Itamaraty's central role in Brazilian foreign trade policymaking does not make the institution immune to political disputes. But compared with the USTR, it has benefited from a margin of autonomy from direct societal influence and interference of other bureaucratic agencies that is unknown in the U.S. trade system. Therefore, Itamaraty cannot be treated as a mere agent representing interests predefined through competition between societal forces.[20] Although its official positions may coincide with the desires of particular economic forces in the country, they do not automatically derive from a prior mandate granted by those same forces. This distinguishing feature limits the application of a pluralist framework that could exaggerate the direct influence of interest groups and underestimate the power of the executive.[21]

However,, Itamaraty's margin of autonomy should not be confused with complete independence, as if the institution were able to extricate itself from Brazilian political life. Under both military and civilian regimes Itamaraty has operated in a context marked by different interests and conflicts of views, and its autonomy has varied according to the level of "synergy" it developed with the presidency.[22] In the next section, the institutional development of Itamaraty is examined in order to show how the institution acquired its status of an intellectual source in the construction of a Brazilian identity to be projected internationally.

Itamaraty: Institutional Autonomy and Legitimacy of a Bureaucratic Agency

During the nineteenth century, in the recently independent nations of Latin America, successful diplomacy required the capacity to blur the distance between imagined nation and the reality of the new states. Considering that in any nation, a unitary interest does not exist a priori, the diplomatic task has always required the ability to shape a coherent notion of national interests and engage with the question of national identity.[23] As a former Brazilian minister of foreign affairs defined, "Foreign policy is an external projection of our national personality in the international sphere."[24]

Brazil achieved independence in 1822 through a negotiated process which outcome was the birth of a newly independent nation under a monarchical regime. At a time when most of its neighbors were facing violent struggles for independence, the Brazilian elite enjoyed a relatively peaceful local environment, in which continental Europe was the predominant source of cultural and intellectual inspiration. For the young men who constituted the local elite,[25] diplomacy was an ideal intellectual occupation. Through their activities, they could promote a nascent nationalism, and contribute to the creation and dissemination of their vision of Brazilian identity. Through their actions, Brazilian diplomats attempted to demonstrate that "not only was [Brazil's] emperor part of the great European royal families, but also that its elites had origins in the nobility of the Old Continent."[26]

The promotion of a national identity by diplomats included contributions to the national culture. An indication of their impact is given by the number of diplomats usually listed among the most important Brazilian writers since independence.[27] During the 1920s and 1930s, Itamaraty became an important center of ideas in the Brazilian state, from which intellectuals produced notions of national culture, values, and institutions, vis-à-vis those prevalent in Europe.[28] In their dissemination of a unified image of Brazil as a giant of the future, diplomats came to enjoy a degree of respect that until very recently was compared only to that enjoyed by the military. The initial installation of the ministry in the Itamaraty Palace, once home to the Republican provisional government, revealed the high status enjoyed by diplomats.[29]

Itamaraty's institutional building process began with the appointment of the Baron of Rio Branco as foreign affairs minister in 1902.[30] Rio Branco, whose achievements included the peaceful annexation of approximately 342,000 square miles to Brazilian territory,[31] inaugurated the tradition of emphasizing conciliation and pacifism in international forums as characteristics of Brazilian diplomacy.[32] He was also responsible for institutional reforms aimed at reinforcing the sense of unity and pride among diplomats. Itamaraty gradually evolved into a solid state institution, freed from the widespread political interference observed in other state agencies.[33] In the 1930s, when the government reformed the public sector, Itamaraty retained control over its professional codes by initiating its own reforms.[34] In 1945, it created its own educational institution—the Rio Branco Institute—to train new entrants into the diplomatic service.[35]

Congruent with the famous saying frequently quoted by Brazilian diplomats, that "the best tradition of the Itamaraty is to know how to renovate itself,"[36] the institution's capacity to adjust in order to preserve its autonomy has been revealed in many instances, including in foreign trade policy.[37] In the 1970s, when Brazilian foreign trade diversified in content and export destinations, Itamaraty created the Trade Promotion Department (*Departamento de Promoção Comercial*) that would become central in improving Brazil's external relations with new markets located in the developing world.[38] In 2001, as specialized knowledge of finance, trade, and investment grew in importance,[39] an organizational reform was carried out in order to increase the technical expertise and coordination among negotiators.[40] Itamaraty has therefore built a strong organizational culture,[41] defended against outside control by regular adjustments to the needs of changing times.[42]

Three main factors help to understand Itamaraty's capacity to remain for most of the twentieth century considerably insulated from interference either by Congress, interest groups, or other bureaucratic agencies. The first factor is related to its organizational structure. Entrants in the career undergo a period of full-time training in the Rio Branco Institute, by the end of which they acquire "a very clear notion, as a group, of their role in the process of construction of the Brazilian nation-state."[43] This professionalism and the esprit de corps among the diplomats, which have justified their comparison with the military in Brazil,[44] are reflected in a high performance of their public duties.

The second reason derives from the role diplomats have played in shaping a vision able to unify Brazilians around shared aspirations for a better future, one in which Brazil's imagined "destiny" of progress and development is realized. In a society still fractured by social and economic disparities and notions of class, this unifying vision has been extremely resilient. To the extent that diplomats have demonstrated the ability to combine perennial and transitory aspirations in the society and represent them through a broadly accepted image of national identity, they have enhanced the social credibility of the institution to which they belong.

According to former minister of foreign affairs, Celso Lafer, it is awareness of historical tradition that gives Itamaraty its coherence, enabling it to convey "a vision of the world."[45] This argument leaves open the question of how multiple readings of history are filtered into a dominant account, a fundamental debate since the scholarship on the history of International Relations in Brazil seems to have evolved without a solid exchange with the scholarship on Brazilian history more broadly.[46] But more revealing, this explanation implies that the legitimacy of the institution's authority is not reduced to its legal-bureaucratic responsibilities.

The third factor, which is particularly relevant to understanding Brazilian foreign trade policies, is related to the fact that until the late 1980s Itamaraty's actions were synchronized with the state-led strategies of national development. By generating foreign policy paradigms[47] that could be adjusted to the predominant development visions of the Brazilian state, Itamaraty made foreign trade policy an effective instrument of the national developmentalist project.

By the mid-1990s, when the FTAA was launched, Brazil was facing simultaneous processes of democratization and economic liberalization,[48] which favored the mobilization of new interest groups.[49] As free market reforms intensified, the corporatist alliances between business, labor, and the Brazilian developmentalist state began to disintegrate, leading to the current situation in which pluralist and corporatist relations coexist.

In parallel with the domestic changes, the end of the cold war, and the global restructuring of production and finance challenged the ability of the Brazilian state to sustain the national developmentalist model. As in most Latin American countries, a space for policy change opened up. While development continued to be a constant reference in national debates, there was no consensus on how best to pursue it. Itamaraty had to search for new responses and again underwent its own transition. It was in this national setting that the FTAA idea was introduced.

Development and Autonomy of a Middle Power

In contrast with countries in which liberal economic ideas have long been influential, in Brazil the belief that the state should play a central role in development has been widespread. Even when different notions of progress and development were disseminated, the state has remained central in framing a coherent image of how Brazil as a nation should pursue development.[50]

The rise of the Brazilian state as a modernizing force began in the 1930s[51] and as in many Latin American countries, expanded after the Second World War.[52] Sikkink argues that the political power of developmentalist ideas in Brazil was enhanced by the fact that they combined a technical approach to development with the role of the state in the economy, both appealing notions to the local insulated bureaucracy.[53] Guided by a "modernizing nationalist ideology,"[54] policymakers implemented a developmental project in which state management of industrialization included guidance of foreign direct investment to and direct state participation in selected sectors, and the use of trade barriers to protect local industries.[55] Trade was subordinated to the broader logic of national industrialization, leading to a situation in which, as a scholar defined, the "the main characteristic of trade policy [through 1988] was its inexistence as such."[56]

This vision of national development, which combined assumptions borrowed from modernization theory with reliance on a supposedly enlightened bureaucracy to implement it, found support in Itamaraty.[57] The next section presents the main paradigms of Brazil's foreign policy, showing how the defense of autonomy from international constraints was harmonious with the state-led project of national development.[58]

Paradigms in Brazilian Foreign Policy

From the times of the Baron of Rio Branco through the late 1980s, two main paradigms dominated Brazilian foreign policy. The first, inaugurated by Rio Branco, was characterized by the idea of a special alliance with the United States. From the late 1950s, a universalist paradigm according to which Brazil's international goals would be better pursued through a worldwide diversification of its relations gained influence.[59]

Beneath these two paradigms lay a set of ideas that have long been perpetuated in Brazilian foreign policy thinking, namely that autonomy from external constraints is necessary to preserve the country's ability to pursue its own strategy of development; the belief that due to Brazil's characteristics, the country should occupy a more relevant place in the international system; and the association of pragmatism with idealism in foreign policy strategies.[60] While these permanent features have provided Brazilian foreign policy with a sense of continuity, the manner in which they have been interpreted and the strategies that originated from these interpretations have varied.

From the early twentieth century until the late 1950s, Brazilian foreign policy was characterized by an alliance with the United States that contrasted markedly with the anti-U.S. position of many Latin American countries at the time.[61] Geopolitical considerations made this alliance particularly valuable, helping Brazil to highlight its position in South America,[62] within which it intended to be recognized as a hegemonic power.[63] Moreover, recognition by the United States was a means to enhance the country's projection as an international actor.

In trade, U.S.-Brazil cooperation allowed Brazilian agricultural products to enter the U.S. market under preferential reduced tariffs.[64] In the area of security, military cooperation during the Second World War[65] turned Brazil into the main recipient of U.S. armaments in Latin America. By the end of the war, Brazil had eclipsed its main rival, Argentina, as the main military power in South America.

In the immediate postwar period, however, Brazil's capacity to attract U.S. attention declined. Caught up in the West-East conflict, Brazil had to redefine its strategy for participation in the international system. At the same time, the project of modernization through industrialization became a national priority. By the 1950s, Brazilian foreign policy gained a more nationalist tone and nonalignment was promoted both as a means of emphasizing the country's sovereignty[66] and as a way to facilitate its development without the ideological constraints of the cold war.

The new paradigm was consolidated during the presidency of Jânio Quadros, inaugurated in January 1961. Quadros and Brazilian diplomats made the first clear rupture in Brazil's policy of alignment with the United States, introducing a new vision that would remain influential in Brazilian foreign policy. Quadros' "Independent Foreign Policy" rested on a combination of ideals and material interests, which merged to serve better the central aspiration of development.[67] It reaffirmed Brazil's identity as a nation with a Christian background and its cultural association with the Western world, but it emphasized economic inequality and underdevelopment as problems shared with the Third World, proposing a stronger association with Asia, Africa, and Latin America. As President Quadros argued, the West should demonstrate that it was "not only Communist planning that promotes the prosperity of national economies."[68]

Although in ideological terms the Independent Foreign Policy reflected a leftist turn in domestic politics,[69] it was not a rejection of the alliance with the United States in favor of communism. By adopting a stance of nonalignment and depicting the cold war as a divide between great powers that did not serve the interests of the underdeveloped world, Brazilian foreign policymakers attempted to preserve the country's autonomy of association with other nations, regardless of ideological positions.

This strategy was closely linked with national priorities. By 1960 Brazil had a fast growing population of about 70 million people. Import-substitution industrialization had fostered a process of intense migration from rural to urban areas and the rapid demographic change had increased pressures for economic growth. The opening of new markets for Brazilian products was fundamental. As President Quadros proposed:

> We shall go out to conquer these markets: at home, in Latin America, in Africa, in Asia, in Oceania, in countries under democracy, and in those that have joined the Communist system. Material interests know no doctrine and Brazil is undergoing a period where its very survival as a nation occupying one of the most extensive and privileged areas of the globe depends on the solution of its economic problems.[70]

The military coup of 1964 abruptly interrupted the call for an independent stance toward the United States. Immediately after the coup, the military shifted to an alliance with the United States, which included, among other things, support for the U.S. invasion of the Dominican Republic in 1965. Conservative civilian and military forces shared the commitment to a dependent model of development, according to which policies favoring the popular classes were seen as a threat.[71]

But the move backwards did not last long. With General Ernesto Geisel (1974–1979), universalism in foreign affairs was consolidated through the "Responsible Pragmatism" policy. As a foreign policy of a right-wing authoritarian regime, it avoided proximity to communist countries.[72] Responsible Pragmatism shared with the Independent Foreign Policy a commitment to nonalignment, nonintervention and the defense of Brazil's right to pursue its international relations independent of the great powers.

With regard to foreign trade, the Responsible Pragmatism policy reflected the transformation in the Brazilian trade structure. The rising importance of manufactured goods in the country's exports, the potential to penetrate new markets worldwide, and the impressive economic growth achieved during the economic miracle in the early 1970s justified the universalist approach to Brazil's participation in the world economy.[73]

At a time when rapid economic growth and industrialization were the driving forces of Brazil's modernization, multilateral commitments risked limiting the country's potential. In this regard, Ambassador Araújo Castro's argument that the great powers were using multilateralism in order to *freeze* the distribution of world power[74] served the double purpose of promoting Brazil as a leading voice in the developing world and minimizing international normative limitations on the country's actions.[75]

In foreign trade policy, this view of international regimes as limiting autonomy of the Third World was advanced through active participation in multilateral forums, from a critical and reactive stance. A member of the GATT since its constitution in 1947,[76] Brazil continuously defended the need to consolidate special and differential treatment mechanisms[77] in the multilateral trading system, and in parallel, pushed development concerns through the United Nations Conference on Trade and Development (UNCTAD) and G77.[78] As a Brazilian trade negotiator commented in 1976:

> there exist two possible forms of interdependence: that which governs the relations between central and peripheral economies...and that which supposes equity and marks the road to independence. The objective of effective international cooperation would thus be to facilitate the transition from the first to the second form of interdependence, and this is the only mode of international cooperation that Brazil judges useful in the agitated world of our days."[79]

Relations with the United States followed the logic of preservation of autonomy of action.[80] In 1975, Brazil signed a nuclear cooperation agreement with West Germany and in 1977 it renounced the military cooperation agreement with the United States that had been in place since 1952.[81]

By the end of the 1970s, Brazil's trade profile confirmed that the Responsible Pragmatism policy had not been simple wishful thinking. Brazilian manufacturing exports rose from US$416 million in 1970 to US$9 billion by 1980. The participation of developing areas as a destination market for Brazilian exports increased from 16.8 percent to 32.3 percent. The U.S. share as export destination declined from 26.1 percent in 1971 to 17.6 percent by 1981, while the participation of Latin America (LAIA/ALADI markets), Africa and the Middle East, and Asia rose respectively from 12.2 percent to 18 percent, 2.3 percent to 7.3 percent, and 3.4 percent to 9.8 percent.[82] Brazil also managed to attract a larger share of investment from West Germany and Japan. At the end of the decade, the country had become the tenth largest economy, with the thirteenth largest industrial sector in the world.[83]

As in the Independent Foreign Policy, the new policy merged a realist orientation with idealist components. Responsible Pragmatism was instrumental in generating economic security and development, but it also reflected the ambition of Brazilian elites to see the country emerge as a middle power. By the late 1970s this view had gained supporters outside the country. One scholar concluded that Brazil was close to becoming "the first Southern

Hemisphere star in the world galaxy and the first new major power to emerge on the international system since the rise of China after the World War II."[84] In an address to the U.S. Congress in 1976, U.S. secretary of state Henry Kissinger declared that "Brazil is becoming a world power, and it does not need our approval to become one, and it is our obligation in the conduct of foreign policy to deal with the realities as they exist."[85]

It appeared that Brazilian military and diplomatic institutions had succeeded in projecting internationally Brazil's identity as a middle power of Western traditions, whose accelerated economic development occurred within the capitalist system, but which would fight against the asymmetric patterns of North-South relations.[86] In this process, their joint commitment to the national development project[87] and mutual institutional respect[88] contributed to the synchronicity between foreign policy actions and domestic priorities.[89]

Nevertheless, the world economic recession that began in the late 1970s proved a major test for Brazilian diplomats, and a deep financial crisis challenged the vision of the country as an emerging world power. Brazil's fight for economic survival and its lack of international credibility in the 1980s showed the distance between the constructed identity of a middle power and the resources needed to sustain it.[90] In trade, diversification did not alter structural asymmetries in its relations with developed countries. While Brazil was sending around 30 percent of its exports to the European Economic Community, it accounted for less than 1 percent of the EEC's exports.[91]

From the postwar period through the 1970s, a foreign trade policy based on the continuous demands on developed countries and protection of the national market suited the national developmentalist paradigm. However, the economic crisis of the 1980s exposed the inefficiencies of Brazilian trade protection and the misuse of trade as a tool to address macroeconomic imbalances. Foreign policymakers would have to find new ways to make Brazil a middle power.

Years of Transition (1980–1994)

As seen in chapter 3, the decade that preceded the launching of the FTAA project was characterized by a series of rapid transformations. Growing international competition and the fear of a world divided into three competing regional blocs contributed to a renascence of trade regionalism. In Latin America, uncertainty was aggravated by a decade of economic exhaustion and political change after which the desire for stability could be felt in both government and society.

As Brazil entered the debt crisis in the early 1980s, reality temporarily interrupted the dream of its consolidation as a middle power. The new civilian government inaugurated in 1985 had to manage a deep economic crisis which exacerbated internal social and political tension. Throughout that decade, the ability of finance ministers to negotiate with external debtors became more important than formal diplomacy in the fight against external intervention in national policies.[92]

Brazil's reconceptualization of relations with Argentina, which until then had been its main rival for regional leadership, was the most relevant change in the country's foreign policy in the period. In the mid-1980s, both countries were in a process of political reconstruction that required national healing and the international projection of a new image. Economic pressures increased the incentives to find in cooperation a way to strengthen their ability to deal with international demands. Following Brazil's logic of being a global player,[93] its economic alliance with Argentina provided an opportunity to gradually adjust its local industrial base and to prepare it for international competition.

On July 29, 1986, Brazil and Argentina signed the *Programa de Integración y Cooperación Económica—PICE* (Integration and Economic Cooperation Program), setting in motion a process of increasing bilateral economic integration and political cooperation that would ultimately lead to the formation of the Southern Common Market (Mercosur) in 1991. Born of a strong political commitment by the parties involved, Mercosur demonstrated the centrality of political leadership in initiating a project of cooperation, which enabled it to overcome the initial disbelief of the Brazilian business sector.[94]

Cooperation with Argentina did not represent an idealist shift to regionalism. Brazil continued to favor a minimalist approach to trade liberalization in the Latin American Integration Association (LAIA/ALADI). It resisted a deep institutionalization of economic integration and, like other Latin American countries, opted for the bilateral negotiation of preferential trade agreements.[95] In the regional trade game, Brazil continued to believe that the advantages that it could obtain through higher institutionalization would not compensate the costs imposed on the country's policy autonomy.

For Brazil, the need to rethink its international role in the post–cold war period became more acute with the debt crisis, which exposed the gap between aspirations for autonomy and the country's actual resources for achieving it.[96] From the mid-1980s the economic crisis led to a decline in the international competitiveness of Brazilian exports and the dismantling of protectionist incentives, which heavily affected the state's capacity to sustain the national developmentalist model.[97]

When Fernando Collor de Mello was elected president in 1989, it seemed that Brazil would finally move toward neoliberal reforms. He introduced a program of rapid unilateral trade liberalization, including a drastic reduction in import tariffs and the elimination of many of the incentive mechanisms that had helped to sustain the national developmentalist project in the previous decades.[98] Concerns about power asymmetry, which had been traditional in Brazilian foreign policy, gave way to a defense of the gains associated with interdependence. In order to promote his view, Collor de Mello attempted to diminish Itamaraty's centrality in foreign policy, acting himself as a diplomatic representative. But his impeachment in 1991 further eroded Brazil's international image.[99]

Following de Mello's short-lived attempt to redirect Brazilian foreign policy toward a liberal view of asymmetrical interdependence, foreign policymakers returned to the pool of ideas accumulated within the diplomatic institution, in search of a strategy appropriate to the new context of the 1990s.[100] As one diplomat explained, in contrast to those groups who tended to nurture "deprecating feelings about Brazil's capacity for projection," foreign policymakers had to be able to look beyond short-term difficulties and see the country's permanent qualities.[101]

Without abandoning a realist perspective,[102] foreign policymakers reinforced the use of discourses and ideas as resources for building international power.[103] As Ambassador Gelson Fonseca Jr. argued, for a country with only limited power, "its ideas, or more precisely, the conceptual bases of its international actions,"[104] were extremely valuable in the legitimization of its actions.

Autonomy, conceived as a country's ability to determine domestic and foreign policies with the least external constraint possible, together with development, continued to be central goals of Brazil's foreign policy, but the strategy deployed to pursue them was modified. In the post–cold war era, the strategy of nonalignment lost value. The idea that Brazil's interests would be better served by participation in the formulation rather than resistance to international norms, gained more credibility among foreign policymakers. Participation, in that context, meant active engagement to influence the content of international regimes. Brazil should act a "mediator" and "consensus builder,"[105] in order to help establish a positive multilateral agenda oriented by the principles of democracy, development, and disarmament (the three "Ds").[106] The leading role assumed by the Brazilian diplomacy in the organization and hosting of the UN Conference on Environment and Development in Rio de Janeiro in 1992 (ECO-92), was one of the first actions that reflected this orientation.

Brazilian foreign policymakers moved from a strategy defined as "autonomy through distance" or "autonomy through detachment," to one of "autonomy through participation" or "autonomy through integration."[107] Thus, in a world of increasing interdependence, commitment to multilateral norms and attempts to change the system from within were seen as the best strategy for preserving autonomy.

At the regional level, relations with South America, particularly the strengthening of Mercosur, gained emphasis. Brazil's attempt to consolidate a position of regional power functioned as leverage for its ambition to consolidate itself as a middle power. Following the announcement of the Enterprise for the Americas Initiative, Brazilian diplomats worked to guarantee that negotiations with the United States would occur with Mercosur as a bloc (format 4+1).[108] In December 1992, President Itamar Franco announced the Amazon's Initiative. Consistent with the shift in Brazil's security focus from the southern borders of the La Plata basin up to the northern Amazon basin, the initiative aimed to improve relations with Bolivia, Colombia, Ecuador, Peru, Venezuela, Guyana, and Suriname.[109] Later, in 1993, Brazil proposed the formation of a South American Free Trade Area (SAFTA). In this period of redefinition of foreign policy strategies, Brazil's ability to innovate was limited by the persistent challenge of managing the domestic economic crisis.

The Cardoso Years. Competitiveness in an International Economic Liberal Order

In Brazil, as in the United States, the FTAA was launched at a time when economic concerns were the main focus of domestic political and policy attention. During the two terms of President Cardoso (1995–1998, 1999–2002), Brazil's participation in the FTAA was characterized by efforts to coordinate the pace of the project according to domestic priorities, and particularly during Cardoso's first term, with the economic reforms.

Social democrat Fernando Henrique Cardoso was elected president in 1994. A sociologist renowned for his work on dependency theory and development in Latin America, Cardoso began his political career in the late 1970s, after returning from exile.[110] In 1988, together with a group of prominent intellectuals from the center-left in Brazil, he founded the Brazilian Social Democratic Party (*Partido da Social Democracia Brasileira*—PSDB). During Itamar Franco's presidency (1992–1994), Cardoso was minister of foreign fafairs and in 1993, he was appointed minister of finance. After a decade of unsuccessful economic plans, it fell upon a sociologist to coordinate Brazil's economic stabilization.[111]

Until 1994, Brazil resisted a radical shift to neoliberalism.[112] In contrast to most Latin American countries, Brazil experimented with heterodox economic programs throughout the 1980s and remained a "maverick...a stumbling block to the international financial community."[113] In Brazil, in contrast to most Latin American countries, the national developmentalist vision had been relatively successful. The proportion of manufactured products of total exports rose from 4 percent in 1964 to about 50 percent by the end of the 1970s.[114] This process evolved within a triangular corporatist system of state-society relations in which the state coordinated relations with organized labor and business. The protectionist system that sustained the development project not only created powerful interest groups in national-owned industry, but also benefited multinational corporations established in an uncompetitive, closed environment. By the end of the 1970s, Brazil had built a diversified industrial base and was among the ten largest economies in the world. This performance lent support to the belief in a positive role for the state in the economy, which continued to be shared by many groups.

In the development of the economic stabilization plan, Cardoso formed a team of nationally renowned economists of unorthodox orientation,[115] including key contributors to neostructuralism.[116] In July 1994, the Real Plan ("Plano Real") was implemented. Inflation rapidly declined and remained at relatively low levels from then on. In the following years, Brazil implemented market-based reforms. In a country in which aversion to radical changes is ingrained in the psychology of the elites,[117] Brazil's transition to neoliberalism would also be conducted gradually.

When the FTAA idea was officially launched in December 1994, Cardoso was president-elect and was invited to accompany President Itamar Franco to the First Summit of the Americas. By then, Brazil was only beginning to recover from more than a decade of economic chaos. In trade, both the government and the private sector faced the accumulated effects of the unilateral liberalization implemented by President Collor de Mello and the commitments undertaken in the Uruguay Round and Mercosur.[118] In this national context, it is not hard to see why the FTAA, as a project requiring further coordination of trade liberalization and concessions in areas still regulated by the state, had little appeal. As Cardoso cautiously commented during the First Summit of the Americas, in order to enhance Brazil's competitiveness by the ambitious FTAA deadline of 2005, substantial technological development and investment would be necessary.[119]

During Cardoso's first term (1995–1998), policy debates concentrated on the implementation and coordination of reforms oriented toward economic liberalization. By his second term (1999–2002), market-based reforms had been implemented, but a new financial crisis in early 1999 exposed again the gap between Brazil's pursued image and outsiders' perceptions about the country. As in the past, foreign policy would be shaped in close relationship with these new conditions.

Cardoso's Foreign Policy

As with domestic policies, foreign policy under Cardoso has been the subject of intense disagreements. While some argue that it lacked a paradigm,[120] others describe it as period of consolidation of "pragmatic institutionalism," according to which Brazil would adopt differentiated degrees of commitment to institutionalism depending on the area in focus.[121] Furthermore, while some see in the shift toward international regimes the consolidation of the idea of "autonomy through integration,"[122] others critically describe it as an almost subordinate attitude of acceptance of neoliberal rules.[123]

Pragmatic institutionalism, when combined with the notion of "autonomy through integration," is a useful description of foreign policy under Cardoso.[124] Following Brazil's self-identification as a global player, multilateral participation remained the priority. In those forums, Brazil attempted to influence the content of multilateral rules as a way to protect its own interests internationally. However, the more constructivist approach to international norms at the multilateral level was not reproduced at the regional level. Under Cardoso, Brazil continued to see regionalism as a platform from which to strengthen its international position and resisted the creation of institutional mechanisms that might limit its scope for autonomous action within the Americas.[125] Within this framework, the FTAA, as a hemispheric-based arrangement that would confirm the United States as the dominant power and lead to a lessening of Brazil's relative power in South America, was unlikely to generate political enthusiasm.

Although universalism, autonomy, and pragmatism continue to be present in Brazilian foreign policy, Cardoso's own ideas and personal style influenced the definition of Brazil's foreign policy priorities. During his two terms in office, a nuanced but significant shift occurred. As in other policy areas, Cardoso attempted to implement his view of how Brazil should participate in the world. That implied distancing foreign policy from the national developmentalist model that still enjoyed support among various domestic sectors. Second, in line with his views of politics as a combination of *virtú* and fortuna,[126] he pragmatically pursued new means for realizing his goals. Cardoso became a de facto "ambassador" for Brazil, promoting through his active international agenda and networks the image he believed Brazil should project. Indeed, his emphasis on presidential diplomacy led to criticisms of what was considered an attempt to reduce Itamaraty's central role in Brazil's diplomacy.[127]

He referred to economic globalization as a process that has limited the margin for national autonomous strategies in areas such as labor policy and macroeconomics, at the same time that it has increased pressure for the creation of internationally uniform regulations. According to Cardoso, recognizing these new conditions required "a sense of realism" that was fundamental to the implementation of adequate political responses.[128] He rejected strategies based on a divisive North-South framework, arguing that rather than reproducing the "illusory dream" of the "new international economic order" of the 1960s and 1970s, the multiple and at times conflicting needs of the developing world had to be discussed with a view to greater insertion in—as opposed to isolation from—the international economy.[129] In a world of increasing technological competition, Cardoso concluded:

> In truth it is a more cruel phenomenon: Either the South (or parts of it) enters the democratic-technological-scientific race and invests massively in R&D, and undergoes "informational" transformations, or it [risks] becoming unimportant, insignificant for the development of the globalized economy.[130]

A similar perspective on development appears in Cardoso's previous work as sociologist in the 1970s, in which he argued that the kind of economic development that Brazil could experience would not occur outside capitalism, but rather in connection with the international expansion of the capitalist system.[131] As he wrote:

> I do not think, though, that the local bourgeoisie, fruit of a dependent capitalism, can accomplish an economic revolution in the strong sense of the concept. Its "revolution" consists of integrating itself to the international capitalism as an associate and dependent. Of course, fighting to obtain the maximum possible benefits. But limited by an objective process: the capitalist accumulation in dependent economies is not fully accomplished.[132]

Given these views, Brazil's pursuit of acceptance and participation in the international liberal economic order was congruent with what Cardoso described as a "viable utopia."[133] The construction and dissemination of this view was facilitated by an ideologically synchronized and stable decision-making team. Career ambassador Luiz Felipe Lampréia[134] was minister of foreign affairs for most of Cardoso's two terms. He was replaced in 2001 by Celso Lafer. Although Lafer was not a career diplomat, he had served as minister of foreign affairs in 1992 and during the two terms of the Cardoso administration had occupied top-level diplomatic positions.[135]

It is in this period that the space for individual leadership in diplomacy became more evident. Since the times of the Baron of Rio Branco, Itamaraty's tradition had combined institutional strength with individual brilliance, to some extent natural in a profession in which intellectual abilities are one of the most important qualities. However, studies of foreign policy under Cardoso usually maintain an institutional focus.[136] Only in a few cases are the roles played by individuals explicitly acknowledged.[137]

While Cardoso's foreign policy maintained concerns with autonomy and preservation of Brazil's status as a global player,[138] the move away from the national developmentalist paradigm, and a more liberal interpretation of international regimes, represented a rupture not unanimously supported within Itamaraty. Although the internal changes that Itamaraty has gone through in the last two decades have not been researched at length, it appears that Cardoso was able to align his visions with those of a like-minded group of senior-level foreign policymakers who recognized that in the post–cold war era Brazil's margin of autonomy was restrained and traditional notions of sovereignty would have to be adjusted for increasing interdependence.[139]

The Cardoso administration was characterized by efforts to reconstruct Brazil's international credibility after a decade of economic turmoil. The previous military government's resistance to international commitments to the monitoring and nonproliferation of nuclear weapons was replaced by cooperation. In 1994, Brazil became a full member of the Treaty of Tlatelolco, and in 1998 it requested accession to the Treaty on the Non-Proliferation of Nuclear Weapons.[140] At the regional level, Mercosur became the first regional bloc of developing countries to insert a democratic clause as a condition for membership. Brazil's acceptance of a series of multilateral treaties in areas as diverse as trade and security reflected a process of identity reconstruction in which the sources of the country's international credibility as a middle power were imagined as resting primarily on its being a liberal democracy and stable market economy.[141]

In trade, the emphasis on integration as a means to defend an increasingly restricted autonomy[142] was translated into simultaneous participation at multiple levels of trade negotiations, ranked according to an assessment of economic and political advantages. Within the paradigm of pragmatic liberalism described above, the multilateral (WTO) and subregional (Mercosur) spheres were prioritized, while bilateral relations were also cultivated.

In contrast to its behavior in multilateral forums, Brazil's actions in South America combined the pursuit of leadership with a resistance to bearing its likely costs. Brazil's relationships with its neighbors were characterized by a lower level of institutionalization of commitments and a resistance to the creation of mechanisms to deal with asymmetries on behalf of the smaller economies. Under Cardoso, Brazilian foreign policymakers pursued a hegemonic position in South America that would to some extent offset the limitations on its autonomy resulting from participation in the global economy. It was only when the 1999 financial crisis exposed the distance between Brazil's self-image and perceptions of outsiders that Brazil shifted more consciously to a policy of cooperation in the subcontinent. In 2000, it hosted the first South American Summit to take place since the independence of the South American countries, with twelve states discussing cooperation in fields such as democracy, trade, and infrastructure.[143]

However, even in Mercosur, resistance to supranational institutions continued to limit the consolidation of the bloc beyond free trade. The fight to preserve policy autonomy, which was particularly strong on the part of the bloc's dominant members Brazil and Argentina, contributed to delays in the ratification of protocols, a reversal of commitments due to "national needs," and increasing criticism from Uruguay and Paraguay.[144]

Despite Mercosur's economic difficulties and structural deficiencies,[145] it has been consistently supported by the Brazilian government. It is not hard to see the value of Mercosur to Brazil. From 1990 to 1996, the bloc's proportion of Brazil's total exports grew from 4.2 percent to 15.5 percent, with imports expanding from 11.2 percent to 15.6 percent. In a period when Brazilian exports to the world grew at an average of 5.0 percent, its exports to Mercosur registered an annual average growth of 33.3 percent.[146] Although lack of coordination in macroeconomic policies slowed this growth in the late 1990s, the initial trade boom was impressive. Moreover, Brazil's economic profile places it in a dominant position within the bloc, and configures an asymmetrical pattern comparable to that observed between the United States and the rest of Latin America. Aware of this, Brazilian foreign policymakers have relied on Mercosur as a building bloc for bargaining in trade negotiations since its formation in 1990.

Implications for the FTAA

Since the early 1990s, Brazilian foreign policy priorities have been linked to multilateral institutions and the consolidation of Mercosur. At both levels, foreign policymakers fought to balance the pace of domestic structural reforms and the pressures deriving from external constraints. It was in a context in which economic stabilization was the political priority, that the idea of a hemispheric free trade area was introduced.

As discussed in chapter 2, Brazil's economic and trade profiles partly explain its lower enthusiasm for the FTAA negotiations, compared with Latin American countries that are highly trade dependent on the United States.

In the 1990s, and particularly from the second half of the decade onwards, the modernization of the Brazilian agricultural sector accelerated.

Between 1990 and 2003, agricultural exports increased from US$8.9 billion to US$21.2 billion. The agribusiness sector, consisting of a sophisticated chain of basic commodities and agro-industrial complexes, emerged as a highly competitive sector globally, placing Brazil among the world leaders in exports of soy, sugar, bovine meat, and tobacco, among other products. By 2003, the leading agro-industrial chains in Brazil were soy (38.2 percent of total agricultural exports), sugar and alcohol (11.6 percent), poultry meat (9.2 percent), bovine meat (7.8 percent), and coffee (7.3 percent). In addition to its role in generating trade surplus, the agricultural sector enhanced Brazil's position as a global player. From 2000 to 2003, although the European Union (EU) continued to be Brazil's most important market for agricultural exports (approximately 40 percent), the most dynamic markets for Brazilian agricultural goods were located in Asia and the Pacific, the Middle East, Northern Africa, Eastern Europe, and the former USSR.[147] In 2009, China was positioned as Brazil's second main trade partner and main destination for its exports, which included products such as iron, soybean, steel, copper, plastic, and airplanes.

Although in 2009 there was a steep fall of 42.4 percent in Brazilian exports to the United States, that country remained as Brazil's most important single trade partner, with a total trade flow of US$ 35.9 billion.[148] Brazilian trade with the United States is also highly diversified: in 2000, approximately 90 percent of Brazil's exports to the United States consisted of semi-manufactured and manufactured products, including technologically-intensive goods such as aircraft.[149]

Although most Brazilian manufactures do not face barriers to the U.S. market, Brazil is a strong competitor with the United States in key markets such as beef, sugar, orange juice, and steel, which are subject to a complex protectionist system of subsidies and selective application of high tariffs, quotas, and antidumping measures.[150] A study of the impact of the FTAA in Brazil-U.S. trade estimated that 43.3 percent of the potential growth in Brazilian exports to the United States would come from the elimination of nontariff barriers.[151] It was therefore expected that in any trade negotiation with the United States, Brazil would demand improved market access to agricultural goods and reform of U.S. antidumping legislation.

If those were the offensive interests of Brazil in a hemispheric free trade area, the country also had strong defensive interests. Its industrial sector continues to benefit from one of the highest average tariff rates in the Americas. Due to the diversification of the industrial base and the high proportion of manufactured products in Brazil's exports, debates on further tariff reductions immediately mobilize groups in the manufacturing sector that can lose in the process. Moreover, because of the corporatist system that prevailed well into the early 1990s, competitive sectors have only in the last decade become more articulated in the push for liberalization. However, despite market deregulation and liberalization, Brazil has resisted international commitments that might reduce its flexibility in defining its own rules with respect to services and investment.

Beyond relations with the United States, Brazilian trade flows into South America are also relevant. South America is the most important market for Brazilian manufactured exports, some of which are not competitive on a world scale. In the LAIA/ALADI system, Brazil has enjoyed preferential access to markets in the region. If for no other reason, Brazil's participation in the FTAA would help the country to avoid discriminatory concessions for the United States in more favorable terms than those made to Brazil.[152]

Against this set of existing incentives and risks, it was hard to assess the likelihood of balanced outcomes before negotiations effectively began. This was particularly valid during the preparatory phase (1995–1998), when countries were mainly evaluating their national situation in the areas covered by the FTAA working groups. In Brazil more detailed evaluations of the FTAA only emerged in the late 1990s. Yet, as seen earlier in chapter 2, since the beginning of the FTAA process Brazil adopted a position of caution and gradualism. It rejected the reproduction of the NAFTA model, insisted on balanced negotiations and, in accord with its emphasis on Mercosur, insisted on the consolidation of the subregional blocs as a base for further hemispheric commitments.

Brazilian foreign policymakers worked to influence the FTAA structure in critical ways. They defended the adoption of the single undertaking principle, and rejected U.S. and Canadian suggestions of an "early harvest" in the negotiations for market access. Moreover, they insisted that the FTAA rules should be "compatible with" rather than more advanced than those prevailing in the WTO.[153] They also opposed the linking of trade sanctions to labor and environmental provisions.[154]

Although this tactic blocked rapid advances in the FTAA process and caused frictions with negotiators from other states, including the United States, synchronicity between presidents Cardoso and Clinton made this gradual approach to the negotiations politically viable. According to Cardoso, despite U.S. state secretary Albright's critical rhetoric Clinton personally voiced on various occasions his support for Brazil's strategy of first strengthening Mercosur.[155]

From 1994 through 2002, Brazilian foreign policymakers participated in the FTAA through a strategy of gradualism that aimed to set a pace for the process that would harm neither the consolidation of Brazil's domestic reforms nor its foreign policy goal to be a global player.[156] Cardoso's rejection of radical moves and his preference for gradualism, which he expressed in domestic policies, was clear in foreign policy. Despite the fact that since its inception, the FTAA idea represented a risk for Brazil's foreign policy ambitions in South America, for almost a decade the diplomatic strategy followed the logic of "autonomy through integration," with attempts to influence the process from within.

Uncertainty was intrinsic to the FTAA negotiations, and policymakers were constantly forced to reassess their positions. The dominant foreign policy view during Cardoso's presidency was that engagement was better than abandonment of the process. As Vigevani describes it, criticism of the asymmetries in the international system continued, but "irremediable tensions—either with the USA or with any other country—[were] avoided at all costs."[157]

Accordingly, Minister Lafer maintained that even though Mercosur was Brazil's "destiny," and the FTAA was only "an option," it was an option that "[could] not be rejected *a priori*."[158] Following his interpretation, if Brazil's demands for market access could be achieved, then the country could indeed benefit, as it would be offering in exchange the consolidation of reforms that would have to be implemented anyway.[159]

This posture of integration into the new international order, which necessarily required the maintenance of good relations with the United States, had to be articulated in a domestic context of rising polarization over the FTAA. Within Brazil, the FTAA public debate over trade issues triggered by the FTAA had no precedent in the history of the country's foreign trade policy. Under the state-led developmentalist model prevalent in the 1980s, corporatism characterized the relationship between the business sector, labor unions, and the state. From 1990 onwards, economic liberalization, the dismantling of traditional mechanisms of industrial protection,[160] and democratization contributed to a system in which corporatist and pluralist practices coexisted,[161] and innovative forms of organizing state-business-labor relations could emerge.

For the private sector, participation in the FTAA evolved in a learning curve.[162] In 1996, under the leadership of the *Confederação Nacional das Indústrias* (National Confederation of Industry—CNI), the *Coalizão Empresarial Brasileira* (Brazilian Business Coalition—CEB) was formed. Conceived as a multisectoral coalition, CEB aimed to improve coordination among the various sectors of the economy and to influence government with a more consolidated business sector position, with initial focus on the FTAA. As could be expected in view of Brazil's industrial structure, CEB faced difficulties due to the conflicts between protectionist *versus* competitive industries and the predominance of the manufacturing sector in the discussions. Despite its deficiencies, CEB inaugurated a new form of organization by the business sector in trade negotiations that contributed to overcoming the limitations of the corporatist model.[163] The most coherent articulation occurred among the competitive exporters in the large-scale agribusiness sector. As the sector with most to win from the removal of barriers to the U.S. market, the agribusiness sector did not suffer the internal divisions of the manufacturing and services industries. Through investment in technical capacity-building and policy influence,[164] it was able to advocate its interests with consistency.

Labor unions also built on their accumulated experience with transnational alliances to organize critical mobilization in the process. In the Belo Horizonte ministerial meeting of 1997, the Brazilian United Central Workers Confederation (*Central Única dos Trabalhadores*—CUT) joined labor organizations from several countries in the hemisphere and presented a common position document in which they emphasized the need to protect workers' rights. But unlike the business sector, CUT's positions in trade negotiations did not follow a strict economic rationale. While it maintained an antagonist attitude during the FTAA negotiations, it adopted a more flexible approach to the WTO negotiations,[165] as well in those between Mercosur and the EU. Since the EU was also demanding strong liberalization in sensitive areas such as services, while at the same time resisting liberalization of its own agricultural sector, CUT's flexible position is more likely to have been related to long-established cooperation with European labor unions and left-wing parties than to a potential better quality of EU's offers.

With regard to the civil society organizations, the involvement of the country in multiple trade negotiations stimulated local NGOs to oppose further trade liberalization. The Brazilian Network for the Integration of the Peoples (REBRIP) became the hub of this movement, bringing together nongovernment organizations (NGO), labor unions, and social movements.[166]

On the state side, the Ministry of Foreign Affairs attempted to coordinate these different views by setting up the *Seção Nacional de Coordenação dos Assuntos Relativos à Alca* (National Section for the Coordination of FTAA-Related Issues—SENALCA) in 1996.[167] SENALCA was promoted as an arena for the discussion of issues covered in the FTAA negotiations, so that the official position would take into consideration contributions from other ministries, Congress and umbrella organizations representing business, labor unions, and civil society.[168] In practice, however, SENALCA did not offer a stable mechanism for participation. Flexibility in the selection criteria for invited organizations, Itamaraty's power to filter access to detailed information, and the lack of consolidated rules for participation, contributed to its fragility.[169] Moreover, the very asymmetrical level of knowledge among participants on the issues under negotiation impaired in-depth discussions, and stakeholders mainly acted to promote their predefined positions.[170]

As the FTAA approached the crucial stage of negotiations in 2002, domestic polarization intensified. The shift to unilateralism in the United States and the introduction of policies such as the U.S. Farm Bill diminished the Brazilian government's margin of maneuver and increased the perception of the FTAA as a U.S.-dominated project. These events occurred at the same time when the government was preparing for the upcoming presidential elections in 2002.

In September 2002, at the peak of the electoral campaign, a coalition of the National Confederation of Bishops of Brazil (CNBB), labor unions, students, the landless movement, and radical left parties, among others, organized a plebiscite to discuss (1) the government's proposal to cede the use of Brazil's *Alcântara* air base to the United States, and (2) the FTAA, under the slogan "Yes to life, no to the FTAA."[171] With approximately 10 million votes registered, about 98 percent agreed that Brazil should not sign the FTAA, and about 85 percent thought that the country should disengage from the negotiations.[172] Regardless of whether the plebiscite reflected real public knowledge of the process, this massive rejection could not be politically dismissed in an election year. Congress also entered the debate, hosting seminars and promoting discussions on ways to enhance the transparency and accountability of the executive in foreign trade policymaking.[173] During 2002, the FTAA became a highly politicized campaign issue; this, together with popular opposition to the project, made advances unlikely.

Lula's Foreign Policy and the National Developmentalist Inspiration

In January 2003, the leader of the Workers' Party (*Partido dos Trabalhadores*—PT), Luiz Inácio Lula da Silva, was elected president. The election of Lula, a former metal-worker and labor union leader, represented a historical turn in Brazil's political life, in which the elite-driven system that had characterized most of the twentieth century was democratically challenged by a working class left-wing leader with little formal education.

In addition to Lula's impressive personal history, the PT's platform gave hope to those who expected a change from the neoliberal orientation of the previous government, toward more socially oriented policies with an emphasis on fighting inequality. The PT, which had once been described as "the largest explicitly socialist political party in South America,"[174] was formed out of the social movements that emerged in the late 1970s in opposition to the authoritarian regime and included progressive sectors of the Catholic church, labor unions, and landless people, among others. Although, the party had emphasized in its early years the fight for "political autonomy of the working class," its diverse constituency transformed it into a broader political umbrella for most forces committed to the struggle for social justice and equality.[175] Since the 1980s, the party had grown and consolidated itself as the main left-wing political force in Brazil. Through its electoral victories in several municipalities, it had also built a reputation in innovative governance oriented to participatory popular democracy.[176]

Lula's victory had an impact beyond Brazil. The popular rejection of neoliberalism in the largest economy in Latin America provided those wanting a shift toward the left in Latin America with hope. It was described by intellectuals outside Brazil as symbolic of "our capacity to be the actors responsible for our history,"[177] an indication of the possibility of "a peaceful transition" toward a "new global financial and economic pact."[178]

However, the PT that arrived in power in 2003 and was reelected in 2006 and 2010, was not the radical party of the early 1980s. Like many Latin American left-wing parties that managed to perform well in elections, PT adjusted its opposition rhetoric to the demands of staying in power. During the presidential campaign, Lula criticized the FTAA as a project that "[was] not about integration but about annexation."[179] Nevertheless, aware of the political implications that a strong anti-FTAA stance could have on the elections and on the perceptions of international investors, PT soon moderated its comments. While it stressed the need for substantial concessions in Brazil's targeted areas in the FTAA, it did not propose a rupture of the process.[180] Moreover, during the campaign, the party reversed its initial decision to participate in the FTAA plebiscite in 2002, leading the plebiscite organizers to criticize the decision as a manifestation of loss of "courage and consistence."[181]

Once in power, Lula worked to convince international investors of the commitment of his government to maintaining the Cardoso administration's economic priorities of fiscal stability and inflation control. Rather than a reversal of his previous positions, Lula's actions reflected his old political views. As he indicated in 1989, when he first competed for the presidency:

> I want the PT to reach office, to see if it can meet the demands we make of the government. Because a party begins to mature not when it becomes moderate, but when it gains consciousness of its responsibilities; that is, when it begins to measure what it says in campaign against what it is going to do after that campaign.[182]

PT's increasing move toward the center[183] caused anxiety among many of its constituents.[184] Apparently, political *maturity* had meant the acceptance of the limits imposed by the neoliberal order. With the recognition of these limits leading to an economic orthodoxy quite different from PT's ideological stance and rhetoric, the new administration found in foreign policymaking the space to promote the party's old agenda. Greater executive control over foreign policymaking facilitated the formulation of policies that preserved ideological consistency and were supported by PT's constituents.[185] This differentiated margin for maneuver between domestic and foreign policies reveals that state autonomy is not a static condition, but must be assessed for particular times and policy areas.[186]

Because the Lula administration maintained emphasis on relations with South America, a cautious view of the FTAA and active participation in multilateral forums, it would be easy to stress continuity with Cardoso's foreign policy. However, a careful examination of the ideas advocated by foreign policymakers and the policies they carried out in Lula's first term (between 2003 and 2006) shows that ideological differences between Cardoso's PSDB and Lula's PT influenced the conduct of Brazilian negotiators in the FTAA. This highlighting of the ideological variable is not intended to ignore the fact that the new administration's foreign policy was heavily influenced by material considerations. What is stressed is that the ideas and ideology prevalent in the new group in power led to different interpretations of gains and risks that consequently influenced their preferences and the choices revealed internationally by the Brazilian state.

Lula's First Term Foreign Policy

At the beginning of his term, President Lula appointed Ambassador Celso Amorim as minister for foreign affairs. A respected career diplomat, Ambassador Amorim had been part of the 1970s Itamaraty generation associated with the Responsible Pragmatism.[187] As foreign minister in 1993 and 1994, he had worked to realign Brazilian diplomacy around the "3Ds" of democracy, development, and disarmament.[188] Although Ambassador Amorim supported Brazil's international engagement, he put particular emphasis on the negative effects of asymmetrical interdependence and defended a qualified type of international participation:

> As we turn our eyes to the international markets of goods, services, and technology, we must ask ourselves whether we should resign ourselves to unqualified attempts at integration in the current context, or if our global insertion presupposes efforts—in coordination with government and non government partners—to promote conditions of more equitable competition and distribution of gains.[189]

This slight variation in emphasis on the negative aspects and risks of interdependence did not conflict with Cardoso's foreign policy and was insufficient to affirm that there would be a major shift in foreign policy. However, the appointment of Ambassador Samuel Pinheiro Guimarães as secretary general of external relations clearly signaled the Lula administration's desire to differentiate itself from the Cardoso administration. A diplomat for more than four decades, Ambassador Guimarães had gained prominence in the FTAA debates through his strong opposition to the project, arguing that the rules that the FTAA would potentially put in place would prevent Brazil from implementing the national policies necessary to overcome the deep social inequalities in the country and its international vulnerability.[190] In early 2001, following diplomatic tensions created by his vehement public criticism of the FTAA, he was dismissed by Minister Lafer from the position of director of the Brazilian Research Institute on International Relations. His subsequent appointment as Secretary General was a signal of the new government's support for his critical stance.

Ambassador Guimarães saw the FTAA as a project against which "Mercosur would not survive" and that could lead to Brazil's 'subordinate and asymmetrical incorporation into the U.S. economic (and political) system."[191] This view that free trade agreements with developed nations constituted a risk was not restricted to the FTAA. In his book *Quinhentos Anos de Periferia* (*Five Hundred Years of Periphery*), Guimarães criticized negotiations within the FTAA and with the EU, arguing that both would reduce Brazil's capacity to implement autonomously the industrial, technological, and trade policies required to "accelerate the internal accumulation of capital, necessary to raise productivity, production, and the income of its expanding population."[192]

In his inaugural speech, Guimarães emphasized the need to address inequalities at the domestic and international levels. Recalling that the United States, China, and Brazil "were the only countries which appear simultaneously on the lists of the ten countries with the largest territory, the largest population, and the largest national product," he advocated a greater status for Brazil in international centers of decision making such as the UN

Security Council and G8, more compatible with its magnitude.[193] This position brought back into Brazilian foreign policy the attempt to guarantee a distinguished international status to Brazil as an intermediary or middle power. While the Cardoso administration had taken a more liberal view of international economic relations, under the Lula administration traditional views of international power and sovereignty would return to the center of Brazil's foreign policy.

Although, Guimarães did not control foreign policy, his influence as Itamaraty's secretary general was significant. Beginning in 2003, an organizational reform was conducted in Itamaraty in order to align diplomatic activities with the new trade priorities. The number of diplomats allocated to South America increased, while the number allocated to Europe was reduced.[194] Moreover, the system of support for trade negotiations that had been implemented under Minister Lafer was dismantled, and the FTAA and Mercosur-EU negotiations were transferred to separate units within a newly established General Sub-Secretariat of South America.[195] For the FTAA, a new coordination team was formed to represent Brazil as cochair in the process.[196]

In early 2005, the proposal to remove the eliminatory character of the English language test in the entrance exam for the diplomatic career led to accusations of anti-American bias.[197] In 2007, in Lula's second term in office, the removal of Brazilian Ambassador to the United States, Roberto Abdenur, further exposed the ideological conflicts within Itamaraty. A career diplomat, Ambassador Abdenur was removed after publicly criticizing Brazil's decision to recognize China as a market economy. In an interview he gave to Brazil's most popular weekly magazine, *Veja*, he argued that the South-South emphasis of the new foreign policy revealed "a backward anti-Americanism," and criticized the admission of Venezuela to Mercosur and the abandonment of the FTAA negotiations. He condemned the process of "indoctrination" in Itamaraty and alignments according to party politics, referring to a "generalized feeling [within the institution] that diplomats are now promoted according to political and ideological affinity, rather than for competence."[198]

Itamaraty also faced inter-bureaucratic disputes. During the preparatory meetings for the FTAA Miami ministerial meeting of November 2003, the ministers of Development, Industry and Foreign Trade; and Agriculture, complained that they had been informed of Brazil's position through the media,[199] despite the existence of formal arenas for coordination of positions such as CAMEX and SENALCA.

For the first time in Brazil's foreign policy history, disagreements over the orientation of foreign policy became an issue of public debate. In the past, different views within Itamaraty had been accommodated through what were unofficially called its "schools," without affecting the coherent image of Brazilian diplomatic action. However, as seen above, the dismantling of the national developmentalist model and the end of the cold war opened up a space for rethinking Brazil's international role. Itamaraty's institutional strength and its traditional aversion to radicalism contributed to a moderate attitude in the early 1990s that contrasted with the foreign policy reorientations observed in countries such as Argentina.[200] Although continuity and consensus were stressed at the rhetorical level, democratization and economic liberalization favored the emergence of new views on the strategies that Brazil should pursue in foreign policy.

Two main lines of thought can be identified among the current foreign policymaking elite.[201] The first consists of the more liberal interpretation prevalent under Cardoso, which emphasizes Brazil's competitive insertion into international regimes and seeks to minimize conflicts with the North. The second, which has gained policy relevance under Lula's administration, is characterized by an emphasis on the limitations on national autonomy imposed by international regimes, and on South-South alliances as a means to promote international recognition of Brazil's leadership power.

Implications for the FTAA

It was at this moment of great domestic polarization over the FTAA and the rise of senior foreign policy officials ideologically committed to national developmentalist ideas[202] that the FTAA reached the stage of exchange of offers. If until then the limited appeal of the FTAA idea had not been sufficient to motivate a rupture with the process, then under this new foreign policy team the perception of the FTAA as a project intended to subordinate Brazil to U.S. interests further reduced the stimulus for advance. Furthermore, the increasing mobilization of opposition to the FTAA by the groups that constituted the PT's electoral base, including labor unions and social movements, created a situation in which concessions in the FTAA would exact a heavy political cost from the party.

In his first month in power, President Lula attended the World Social Forum (WSF) held in Porto Alegre, an event of strong symbolic power. The WSF, an international gathering of NGOs, left-wing parties, social movements, and intellectuals sharing a critical view of neoliberalism, had first met in 2001 in Brazil with the support of PT's local government in the city of Porto Alegre. Two years later, it saw Lula, one of its activists, returning in the capacity of Brazilian president.[203] During the meeting, an anti-FTAA march was organized with thousands of participants. For the new government, defense of the FTAA had become politically costly.[204]

When the United States made offers that discriminated against Mercosur,[205] the FTAA was doomed. It is hard to know whether the United States differentiated offer derived from a miscalculation of its ability to pressure Brazil or was an indication of its bilateral ambitions. The net result, however, was that Brazilian foreign policymakers were provided publicly with a reason to reject the process and to transform such a rejection into a domestic political victory.

After the initial U.S. offer, Brazilian negotiators began openly to defend the long-cherished solution of bilateral Mercosur-U.S. negotiations. In parallel, they focused on the ongoing negotiations with the European Union and the WTO Doha Round as more promising alternatives. Throughout 2003 the sense of a developing crisis increased. In Brazil, the intense press coverage of the FTAA transformed the negotiations into an issue of public debate[206] and critical views of the FTAA predominated. By the time the Miami ministerial meeting was held in November, Brazil had already negotiated U.S. support for its proposal to fragment the negotiations.[207]

When all countries met for the Fourth Summit of the Americas in Puebla in February 2004, it was clear that Brazil had no intention of moving forward with the FTAA. Other Latin American countries questioned whether Mercosur had the actual means to implement the new approach to negotiations but no satisfactory clarification was given. Although diplomatic formalities prevented an official declaration of paralysis, Brazil's refusal to provide detailed references to the FTAA in the Summit's declaration and the lack of enthusiasm shown by the country's diplomats in the meetings[208] meant that in practice, the FTAA process had been paralyzed.

In the aftermath of the Miami ministerial meeting, Brazilian foreign policy did not move to an isolationist position. The abandonment of the FTAA was followed by the intensification of actions to construct multiple alliances, particularly along the South-South axis. The Lula administration continued to push for greater cooperation with South American countries in matters of infrastructure, trade, and security. Mercosur moved forward in trade negotiations with the Andean Community. Despite the fact that the negotiations were held between the two blocs, concession lists were exchanged bilaterally and guided by a product-by-product method, leading to seventy-seven schedules of tariff elimination. In an indication of Brazil's political will in the negotiations, the government reversed the position that had prevailed during the Cardoso administration. The principle of asymmetrical reciprocity was incorporated, and both Brazil and Argentina committed to remove most of their tariffs in a shorter timeframe than the Andean countries.[209] This approach contrasted markedly with the U.S. approach to asymmetries—since NAFTA, the United States had used its economic attractiveness to pressure the weaker parties into make greater concessions.

Together with other Mercosur members, Brazil attempted to strengthen alliances with South and North. On the South-South axis, it signed preferential trade agreements with India and the South African Customs Union (SACU) in 2004,[210] and formalized its intention to negotiate a free trade agreement with the Persian Gulf nations.[211] On the North-South axis, it demonstrated a high level of political willingness to reach a Mercosur-EU free trade agreement in the future, despite the fact that, as with the United States, the EU demanded major concessions in services and showed no willingness to change its agricultural subsidies policies. Many of the restrictions on regulatory autonomy that the EU expected were similar to those that would likely have emerged from the FTAA. Brazil's risk-taking approach with the EU appears to have been grounded more on a desire for the kind of balance of power that would derive from association with a powerful player, than on the actual negotiation conditions.

Moreover, Brazil set up a trilateral forum with India and South Africa in 2003 (IBSA), targeting cooperation over economic issues, security and health. Considering the prominence of these three countries in the WTO agricultural coalition of developing countries, the G20, the forum was also expected to assist in the coordination of trade positions in the multilateral negotiations.[212]

Critics of this new foreign trade policy pointed out that it would not lead to effective trade gains to the country, with only a small percentage of trade being covered by the new trade deals.[213] At the same time, at the Doha Round and in negotiations with the EU, Brazil's willingness to advance was not reciprocated.[214] Agriculture continued to block multilateral negotiations and with the demise of the FTAA the EU's interest in an agreement declined considerably.

When the interviews for this book were conducted in 2006, the vast majority of participants denied that Brazil was a leader in South America, citing lack of material resources, fear of Brazil's hegemonic intentions, and stronger links between individual countries and the United States as the main limitations to such leadership. In fact, in 2005 Brazil was unable to secure support for its candidature for head of the Inter-American Development Bank and Director-General of the WTO. The country was also denied support from Argentina, Colombia, and the United States for its bid to obtain a permanent seat in an expanded UN Security Council. In Lula's second term, however, Brazil has consistently attempted to engage with its neighbors with due recognition of the need to address asymmetries. Brazil's investment in physical integration in South America, efforts to mediate conflicts, and human and financial assistance in emergency situations such as that faced by Haiti after the hurricane, may lead to a more positive kind of leadership and effective cooperation.

The foreign policymakers empowered during the Lula administration continued the tradition of pursuing global partnerships as a means of promoting Brazil's claim to middle power status, as shown in their engagement in the BRIC (Brazil, Russia, India, and China) Summit, held in Russia in June 2009. However, in view of their emphasis on the risks of interdependence and their belief in the Brazil's potential to play a leading role in the developing world, the idea of a hemispheric project in which the United States would be the most relevant actor had no appeal.

In the years following the Miami deadlock, the FTAA was referred to only sporadically and without political enthusiasm. The expectation that in a Mercosur-U.S. negotiation, sensitive issues could be accommodated more easily never found a positive response from the United States.[215] During a congress of the Interamerican Regional Organization of Workers in 2005, Lula declared that the project had been removed from Brazil's agenda, and instead, priority would be given to the consolidation of Mercosur and the strengthening of relations with South America.[216] Brazilian authorities were still referring to the FTAA as "an abstraction."[217]

Ideas and ideology played a role in conjunction with, not to the exclusion of, a pragmatic view of foreign affairs. As in most periods of Brazil's foreign policy history, bilateral negotiations remained the preferred choice in its relations within the Western Hemisphere. In early 2007, the Brazilian government celebrated the signature of a bilateral agreement with the United States for cooperation on research and production of biofuel ethanol. During the negotiations for the bilateral deal, Minister Amorim commented that any attempt to "resuscitate the FTAA" would demand great effort and it would be better for Mercosur to consider bilateral associations.[218]

Brazilian foreign policy decision makers were not driven by anti-American ideology. The ideology that could be identified was one influenced predominantly by realism, in which a traditional interpretation of sovereignty led to an emphasis on asymmetrical interdependence as a zero-sum game. In order to defend Brazil's autonomy to shape its domestic and foreign policies, foreign policymakers had to work to diminish Brazil's dependence through diversification of relations and the consolidation of the country's position in relationships in which it held greater relative power.

Finally, in regard to relations with civil society, following the pressures for the democratization of foreign trade policymaking initiated by Cardoso's government, the Lula administration had to combine the definition of external priorities with rising domestic pressure for information and transparency. But, while under Cardoso informal networks with business groups and ideological identification with the PSDB facilitated inputs from the business sector into trade policy, under Lula the emphasis turned to groups with which the PT had ideological and personal links.[219] As might be expected, during the Lula administration, NGOs, social movements, and labor unions gained more space to participate.

Still, foreign policymakers retained the ability to adjust the degree of participation according to the trade negotiations under debate. Business representatives were keen to note that their positive interaction with diplomats during the WTO Doha Round was maintained under Lula, but the same was not true during the FTAA process. In contrast, NGOs complained that the high level of access they had enjoyed in the FTAA negotiations was not reproduced in the Mercosur-EU negotiations, a sphere in which the Lula administration eagerly pursued a successful agreement.

Conclusion

As in the case of the United States, Brazilian foreign trade policies evolved in direct connection with transformations occurring at national and international levels. From the postwar period through the 1980s, the state managed foreign trade policy as an instrument to assist in national development through industrialization in a closed economy.

Until the 1980s, this goal and the visions of foreign policymakers about how to promote autonomy coincided. Concern with autonomy was central to the attempt to ensure for Brazil the space it wanted in order to develop and consolidate itself as a middle power. In foreign trade, the defense of differentiated treatment according to development levels, the reactive stance against rules shaped by the most powerful nations, and the pursuit of diversified trade relations, exemplified the links between foreign trade policy and national development priorities. In this process, Itamaraty's professionalism and its commitment to constructing Brazil's international identity, combined with its relative insulation from direct societal pressure, substantially contributed to promoting consistency and continuity in foreign policy ideas.

With the debt crisis and economic liberalization, the national developmentalist project was threatened. Still, within society, support for state intervention in the economy and negative perceptions of free trade remained strong. In Brazil the free trade idea has never attracted the level of domestic support that existed in the postwar period in the United States.

In the 1980s, in addition to considering the domestic economic and political transitions, foreign policymakers had to operate in an international context in which the old strategies were no longer viable. In the uncertain international context of the post–cold war period, in which economic power defined even more the ability of a country to occupy a relevant position, Brazil's search for recognition as a middle power depended heavily on its capacity to resume economic growth within the new framework of a liberal economy.

During the Cardoso administration, acceptance of international norms and of competitive insertion in the international economy provided the rationale for Brazil's multilateral approach. This vision was not driven by idealism, but rather emerged in the search for how to best satisfy Brazil's goals of economic stability and growth, and international recognition. In this regard, the most obvious signal of pragmatism was how the same foreign policymakers approached relations within South America differently, attempting to consolidate Brazil's dominant economic position while incurring the lowest cost possible.

Within this overall strategy, the FTAA held little appeal. It represented more pressure on a state that was undergoing a politically difficult process of neoliberal reform. At the international level, the FTAA represented a threat to Brazil's ambitions in South America. Nevertheless, following the dominant vision under Cardoso—that the government should pursue participation in the international system through the negotiation of its rules—Brazil remained engaged with the FTAA. Cardoso himself manifested this belief in engagement as a better option than a rupture of the process. After criticizing the groups in Brazil that described the FTAA as "annexation," he argued that under the Lula administration, the difficulties in advancing in the negotiations gave way to "a fundamental change of posture," with the United States and Brazil abandoning the idea of a single undertaking in favor of fragmentation.[220]

With the arrival of Lula to power in 2003, at a moment of high domestic polarization over the FTAA idea, the already fragile incentive for the FTAA project disappeared. The Workers' Party's ideological stance influenced foreign policy. It led to the political empowerment of the group within Itamaraty that continued to value the national developmentalist project and emphasized the risk of interdependence to national autonomy. For this group, Brazil's consolidation as a middle power required economic growth and stability, but this should not lead to what they perceived as unqualified terms for cooperation. As with the Cardoso administration, pragmatism remained a characteristic of Brazilian foreign policy, as the Brazil-U.S. cooperation agreement on ethanol shows. But within the new visions of how to best realize Brazil's potential, the assessment of the country's interests changed. For the new government and its foreign policy team, Brazil's ability to stop the FTAA demonstrated the country's power and capacity to reject U.S. unilateral pressure, and in that regard could be celebrated as a political victory at the national and international levels.

The failure of the FTAA to capture the support of decision makers in Brazil can then be better understood through considering it within the universe of the foreign policy paradigms that have predominated in the country. The Brazilian foreign policy-making elite reject the notion that the country's position in the international system is structurally fixed, and it has attempted to guarantee the greatest possible degree of autonomy from external constraints in order to pursue development. While for many outsiders, Brazil's repeated emphasis on autonomy may sound somewhat idealistic and perhaps rhetorical, the idea has evolved in tandem with national processes that have given it social legitimacy far beyond the restricted circles of foreign policy-making. In Brazil's self-constructed identity, the preservation of autonomy in the face of externally imposed limits has symbolized the country's capacity to fight for its own path to development.

In the process of reassessment of economic policies triggered by the financial crisis of late 2008, Brazil has emerged as a relatively stable country, an emerging economy with prospects for an expanding role in central areas of concern for international security, such as energy and environmental issues. If international cooperation moves toward a less asymmetrical pattern between North and South, Brazil may finally gain the space it has been pursuing for decades.[221]

Part V

Conclusion

Conclusion

In the international political economy scholarship, globalization is often identified as the driving force behind states' pursuit of trade regionalism. The mainstream perspective argues that the phenomenon is a necessary state response to the challenges created by rising international competition. Cooperation among states for regional trade integration thus becomes a way to improve individual states' capacity to compete and to adjust to a neoliberal economic order. Advocates of trade regionalism describe it as a second-best choice to curb the prolonged and politically complex process of multilateral trade liberalization that characterizes negotiations under the GATT/WTO system. For those taking a critical stand on globalization, trade regionalism is defined either as a mechanism used by powerful states to consolidate their hegemonic power, or, in the case of South-South initiatives, as a form of contestation of such hegemony.

These perspectives help to understand particular cases of trade regionalism, but as this book hoped to have shown, they cannot be generalized. Indeed, if there is one generalization that can be drawn from case studies, it is that while globalization has pushed states to rethink their strategies for participation in the world economy, governments have differed considerably in how they interpret the new international conditions and evaluate the international potential of their individual countries. The recognition that different logics may have been guiding states' behavior in trade regionalism is particularly valuable in the case of the FTAA. While variations in national rationales may to some extent be disregarded in situations where states successfully reach agreement, they are crucial to understanding situations where states fail to cooperate.

The stagnation of the WTO Doha Round provides a good example of the analytical puzzle that cases of failure create. In the Doha Round, ten years after its launching and following two decades in which the liberal economic order was hegemonic, the deadlock in the negotiations challenges the notion that states have acted consistently for the consolidation of such a liberal order. At the core of the Doha Round's stagnation is the dilemma that states have faced for more than a century, namely, what degree of economic liberalization they aspire once political and social considerations are taken into consideration.

This book examined the failed attempt at trade cooperation in the Americas, focusing on the interface between national and international political economy. Running counter to the notion that states follow a predictable path in order to cope with high international competitiveness and the proliferation of regional trade initiatives, the FTAA provided a good case to test the limits between states' agency and international structures in trade negotiations. Moreover, due to the presence of the United States as a central player, it allowed examination of the implications for trade cooperation of high asymmetry of power. These two broad components—the links between national and international processes, and the space for agency in conditions of high power asymmetry—were central to the analytical framework adopted in this book.

It was argued that the failure of the FTAA derived from the fact that, as an inter-American policy idea requiring the cooperation of thirty-four countries, the FTAA was incompatible with the predominant views of U.S. and Brazilian foreign trade policymakers of how the interests of their countries could and should be pursued within the Americas. As explained in chapter 1, the book repositioned human action at the center of analyses of international political economy. Rather than beginning with the state as a unit, the state is approached with analytical curiosity, on the assumption that what is revealed internationally as a state preference derives mainly from domestic political processes in which the struggle for power and ideas remains central.

As discussed in chapter 2, sustained political will was a challenge from the beginning of the FTAA project in 1994. Despite the enthusiasm it engendered among several Latin American governments, the FTAA failed to become a "grand vision" for the main players in the negotiations. For both Brazil and the United States, trade bilateralism was initially the preferred option in the Americas. By late 1994, only a few weeks before the FTAA was launched, the most widely disseminated idea within the U.S. administration was the expansion of free trade with Latin America through accession to NAFTA. Brazil, in contrast, manifested on several occasions its preference for negotiations between the United States and Mercosur. A compromise with a collective process of negotiation involving thirty-four parties did occur, but to the extent that it created a prolonged process of trade negotiations, it benefited both states by putting off concrete decisions to a distant future. From 2002, political changes worked against the FTAA and ultimately led to the deadlock of the negotiations in late 2003.

Chapter 3 explored how international conditions and domestic political changes created for the first time in the history of inter-American relations, greater convergence among governments around the ideas of free markets and democracy. It detailed the profound shift in economic paradigms in Latin America, from national developmentalism to neoliberalism, which became more explicit during the debt crisis of the 1980s. Together with the transition to electoral democracy, the acceptance by Latin American government elites of market-based reforms as a means of survival in the global economy created an environment receptive to the idea of hemispheric free trade, which had been unimaginable a few years earlier. As shown in chapter 4, this political will contrasted markedly with the mutual distrust that had prevailed in previous attempts at inter-American economic cooperation. And as the cases of CUFSTA and NAFTA demonstrated, the Canadian and Mexican governments' changing perceptions of the value of stronger economic relations with the United States were central to the achievement of a cooperative solution in both negotiations. By moving from a position of fear of deepened economic dependence on the United States to one of expected benefits, these governments provided the political support necessary for trade negotiations with the United States to succeed.

Chapters 5 and 6 examined the difficulties in creating and sustaining political enthusiasm for the FTAA in the United States and Brazil respectively. Both chapters offered historical narratives that evolved around dominant foreign trade policy ideas, demands for change emerging at different periods of history, and the corresponding adjustment of national foreign trade policy institutions to new social and political conditions.

In the United States, freer trade—support for trade liberalization but with margin for selective protectionism—has remained at the core of foreign trade policies though its mode of implementation has varied. In trade, U.S. decision makers have dealt with the increasing international competition brought by globalization by moving away from their strong commitment to a multilateral approach to trade liberalization toward the unilateral approach embedded in the strategy of competitive liberalization. This turn, pushed by Treasury and later State Secretary James Baker, could have been interpreted as a temporary policy solution to the problems of economic recession and global international competition. However, with the administration of George W. Bush, the strategy was resumed and unilateralism was recognized as the guiding principle of U.S. foreign trade policy. For the neoconservative decision makers who came to power in 2001, free trade agreements were seen as a highly valued prize that the United States could offer its cooperative partners whose value went beyond trade considerations. While this new mindset considerably restricted the possibility of balanced negotiations with the United States, the fact that U.S. foreign trade policymakers did not see Latin America as a priority diminished even further the prospect of U.S. concessions.

In Brazil, foreign trade policies were always coupled with the broader priorities of economic development and the preservation of the highest degree of state autonomy possible in the international system. Unlike in the United States, in Brazil trade protectionism was the most supported principle up to the 1980s. This predominance only began to be challenged with the debt crisis of the 1980s and the simultaneous economic pressures posed by rising international competition. Throughout the 1990s, the Brazilian government responded to the challenges posed by globalization with a politics of accommodation to the neoliberal order, rather than contestation. In that period, Mercosur was consolidated as the most important manifestation of Brazil's embrace of trade regionalism. The Southern

Cone bloc not only provided Brazil with a base for improving its economic competitiveness but, from a foreign policy perspective, was also a means to strengthen the country's relative power. In these circumstances, the FTAA, as a hemispheric endeavor centered on the United States, was addressed with caution. With the election of the left-wing Workers' Party to power in Brazil in 2003, caution gave way to complete rejection of the project. For the new team of decision makers, the U.S. imposition of asymmetrical terms for the negotiations was a manifestation of hegemonic intentions that Brazil should reject.

Brazilian and U.S. decision makers rationally assessed the material incentives in the FTAA through their particular interpretations of the value of proceeding and their scope for action. In this process of rational choice, ideas were not simple instruments applied to a predefined set of interests, but were fundamental to the very definition of what those interests were.

In the end, the potential economic efficiencies that a hemisphere-based agreement could bring for each party were considered less valuable than the preservation of their freedom to use bilateralism in their foreign trade policy strategies in the Americas. If the negotiation framework initially defined by the thirty-four parties in the FTAA is taken as the parameter, it is clear that fragmentation marked the collapse of the cooperative process of negotiation initially envisioned.

The Political Economy of Trade Regionalism

For Brazil and the United States, assessments of the value of trade regionalism went beyond trade considerations. The FTAA shows that there is no predictable path between international constraints or incentives and state choices. Although globalization has affected all states, it has influenced them in ways that vary according to economic characteristics and to how individual governments design their policy responses to international changes. Based on some of the experiences referred to in this book, it is possible to say that,

a. In CUSFTA and NAFTA, globalization functioned simultaneously as a stimulus and as a pressure on national governments to opt for trade regionalism, for all parties involved;
b. For most governments of the small economies of Latin America and the Caribbean, trade regionalism has become a necessity to avoid further isolation from the international economy. In these cases, it is hard to know whether states ideologically support a liberal economic order, or are simply adopting a survival strategy;
c. For the United States, following the consolidation of its economic hegemony in North America through NAFTA, further trade pacts with Latin America are not important from the perspective of improving U.S. international competitiveness. Despite the lack of strong economic incentives, during the George W. Bush administration, these pacts regained strategic

value as instruments for achieving cooperation in other foreign policy areas; and
d. In Brazil, different models of trade regionalism have been adopted in an attempt to improve Brazil's international position with the minimum limitations to its autonomy over national policies. Under the Workers' Party administration, efforts to reaffirm Brazil as a middle power in a global economy have raised the appeal of South-South trade pacts. Here, the logics of survival, regional hegemony aspiration, and resistance to the dominant economic powers, all merged.

In addition to exposing variations in motives and responses through trade regionalism, the FTAA experience demonstrates that even when states are initially inclined to engage in trade regionalism, the negotiation of the terms of cooperation is uncertain. Its outcomes are heavily influenced by the subjective parameters that decision makers apply when assessing whether the interests of the state they represent are satisfactorily met. If this evaluation turns out to be negative, states show less flexibility in making concessions. It was this perceived lack of incentives by U.S. and Brazilian decision makers that created a process in which, in contrast to the European integration, sustained political leadership was absent. By the time the FTAA negotiations were fragmented, this crisis of leadership was explicit.

As the years passed without indication that the process would be resumed, Brazilian diplomats and media frequently repeated the version that because of the U.S. behavior, Brazil had no other option. However, the long list of states that have accepted U.S. conditions for bilateral free trade agreements is evidence that the Brazilian government *strategically chose* fragmentation of the FTAA process as the most acceptable solution.

It is by considering how national decision makers interpret external conditions and articulate responses that discussions on the new trade regionalism can avoid the risk of mechanistic interpretations. Why have states as different as Canada, Chile, Mexico, and Australia, with their varied levels of development, geopolitical interests, and interdependence with the United States, chosen to sign free trade pacts with the United States whose main shared characteristic is the U.S. ability to extract more concessions than it has given? Why do some states voluntarily commit to highly asymmetrical trade relations while others continue to see power asymmetry as a central problem to the way in which they conceive their international relations?

The variations in state reactions show that while the distribution of power in international relations continues to be highly unequal, this condition is not static. The degree to which the most powerful states are able to sustain a hegemonic status is still influenced by how individual states relate to that condition. It is this space for foreign policymaking, in which ideas, ideology, and beliefs come to affect external processes such as trade negotiations that link the political economy scholarship on trade regionalism with policy studies.

Policy Ideas

As the existing literature on the role of ideas in policymaking would predict, many of the ideas that influenced decision makers in the FTAA were not a complete innovation in policy thinking. Within the world of historically constructed ideas that states hold about their role in the Americas, tensions have originated from misconceptions about "others" as much as from the unequal distribution of material resources between states. The common belief among U.S. policymakers in the superiority of the U.S. political and economic systems has frequently led to interventionist foreign policies on Latin America, even when that was not their original intention. On the other hand, in Latin America, intra-regional competition and a search for privileged associations with the United States have limited regional cooperation on various occasions.

In regard to the idea of hemispheric trade integration, the FTAA could be described as a modern version of the proposal advanced in the First International Conference of American States a century earlier. What was new was the support that various governments in the Americas gave to the idea in the early 1990s. The profound transformation in the international economy brought about by globalization, and the deep crisis of economic policy paradigms in the 1980s, affected all states in the hemisphere and opened up an opportunity for foreign policy innovation. In line with the conclusions made in several policy studies, a crisis of credibility of the old policies was necessary to trigger a rethinking of foreign policy directions. In this regard, the economic downturn initiated with the crisis of late 2008 also provided a window for a critical review of the neoliberal dogma, but that opportunity remains to be explored.

Finally, in the crisis of the FTAA, both the United States and Brazil's positions reflected the rise of certain foreign policy views out of a pool of ideas available within their foreign trade policy institutions. Institutions, which Polanyi has elegantly defined as "embodiments of human meaning and purpose,"[1] can be imagined as hosts of ideas and visions accumulated throughout history. Ultimately, however, the "empowerment" of specific ideas—their conversion into actual policy—depends on whether those in charge of making policies perceive them as compatible with their beliefs, as suitable approaches to address a complex reality.

Future Research Agenda

Since this book covers only one case of failed trade negotiations, it does not allow for generalization of results. I accepted this limitation for what I hope has been a more refined consideration of the multiple aspects that affect the behavior of states in trade cooperation. Neither the book places great emphasis on the asymmetry of power that characterizes the relationship between the United States and Latin America. However, due to a tendency scholarship to see developing states as so sufficiently similar to be placed in a single broad analytical category, I highlighted the scope for agency in order to provide a richer picture of ideas and foreign policy in a developing context.

In the future, more empirical studies of initiatives for trade cooperation between developed and developing states can correct some of these shortcomings. In international political economy, a more careful examination of the interaction between politics and economics in developing states is an urgent task, due to their increasing capacity to affect debates on prominent global issues such as renewable energy, the environment, and trade. Among the variety of approaches available to guide such examination, multidisciplinary perspectives that focus on identifying the national forces that influence state behavior can open doors to a better understanding of the formation of state interests in developing contexts. If this book has been able to show that ideas and ideology continue to matter, not only as instruments for human action in a materially driven world, but as its constitutive force, it will have achieved its main objective.

Appendices

Appendix A

Questionnaire

Question 1. Please indicate your nationality:

Question 2. Please indicate which category best describes your affiliation

__government	__ business sector	__ international organization
__ non governmental organization	__ labor unions	__ academia/think tank

Question 3. Rank the alternatives, in order of importance (ranging from 1 to 4, with 1 for the most relevant factor and 4 for the least relevant factor)

The driving force behind the new wave of trade regionalism in the Americas is:

__ to guarantee access to the U.S. market
__ geopolitical
__ to attract more investment to the region
__ to enhance the ties between trade and non-trade regional issues (*e.g.* drugs, immigration)

Question 4. Regional trade agreements will help Latin American and Caribbean countries to become more competitive at the global level.
__ I agree __ I partially agree __ I disagree

Question 5. You consider that the package of issues covered in U.S. free trade agreements– *e.g.* liberalization of services, stricter rules in intellectual property and investment:
__ will have a net positive impact on the poor in Latin American and the Caribbean countries.

__ will have different impacts depending on the ability of domestic governments to implement complementary policies.
__ will have a net negative impact on the poor in Latin American and the Caribbean countries.

Question 6. "*In the First Summit of the Americas in 1994, beyond the rhetoric, the launching of the FTAA represented an attempt to build more cooperative relations in the Americas, through trade integration.*"
__ I agree   __ I partially agree   __ I disagree

Question 7. "*While most Latin American countries have a clear economic motive to pursue the FTAA, the U.S. motives are mainly political.*"
__ I agree   __ I partially agree   __ I disagree

Question. 8. The idea of trade integration in the Western Hemispheric through bilateral agreements with the United States:
__ contradicts the cooperation envisioned when negotiations were first initiated
__ is harmonious with the format of trade integration planned when the FTAA negotiations were launched

Question 9. Bilateralization of trade agreements with the United States will:
__ provide similar economic gains for the countries signing the agreements as a broad regional agreement could provide
__ provide more economic gains for the countries signing the agreements, than a broad regional agreement could provide
__ provide less economic gains for the countries signing the agreements, than a broad regional agreement could provide

Question 10. The deadlock in the FTAA negotiations can be attributed mainly to:
__ the lack of commitment from the United States
__ the lack of commitment from Brazil
__ the lack of commitment from Brazil and the United States
__ None of the above

Question 11. In order to explain the deadlock in the FTAA negotiations, the U.S. domestic politics is:
__ decisive
__ of moderate relevance
__ not relevant

Question 12. In terms of the interests of Latin American and Caribbean countries:
__ A U.S. Republican administration is better
__ A U.S. Democratic administration is better
__ The party in power does not make a substantial difference in the U.S. foreign trade policy

Questionnaire results

1. Nationality

Respondents/total interviews = 56 % Americans = 35.7% Brazilians = 42.8% Others in the Americas = 21.5%

Question 2. Please indicate which category best describes your affiliation

Government	3
Business	5
NGO	2
Labor	1
International organization	1
Academia/think tank	2

Question 3. Rank the alternatives, in order of importance (ranging from 1 to 4, with 1 to the most relevant factor and 4 to the least relevant factor)

The driving force behind the new wave of trade regionalism in the Americas is:
2 most cited answers (either as first or second reason):
   1st) to attract more investment to the region (10)
   2nd) to guarantee access to the U.S. market (9)

Question 4. Regional trade agreements will help Latin American and Caribbean countries to become more competitive at the global level

Agree	10
Partially Agree	3
Disagree	1

Question 5. You consider that the package of issues covered in U.S. free trade agreements– e.g. liberalization of services, stricter rules in intellectual property and investment:

will have a net positive impact on the poor in Latin American and the Caribbean countries	1
will have different impacts depending on the ability of domestic governments to implement complementary policies	12
will have a net negative impact on the poor in Latin American and the Caribbean countries	1

Question 6. "In the First Summit of the Americas in 1994, beyond the rhetoric, the launching of the FTAA represented an attempt to build more cooperative relations in the Americas, through trade integration."

Agree	11
Partially agree	2
Disagree	0
Not answered	1

Question 7. While most Latin American countries have a clear economic motive to pursue the FTAA, the U.S. motives are mainly political.

Agree	2
Partially agree	7
Disagree	4
Not answered	1

Question. 8. The idea of trade integration in the Western Hemispheric through bilateral agreements with the United States:

Contradicts the cooperation envisioned when negotiations were first initiated	8
Is harmonious with the format of trade integration planned when the FTAA negotiations were launched	4
Not answered	2

Question 9. Bilateralization of trade agreements with the United States will:

provide similar economic gains for the countries signing the agreements as a broad regional agreement could provide	3
provide more economic gains for the countries signing the agreements, than a broad regional agreement could provide	0
provide less economic gains for the countries signing the agreements, than a broad regional agreement could provide	8
Not answered	3

Question 10. The deadlock in the FTAA negotiations can be attributed mainly to:

the lack of commitment from the United States	0
the lack of commitment from Brazil	3
the lack of commitment from Brazil and the United States	10
Not answered	1

Question 11. In order to explain the deadlock in the FTAA negotiations, the U.S. domestic politics is:

Decisive	8
of moderate relevance	5
Not relevant	1

*Question 12. In terms of the interests of Latin American and Caribbean countries:**

A U.S. Republican administration is better	7
A U.S. Democratic administration is better	1
The party in power does not make a substantial difference in the U.S. foreign trade policy	6

(Some respondents emphasize that the answer was in regard to trade policy only)

Appendix B

First Summit of The Americas

Miami, Florida December 9–11, 1994

The following document is the complete text of the Declaration of Principles signed by the Heads of State and Government participating in the First Summit of the Americas.

Declaration of Principles[1]
Partnership for Development and Prosperity: Democracy, Free Trade and Sustainable Development in the Americas

The elected Heads of State and Government of the Americas are committed to advance the prosperity, democratic values and institutions, and security of our Hemisphere. For the first time in history, the Americas are a community of democratic societies. Although faced with differing development challenges, the Americas are united in pursuing prosperity through open markets, hemispheric integration, and sustainable development. We are determined to consolidate and advance closer bonds of cooperation and to transform our aspirations into concrete realities.

We reiterate our firm adherence to the principles of international law and the purposes and principles enshrined in the United Nations Charter and in the Charter of the Organization of American States (OAS), including the principles of the sovereign equality of states, non-intervention, self-determination, and the peaceful resolution of disputes. We recognize the heterogeneity and diversity of our resources and cultures, just as we are convinced that we can advance our shared interests and values by building strong partnerships.

To Preserve and Strengthen the Community of Democracies of the Americas

The Charter of the OAS establishes that representative democracy is indispensable for the stability, peace and development of the region. It is the sole political system that guarantees respect for human rights and the rule of law; it safeguards cultural diversity, pluralism, respect for the rights of minorities, and peace within and among nations. Democracy is based, among other fundamentals, on free and transparent elections and includes the right of all citizens to participate in government. Democracy and development reinforce one another.

We reaffirm our commitment to preserve and strengthen our democratic systems for the benefit of all people of the Hemisphere. We will work through the appropriate bodies of the OAS to strengthen democratic institutions and promote and defend constitutional democratic rule, in accordance with the OAS Charter. We endorse OAS efforts to enhance peace and the democratic, social, and economic stability of the region.

We recognize that our people earnestly seek greater responsiveness and efficiency from our respective governments. Democracy is strengthened by the modernization of the state, including reforms that streamline operations, reduce and simplify government rules and procedures, and make democratic institutions more transparent and accountable. Deeming it essential that justice should be accessible in an efficient and expeditious way to all sectors of society, we affirm that an independent judiciary is a critical element of an effective legal system and lasting democracy. Our ultimate goal is to better meet the needs of the population, especially the needs of women and the most vulnerable groups, including indigenous people, the disabled, children, the aged, and minorities.

Effective democracy requires a comprehensive attack on corruption as a factor of social disintegration and distortion of the economic system that undermines the legitimacy of political institutions.

Recognizing the pernicious effects of organized crime and illegal narcotics on our economies, ethical values, public health, and the social fabric, we will join the battle against the consumption, production, trafficking and distribution of illegal drugs, as well as against money laundering and the illicit trafficking in arms and chemical precursors. We will also cooperate to create viable alternative development strategies in those countries in which illicit crops are grown. Cooperation should be extended to international and national programs aimed at curbing the production, use and trafficking of illicit drugs and the rehabilitation of addicts.

We condemn terrorism in all its forms, and we will, using all legal means, combat terrorist acts anywhere in the Americas with unity and vigor.

Recognizing the important contribution of individuals and associations in effective democratic government and in the enhancement of cooperation among the people of the Hemisphere, we will facilitate fuller participation of our people in political, economic and social activity, in accordance with national legislation.

To Promote Prosperity through Economic Integration and Free Trade

Our continued economic progress depends on sound economic policies, sustainable development, and dynamic private sectors. A key to prosperity is trade without barriers, without subsidies, without unfair practices, and with an increasing stream of productive investments. Eliminating impediments to market access for goods and services among our countries will foster our economic growth. A growing world economy will also enhance our domestic prosperity. Free trade and increased economic integration are key factors for raising standards of living, improving the working conditions of people in the Americas and better protecting the environment.

We, therefore, resolve to begin immediately to construct the "Free Trade Area of the Americas" (FTAA), in which barriers to trade and investment will be progressively eliminated. We further resolve to conclude the negotiation of the "Free Trade Area of the Americas" no later than 2005, and agree that concrete progress toward the attainment of this objective will be made by the end of this century. We recognize the progress that already has been realized through the unilateral undertakings of each of our nations and the subregional trade arrangements in our Hemisphere. We will build on existing subregional and bilateral arrangements in order to broaden and deepen hemispheric economic integration and to bring the agreements together.

Aware that investment is the main engine for growth in the Hemisphere, we will encourage such investment by cooperating to build more open, transparent and integrated markets. In this regard, we are committed to create strengthened mechanisms that promote and protect the flow of productive investment in the Hemisphere, and to promote the development and progressive integration of capital markets.

To advance economic integration and free trade, we will work, with cooperation and financing from the private sector and international financial institutions, to create a hemispheric infrastructure. This process requires a cooperative effort in fields such as telecommunications, energy and transportation, which will permit the efficient movement of the goods, services, capital, information and technology that are the foundations of prosperity.

We recognize that despite the substantial progress in dealing with debt problems in the Hemisphere, high foreign debt burdens still hinder the development of some of our countries.

We recognize that economic integration and the creation of a free trade area will be complex endeavors, particularly in view of the wide differences in the levels of development and size of economies existing in our Hemisphere. We will remain cognizant of these differences as we work toward economic integration in the Hemisphere. We look to our own resources, ingenuity, and individual capacities as well as to the international community to help us achieve our goals.

To Eradicate Poverty And Discrimination In Our Hemisphere

It is politically intolerable and morally unacceptable that some segments of our populations are marginalized and do not share fully in the benefits of growth. With an aim of attaining greater social justice for all our people, we pledge to work individually and collectively to improve access to quality education and primary health care and to eradicate extreme poverty and illiteracy. The fruits of democratic stability and economic growth must be accessible to all, without discrimination by race, gender, national origin or religious affiliation.

In observance of the International Decade of the World's Indigenous People, we will focus our energies on improving the exercise of democratic rights and the access to social services by indigenous people and their communities.

Aware that widely shared prosperity contributes to hemispheric stability, lasting peace and democracy, we acknowledge our common interest in creating employment opportunities that improve the incomes, wages and working conditions of all our people. We will invest in people so that individuals throughout the Hemisphere have the opportunity to realize their full potential.

Strengthening the role of women in all aspects of political, social and economic life in our countries is essential to reduce poverty and social inequalities and to enhance democracy and sustainable development.

To Guarantee Sustainable Development and Conserve Our Natural Environment for Future Generations

Social progress and economic prosperity can be sustained only if our people live in a healthy environment and our ecosystems and natural resources are managed carefully and responsibly. To advance and implement the commitments made at the 1992 United Nations Conference on Environment and Development, held in Rio de Janeiro, and the 1994 Global Conference on the Sustainable Development of Small Island Developing States, held in Barbados, we will create cooperative partnerships to strengthen our capacity to prevent and control pollution, to protect ecosystems and use our biological resources on a sustainable basis, and to encourage clean, efficient and sustainable energy production and use. To benefit future generations through environmental conservation, including the rational use of our ecosystems, natural resources and biological heritage, we will continue to pursue technological, financial and other forms of cooperation.

We will advance our social well-being and economic prosperity in ways that are fully cognizant of our impact on the environment. We agree to support the Central American Alliance for Sustainable Development, which seeks to strengthen those democracies by promoting regional economic and social prosperity and sound environmental management. In this context, we support the convening of other regional meetings on sustainable development.

Our Declaration constitutes a comprehensive and mutually reinforcing set of commitments for concrete results. In accord with the appended Plan of Action, and recognizing our different national capabilities and our different legal systems, we pledge to implement them without delay.

We call upon the OAS and the Inter-American Development Bank to assist countries in implementing our pledges, drawing significantly upon the Pan American Health Organization and the United Nations Economic Commission for Latin America and the Caribbean as well as sub-regional organizations for integration.

To give continuity to efforts fostering national political involvement, we will convene specific high-level meetings to address, among others, topics such as trade and commerce, capital markets, labor, energy, education, transportation, telecommunications, counter-narcotics and other anti-crime initiatives, sustainable development, health, and science and technology.

To assure public engagement and commitment, we invite the cooperation and participation of the private sector, labor, political parties, academic institutions and other non-governmental actors and organizations in both our national and regional efforts, thus strengthening the partnership between governments and society.

Our thirty-four nations share a fervent commitment to democratic practices, economic integration, and social justice. Our people are better able than ever to express their aspirations and to learn from one another. The conditions for hemispheric cooperation are propitious. Therefore, on behalf of all our people, in whose name we affix our signatures to this Declaration, we seize this historic opportunity to create a Partnership for Development and Prosperity in the Americas.

Appendix C

Free Trade Area of The Americas

EIGHTH MINISTERIAL MEETING

MIAMI, USA
NOVEMBER 20, 2003

MINISTERIAL DECLARATION[2]

Introduction

1. We, the Ministers Responsible for Trade in the Hemisphere, representing the 34 countries participating in the negotiations of the Free Trade Area of the Americas (FTAA) held our Eighth Ministerial Meeting in Miami, United States of America, on November 20–21, 2003, in order to provide guidance for the final phase of the FTAA negotiations.
2. We recognize the significant contribution that economic integration, including the FTAA, will make to the attainment of the objectives established in the Summit of the Americas process: strengthening democracy, creating prosperity and realizing human potential. We reiterate that the negotiation of the FTAA will continue to take into account the broad social and economic agenda contained in the Miami, Santiago and Quebec City Declarations and Plans of Action with a view to contributing to raising living standards, increasing employment, improving the working conditions of all people in the Americas, strengthening social dialogue and social protection, improving the levels of health and education and better protecting the environment. We reaffirm the need to respect and value cultural diversity as set forth in the 2001 Summit of the Americas Declaration and Plan of Action.
3. We reiterate that the FTAA can co-exist with bilateral and sub-regional agreements, to the extent that the rights and obligations under these agreements are not covered by or go beyond the rights and obligations of the FTAA. We also reaffirm that the FTAA will be consistent with the rules and disciplines of the World Trade Organization (WTO).

4. Commitments assumed by the countries of the FTAA must be consistent with the principles of the sovereignty of States and the respective constitutional texts.

The Vision of the FTAA

5. We, the Ministers, reaffirm our commitment to the successful conclusion of the FTAA negotiations by January 2005*, with the ultimate goal of achieving an area of free trade and regional integration. The Ministers reaffirm their commitment to a comprehensive and balanced FTAA that will most effectively foster economic growth, the reduction of poverty, development, and integration through trade liberalization. Ministers also recognize the need for flexibility to take into account the needs and sensitivities of all FTAA partners.
6. We are mindful that negotiations must aim at a balanced agreement that addresses the issue of differences in the levels of development and size of economies of the hemisphere, through various provisions and mechanisms.
7. Taking into account and acknowledging existing mandates, Ministers recognize that countries may assume different levels of commitments. We will seek to develop a common and balanced set of rights and obligations applicable to all countries. In addition, negotiations should allow for countries that so choose, within the FTAA, to agree to additional obligations and benefits. One possible course of action would be for these countries to conduct plurilateral negotiations within the FTAA to define the obligations in the respective individual areas.
8. We fully expect that this endeavor will result in an appropriate balance of rights and obligations where countries reap the benefits of their respective commitments.

General Instructions

9. The Agreement will include measures in each negotiating discipline, and horizontal measures, as appropriate, that take into account the differences in the levels of development and the size of the economies, and are capable of implementation. Special attention will be given to the needs, economic conditions (including transition costs and possible internal dislocations) and opportunities of smaller economies, to ensure their full participation in the FTAA process.
10. We instruct the Trade Negotiations Committee (TNC) to develop a common and balanced set of rights and obligations applicable to all countries. The negotiations on the common set of rights and obligations will include provisions in each of the following negotiating areas: market access; agriculture; services; investment; government procurement; intellectual property; competition policy; subsidies, antidumping, and countervailing duties; and dispute settlement. On a plurilateral

basis, interested parties may choose to develop additional liberalization and disciplines. The TNC shall establish procedures for these negotiations that shall, among other things, provide that: countries negotiating additional obligations and benefits within the FTAA shall notify the Co-Chairs of their intention to do so before the outset of the negotiations; and any country not choosing to do so may attend as an observer of those additional negotiations. Observers, by notifying the Co-Chairs, may become participants in these negotiations at any time thereafter. The results of the negotiations must be WTO compliant. These instructions are to be delivered by the TNC to the Negotiating Groups and the Technical Committee on Institutional Issues (TCI), no later than the seventeenth meeting of the TNC to enable the negotiations to proceed simultaneously and to be completed according to the schedule.

Guidance on text issues

11. We instruct the TCI to present to the eighteenth TNC meeting its draft text as well as its recommendations on the institutions required to implement the FTAA Agreement, including proposals on the funding mechanisms, the administrative rules and the implications for human resources for the functioning of the institutional structure of the FTAA Agreement.
12. We direct the TCI with due regard to the provisions contained in this Declaration to provide to the TNC, as soon as possible, a proposal on the process for finalizing the agreement. This proposal shall contain, *inter alia*, specific steps, including legal review, translation, verification and authentication, necessary to finalize the text of the agreement, as well as the process and timetable for the completion of those steps.

Guidance on market access negotiations

13. We instruct that the negotiations on market access be conducted at a pace that will lead to the conclusion of those negotiations by September 30, 2004.

Differences in levels of development and size of economies

14. We acknowledge the differences in the levels of development and size of economies in the hemisphere and the importance of all the countries participating in the FTAA to attain economic growth, improved quality of life for their people, and balanced and sustained social and economic development for all its participants. We therefore reaffirm our commitment to take into account in designing the FTAA, the differences in levels of development and size of economies in the hemisphere to create opportunities for their full participation and increase their level of development. We will establish mechanisms that complement and enhance

the measures that address differences in the level of development and size of economies, in particular smaller economies, in order to facilitate the implementation of the Agreement and to maximize the benefits that can be derived from the FTAA. Such measures shall include but not be limited to technical assistance and transitional measures including longer adjustment periods.

15. We take note of the TNC Report on the results of the progress achieved in relation to the treatment of differences in the levels of development and the size of economies in each of the Negotiating Groups, and we instruct these entities to continue their work on this issue. We have made this report available to the public on the official FTAA website. We note with concern that while text negotiations have progressed, proposals aimed at giving expression to treatment of the differences in levels of development and size of economies are bracketed across all the negotiating disciplines. We therefore reiterate our instruction to the TNC and to all the negotiating groups, in particular those undertaking market access negotiations, to translate this principle into specific measures so that they are reflected in the results of the negotiations. We instruct the Consultative Group on Smaller Economies (CGSE) to keep this report up to date, with the support of the Tripartite Committee, and to submit it to us at our next meeting.

16. With a view to providing appropriate follow-up of the activities underway within the CGSE and in order to achieve the full participation of all countries in the FTAA, we instruct the CGSE to make recommendations to the TNC, at its next meeting and in coordination with the TCI, on the characteristics of a Permanent Committee on the application of the treatment of differences in the level of development and size of economies so that it forms part of the institutional framework of the FTAA.

Hemispheric Cooperation Program

17. We recognize that trade can play a major role in the promotion of economic development and the reduction of poverty. Therefore, we underscore that the commitment of countries to integrate trade into their national development plans, such as Poverty Reduction Strategies, is central to ensuring the role of trade in development and securing increased trade-related assistance in the region.

18. We recognize that smaller and less developed economies will require financial support to assist in the process of adjustment resulting from hemispheric integration. We therefore instruct the CGSE, based on its current work on the subject and with the support of the Tripartite Committee, to present recommendations to the TNC at its eighteenth meeting on financing methods and facilities to address the adjustment needs resulting from the differences in the levels of development and size of the economies of the hemisphere.

19. We welcome the efforts of the CGSE, with the assistance of the Tripartite Committee, to implement the Hemispheric Cooperation Program (HCP). Important steps took place at the Washington, D.C. meeting on October 14 and 15, hosted by the Inter-American Development Bank (IDB), with relevant donor institutions and in the preparation of trade capacity building strategies (TCB) by governments, which were the focus of discussion at the donors" roundtable. These strategies are critical to identifying effective programs and appropriate funding sources. These steps constitute a beginning to the process of enhancing the capacity of the countries that are seeking assistance to complete negotiation of the FTAA Agreement, prepare to implement its terms, and to enhance their capacity to trade, and successfully adapt to integration.
20. Based on the discussions and the TNC Report on progress in the implementation of the HCP and the initial meeting with donors, we encourage the countries with the help of the Tripartite Committee to finalize the TCB strategies as appropriate and to organize sub-regional meetings with donors to continue discussions on the TCB strategies. The first sub-regional meetings with donors should be held within four to six months.
21. We reiterate our agreement at Quito that the HCP will respond to the immediate assistance needs for the purpose of strengthening the participation of countries in the negotiations. We note with concern the slow progress in addressing these immediate needs and call on the donor community to urgently provide predictable and multifaceted financial and non-financial support, in particular non-reimbursable financing, for meeting the objectives and capacity-building priorities set out in the national and sub-regional capacity building strategies and action plans under the HCP. In this connection, we welcome the contributions, including non-reimbursable financing, already made.
22. We also instruct the TNC with the support of the CGSE to further develop the HCP by identifying the modalities and procedures for the management and implementation of the HCP once the FTAA negotiations are completed. We instruct the CGSE to report to the TNC throughout the year on progress under the HCP. We have made the TNC Report on the Implementation of the HCP available to the public on the official FTAA website.

Transparency and the Participation of Civil Society

23. In accordance with our commitment to transparency assumed at the Santiago and Quebec City Summits, we have made the third draft of the chapters of the FTAA Agreement available to the public on the official FTAA website in the four official languages today.
24. We also welcome receipt of the report on Best Practices and Illustrative Examples of Consultations with Civil Society at the National/Regional Level that was prepared by the Committee of Government Representatives

on the Participation of Civil Society (SOC) and that highlights best practices for disseminating information to civil society and to increase their participation in the FTAA process. We note the breadth and diversity of the measures and activities that have been undertaken by our various national governments in order to enhance communication with our respective civil societies. In addition, we note that this document is available to the public on the official FTAA Website. Furthermore, we instruct the SOC to make recommendations to the TNC on the means to broaden the mechanisms for disseminating information on the discussions, drawing upon the experiences of countries for distributing information to their civil societies.

25. In regard to this enhanced participation of different sectors of civil society in the hemispheric initiative and increased and sustained two-way communication with civil society, we take particular note of the decision to hold meetings with civil society, in conjunction with the regular meetings of the SOC, focusing on issues that are topics of discussion in these negotiations. In the past year, two such meetings have been held, one in Sao Paulo, Brazil on agriculture and the other in Santiago, Chile on services. We note that these meetings included a broad representation of FTAA government officials and civil society including business, labor, agricultural producers, NGOs, academics, rural and indigenous groups. Reports of the meetings from the SOC, including the statements of civil society, were made available to the public on the official FTAA website. We are pleased that at least two such meetings are planned in 2004, one in the Dominican Republic on the topic of intellectual property rights and one in the United States on the topic of market access, including small business issues.

26. We appreciate the views that various sectors of civil society have provided us in the last year and a half and especially in parallel to the Mexico and San Salvador Vice Ministerial meetings. We appreciate the recommendations made by the Eighth Americas Business Forum and the First Americas Trade and Sustainable Development Forum, organized with a broad representation of civil society, and with whom we met here in Miami, Florida. We encourage the holding of similar events organized parallel to all Ministerial and Vice Ministerial meetings and recommend that they include broad representation from civil society. We also take note of the regional seminar on the FTAA held by the Andean Community in Lima, Peru. The views expressed at these events constitute a valuable contribution to the negotiations, and we urge civil society to continue to make contributions in a constructive manner.

27. We welcome the Fourth Report of the SOC, which describes the activities of the SOC as well as the range of contributions received during this phase. We have made this report available to the public on the official FTAA website. We further instruct the SOC to continue to forward contributions to FTAA entities as well as to submit a new report

for our next meeting outlining its activities and the range of views it has received from individuals and organizations in the hemisphere, as well as the manner in which these have been considered in the FTAA negotiations.
28. We express our interest in creating a civil society consultative committee within the institutional framework of the FTAA upon the Agreement's entry into force. Such a committee could contribute to transparency and the participation of civil society on an on-going basis as the FTAA is being implemented. We instruct the Committee on Government Representatives on the Participation of Civil Society, in coordination with the TCI, to continue to study the issue and make recommendations to the TNC concerning it. We ask the TNC to review these recommendations and make a proposal concerning this matter for our future consideration.

Working Languages

29. We reiterate our current operating procedure, which is to conduct Ministerial level meetings with interpretation in English, Spanish, French, and Portuguese, and to release to the public the Ministerial Declaration and the texts of the Draft FTAA Agreement in these four languages. We agree that TNC meetings will be conducted with interpretation in English, Spanish, French, and Portuguese, and reiterate the existing procedure that meetings of the other Committees and the Negotiating Groups will be conducted with interpretation in the working languages of English and Spanish and that documents in these meetings and the TNC will be translated into the two working languages.

Appointment of Entity Chairs

30. We recognize the work completed by the Chairs and Vice Chairs of the different Negotiating Groups and other FTAA entities during this phase of the negotiations, whose support has been crucial to the advances made in the process. In accordance with the terms agreed at the San Jose Meeting, we approve the new roster of Chairs and Vice Chairs for the various FTAA entities who will serve during the next phase of negotiations, which is submitted as the Annex to this Declaration. In the case of the resignation or permanent absence of a Chair of an FTAA entity, the Vice Chair will act as Chair.

Schedule of Meetings

31. We instruct the TNC to convene at least 3 meetings before the next Ministerial Meeting; the meetings shall be held in the cities of Puebla and Panama City, and in Trinidad and Tobago, respectively.

Candidate cities for the FTAA Secretariat Site

32. We note that the following cities have asked to be considered for the permanent site of the FTAA Secretariat and have so notified the TNC Co-Chairs: Atlanta, USA; Cancun, Mexico; Chicago, USA; Colorado Springs, USA; Galveston, USA; Houston, USA; Miami, USA; Panama City, Panama; Port of Spain, Trinidad and Tobago; Puebla, Mexico; and San Juan of Puerto Rico, USA.[1] This is the final list of candidate cities. In order to facilitate our decision-making on this matter, we request that these cities provide to the FTAA Secretariat the information described in document FTAA.TNC/26 "Elements for Consideration in the Evaluation of the Candidate Sites for the FTAA Secretariat," by March 1, 2004, for dissemination to all delegations.[2]
33. We agree that the elements developed by the Sub-Committee on Budget and Administration (ADM) for evaluating candidate sites for the FTAA Secretariat are for information only to serve as a guide, and which may be used by countries in the selection process.
34. We agree that the decision on the site of the FTAA Secretariat will be taken at our ninth meeting.

Tripartite Committee

35. Once again, we express our appreciation for the support provided by the Tripartite Committee (the Inter-American Development Bank (IDB), the Organization of American States (OAS), and the United Nations Economic Commission for Latin America and the Caribbean (ECLAC)) to the FTAA negotiations and their technical, analytical, and financial contribution to the hemispheric integration process. We also thank the IDB, ECLAC, and the OAS for the support provided to the Hemispheric Cooperation Program, and to the issue meetings of civil society, and for redesigning and maintaining the official FTAA website. We encourage the Tripartite Committee to continue to support the negotiations and the HCP, and reiterate the need for their continued collaboration during this final stage of the negotiations.

FTAA Administrative Secretariat

36. We appreciate the invaluable and substantial support provided by the Administrative Secretariat to these negotiations. We also convey our appreciation to the Government of Mexico and the Tripartite Committee for the steps taken to cover the costs of the transfer of the Administrative Secretariat from Panama City to Mexico, and the costs of the operation of the Administrative Secretariat in the city of Puebla during the final stage of the negotiations. Finally, we thank the Government of Mexico for providing the facilities within which the negotiations are held and the Administrative Secretariat is functioning during this final phase.

Acknowledgments

37. We express our appreciation to the Ministers of Labor from Brazil, Canada and Mexico for providing their views on the work of the Inter-American Conference of Ministers of Labor, and for providing for our consideration the Report from the Working Group on Labor Dimensions of the Summit of the Americas Process established by the Inter-American Conference of Ministers of Labor (IACML) on the results of its examinations of, inter alia, questions of globalization related to employment and labor. We note that the IACML will deepen its enquiry into key aspects of the labor dimensions of economic integration, and request that the IACML Ministers keep us informed of the results through the FTAA Co-Chairs. We share their views, as expressed in the Salvador Declaration.
38. We thank the Governments of Mexico, El Salvador, Trinidad and Tobago, and the United States for organizing the meetings of the TNC during this period and the Government of the United States for the organization of this Eighth Ministerial Meeting. We also express thanks to the United States and Brazil for serving as the co-chairs of the FTAA during this final phase of the negotiations.

Future Meetings

39. We shall hold our next meeting in Brazil in 2004.

(*) Venezuela reiterates its reservation expressed in the Quebec City Declaration, with respect to the entry into force of the FTAA in 2005.
(1) The phrase "and San Juan of Puerto Rico, USA" was incorporated into the original text to reflect receipt of the necessary notification from San Juan prior to the deadline of midnight, November 20, 2003.
(2) The phrases "FTAA" and "Consideration in" were incorporated into the original text as corrections to the document title.

Notes

Introduction

1. Antigua and Barbuda, Argentina, Bahamas, Barbados, Belize, Bolivia, Brazil, Canada, Chile, Colombia, Costa Rica, Dominica, Dominican Republic, Ecuador, El Salvador, Grenada, Guatemala, Guyana, Haiti, Honduras, Jamaica, Mexico, Nicaragua, Panama, Paraguay, Peru, St. Vincent and the Grenadines, St. Lucia, St. Kitts and Nevis, Suriname, Trinidad and Tobago, the United States, Uruguay, and Venezuela. Cuba was the only country in the Americas excluded from the summit.
2. For an exception, see Justin Robertson and Maurice A. East, eds., *Diplomacy and Developing Nations. Post-Cold War Foreign Policy-Making Structures and Processes* (Abington: Taylor & Francis; New York: Routledge, 2005), which introduces analytical categories of foreign policymaking and their application to a broad range of countries, including China, Brazil, Ghana, and Malaysia. For earlier studies on the experience of developing states, see Alberto van Klaveren, "The Analysis of Latin American Foreign Policies. Theoretical Perspectives," in *Latin American Nations in World Politics*, ed. Heraldo Muñoz and Joseph S. Tulchin (Boulder, CO: Westview Press, 1984), 1–21; Jeane A.K. Hey, "Foreign Policy in Dependent States," in *Foreign Policy Analysis. Continuity and Change in its Second Generation*, ed. Laura Neack, Jeanne A.K. Hey, and Patrick J. Haney (Englewood Cliffs, NJ: Prentice Hall, 1995), 201–213.
3. John S. Odell and Susan K. Sell, "Reframing the Issue: The WTO Coalition on Intellectual Property and Public Health, 2001," in *Negotiating Trade. Developing Countries in the WTO and NAFTA*, ed. John S. Odell (Cambridge: Cambridge University Press, 2006), 85–114.
4. WTO website, http://www.wto.org/english/tratop_e/region_e/region_e.htm
5. John H. Barton et al., *The Evolution of the Trade Regime. Politics, Law and Economics of the GATT and the WTO* (Princeton and Oxford: Princeton University Press, 2006), 2.
6. John G. Ruggie, "International Regimes, Transactions, and Change: Embedded Liberalism in the Postwar Economic Order," *International Organization* 36.2 (Spring 1982), 379–415.
7. Since trade agreements are preceded by intense negotiations between states, a WTO decision to outlaw an agreement already concluded would be too costly politically. The institution's efforts have thus concentrated on the

issue of transparency and trade data information related to such arrangements. WTO Decision of December 14, 2006, "Transparency Mechanism for Regional Trade Agreements" (WT/L/671).
8. Economic Commission for Latin America and the Caribbean (ECLAC), *Open Regionalism in Latin America and the Caribbean* (Santiago, Chile: United Nations, 1994); C. Fred Bergsten, "Open Regionalism," Working Paper 97-3, Peterson Institute for International Economics, Washington, DC, 1997, http://www.petersoninstitute.org/publications/wp/wp.cfm?Research ID=152
9. For the link between autonomous trade reforms and cooperation in the new regionalism, see Stephan Haggard, "The Political Economy of Regionalism in Asia and the Americas," in *The Political Economy of Regionalism*, ed. Edward D. Mansfield and Helen V. Milner (New York: Columbia University Press, 1997), 20–48.
10. For a comparison of the experiences in the two regions, see Ramiro Pizarro, *Comparative Analysis of Regionalism in Latin America and Asia-Pacific*. CEPAL Serie Comercio Internacional No. 6 (Santiago, Chile: United Nations, 1999), http://www.eclac.cl/publicaciones/xml/5/4285/lcl1307i.pdf
11. Services, for instance, were only added to the scope of the multilateral trading system in the Uruguay Round. On the pressures by OECD countries to include services as part of the trade concept, see William J. Drake and Kalypso Nicolaidis, "Ideas, Interests, and Institutionalization: Trade in Services and the Uruguay Round," *International Organization* 46.1 (Winter 1992), 37–100.
12. Economist Robert Z. Lawrence suggests that developing countries may benefit from "'importing' new institutions and regulatory systems" that "have been pretested in the international arena and are compatible with its norms," in *Regionalism, Multilateralism, and Deeper Integration* (Washington, DC: The Brookings Institution, 1996), 17. See also "Conclusions," in Gary Sampson and Stephen Woolcock, eds., *Regionalism, Multilateralism, and Economic Integration: The Recent Experience* (New York: United Nations University Press, 2003), 336–339. A more critical perspective, highlighting the risk of rising constraints on national policies, is offered by Robert M. Hamwey in "Expanding National Policy Space for Development: Why the Multilateral Trading System Must Change," Working Paper 25, South Centre, September 2005, http://www.southcentre.org/publications/workingpapers/wp25.pdf
13. The literature on the issue is vast. For a critical view of the phenomenon, see Jagdish Bhagwati, *The World Trading System at Risk* (Princeton, NJ: Princeton University Press, 1991); Jagdish Bhagwati and Arving Panagaryia, eds., *Free Trade Areas or Free Trade? The Economics of Preferential Trade Arrangements* (Washington, DC: AEI Press, 1995); and Jaime de Mello and Arvind Panagaryia, eds., *New Dimension in Regional Integration* (Cambridge: Cambridge University Press, 1993). For the WTO's perspective, see *Regionalism and the World Trading System* (Geneva: World Trade Organization, 1995).
14. As the WTO Director General Pascal Lamy proposed, "We often think and talk about how regionalism might be hurting multilateralism.... what I would like to do is turn the question around. I would like to ask what the WTO

might do to help avoid a situation in which these negative aspects of regional agreements prevail, and ultimately to promote multilateralization." Speaking points at the opening of the WTO's sponsored conference "Multilateralizing Regionalism," September 2007, Geneva, Switzerland, http://www.wto.org/english/news_e/sppl_e/sppl67_e.htm

15. The concept of regionalism is contested and some scholars prefer to use the term in the plural in order to capture the diversity of responses coming from states, firms and civil society. See Morten Bøås, Marianne H. Marchand, and Timothy M. Shaw, "The Weave-World: The Regional Interweaving of Economies, Ideas and Identities," in *Theories of New Regionalism. A Palgrave Reader*, ed. Fredrik Söderbaum and Timothy M. Shaw (Basingstoke; New York: Palgrave Macmillan, 2003), 197–210.

16. Alan L. Winters, "Regionalism vs. Multilateralism," in *Market Integration, Regionalism and the Global Economy*, ed. Richard Baldwin et al. (Cambridge: Cambridge University Press, 1999), 8–10.

17. WTO website, Regional Trade Agreements session, http://www.wto.org/english/tratop_e/region_e/scope_rta_e.htm

18. Regionalization can be described as a localized manifestation of globalization. Although states matter, neither of these processes necessarily relies on a state decision in order to continue. For conceptual reviews of the terms globalization/regionalization and globalism/regionalism, see Michael Schultz, Fredrik Söderbaum, and Joakim Öjendal, "Key Issues in the New Regionalism: Comparisons from Asia, Africa and the Middle East," in *Comparing Regionalisms: Implications for Global Development*, ed. Björn Hettne, András Inotai, and Osvaldo Sunkel (Basingstoke; New York: Palgrave, 2001), 234–276; Andrew Gamble, "Regional Blocs, World Order and the New Medievalism," in *European Union and New Regionalism: Regional Actors and Global Governance in a Post-hegemonic Era*, ed. Mario Telò (Aldershot: Ashgate, 2001), 21–37. Phillips refers to the case of Mercosur to show how regionalization has occurred despite the skepticism of those concentrating on the problems of intergovernmental coordination. See "The Rise and Fall of Open Regionalism? Comparative Reflections on Regional Governance in the Southern Cone of Latin America," *Third World Quarterly* 24.2 (2003), 217–234. For a definition of regionalization that places it closer to the idea of regional integration, see Alex Warleigh-Lack, "Toward a Conceptual Framework of Regionalisation: Bridging 'New Regionalism' and 'Integration Theory'," *Review of International Political Economy* 13.5 (December 2006), 750–771.

19. Victor Bulmer-Thomas lists eight dimensions of globalization affecting how new trade regionalism is developing, namely, liberalization of trade in goods, liberalization of trade in services, liberalization of capital flows, rearrangements in the allocation of foreign direct investment, adoption of the WTO rules as the basis for dispute resolution in trade; the rising importance of patents and intellectual property rules, free movement of labor, and environmental concerns. See "Introduction" to his edited volume, *Regional Integration in Latin America and the Caribbean: The Political Economy of Open Regionalism* (London: Institute of Latin American Studies, University of London., 2001), 1–13.

20. For instance, Japanese firms involved in integrated production and investment with other countries have pressured the Japanese government to

move toward bilateral trade agreements when the lack of such agreements could lead to a loss of competitiveness for those firms. In Mark S. Manger, "Competition and Bilateralism in Trade Policy: The Case of Japan's Free Trade Agreements," *Review of International Political Economy* 15.5 (December 2005), 804–828.
21. Dilip K. Das, *Regionalism in Global Trade* (Cheltenham, UK; Northampton, MA: Edward Elgar, 2004), 25–56; Brigid Gavin, and Luk Van Langenhove, "Trade in a World of Regions," in Sampson and Woolcock, *Regionalism, Multilateralism, and Economic Integration*, 284.
22. Diane Tussie, "Regionalism: Providing a Substance to Multilateralism?," in Söderbaum and Shaw, *Theories of New Regionalism*, 313.
23. Stefan Schirm, *Globalization and the New Regionalism. Global Markets, Domestic Politics and Regional Cooperation* (Cambridge: Polity Press, 2002), 13–14.
24. For recent studies on the new regionalism in Asia, see Charles Harvie, Fukunari Kimuar, and Hyun-Hoon Lee, eds., *New East Asian Regionalism. Causes, Progress and Country Perspectives* (Cheltenham, UK; Northampton, MA: Edward Elgar, 2005), particularly the Introduction; Fu-Kuo Liu and Philippe Régnier, eds., *Regionalism in East Asia: Paradigm Shifting?* (London; New York: Routledge Curzon, 2003); Shaun Narine, *Explaining ASEAN: Regionalism in the Southeast Asia* (Boulder, CO: Lynne Rienner, 2002). For studies including the Pacific, see Jenny Bryant-Tokalau and Ian Frazer, eds., *Redefining the Pacific?: Regionalism. Past, Present and Future* (Aldershot, Hampshire; Burlington, VT: Ashgate, 2006).
25. Nick Bisley, "East Asia's Changing Regional Architecture: Toward an East Asian Economic Community," *Pacific Affairs* 80.4 (2007), 603–625.
26. A recent evaluation of APEC challenges is offered by Lorraine Elliot et al., *APEC and the Search for Relevance: 2007 and Beyond* (Canberra: The Australian National University/RSPAS, 2006), http://rspas.anu.edu.au/ir/pubs/keynotes/documents/Keynotes-7.pdf.
27. On the new regionalism at APEC, see Ross Garnaut, *Open Regionalism and Trade Liberalization. An Asia-Pacific Contribution to the World Trade System* (Sydney, NSW: Allen & Unwin, 1996), 1.
28. Winters, "Regionalism vs. Multilateralism," 7–52.
29. The Australia-U.S. free trade agreement, signed in 2004, provides another example of the greater weight of political motivations than economic incentives, from the Australian government viewpoint. Garnaut offers an economic critique of the agreement in "Australian Security and Free Trade with America," in *Balancing Act: Law, Policy and Politics in Globalisation and Global Trade*, ed. Jianfu Chen and Gordon Walker (Leichhardt, N.S.W.: The Federation Press, 2004), 53–74. For a detailed analysis of the political economy of the negotiations, see Ann Capling, *All the Way with the USA: Australia, the US and Free Trade* (Sydney: University of NSW, 2005).
30. For a collection of contributions aligned with the critical approach to the new regionalism, see Söderbaum and Shaw, *Theories of New Regionalism*.
31. Robert W. Cox, "Social Forces, States and World Orders: Beyond International Relations Theory," *Millenium: Journal of International Studies* 10. 2 (1981), 126–155.
32. Regions are understood not only in geographic terms, but as a "social and cognitive construct," grounded in "political processes." See Peter Katzenstein,

"Regionalism and Asia," in *New Regionalisms in the Global Political Economy*, ed. Shaun Breslin et al. (London; New York: Routledge, 2002), 105. Also, Iver Newumann, "A Region-Building Approach," in Söderbaum and Shaw, *Theories of New Regionalism*, 160–178; Takashi Terada, "Constructing an "East Asian" Concept and Growing Regional Identity: from EAEC to ASEAN+3," *The Pacific Review* 16.2 (2003), 251–277.

33. John MacLean, "Toward a Political Economy of Agency in Contemporary International Relations," in *Politics and Globalisation. Knowledge, Ethics and Agency*, ed. Martin Shaw (London; New York: Routledge, 1999), 180–181.
34. The New Regionalism Approach originated from an international research project, sponsored by the United Nations University/World Institute for Development Economics Research (WIDER). The research results were organized in five volumes, edited by Björn Hettne, András Inotai, and Osvaldo Sunkel, and published by Palgrave Macmillan under WIDER's New Regionalism Series: *Globalism and the New Regionalism* (1999), *National Perspectives on the New Regionalism in the North* (2000), *National Perspectives on the New Regionalism in the South* (2000), *The New Regionalism and the Future of Security and Development* (2000), and *Comparing Regionalisms: Implications for Global Development* (2001).
35. Björn Hettne draws a parallel with Karl Polanyi's double movement and the new regionalism, arguing that the new wave of regionalism would consist of a political reaction aimed at bringing back the social and political dimensions ignored by the market forces. In Björn Hettne, "The New Regionalism Revisited," in Söderbaum and Shaw, *Theories of New Regionalism*, 26–42.
36. Björn Hettne, "Beyond the "New" Regionalism," in *Key Debates n New Political Economy*, ed. Anthony Payne (London: Routledge, 2006), 137.
37. Andrew Gamble and Anthony Payne, "Introduction" and "Conclusion," in their edited volume, *Regionalism & World Order* (Basingstoke: Macmillan, 1996).
38. Hegemony is used here to refer to both the material and ideological components of dominance. See Robert W. Cox, "Gramsci: Hegemony and International Relations: An Essay on Method," *Millenium: Journal of International Studies* 12.2 (1983), 162–175.
39. Andrew Gamble and Anthony Payne, "The World Order Approach," in Söderbaum and Shaw, *Theories of New Regionalism*, 52.
40. The scarcity of empirical studies is particularly noticeable in the experiences of developing countries. See Schultz, Söderbaum, and öjendal, "Key Issues in New Regionalism," 270–272.
41. An exception is Jean Grugel and Wil Hout, "Regions, Regionalism and the South," in *Regionalism across the North-South Divide: State Strategies and Globalization*, ed. Jean Grugel and Wil Hout (London; New York: Routledge, 1999), 3–13. They explicitly reject the idea that developing countries are completely deprived of the means to design economic and political strategies. For the variations among states in the construction of regionalism in East Asia, see Liu and Régnier, *Regionalism in East Asia*.
42. Wil Hout, "Theories of International Relations and the New Regionalism," in Grugel and Hout, *Regionalism across the North-South*, 14–28. A similar criticism is offered by Nicola Phillips, "Whither IPE?," in her edited volume, *Globalizing International Political Economy* (Basingstoke; New York: Palgrave Macmillan, 2005), 246–269.

1 Trade Cooperation as a Policy Idea

1. Hugh Heclo, Modern Social Politics in Britain and Sweden. From Relief to Income Maintenance (New Haven; London: Yale University Press, 1974), 313.
2. Nicholas G. Onuf, *World of our Making: Rules and Rule in Social Theory and International Relations* (Columbia, SC: University of South Carolina Press, 1989); Alexander Wendt, "Anarchy is what States Make of it: the Social Construction of Power Politics," *International Organization* 46.2 (1992), 391–425; *Social Theory of International Politics* (Cambridge: Cambridge University Press, 1999); Peter Katzenstein, ed., *The Culture of National Security: Norms and Identity in World Politics* (New York: Columbia University Press, 1996).
3. On the subjective utility of the various options in negotiations, see Judith Goldstein and Robert Keohane, "Ideas and Foreign Policy. An Analytical Framework," in *Ideas and Foreign Policy. Beliefs, Institutions, and Political Change*, ed. authors (Ithaca, NY: Cornell University Press, 1993), 3–30; Maxwell A. Cameron and Brian W. Tomlin, *The Making of NAFTA: How the Deal was Done* (Ithaca, NY: Cornell University Press, 2000), 26. According to Cardenas and Ostrom, actors inform their decision based on three layers of information, consisting of the material game payoffs, a group-context layer, and an identity layer, which includes values. In Juan-Camilo Cárdenas and Elinor Ostrom, "What Do People Bring into the Game: Experiments in the Field about Cooperation in the Commons," CAPRI Working Paper No.32, International Food Policy Research Institute, Washington, DC, June 2004, http://www.capri.cgiar.org/pdf/capriwp32.pdf
4. On the relevance of perceptions and image interpretation in foreign policy-making, see Robert Jervis, *The Logic of Images in International Relations* (Princeton: Princeton University Press, 1970); Robert Jervis, Richard N. Lebow, and Janice Gross Stein, eds., *Psychology and Deterrence* (Baltimore; London: The Johns Hopkins University Press, 1985).
5. Robert O. Keohane, *After Hegemony: Cooperation and Discord in the World Political Economy* (Princeton, NJ: Princeton University Press, 1984), 51.
6. Robert Axelrod and Robert O. Keohane, "Achieving Cooperation under Anarchy: Strategies and Institutions," *World Politics* 38.1 (October 1985), 226.
7. For instance, Kenneth N. Waltz, *Theory of International Politics* (Reading, MA: Addison-Wesley, 1979); Robert Gilpin, *War and Change in World Politics* (Cambridge, MA: Cambridge University Press, 1981); Charles Lipson, "International Cooperation in Economic and Security Affairs," *World Politics* 37 (October 1984), 1–23; Joseph M. Grieco, "Anarchy and the Limits of Cooperation: A Realist Critique of the Newest Liberal Institutionalism," *International Organization* 42.3 (Summer 1988), 485–507; and his application of the approach to international trade negotiations in *Cooperation Among Nations: Europe, America, and Non-Tariff Barriers to Trade* (Ithaca, NY: Cornell University Press, 1990). For a critical appraisal of the relative gains argument, see Duncan Snidal, "Relative Gains and the Pattern of International Cooperation," *American Political Science Review* 85.3 (1991), 701–726.
8. Robert O. Keohane and Joseph S. Nye, *Power and Interdependence*, 3rd ed. (New York and San Francisco: Longman, 2001 [1st ed. 1977]), 8.

9. Ernst Haas, "Turbulent Fields and the Theory of Regional Integration," *International Organization* 30.2 (Spring 1976), 173–178; Keohane and Nye, *Power and Interdependence*, 8.
10. See David A. Baldwin, "Neoliberalism, Neorealism, and World Politics," 9; and Robert O. Keohane, "Institutional Theory and the Realist Challenge After the Cold War," 271; both in *Neorealism and Neoliberalism. The Contemporary Debate*, ed. David A. Baldwin (New York: Columbia University Press, 1993).
11. Robert W. Cox, "Critical Political Economy," in *International Political Economy Understanding Global Disorder*, ed. Björn Hettne (London; New Jersey: Zed Books, 1995), 31–45.
12. According to Cox, world hegemony necessarily involves three structures—social, economic, and political—and is manifested through "universal norms, institutions and mechanisms which lay down general rules of behavior for states and for those forces of civil society that act across national boundaries—rules which support the dominant mode of production." In Robert W. Cox, "Gramsci: Hegemony and International Relations," 172. For a recent analysis, see Robert W. Cox, "Beyond Empire and Terror: Critical Reflections on the Political Economy of World Order," *New Political Economy* 9.3 (2004), 307–323.
13. Jean Grugel, "Democratization and the Realm of Politics in International Political Economy," in Phillips, *Globalizing International Political Economy*, 210.
14. Axelrod and Keohane, "Achieving Cooperation," 231. See also Kenneth A. Oye, "Explaining Cooperation under Anarchy: Hypotheses and Strategies," in *Cooperation under Anarchy*, ed. author (Princeton, NJ: Princeton University Press, 1986).
15. Schelling points out that in setting the limits of what is acceptable, actors will evaluate the potential of retaliation, using history as one source. See Thomas C. Schelling, *The Strategy of Conflict* (Cambridge, MA: Harvard University Press, 1960), 107.
16. Hirschman offered one of the most enduring contributions to understanding the tenuous between cooperation and coercion in trade relations. Albert Hirschman, *National Power and the Structure of Foreign Trade* (Berkeley and Los Angeles: University of California Press, 1969), 14–17.
17. Richard Snyder, H.W. Bruck, and Burton Sapin, "Decision-Making as an Approach to the Study of International Politics," Foreign Policy Analysis Project no.3 (1954). Reprinted in Richard Snyder, H.W. Bruck, and Burton Sapin, *Foreign Policy Decision-Making (Revisited)* (Basingstoke; New York: Palgrave Macmillan, 2002), 59.
18. See, for instance, Jervis, *Logic of Images*, on the importance of perceptions and images decision makers project at the international level; Graham T. Allison, *Essence of Decision. Explaining the Cuban Missile Crisis* (Boston: Little Brown, 1971), which emphasizes the impact of inter-bureaucratic disputes on foreign policy; Robert Putnam's two-level game, in "Diplomacy and Domestic Politics: the Logic of Two-level Games," *International Organization* 42.3 (Summer 1988), 427–460.
19. Andrew Moravcsik, "Introduction," in *Double-Edged Diplomacy. International Bargaining and Domestic Politics*, ed. Peter B. Evans, Harold K. Jacobson, and Robert D. Putnam (London; Berkeley and Los Angeles: University of California Press, Ltd., 1993), 9.

20. Putnam, "Diplomacy and Domestic Politics."
21. Putnam touches on the issue when he argues, for instance, that the less democratic is a state, the lower the chances its negotiators will be able to convince others of the constraints they face domestically. On "Diplomacy and Domestic Politics," 449.
22. See collection of case studies based on the two-level game organized by Peter B. Evans, Harold K. Jacobson, and Robert D. Putnam, eds., *Double-Edged Diplomacy. International Bargaining and Domestic Politics* (London; Berkeley and Los Angeles: University of California Press, Ltd., 1993); Cameron and Tomlin, *Making of NAFTA*; Inter-American Development Bank, Inter-American Dialogue and Munk Centre for International Studies, eds., *The Trade Policy-Making Process. Level One of the Two-Level Game: Country Studies in the Western Hemisphere* (Buenos Aires: INTAL, ITD, STA, 2002).
23. For Latin America, see Sebastián Sáez, "Trade Policymaking in Latin America: A Compared Analysis," CEPAL Serie Comercio Internacional No. 55 (Santiago, Chile: United Nations, 2005), 21, http://www.eclac.org/publicaciones/xml/8/23238/lcl2410i.pdf
24. In addition to the two-level game, see Moravicsik, "Preferences and Power in the European Community: A Liberal Intergovernmental Approach," *Journal of Common Market Studies* 31.4 (December 1993), 473–524; and Helen Milner, *Interests, Institutions and Information* (Princeton, New Jersey: Princeton University Press, 1997).
25. Miles Kahler addressed the problem of aggregation of preferences in "Rationality in International Relations," *International Organization* 52.4 (Autumn 1988), 929–932.
26. See John Gerard Ruggie, "What Makes the World Hang Together? Neo-Utilitarianism and the Social Constructivist Challenge," *International Organization* 52.4 (Autumn 1998), 855–885.
27. As Watson reminds us, the market does not act, but it is an arena where human beings can act. In Matthew Watson, *Foundations of International Political Economy* (Houndmills, Basingstoke; New York: Palgrave Macmillan, 2005), 178.
28. On the distinction between the definition of rationality in economics in contrast to other social sciences, and its analytical implications, see Herbert A. Simon, "Rationality as Process and as Product of Thought," *The American Economic Review* 68.2 (May 1978), 1–16.
29. In the words of philosopher John Ralston Saul, "because that consciousness (of the "marriage between thought and *the other* which makes reason both conscious and intelligent") has so often been abandoned for absolute truths and methodology, reason has often rightly been criticized from the left and the right for having failed. Sometimes these criticisms will themselves be so ideological as to confuse what reason has become versus what it can be." In *On Equilibrium* (Toronto: Penguin Books, 2001), 283. For a suggestion of a new approach to rationality, drawing on non-Western traditions, see Peter J. Sheehan, "Reason, Values and Public Policy," Working Paper No.3, Centre for Strategic Economic Studies, Victoria University of Technology, Melbourne, March 1995, http://www.cfses.com/documents/wp3cses.pdf
30. See, for instance, Robert Jervis, *Perception and Misperception in International Politics* (Princeton: Princeton University Press, 1976); Axelrod and Keohane, "Achieving Cooperation," Schelling, *The Strategy of Conflict*.

31. According to Judith Goldstein, the struggle is not only about which interests should prevail, but about the methods to realize them. In "Creating the GATT Rules: Politics, Institutions, and American Policy," in *Multilateralism Matters. The Theory and Praxis of an Institutional Form*, ed. John Ruggie (New York: Columbia University Press, 1993), 203.
32. On beliefs, see Keohane and Nye, *Power and Interdependence*, 8; Goldstein and Keohane, "Ideas and Foreign Policy"; and Jerel A. Rosati, "A Cognitive Approach to the Study of Foreign Policy," in *Foreign Policy Analysis. Continuity and Change in Its Second Generation*, ed. Jeanne A.K. Hey, and Patrick J. Haney (Englewood Cliffs, NJ: Prentice Hall, 1995), 49–70. On historical memory, see Schelling, *The Strategy of Conflict*, 107; Susan Strange, *States and Markets*, 2nd ed. (London; New York: Pinter Publishers, 1988), 36. For the weight of emotions in international politics, see Richard Ned Lebow, "Reason, Emotion and Cooperation," *International Politics* 42 (2005), 283–313; Neta C. Crawford, "The Passion of World Politics: Propositions on Emotion and Emotional Relationships," *International Security* 24 (Spring 2000), 116–156.
33. Arthur T. Denzau and Douglass G. North, "Shared Mental Models: Ideologies and Institutions," *Kyklos* 47 (1994), 4. For a recent reflection on the model, see Arthur Denzau, Douglass G. North, and Ravi K. Roy, "Shared Mental Models: a Postcript," in *Neoliberalism. National and Regional Experiments with Global Ideas*, ed. Ravi K. Roy, Arthur T. Denzau, and Thomas D. Willett (Abingdon; New York: Routledge, 2007), 14–25. The volume also includes various case studies applying the shared mental model.
34. Denzau and North, "Shared Mental Models," 4.
35. Ibid., 4.
36. Albert S. Yee, "Thick Rationality and the Missing 'Brute Fact': The Limits of Rationalist Incorporation of Norms and Ideas," *The Journal of Politics* 59.4 (1997), 1001–1039; and Eric Helleiner, "Preface," to Roy, Denzau, and Willett, *Neoliberalism*, xviii–xx.
37. The normativism is explicit in expressions such as "wrong model of the world," "start out wrong," or "one never sees things as they are, but rather only through the lens of the mental models shared in our heads." See Denzau, North, and Roy, "Share Mental Models," 14–15.
38. Gilbert R. Winham, *International Trade and the Tokyo Round Negotiation* (Princeton, NJ: Princeton University Press, 1986), 58.
39. On the need for further investigation on the role of economic ideas in International Relations, see Ngaire Woods, "Economic Ideas and International Relations: Beyond Rational Neglect," *International Studies Quarterly* 39.2 (June 1995), 161–180.
40. Emanuel Adler, *The Power of Ideology. The Quest for Technological Autonomy in Argentina and Brazil* (Berkeley: University of California Press, 1987); Peter Hall, ed., *The Political Power of Economic Ideas* (Princeton: Princeton University Press, 1989); Michael Pusey, *Economic Rationalism in Canberra: A Nation-building State Changes Its Mind* (Cambridge, UK: Cambridge University Press, 1991); Kathryn Sikkink, *Ideas and Institutions. Developmentalism in Brazil and Argentina* (Ithaca, NY: Cornell University Press, 1991); Judith Goldstein, *Ideas, Interests, and American Trade Policy* (Ithaca: Cornell University Press, 1993); Eric Helleiner, *States and the Re-emergence of Global Finance: From Bretton Woods to the 1990s* (Ithaca,

NY: Cornell University Press, 1994); Kathleen R. McNamara, *The Currency of Ideas: Monetary Politics and the European Union* (Ithaca, NY: Cornell University Press, 1998); Frank Trentmann, "Political Culture and Political Economy: Interest, Ideology, and Free Trade," *Review of International Political Economy* 5.2 (Summer 1998), 217–251; Shaun Goldfinch, *Remaking New Zealand and Australian Economic Policy: Ideas, Institutions and Policy Communities* (Wellington, NZ: Victoria University Pres, 2000); Glen Biglaiser, *Guardians of the Nation? Economists, Generals and Economic Reform in Latin America* (Notre Dame, IN: University of Notre Dame Press, 2002); Mark Blyth, *Great Transformations. Economic Ideas and Institutional Change in the Twentieth Century* (Cambridge, UK: Cambridge University Press, 2002); Esteban Pérez Caldentey and Matías Vernengo, "Ideas, Policies and Economic Development in the Americas," in *Ideas, Policies and Economic Development in the Americas*, ed. authors (Abingdon; New York: Routledge, 2007); John Quiggin, "Economic Liberalism" Fall, Revival and Resistance," in Peter Sandlers and James Walter, eds., *Ideas and Influence. Social Science and Public Policy in Australia* (Sydney, NSW: UNSW Press, 2005), 21–43.

41. Under the umbrella of the new institutionalism, rational choice institutionalism mainly draws on institutions as constraints to choices or as coordination mechanisms, while historical institutionalism focuses on institutions per se, their construction and historical development, and effects on the creation and reproduction of patterns of norms and policy ideas. For comparisons of the different lines within the new institutionalism, see Peter A. Hall and Rosemary C.R. Taylor, "Political Science and the Three New Institutionalisms," *Political Studies* XLIV (1996), 936–957; Kathleen Thelen, "Historical Institutionalism in Comparative Politics," *Annual Review of Political Science* 2 (1999), 369–404.

42. Mark Blyth, "Any More Bright Ideas? The Ideational Turn of Comparative Political Economy," *Comparative Politics* 29.2 (January 1997), 229–250.

43. Goldstein, *Ideas, Interests*, 250.

44. For an early collection on historical institutionalism, see Sven Steinmo, Katheen Thelen, and Frank Longstreth, eds., *Structuring Politics: Historical Institutionalism in Comparative Perspective* (Cambridge: Cambridge University Press, 1992). For a critical review, highlighting the role of political conflicts and ideas in institutional change, see B. Guy Peters, Jon Pierre, and Desmond S. King, "The Politics of Path Dependence: Political Conflict in Historical Institutionalism," *The Journal of Politics* 67.4 (November 2005), 1275–1300.

45. Margareth Weir, "Ideas and the Politics of Bounded Innovation," in Steinmo, Thelen, and Longstreth, *Structuring Politics*, 189.

46. Thomas Risse-Kappen, "Ideas Do Not Float Freely: Transnational Coalitions, Domestic Structures and the End of the Cold War," *International Organization* 48.2 (Spring 1994), 185–214.

47. See Hugh Heclo, "Issue Networks and the Executive Establishment," in *The New American Political System*, ed. Anthony King (Washington, DC: American Enterprise Institute, 87–124); John Kingdon, *Agendas, Alternatives, and Public Policies* (Boston: Little Brown, 1984).

48. Keohane and Nye deal with transnational informal networks of government members, within which exchange of information and ideas occur. In *Power and Interdependence*, 21. On transnational networks, including

non-governmental actors, see Hall, "Conclusion"; Andreas Nölke, "The Relevance of Transnational Policy Networks: Some Examples from the European Commission and the Bretton Woods Institutions," *Journal of International Relations and Development* 6.3 (2003), 276–298.

49. Margareth Weir, "Ideas and Politics: The Acceptance of Keynesianism in Britain and the United States" (54–56) and Peter Hall, "Conclusion: The Politics of Keynesian Ideas" (373–376), both in Hall, *The Political Power*; Peter Hay, "Contemporary Capitalism, Globalization, Regionalization and the Persistence of National Variation," *Review of International Studies* 26 (2000), 509–531; Goldstein, *Ideas, Interests*, 15.
50. Peter Hall, "Policy Paradigms, Social Learning, and the State: The Case of Economic Policymaking in Britain," *Comparative Politics* 25.3 (1993), 275–296; Lisbeth Aggestam, "Role Theory and European Foreign Policy. A Framework of Analysis," in *The European Union's Roles in International Politics. Concepts and Analysis*, ed. Ole Elgström and Michael Smith (London: Routledge, 2006), 11–29.
51. Karl Polanyi, *The Great Transformation* (Boston: Beacon Press, 1957), 254.
52. Goldstein, *Ideas, Interests*, 13–14; Hall, "Conclusion," 386–389.
53. In his reflections on scientific development, Thomas S. Khun highlighted the role of crisis in stimulating theoretical advances, pointing out that in most cases, the solutions "had been partly anticipated" but had remained ignored until a crisis created an opportunity for those solutions to be considered. In Thomas S. Khun, *The Structure of Scientific Revolution* (Chicago, IL: The University of Chicago Press, 1970), 75.
54. Ibid., 27.
55. The emphasis on central beliefs is required to differentiate that set of beliefs as reflecting "fundamental normative and ontological axioms that define a person's underlying personal philosophy," from beliefs related to strategies and instruments to be applied in the pursuit of the goals associated to the central beliefs and which, unlike the former, are less resistant to change. Paul A. Sabatier and Hank C. Jenkins-Smith, *Policy Change and Learning: An Advocacy Coalition Approach* (Boulder, CO: Westview Press, 1993), 30–31.
56. On the possibility of biased views arising in knowledge-based groups, see Sabatier and Jenkins–Smith, *Policy Change*, 54–55; Anne Schneider and Helen Ingram, "Systematically Pinching Ideas: A Comparative Approach to Policy Design," *Journal of Public Policy* 8.1 (1988), 61–80. On the relation between beliefs and knowledge validation, see Thomas Khun, "The Trouble with the Historical Philosophy of Science," in *The Road since Structure* (Chicago: University of Chicago Press, 2000), 105–120.
57. Blyth, *Great Transformations*, 29–30; John, "Is There Life After Policy Streams?."
58. Data based on GDP at purchasing power parity. World Bank, World Development Indicators Database, April 19, 2010, viewed June 24, 2010, http://siteresources.worldbank.org/DATASTATISTICS/Resources/GDP_PPP.pdf
59. On bounded innovation deriving from the relationships between ideas and the political setting in which they manifest, see Weir, "Ideas and the Politics."

60. Distribution of interviewees, according to affiliation: government (8), business (5), organized labor (1), trade adviser (7), civil society, including members from academia, nongovernmental organizations, and media (4).
61. A gradual move toward broader public access seems to be occurring. In 2006, the Brazilian Ministry of Foreign Affairs and the Brazilian Federal Police decided to transfer to the national archives, formerly secret documents from the military period. Josias de Souza, "Itamaraty Libera Materiais de Arquivo do Tempo da Ditadura," May 31, 2006, posted by Paulo Roberto de Almeida, http://diplomatizando.blogspot.com/2006/05/453-itamaraty-libera-materiais-de.html
62. Henrique Altemani de Oliveira, "Apresentação," to *A Política Externa Brasileira na Visão dos Seus Protagonistas*, ed. Henrique Altemani de Oliveira and José A. Guilhon Albuquerque (Rio de Janeiro: Editora Lumen Juris, 2005), xiii; Leticia Pinheiro, "How Much Foreign Policy Teaching Can Be Foreign Policy Making?" (paper delivered at the 4th Annual APSA Conference on Teaching and Learning in Political Science, Charlotte, North Carolina, February 9–11, 2007). For critical comments by diplomats, see Gelson Fonseca Jr., "O Pensamento Brasileiro em Relações Internacionais: O Tema da Identidade Nacional (1950–1995)," in *A Legitimidade e Outras Questões Internacionais* (Sao Paulo: Paz e Terra, 1998); Paulo Roberto de Almeida, "Preface" to *Relações Internacionais e Oolítica Externa do Brasil. História e Sociologia da Diplomacia Brasileira*, 2nd ed. (Porto Alegre: Editora da UFRGS, 2004).

2 The FTAA Negotiations

1. Ten out of the fourteen participants who answered the questionnaire cited lack of commitment from both the United States and Brazil, as the main reason for the FTAA deadlock, while three attributed the responsibility exclusively to Brazil. See questionnaire results, question 10, in Appendix A.
2. *Mexico-United States Joint Statement on Negotiation of a Free Trade Agreement*, June 11, 1990. Available from the George Bush Presidential Library Museum, http://bushlibrary.tamu.edu/research/public_papers.php?id=1979&year=1990&month=6
3. George H.W. Bush, *Remarks Announcing the Enterprise for the Americas Initiative*, White House, June 27, 1990. Available at The American Presidency Project, http://www.presidency.ucsb.edu/ws/index.php?pid=18644
4. Roger Porter, "The Enterprise for the Americas Initiative. A New Approach to Economic Growth," *Journal of Interamerican Studies and World Affairs* 32.4 (Winter 1990), 7.
5. The reliance on economic growth and private enterprise predominated despite indications that the profound asymmetries among the parties required cooperation in various institutional areas such as education, research, and development. Fernando Fajnzylber, "Technical Progress, Competitiveness and Institutional Change," in *Strategic Options for Latin America in the 1990s*, ed. Colin I. Bradford Jr. (Paris: Organization for Economic Co-operation and Development, 1992), 121.
6. A list of the trade agreements in force in the Americas is available at the OAS Foreign Trade Information System's website, http://www.sice.oas.org

7. Inter-American Development Bank (IDB), *Mas Allá de las Fronteras. El Nuevo Regionalismo en América Latina* (Washington, DC: IDB, 2002), 37.
8. This factor is reinforced by studies that show, in the few cases in which foreign direct investment has increased, that there has been no evidence that trade agreements have been the cause. Sheila Page, "Regional Integration and the Investment Effect," in *Regional Integration in Latin America and the Caribbean: The Political Economy of Open Regionalism*, ed. Victor Bulmer-Thomas (London: Institute of Latin American Studies, University of London, 2001), 45–64. On the relevance of macroeconomic performance as the main variable in the attraction of foreign direct investment in Latin America, see Alfredo P. Montero, "Macroeconomic Deeds, Not Reform Words: The Determinants of Foreign Direct Investment in Latin America," *Latin American Research Review* 43.1 (2008), 55–77.
9. For an analysis of the conflict between centripetal and centrifugal forces in the FTAA project, see Diana Tussie and Ignacio Labaqui, "The Free Trade Area of the Americas: the Hunt for the Hemispheric Grand Bargain," in Fawcett and Serrano, *Regionalism and Governance*, 71–92.
10. See Roberto Bouzas and Jaime Ros, eds., *Economic Integration in the Western Hemisphere* (Notre Dame, IN; London: University of Notre Dame Press, 1994) for an early study containing data on individual trade blocs in the continent, with a cautionary view on the implications of hemispheric integration. Gary Hufbauer and Jeffrey Schott, *Western Hemisphere Economic Integration* (Washington, DC: Institute of International Economics, 1994) addresses the question of hemispheric trade integration, but the focus is predominantly on potential gains.
11. Hufbauer and Schott, *Western Hemisphere*, 25–49.
12. Helio Jaguaribe, "A View from the Southern Cone," in *Latin America in a New World*, ed. Abraham Lowenthal and G.Treverton (Boulder, CO: Westview Press, 1994), 57.
13. Patrice M. Franko, *Toward a New Security Architecture in the Americas. The Strategic Implications of the FTAA* (Washington, DC: CSIS Press, 2000).
14. Raymond J. Ahearn and Alfred Reifman, *US Interest in Western Hemisphere Free Trade*, U.S. Congressional Research Service Report, November 12, 1993 (Washington, DC: U.S. Library of Congress/CRS, 1993).
15. George Bush, *Remarks Announcing the Enterprise for the Americas Initiative*, June 27, 1990, available at The American Presidency Project, http://www.presidency.ucsb.edu/ws/index.php?pid=18644
16. Tussie and Labaqui, "Free Trade Area of the Americas," 75.
17. A collection of articles exploring the meanings of democracy promotion in the U.S. foreign policy strategy is offered in Michael Cox, G. John Ikenberry, and Takashi Inoguchi, eds., *American Democracy Promotion. Impulses, Strategies and Impacts* (New York: Oxford University Press, 2000).
18. Personal interview with Professor Louis Bélanger (Université Laval), Washington, DC, March 30, 2006.
19. President Reagan inaugurated the Caribbean Basin Initiative in 1983, as part of his foreign policy strategy in Central America. It comprises the Caribbean Basin Economic Recovery Act (CBERA) of 1983, its extension of 1990, and the Caribbean Trade Partnership Act (CBTPA) of 2000. It establishes U.S. nonreciprocal concessions of trade preferences to selected countries located in Central America and the Caribbean. The CBTPA upgraded the program,

providing parity to NAFTA in market access for selected sectors. However, unlike the permanent concessions of the CBERA, those created by the CBTPA were due to expire in September 2008 or upon the entry into force of a free trade agreement between the beneficiaries and the United States.

20. Pablo Rodas-Martini describes "dwarf regionalism" as a kind of regionalism that does not fit into the old mode of inward-orientation nor in the more optimistic views surrounding open regionalism, but which is commonly found in small economies heavily linked to a country in the North. In Pablo Rodas-Martini, "Central America: Toward Open Regionalism or Toward an Opening without Regionalism?," in *Regional Integration in Latin America and the Caribbean: The Political Economy of Open Regionalism*, ed. Victor Bulmer-Thomas (London: Institute of Latin American Studies, University of London., 2001), 268.

21. S.R. Insanally, "Multilateralism in International Relations: Past Practice and Future Promise," in *Caribbean Imperatives. Regional Governance and Integrated Development*, ed. Kenneth Hall and Denis Benn (Kingston, Jamaica: Ian Randle Publishers, 2005), 275.

22. CARICOM also benefits from unilateral preferential market access to Canada, through the CARIBCAN program, and the European Union, through the Lomé Conventions.

23. Richard Bernal, "CARICOM: Externally Vulnerable Regional Economic Integration," in Bouzas and Ros, *Economic Integration*, 171–202.

24. Winston Fritsch and Alexandre A. Tombini, "The Mercosul: An Overview," in Bouzas and Ros, *Economic Integration*, 81–99.

25. For a perspective from Argentina, see former Minister of Industry and Foreign Trade during the negotiations of the sectoral agreements with Brazil, Roberto Lavagna, *Argentina, Brasil, Mercosur. Una Decisión Estratégica, 1986–2001* (Buenos Aires: Ciudad Argentina, 1998).

26. For transformations in the Uruguayan foreign policy in the period, see Lincoln Bizzozero, "Uruguayan Foreign Policies in the 1990s: Continuities and Changes with a View to Recent Regionalisms," in *National Perspectives on the New Regionalism in the South*, ed. Björn Hettne, András Inotai, and Osvaldo Sunkel (Basingstoke; New York: Palgrave Macmillan, 2000), 177–197.

27. For a brief comment on the differences between Argentinean and Brazilian foreign policy orientation in the period, see Monica Hirst, "Mercosur's Complex Political Agenda," in *Mercosur: Regional Integration, World Markets*, ed. Riordan Roett (Boulder, CO: Lynne Rienner Publishers, Inc., 1999), 35–47.

28. Fritsch and Tombini, "Mercosul," 82.

29. For an analysis of the reorientation of the Argentinean foreign policy under Carlos Menem, see Janina Onuki, "As Mudanças da Política Externa Argentina no Governo Menem" (PhD diss., Political Science Department, Universidade de São Paulo, 2002).

30. Rubens A. Barbosa and Luís Fernando Panelli César, "A Integração Sub-Regional, Regional e Hemisférica: O Esforço Brasileiro," in *Temas da Política Externa Brasileira II*, ed. Gelson Fonseca Jr. and Sergio Henrique Nabuco de Castro (Sao Paulo: Paz e Terra, 1994), 301.

31. Pedro da Motta Veiga, "Brazil in Mercosur: Reciprocal Influence," in Roett, *Mercosur*, 25–33.

32. In 1996, the Andean Group, also referred to as Andean Pact, changed its denomination to Andean Community.
33. José Antonio Ocampo and Pilar Esguerra, "The Andean Group and Latin American Integration," in Bouzas and Ros, *Economic Integration*, 122–145.
34. Mauricio Reina and Gladys Cristina Barrera, "An Analysis of Colombian Reactions to the EAI: Prospects for Success," in *The Enterprise for the Americas Initiative. Issues and Prospects for a Free Trade Agreement in the Western Hemisphere*, ed. Roy E. Green (Westport, CT: Praeger, 1993), 185.
35. An example of the merging of political and trade interests is the U.S. unilateral trade preferences program to the Andes. Created in 1991, the program aimed to assist in the diversification of exports and reduction of crops cultivated for drug-production purposes. For an evaluation of the program, see Zuleika Arashiro, "Preferências Comerciais Unilaterais: Cooperação ou Coerção? O Caso do Programa de Preferências Comerciais para os Andes" (Master's diss., Fundação Getúlio Vargas/EAESP, São Paulo, 2004).
36. Jean Grugel, "The Chilean State and New Regionalism: Strategic Alliances and Pragmatic Integration," in *Regionalism across the North-South Divide: State Strategies and Globalization*, ed. Jean Grugel and Wil Hout (London: Routledge, 1999), 62–78.
37. Malcolm D. Rowat, "Future Accession to NAFTA: The Case of Chile and the Mercosur," in *Beyond NAFTA: An Economic, Political and Sociological Perspective*, ed. A.R. Riggs and Tom Velk (Vancouver, BC: The Fraser Institute, 1993), 198.
38. Grugel, "Chilean State," 67.
39. Personal interview with a Chilean government's adviser, Washington, DC, March 23, 2006.
40. Alberto van Klaveren, "Chile: The Search for Open Regionalism," in Hettne, Inotai, and Sunkel, *National Perspectives on the New Regionalism in the South*, 133–155.
41. G. John Ikenberry, "America's Liberal Grand Strategy: Democracy and National Security in the Post-war Era," in Cox, Ikenberry, and Inoguchi, *American Democracy*, 125.
42. Michael Cox, "Wilsonianism Resurgent? The Clinton Administration and the Promotion of Democracy," in Cox, Ikenberry, and Inoguchi, *American Democracy*, 219–239. For a defense of Clinton's foreign policy views, see Stephen M. Walt, "Two Cheers for Clinton's Foreign Policy," *Foreign Affairs* 79.3 (2000), 63–79. A critical evaluation is found in Richard Haas, *The Reluctant Sheriff: The United States After the Cold War* (New York: Council on Foreign Relations Press, 1997).
43. William J. Clinton, *Address to the Nation on Haiti*, September 15, 1994, http://www.presidency.ucsb.edu/ws/index.php?pid=49093
44. In June 1991, the OAS members adopted the Santiago Commitment to Democracy and the Renewal of the Inter-American System and, through the OAS Resolution 1080, agreed upon a mechanism for collective action in case of disruption of democracy in any of the organization's members. For a discussion on the achievements and limitations of the democracy cause as advanced by the OAS, see Andrew F. Cooper and Thomas Legler, "The OAS Democratic Solidarity Paradigm: Questions of Collective and National Leadership," *Latin American Politics and Society* 43.1 (Spring 2001), 103–126.

45. See Richard E. Feinberg, *Summitry of the Americas. A Progress Report* (Washington, DC: Institute for International Economics, 1997), 53. Feinberg, former Special Assistant to the President and Senior Director of Inter-American Affairs at the National Security Council (1993–1996). The book contains a detailed narrative of the summit process, including the origin and rise of the idea within the U.S. administration.
46. Ibid., 56–57.
47. Scott Otteman, "Clinton announces USTR-led effort to design post-NAFTA trade path," *Inside US Trade*, December 3, 1993.
48. William J. Clinton, *Remarks to the Executive Committee of the Summit of the Americas*

    in Miami, Florida, July 18, 1994, http://www.presidency.ucsb.edu/ws/index.php?pid=50504&st=Remarks+to+the+Executive+Committee+of+the+Summit+of+the+Americas&st1
49. Howard Wiarda, "After Miami: The Summit, the Peso Crisis, and the Future of US-Latin American Relations," *Journal of Interamerican Studies and World Affairs* 37.1(1995), 43–68.
50. Ambassador Charles Gillespie, Jr.'s interview with David Scott Palmer, Washington, DC, February 14, 2002. Cited in David Scott Palmer, *US Relations with Latin America during the Clinton Years* (Gainesville: University Press of Florida, 2006), 108, fn.6 to chapter 5.
51. Inside U.S. Trade, "US shows early favour for NAFTA expansion over separate pacts," January 14, 1994.
52. Feinberg, *Summitry of the Americas*, 53.
53. Personal interview with a national security adviser for the Clinton administration, Washington, DC, March 21, 2006.
54. Inside U.S. Trade, "US seeks to build 'Americas Free Trade Area' at Miami Summit," November 18, 1994.
55. The Rio Group was formed in 1986, out of the joint efforts of some Latin American countries to assist in the peace process in Central America. It included members of the Contadora Group—Venezuela, Mexico, Panama, and Colombia—and the support group—Argentina, Brazil, Peru, and Uruguay. The Group was designed as a dialogue forum for Latin American countries separated from the OAS and from U.S. influence. Its current membership includes: all South American states with the exception of Suriname and Guyana, Central America, except Belize, Dominican Republic, Mexico, and a rotative representative from CARICOM. Alicia Frohmann, "Regional Initiatives for Peace and Democracy: The Collective Diplomacy of the Rio Group," in *Responses to Regional Problems: The Case of Latin America and the Caribbean*, ed. Carl Kaysen, Robert A. Pastor, and Laura W. Reed (Cambridge: American Academy of Arts and Sciences, 1994), 129–141.
56. Scott Otteman, "U.S. proposal for Americas' free trade area relies on Bush Initiative," *Inside US Trade*, November 25, 1994.
57. Antigua and Barbuda, Argentina, Bahamas, Barbados, Belize, Bolivia, Brazil, Canada, Chile, Colombia, Costa Rica, Dominica, Dominican Republic, Ecuador, El Salvador, Grenada, Guatemala, Guyana, Haiti, Honduras, Jamaica, Mexico, Nicaragua, Panama, Paraguay, Peru, St. Vincent and the Grenadines, St. Lucia, St. Kitts and Nevis, Suriname, Trinidad and Tobago, the United States, Uruguay, and Venezuela. Cuba was the only state in the hemisphere excluded from the initiative.

58. Feinberg and Corrales, "Why Did It Take 200 Years?," 7–38.
59. The official documents produced throughout the FTAA process, and referred to in this work, are available in four languages (English, Spanish, Portuguese, and French) at the official FTAA website, www.ftaa-alca.org.
60. A detailed account of the FTAA process through the Third Trade Ministerial Meeting of May 1997 is offered by Pedro da Motta Veiga in "El Mercosur y el proceso de construcción del ALCA," *Revista Integración & Comercio* 3 (September-December 1997), 3–31.
61. In regard to the WTO, Justin Robertson recalls that "one-third of members from the developing world are not physically present in Geneva and only twenty to twenty-five developing nations are actively engaged in WTO deliberations." In Justin Robertson and Maurice A. East, "Introduction" to *Diplomacy and Developing Nations. Post-Cold War Foreign-Policy Making Structures and Processes* (Abington; New York: Routledge, 2005), 23.
62. John S. Odell, "Introduction," to *Negotiating Trade. Developing Countries in the WTO and NAFTA* (Cambridge, UK: Cambridge University Press, 2006), 1–38.
63. Scott Otteman, "Confidential U.S. Plan sets out steps toward 'foundation' of FTAA," *Inside US Trade*, May 5, 1995; Scott Otteman, "US curtails labor, green language to gain FTAA consensus in Denver," *Inside US Trade*, June 16, 1995.
64. According to the WTO, the single undertaking principle implies that "nothing is agreed until everything is agreed." Negotiations guided by this principle require countries to negotiate commitments across areas before a balanced agreement can be reached. Nevertheless, early agreements on specific topics are possible as long as all negotiating parties agree. For a critical analysis of the implications of the single undertaking for developing countries, see Chandrakant Patel, "Single Undertaking: A Straitjacket or a Variable Geometry?" *Trade-Related Agenda, Development and Equity (T.R.A.D.E) Working Papers* no.15, South Centre, May 2003, http://www.southcentre.org/index.php?option=com_content&task=view&id=363&Itemid=67
65. See Paragraph 5 of the Denver Trade Ministerial Declaration, June 30, 1995.
66. Stephen Haggard, "The Political Economy of Regionalism in the Western Hemisphere," in *The Post-NAFTA Political Economy. Mexico and the Western Hemisphere*, ed. Carol Wise (University Park, PA: The Pennsylvania State University Press, 1998), 331.
67. With regard to the structure for the negotiations, the parties agreed to immediately form seven working groups: market access, customs procedures, and rules of origin; investment; standards and technical barriers to trade; sanitary and phytosanitary measures; subsidies, antidumping and countervailing duties, and working group on smaller economies. The creation of the U.S.-suggested working groups on government procurement, intellectual property rights, services, competition policy, was delayed. See paragraph 5 of the Denver Trade Ministerial Declaration, June 30, 1995.
68. Inside U.S. Trade, "Senior officials unable to bridge gap on hemispheric trade statement," March 15, 1996.
69. Inside U.S. Trade, "Hemispheric trade ministers reach agreement on FTAA declaration," March 22, 1996.

70. Second Ministerial Trade Meeting Joint Declaration, Cartagena, Colombia, March 21, 1996. Working groups on government procurement, intellectual property rights, services, and competition policy were established.
71. O Estado de S. Paulo, "Temas bilaterais dominam reunião da Alca," April 17, 1997.
72. Personal interview with Thea Lee, Policy Director for the Legislation Department, AFL-CIO, Washington, DC, March 26, 2006. Lee described the process as an exercise of cooperation among trade unions in the Americas, with impressive collaboration during the simultaneous drafting of the declaration in various languages.
73. A history of actions of the Hemispheric Social Alliance can be found in the Alliance's website, http://www.asc-hsa.org/
74. Fourth Trade Ministerial Joint Declaration, San José, Costa Rica, March 19, 1998. For the first time in trade negotiations, a joint public-private sector committee of experts in electronic commerce was created. Additionally, the parties established a Consultative Group on Smaller Economies, and a Committee of Government Representatives on the Participation of Civil Society.
75. A trade adviser in the FTAA process pointed out during interview that the wisdom of that decision may have been challenged by the deadlock in the negotiations, which raised the question of whether it would have been more appropriate to have one of the highly committed countries—such as Chile or Costa Rica—as part of the coordination of the final stage of negotiations.
76. Inés Bustillo and José Antonio Ocampo highlight the need to address asymmetries, including in technical capacity, in order to allow smaller economies to actually benefit from the FTAA. In "Asymmetries and Cooperation in the FTAA," in *Integrating the Americas. FTAA and Beyond*, ed. Antoni Estevadeordal, Dani Rodrik, Alan M. Taylor, and Andrés Velasco (Cambridge, MA: Harvard University Press, 2004), 723–754.
77. See references to Costa Rican Foreign Trade Minister, José Manuel Salazar, in Scott Otteman, "FTAA officials say talks must offer quick results to keep interest," *Inside US Trade*, February 20, 1998.
78. Robert Devlin and Ricardo Ffrench-Davis, Working Paper 2, Institute for the Integration of Latin America and the Caribbean, and Integration, Trade and Hemispheric Issues Division, Buenos Aires, December 1998, http://www.iadb.org/intal/aplicaciones/uploads/publicaciones/i_intalitd_wp_02_1998_devlin.pdf
79. Gary Hufbauer, Jeffrey J. Schott, and Barbara Kotschwar, "US Interests in Free Trade in the Americas," in *The United States and the Americas: A Twenty-First Century Viewi*, ed. Albert Fishlow and James Jones (New York: W.W. Norton & Co., 1999), 58–78.
80. The FTAA was only one component of the Summit of the Americas' process. For an evaluation of the achievements and limitations in other areas, see Leadership Council for Inter-American Summitry, *An Evaluation of the Santiago Summit of the Americas and Its Aftermath*, Policy Report II, North South Center, University of Miami, Florida, March 1999.
81. Inside U.S. Trade, "Deputy USTR sees 'negotiation overload' slowing FTAA progress," August 6, 1999.
82. The First South American Summit took place in August 2000 in Brazil. The rationale for the summit was summarized by the Brazilian Minister of

Foreign Relations, Luiz Felipe Lampréia, "Cúpula da América do Sul," O Estado de S. Paulo, March 30, 2000.
83. George W. Bush, *Century of the Americas*, Florida International University, Miami, Florida, August 25, 2000. Reprinted in *The George W. Bush Foreign Policy Reader. Presidential Speeches with Commentary*, ed. John W. Dietrich (New York: M.E. Shapiro, 2005), 34–37.
84. Inside U.S. Trade, "NGO Alliance calls for release of FTAA negotiating texts," November 10, 2000. Among the most articulate alliances emerging in connection to the FTAA process is the Hemispheric Social Alliance (http://www.asc-hsa.org/), whose origins are found in the meeting of civil society organizations that took place parallel to the Belo Horizonte Trade Ministerial Meeting in 1997.
85. See section on "Transparency and participation of civil society" of the Sixth Ministerial Trade Meeting Declaration, Buenos Aires, April 7, 2001.
86. The clause establishes that "any unconstitutional alteration or interruption of the democratic order in a state of the Hemisphere constitutes an insurmountable obstacle to the participation of that state's government in the Summit of the Americas process." As seen in the footnotes to the Declaration, Venezuela was the only country which expressed discordance in relation to the final text. Declaration of Quebec City, April 22, 2001.
87. George W. Bush, speech delivered at the Third Summit of the Americas, Quebec City, April 21, 2001. Reprinted in Dietrich, *George W. Bush*, 281–283.
88. Dietrich, *George W. Bush*, 267.
89. Section 2, Division B of the 2002 Trade Act (P.L 107–210).
90. Robert B. Zoellick, "A Republican Foreign Policy," *Foreign Affairs* 79.1 (January/February 2000), 63–78.
91. James Baker, quoted in Kenneth Kidd, "Baker says free trade may prod other nations. Pact could result in 'market liberalization club'," *Toronto Star*, June 23, 1988, ME2.
92. Trade Negotiations Committee, *Methods and Modalities for Negotiations* (FTAA.TNC/20/Rev.1), derestricted October 18, 2002.
93. A study on the impact of U.S. antidumping and countervailing duty measures imposed against Brazilian exports revealed that, during the year of investigation, exporters should expect to lose approximately 59 percent of its exports to that country. Aluisio de Lima-Campos, and Adriana Vito, "the Impact of Anti-dumping and Countervailing Duty Proceedings on Brazilian Exports to the United States," *Journal of World Trade* 38.1 (2004), 37–68.
94. Rubens A. Barbosa, "A View from Brazil," *The Washington Quarterly* 24.2 (2001), 149–157.
95. Celso Lafer, "Novos Cenários de Negociação," address delivered during the Seminar "Doha e o Pós-Doha: Novos Desafios da Negociação Comercial Internacional," São Paulo, January 24, 2002. Reprinted in Celso Lafer, *Mudam-se os Tempos. Diplomacia Brasileira, 2001–2002* (Brasília: Fundação Alexandre de Gusmão/ Instituto de Pesquisa de Relações Internacionais, 2002), 257. Original in Portuguese: "Não acredito...que se deva olhar para a Alca como um exercício fadado a uma confrontação insolúvel."
96. Jornal do Brasil, "Canadá ofrece ao Brasil acordo comercial alternativo à Alca," May 9, 2002.

97. For a coverage of the reactions in Brazil, see Patricia Campos Mello, "Especialista ve armadilhas para o Brasil," O Estado de S. Paulo, February 12, 2003; Vladimir Goltia, "Alca: proposta americana é discriminatória," O Estado de S. Paulo, February 14, 2003.
98. Denise Chrispim Marin, "Itamaraty quer negociar diretamente com os EUA," O Estado de S. Paulo, May 12, 2003, B5.
99. Denise Chrispim Marin, "Zoellick exige ALCA e descarta EUA-Mercosul," O Estado de S. Paulo, May 28, 2003, B1.
100. Denise Chrispim Marin, "Fracassa nova proposta brasileira para a Alca," O Estado de S. Paulo, July 16, 2003, B5.
101. From Brazilian perspective, the "FTAA lite" had been already configured by the U.S. resistance in a full liberalization in agriculture. The comment was that an FTAA in which Brazilian sugar could not benefit from full access to the U.S. market was already a "light" (sugar-free) FTAA.
102. Jamil Chade, "México e EUA rejeitam proposta de 'Alca light'," O Estado de S. Paulo, June 21, 2003, B5; Denise Chrispim Marim, "Fracassa nova proposta brasileira para a Alca," O Estado de S. Paulo, July 16, 2003, B5..
103. Oxfam released a report prior to the Cancún Meeting, in which it pointed out the negative effects, for developing countries, of a failure in Cancún. See Oxfam, "Running into Sand. Why Failure at the Cancún Trade Talks Threatens the World's Poorest People," *Briefing Paper* 53, August 2003.
104. In October 2003, Colombia and Peru left the G20, under the U.S. offer of a bilateral trade deal.
105. See opinion article by Paulo Nogueira Baptista Jr., "A Alca depois de Cancún," Folha de São Paulo, October 2, 2003.
106. Paulo Sotero, "Brasil lidera 'ufanismo'," diz assessor de Zoellick," O Estado de S. Paulo, September 30, 2003, B14.
107. Chile, Costa Rica, Canada, Mexico, and Uruguay were among the countries which expressed disappointment with the bilateral solution. Sergio Leal, "Países da Futura Alca criticam acordo Brasil-Estados Unidos," Valor Econômico, November 17, 2003; Denise Chrispim Marin, "Uruguay desaprova modelo proposto por Brasil e EUA," O Estado de S. Paulo, November 18, 2003.
108. Eight Ministerial Meeting Declaration, Miami, November 20, 2003.
109. Valor Econômico, "Estados Unidos partem para ofensive de acordos," November 19, 2003.
110. Clovis Rossi, "Mercosur e G-3 duelam na reuniao da Alca," Folha de Sao Paulo, February 2, 2004; Clovis Rossi, "Surpreendido, Mercosul teve que sair ao ataque," Folha de Sao Paulo, February 8, 2004.
111. O Estado de S. Paulo, "Um jogo de alto risco em Puebla," February 3, 2004, A3.
112. The risk of failure, due to lack of political leadership to guide the FTAA was pointed out by I. M. Destler, "The United States and a Free Trade Area of the America. Notes toward a Political-Economic Analysis," Notes of presentation delivered on June 1, 2002; Donald R. Mackay, "Challenges Confronting the Free Trade Area of the Americas," FOCAL *Policy Papers* 02–7 (June 2002).
113. Peter H. Smith, *The Talons of the Eagle. Latin America, the United States, and the World*, 3rd ed. (Oxford; New York: Oxford University Press, 2008), 342–343. Between 1998 and 2006, candidates associated to center-left and left-wing parties, won elections in Argentina, Bolivia, Brazil, Chile, Ecuador, Nicaragua, Uruguay, and Venezuela.

114. Monte Reel and Michael A. Fletcher, "Anti-US Protests Flare at Summit," *Washington Post*, November 5, 2005, A01.
115. For a reflection on the social significance of the protests, see Jerónimo Montero, "Cumbre de las Américas en Mar del Plata: Victorias, Debates y Limitaciones de la Oposición," *ACME: An International E-Journal for Critical Geographies* 6.1 (2007), 124–130, http://www.acme-journal.org/vol6/JM_s.pdf
116. See "Declaration of Commitment of Port of Spain. Securing our 'Citizens' Future by Promoting Human Prosperity, Energy Security and Environmental Sustainability," Fifth Summit of the Americas, Trinidad, and Tobago, April 19, 2009, http://www.summit-americas.org/V_Summit/decl_comm_pos_en.pdf
117. C. Fred Bersgten, "A Renaissance for U.S. Trade Policy?," *Foreign Affairs* 81.6 (November/December 2002), 86–98. Bergsten used the term competitive liberalization back in the mid-1990s, to celebrate the kind of liberalization taking place through multiple regional trade agreements, and guided by fierce competition among countries. See C. Fred Bergsten, "Globalizing Free Trade," *Foreign Affairs* 75.3 (May/June 1996), 105–120.
118. Aggarwal and Lin argue that competitive liberalization, by offering specific sectors a prize through bilateral trade agreements, contributes to weaken domestic pro-free trade coalitions. As a result, protectionist forces can pressure on governments without facing much opposition. In Vinod Aggarwal and Kun-Chin Lin, "Strategy without Vision: The U.S. and Asia-Pacific Economic Cooperation," in *APEC: The First Decade*, ed. Jürgen Rüland, Eva Manske, and Werner Draguhn (London: Curzon Press, 2002), 91–122.
119. Dick K. Nanto and Thomas Lum, "US International Trade: Data and Forecasts," Congressional Research Service Report No.IB96038 (Washington, DC: U.S. Library of Congress/CRS, 2003).
120. See Björn Hettne, "Regionalism, Security and Development: A Comparative Perspective," in *Comparing Regionalisms: Implications for Global Development*, ed. Björn Hettne, András Inotai, and Osvaldo Sunkel (Basingstoke; New York: Palgrave Macmillan, 2001), 34; Helge Hveem, "The Regional Project in Global Governance," in *Theories of New Regionalism. A Palgrave Reader*, ed. Fredrik Söderbaum and Timothy M. Shaw (Basingstoke; New York: Palgrave Macmillan, 2003), 97.
121. Manger, Pickup and Snijders" analysis of networks of preferential trade agreements indicates that they tend to generate fragmented systems with a hub-and-spoke orientation, in which major economic powers and middle powers are somehow linked, but smaller economies are excluded. If this picture is accurate, it should be expected that in order to be considered, less powerful economies will be likely to face even more asymmetrical terms in negotiations. In Mark S. Manger, Mark A. Pickup, and Tom Snijders, "When Country Interdependence is not a Nuisance: The Longitudinal Network Approach," Working paper in progress, 2008.

3 Economic Paradigms and Trade Regionalism in Latin America

1. Victor Bulmer-Thomas, *The Economic History of Latin America since Independence*, 2nd ed. (Cambridge: Cambridge University Press, 2003), 354. Also, Robert Devlin and Paolo Giordano, "The Old and New Regionalism: Benefits, Costs, and Implications for the FTAA," in *Integrating the Americas*,

ed. Antoni Estevadeordal, Dani Rodrik, Alan M. Taylor, and Andrés Velasco (Cambridge, MA: Harvard University Press, 2004), 143–186.
2. President Luis Lacalle, quoted in *The New York Times*, "Bush's Trade Offer Gets a Warm Latin Reception," August 26, 1990, A23.
3. The term paradigm is used here in a similar way as applied by Albert Hirschman, to refer to those sets of "cognitive styles," which become widespread but which can sometimes hinder understanding. See Albert O. Hirschman, "The Search for Paradigms as a Hindrance to Understanding," *World Politics* 22.3 (April 1970), 329–343. Therefore, the term is applied in a more flexible manner than in Thomas S. Kuhn's scientific definition, according to which a paradigm consists of an achievement "sufficiently unprecedented" to gain solid support from the scientific community but which, at the same time, remains "sufficiently open-ended" so that practitioners can still engage in solving the new emerging questions. Thomas S. Kuhn, *The Structure of Scientific Revolution* (Chicago: The University of Chicago Press, 1970), 10.
4. Inter-American Development Bank, *Mas Allá de las Fronteras. El Nuevo Regionalismo en América Latina* (Washington, DC: Inter-American Development Bank, 2002).
5. John Williamson first applied the term "Washington Consensus" to refer to a set of ten adjustment policies prescribed by the U.S. government and multilateral financial institutions to Latin America, during the 1980s. The policies covered: fiscal discipline, prioritization of expenditure in health and education and removal of subsidies, tax reform, financial liberalization, unification of exchange rate, trade liberalization, foreign direct investment, privatization, deregulation and property rights. In John Williamson, *Latin American Adjustment: How Much Has Happened?* (Washington, DC: Institute for International Economics, 1990).
6. John Coatsworth, "Structures, Endowments, and Institutions in the Economic History of Latin America," *Latin American Research Review* 40.3 (2005), 126. For detailed reviews of Latin American economic history in the twentieth century, see Rosemary Thorp, *Progress, Poverty and Exclusion: An Economic History of Latin America in the 20th Century* (Washington, DC: Inter-American Development Bank, 1998); Bulmer-Thomas, *Economic History*, 295.
7. Joseph L. Love and Nils Jacobsen, "Preface" to *Guiding the Invisible Hand. Economic Liberalism and the State in Latin American History* (New York: Praeger Publishers, 1988), viii.
8. For a collection of case studies, see Love and Jacobsen's edited volume, *Guiding the Invisible Hand*; Vincent C. Peloso and Barbara A. Tenenbaum, eds., *Liberals, Politics and Power. State Formation in Nineteenth-Century Latin America* (Athens: The University of Georgia Press, 1996).
9. John H. Coatsworth and Jeffrey G. Williamson point out that by the First World War, Latin America accounted for the highest import tariffs among all world regions, with import tariff revenues playing a fundamental role in funding security-related expenditures. In "Always Protectionist? Latin American Tariffs from Independence to Great Depression," *Journal of Latin American Studies* 36 (2004), 205–232.
10. :James F. Rippy, *Latin America. A Modern History* (Ann Arbor: The University of Michigan Press, 1968), Statistical Tables, 577.

11. Osvaldo Sunkel and Pedro Paz, *El Subdesarrollo Latinoamericano y la Teoría del Desarrollo* (Mexico, DF: Siglo XXI Editores, 1970), 346–355.
12. A collection of studies on the worldwide diffusion of Keynesianism is offered in Peter A. Hall, ed., *The Political Power of Economic Ideas: Keynesianism across Nations* (Princeton, NJ: Princeton University Press, 1989).
13. Eduardo D. Valdés, "O Pensamento Nacionalista na América Latina e a Reivindicação da Identidade Econômica (1920–1940)," *Estudos Históricos* 20 (1997), 1–19.
14. In this work I opted for the use of the term in Spanish, CEPAL (*Comisión Económica para América Latina*), as it better reflects its regional purpose and the local emphasis of its school of thought. In 1984, the Caribbean was brought under the scope of the organization, and CEPAL currently stands for *Comisión Económica para América Latina y el Caribe*.
15. The United Nations set up five regional commissions: Economic Commission for Europe (ECE) and Economic and Social Commission for Asia and the Pacific (ESCAP), established in 1947, Economic Commission for Latin America (ECLA, 1948), Economic Commission for Africa (ECA, 1958), and Economic and Social Commission for Western Asia (ESCWA, 1973).
16. See Ricardo Bielschowsky, "Evolución de las Ideas de la CEPAL," Revista de la CEPAL, Número Extraordinario, *CEPAL. Cincuenta Años. Reflexiones sobre América Latina y el Caribe*. United Nations, Santiago, October 1998. For a study on the impact of structuralism and dependency in Spain and Portugal, see Joseph Love, "Structuralism and Dependency in Peripheral Europe: Latin American Ideas in Spain and Portugal," *Latin American Research Review* 39.2 (2004), 114–140.
17. For a review on structuralism, see Nora Lustig, "From Structuralism to Neostructuralism: The Search for a Heterodox Paradigm," in *The Latin American Development Debate. Neostructuralism, Neomonetarism, and Adjustment Processes*, ed. Patricio Meller (Boulder, CO: Westview Press, 1991), 27–42.
18. Jacob Viner, "Conflicts of Principle in Drafting a Trade Charter," *Foreign Affairs* 25.4 (July 1947), 628–629.
19. Nora Lustig identifies the official birth of structuralism in two documents published by CEPAL, at the end of 1949 and early in 1950, and to which Raúl Prebisch was the main contributor: "The Economic Development of Latin America and Some of Its Main Problems" and "The Economic Study of Latin America 1949." In Lustig, "From Structuralism to Neostructuralism," 30.
20. Raúl Prebisch, "Five Stages in my Thinking on Development," in *Pioneers of Development*, ed. Gerald M. Meier and Dudley Seers (Oxford: Oxford University Press, 1984), 175–189.
21. Raúl Prebisch, *The Economic Development of Latin America and Its Principal Problems* (Lake Success, NY: United Nations Department of Economic Affairs, 1950). At the same time, economist Hans Singer was coming to similar conclusions in his studies. See Hans W. Singer, "The Distribution of Gains between Investing and Borrowing Countries," *American Economic Review* XL (May 1950), 433–485.
22. Osvaldo Sunkel and Michael Mortimore, "Transnational Integration and National Disentegration Revisited," in Hettne, Inotai, and Sunkel, *Comparing Regionalism*, 54–92; Daniel Kerner, "La CEPAL, las

Empresas Transnacionales y la Búsqueda de una Estrategia de Desarrollo Latinoamericano," *Revista de la CEPAL* 79 (2003), 85–99.
23. See Celso Furtado, *Economic Development of Latin America. A Survey from Colonial Times to the Cuban Revolution* (New York: Cambridge University Press, 1970).
24. Sunkel and Paz, *El Subdesarrollo Latinoamericano*, 366–371.
25. Statement made by Mr. Raúl Prebisch, Executive Secretary of the Economic Commission for Latin America, at the second session of the Special Committee to study the Formulation of New Measures for Economic Cooperation, of the Organization of American States, Buenos Aires, 28 April 1959. Reproduced in ECLA, *The Latin American Common Market* (s.l.: United Nations Department of Economic and Social Affairs, 1959), 146.
26. José Manuel Salazar-Xirinachs, "The Integrationist Revival: A Return to Prebisch's Policy Prescription," *CEPAL Review* 50 (1998), 21–40.
27. For an early assessment of LAFTA's prospects, contrasting its political dynamic with the European case, see Ernst B. Haas and Philippe C. Schmitter, "Economics and Differential Patterns of Political Integration: Projections about Unity in Latin America," *International Organization* 18.4 (Autumn 1964), 705–737.
28. For an analysis of the first years of the Andean Pact, see Roger W. Fontaine, *The Andean Pact: A Political Analysis*. The Washington Papers, Vol.5, No.45 (Beverly Hills and London: Sage Publications, 1977).
29. CARICOM's members are: Antigua and Barbuda, the Bahamas, Barbados, Belize, Dominica, Grenada, Guyana, Haiti, Jamaica, Montserrat, Saint Lucia, St. Kitts and Nevis, St. Vincent and the Grenadines, Suriname, and Trinidad and Tobago.
30. On the institutional evolution in the CACM, the Andean Group and CARICOM, see Shelton Nicholls et al., "Open Regionalism and Institutional Development among the Smaller Integration Schemes of CARICOM, the Andean Community and the Central American Common Market," in *Regional Integration in Latin America and the Caribbean: The Political Economy of Open Regionalism*, ed. Victor Bulmer-Thomas (London: Institute of Latin American Studies, University of London, 2001), 141–164.
31. Angus Cameron and Ronen Palan, "The National Economy in the Contemporary Global System," in *Politics and Globalisation. Knowledge, Ethics and Agency*, ed. Martin Shaw (London: Routledge, 1999), 37–54.
32. Kathryn Sikkink notes that despite some variations, all developmentalist streams that emerged in the 1950s and 1960s shared three policy characteristics: (i) a focus on ISI; (ii) expansion of capital accumulation to support industrialization; and (iii) rising state intervention in the economy with the purpose of promoting development. In Sikkink, *Ideas and Institutions*, 3–4.
33. Peter Evans' analysis of the Brazilian case is illustrative of the complex relations which sustained the pact between state, local and foreign capital in a highly unequal society. See *Dependent Development. The Alliance of Multinational, State, and Local Capital in Brazil* (Princeton, N.J: Princeton University Press, 1979).
34. Guillermo A. O"Donnell, *Bureaucratic Authoritarianism. Argentina, 1966–1973, in Comparative Perspective* (Berkeley: University of California Press, 1986).

35. Veronica Montecinos and John Markoff, "From the Power of Economic Ideas to the Power of Economists," in *The Other Mirror. Grand Theory through the Lens of Latin America,* ed. Miguel A. Centeno and Fernando Lopez-Alves (Princeton, NJ; Oxford: Princeton University Press, 2001), 105–150.
36. Fernando Fajnzylber, *Industrialización en América Latina: de la "Caja Negra" al "Casillero Vacio": Comparación de Patrones Contemporáneos de Industrialización* (Santiago: ECLAC, 1989).
37. Fernando Henrique Cardoso and Enzo Faletto wrote the book that would become a central reference in the dependency scholarship, *Dependencia y Desarrollo en América Latina: Ensayos de Interpretación Sociológica* (Mexico, DF: Siglo XXI, 1969). Cardoso and Faletto, *Dependencia y Desarrollo en América Latina*; Gary Gereffi and Peter Evans, "Transnational Corporations, Dependent Development, and State Policy in the Semi-periphery: A Comparison of Brazil and Mexico," *Latin American Research Review* 16.3 (1981), 31–64. On the Mexican case, see John Minns, *The Politics of Developmentalism. The Midas States of Mexico, South Korea, and Taiwan* (Basingstoke; New York: Palgrave Macmillan, 2006), 88–117.
38. Victor Bulmer-Thomas, *Economic History,* 295.
39. Sebastian Edwards "The United and Foreign Competition in Latin America," in *The United States in the World Economy,* ed. Martin Feldstein (Chicago; London: The University of Chicago Press, 1988), 30–33.
40. See M. Leann Brown, *Developing Countries and Regional Economic Cooperation* (Westport, CT: Praeger Publishers, 1994), 43–72, on Chile's decision to leave the Andean Pact.
41. Constantino V. Vaitsos, *Crisis en la Cooperación Económica Regional. La Integración entre Países Subdesarrollados* (Mexico, D.F.: Instituto Latinoamericano de Estudios Transnacionales, 1978).
42. Celso Furtado, *Teoria e Política do Desenvolvimento Económico,* 4th ed. (Sao Paulo: Editora Nacional, 1971), 292–294.
43. For an analysis of the reasons for the failure of the ALADI scheme, with an emphasis on the Brazilian rationale, see Rubens Barbosa, "O Brasil e a Integração Regional: a ALALC e a ALADI (1960–1990)," in *Diplomacia para o Desenvolvimento. Sessenta Anos de Política Externa Brasileira (1930–1990),* vol. 2, ed. José A. Guilhon Albuquerque (Sao Paulo: Cultura/NUPRI-USP, 1996), 135–168.
44. José A. Ocampo points out the distinction adopting the term "state-led industrialization" to characterize to the period between the 1930s and 1970s. See José A. Ocampo, "Lights and Shadows in Latin American Structural Reforms," in *Economic Reforms, Growth and Inequality in Latin America. Essays in Honor of Albert Berry,* ed. Gustavo Indart (Aldershot; Burlington: Ashgate, 2004), 31, fn.2.
45. For a recent essay pointing out the importance of the Latin American intellectual initiative to construct locally grounded theories, see Raewyn Connell, "Dependency, Autonomy and Culture," in *Southern Theory. The Global Dynamics of Knowledge in Social Science* (Crows Nest, NSW: Allen & Unwin, 2007), 139–163; Joseph Love, "The Rise and Decline of Economic Structuralism in Latin America: New Dimensions," *Latin American Research Review* 40.3 (2005), 100–125; Cristóbal Kay, "Relevance of Structuralist and Dependency Theories in the Neoliberal Period: A Latin American

Perspective," Working Paper Series No.281, Institute of Social Sciences, The Hague, Netherlands, October 1998.
46. A general evaluation of the post–Washington Consensus scenarios are offered in Nancy Birdsall, Augusto de la Torre with Rachel Menezes, *Washington Contentious: Economic Policies for Social Equity in Latin America* (Washington, DC: Carnegie Endowment for International Peace and Inter-American Dialogue, 2001); ECLAC, *Una Década de Luces y Sombras: América Latina y el Caribe en los Años Noventa* (Bogotá: ECLAC and Alfaomega, 2001); Indart, *Economic Reforms*.
47. World Bank, "Swimming against the Tide: How Developing Countries are Coping with the Global Crisis," Background paper prepared by World Bank staff for the 20 Finance Ministers and Central Bank Governors Meeting, Horshmam, United Kingdom, March 13–14, 2009.
48. In the mid-1980s, a reformed version of structuralism was proposed. Neostructuralism retained the emphasis on structural conditions as relevant to economic analysis, and accepted a larger space for state action than that admitted under neoliberalism. See Nora Lustig, "From Structuralism to Neostructuralism." Fernando Ignacio Leiva offers a critical comparison of neoliberalism and neostructuralism, arguing that they have coincided particularly in their defense of flexibilization of labor markets and social demobilization. In *Latin American Neostructuralism. The Contradictions of Post-Neoliberal Development* (Mnneapolis, MN: University of Minnesota Press, 2008).
49. Colin Hay refers to a process of "normalization" of neoliberalism, in which the ideology is diffused as a rational, logic step, rather than as a political choice. See "The Genealogy of Neoliberalism," in, *Neoliberalism. National and Regional Experiments with Global Ideas*, ed. Ravi K. Roy, Arthur T. Denzau, and Thomas D. Willett (Abingdon; New York: Routledge, 2007), 51–70.
50. See, for a combination of general essays and country cases, Henk Overbeek, ed., *Restructuring Hegemony in the Global Political Economy. The Rise of Transnational Liberalism in the 1980s* (London; New York: Routledge, 1993).
51. Taiwan, South Korea, Hong Kong, Singapore, Malaysia, Thailand, and the Philippines.
52. Michael Mortimore argues that the origin of foreign direct investment, and transfer of technology, have played a crucial role in the contrasting performances of Asia and Latin America. In "Flying Geese or Sitting Ducks? Transnational and Industry in Developing Countries," *CEPAL Review* 51 (December 1993), 15–34. For detailed comparisons of the development paths between the two regions, see Gary Gereffi and Donald L. Wyman, eds., *Manufacturing Miracles. Paths of Industrialization in Latin America and East Asia* (Princeton: Princeton University Press, 1990); Minns, *The Politics of Developmentalism*.
53. Thorp, *Progress, Poverty, and Exclusion*, 215.
54. Bulmer-Thomas, *Economic History*, 355–356.
55. Ibid., 358.
56. Julio J. Nogués, Andrzej Olechowski, and L. Alan Winters, "The Extent of Nontariff Barriers to Industrial Countries' Imports," *The World Bank Economic Review* 1.1 (1986), 181–199; Edwards "The United and Foreign Competition in Latin America."

57. Nogués, Olechowski, and Winters, "The Extent of Nontariff Barriers," 195.
58. According to John Williamson, multilateral financial institutions apply the term "structural adjustments" to refer to the "opening the economy plus reordering public expenditure priorities, financial liberalization, privatization, deregulation and the provision of an enabling environment for the private sector." In John Williamson, *The Progress of Policy Reform in Latin America* (Washington, DC: Institute for International Economics,1990), 61.
59. Chile, Argentina, and Uruguay experimented with market-oriented reforms in the 1970s, but only in Chile the military was able to sustain it. Comparative studies can be found in Glen Biglaiser, *Guardians of the Nation? Economists, Generals, and Economic Reform in Latin America* (Notre Dame, IN: University of Notre Dame Press, 2002); Alejandro Foxley, *Latin American Experiments in Neoconservative Economics* (Berkeley and Los Angeles; London: University of California Press, 1983). For the political economy of the reforms in Chile, see Genaro Arriagada, *Pinochet. The Politics of Power* (Boston, MA: Allen & Unwin, 1988); Juan Gabriel Valdés, *Pinochet's Economists. The Chicago School in Chile* (Cambridge; New York: Cambridge University Press, 1995).
60. In Australia, Prime Minister Paul Keating (1991–1996) was the most prominent political representative of this ideological alignment. In his efforts to avoid Australia being transformed in a "banana republic," he moved into orthodoxy. As he declared, "what my party [Labor] wanted was to have the treasury brought back into the mainstream of economic thinking...this is the mission I was given and it has been achieved." Quoted in Paul Kelly, *The End of Certainty. Power, Politics and Business in Australia* (Sydney, NSW: Allen & Unwin Pty Ltd., 1994), 69–70. For the rise of economists in Australia, see Greg Whitwell, *The Treasury Line* (Sydney, NSW: George Allen & Unwin, 1986); Michael Pusey, *Economic Rationalism in Canberra: A Nation-Building State Changes its Mind* (Cambridge, UK: Cambridge University Press, 1991).
61. Lynne Phillips, "Introduction: Neoliberalism in Latin America," in *The Third Wave.of Modernization in Latin America: Cultural Perspectives on Neoliberalism*, ed. author (Wilimington, DE: Scholarly Resources, Inc., 1998), xvii.
62. On the influence of ideology in international policy transfer, see Mark Evans and Jonathan Davies, "Understanding Policy Transfer: A Multi-Level, Multi-Disciplinary Perspective," *Public Administration* 77.2 (1999), 380.
63. See Pusey, *Economic Rationalism*, on the Australian case; Shaun Goldfinch, *Remaking New Zealand and Australian Economic Policy: Ideas, Institutions and Policy Communities* (Wellington, NZ: Victoria University Press, 2000); Glen Biglaiser, *Guardians of the Nation? Economists, Generals and Economic Reform in Latin America* (Notre Dame, IN: University of Notre Dame Press, 2002); Miguel A. Centeno, *Democracy Within Reason: Technocratic Revolution in Mexico* (University Park: Pennsylvania State University Press, 1994); Sarah Babb, *Managing Mexico. Economists from Nationalism to Neoliberalism* (Princeton: Princeton University Press, 2001); Maria Rita Loureiro in *Os Economistas no Poder* (Sao Paulo: Editora da Fundação Getúlio Vargas, 1997), on the Brazilian case.
64. James Petras offers a critical view of the phenomenon in "The Metamorphosis of Latin America's Intellectuals," *Latin American Perspectives* 17.2 (Spring 1990), 102–112.

65. Montecinos and Markoff, "From the Power of Economic Ideas," 128–129.
66. The first representative case took place early in the 1970s, with the empowerment of economists trained in the University of Chicago (the "Chicago Boys"), who conducted the orthodox economic during the military regime of General Augusto Pinochet. For a detailed study on the Chilean case, see Valdés, *Pinochet's Economists*.
67. The term "technopols" was coined by Richard Feinberg and Jorge I. Domínguez. Among the individuals identified as technopols were Pedro Aspe (Mexico's Finance Minister, 1988–1994), Fernando Henrique Cardoso (Brazil's president, 1994–2002), and Alejandro Foxley (Chile's Finance Minister, 1990–1994). In Jorge Domínguez, ed., *Technopols. Freeing Politics and Markets in Latin America in the 1990s* (University Park: The Pennsylvania State University Press, 1997).
68. Domínguez, *Technopols*, 3.
69. John Williamson, "In Search of a Manual for Technopols," in *The Political Economy of Policy Reform*, ed. author (Washington, DC: Institute for International Economics, 1994), 11.
70. Peter Haas defines epistemic community as "networks of experts in specific policy issues, who share fundamental normative assumptions and causal beliefs, as well as knowledge validity criteria, and work toward a "common policy enterprise." In Peter Haas, "Introduction: Epistemic Communities and International Policy Coordination," *International Organization* 46.1 (1992), 1–35.
71. Judith Teichman, *The Politics of Freeing the Markets in Latin America. Chile, Argentina, and Mexico* (London; Chapel Hill: The University of North Carolina, 2001), 15–22.
72. Arminio Fraga, "A Fork in the Road," *Finance and Development* 42.4, December 2005, http://www.imf.org/external/pubs/ft/fandd/2005/12/fraga.htm
73. For an analysis of the social impact, see Sebastian Edwards, *Crisis and Reform in Latin America. From Despair to Hope* (New York: Oxford University Press, 1995), 252–292.
74. Dani Rodrik, "The Rush to Free Trade in the Developing World: Why So Late? Why Now? Will it Last?," in *Voting for Reform. Democracy, Political Liberalization, and Economic Adjustment*, ed. Stephan Haggard and Steven B. Webb (New York: Oxford University Press, 1994), 61–88.
75. Francisco Rodríguez and Dani Rodrik, "Trade Policy and Economic Growth: A Skeptic's Guide to the Cross-National Evidence," in *NBER Macroeconomics Annual 2000*, ed. Ben Bernanke and Kenneth S. Rogoff (Cambridge, MA: MIT Press for National Bureau of Economic Research, 2001); Robert E. Baldwin, "Openness and Growth: What's the Empirical Evidence?," *NBER Working Paper* No. 9578, National Bureau of Economics Research, Cambridge, March 2003, http://www.nber.org/papers/w9578.pdf?new_window=1
76. Manuel R. Agosin and Ricardo French-Davis, "Trade Liberalization in Latin America," *CEPAL Review 50* (August 1993), 42.
77. Beth A. Simmons and Zachary Elkins argue that the diffusion of liberal economic ideas was influenced both by international competition for capital and by learning from countries with similar social and cultural characteristics. In "The Globalization of Liberalization: Policy Diffusion in the

International Political Economy," *American Political Science Review* 98.1 (February 2004), 171–189.
78. Babb, *Managing Mexico*, 183. Ideological commitment was also emphasized by Manuel Pastor and Carol Wise, "The Origins and Sustainability of Mexico's Free Trade Policy," *International Organization* 48.3 (Summer 1994), 469–470.
79. Bulmer-Thomas lists eight new conditions: (i) the increase in trade faster than growth in production, (ii) the growing importance of trade in services, (iii) liberalization of financial capital flows, (iv) the expanding role of transnational corporations in the allocation of foreign direct investment, (v) growing membership in the multilateral system and expansion of multilateral regulations on trade-related areas, (vi) addition of intellectual property to the trade agenda, (vii) movement of labor, and (viii) environmental issues. In "Introduction," in Bulmer-Thomas, *Regional Integration*, 1–13.
80. ECLAC, *Relaciones Económicas Internacionales y Cooperación Regional de América Latina y el Caribe*. Estudios e Informes de la CEPAL 63 (Santiago, Chile: United Nations, 1987), 219–220.
81. As seen in the Introduction, the discussion over the actual benefits of regional trade agreements has been subject to an intense debate among economists. A critical analysis raising the risks of trading blocs is found in Jaime de Melo and Arvind Panagariya, *New Dimensions in Regional Integration* (Cambridge: Cambridge University Press, 1993).
82. ECLAC, *Open Regionalism in Latin America and the Caribbean. Economic Integration as a Contribution to Changing Productions Patterns with Social Equity* (Santiago: United Nations, 1994).
83. Ross Garnaut, *Open Regionalism and Trade Liberalization. An Asia-Pacific Contribution to the World Trade System* (Singapore: Institute of South Asian Studies; Sydney, NSW: Allen & Unwin, 1996), 16–41.
84. On the advocacy dimension in the East Asian new regionalism, see Jörn Dosch, "The Post Cold-War Development of Regionalism in East Asia," in *Regionalism in East Asia. Paradigm Shifting?*, ed. Fu-Kuo Liu and Philippe Régnier (London; New York: Routledge Curzon, 2003), 30–51.
85. Robert Devlin and Ricardo Ffrench-Davis, "Toward an Evaluation of Regional Integration in Latin America in the 1990s," Working Paper 2, Institute for the Integration of Latin America and the Caribbean, and Integration, Trade and Hemispheric Issues Division, Buenos Aires, December 1998, http://www.iadb.org/intal/aplicaciones/uploads/publicaciones/i_intalitd_wp_02_1998_devlin.pdf
86. Jean Grugel, "Latin America and the Remaking of the Americas," in *Regionalism and World Order*, ed. Andrew Gamble and Anthony Payne (Basingstoke: Macmillan, 1996), 142.
87. Peru delayed its process of integration but joined the free trade area in 1997. In 1996, as part of an institutional reorganization, the Andean Group became the Andean Community (*Comunidad Andina* or CAN, in Spanish). A chronology of decisions is available at the website of the Andean Community, http://www.comunidadandina.org
88. See "Protocolo de Tegucigalpa para la Carta de la Organización de Estados Centraoamericanos," December 13, 1991. Available from *Sistema de la Integración Centroamericana*, http://www.sica.int/busqueda/centro%20de%20documentación.aspx?IdItem=372&IdCat=8&IdEnt=401

89. Georges Fauriol, "The Shadows of Latin America Affairs," *Foreign Affairs* 69.1 (1989/1990), 116–134; Robert Pastor, "The Bush Administration and Latin America: The Pragmatic Style and the Regionalist Option," *Journal of Interamerican Studies and World Affairs* 33.3 (1991), 1–34; Abraham Lowenthal, "Latin America: Ready for Partnership?," *Foreign Affairs* 72.1 (1993), 74–92; Jonathan Hartlyn, Lars Schoultz, and Augusto Varas, eds., *The United States and Latin America in the 1990s: Beyond the Cold War* (Chapel Hill: University of North Carolina Press, 1992).
90. Andrew Hurrell, "Hegemony and Regional Governance in the Americas," in *Regionalism and Governance in the Americas Continental Drift*, ed. Louise Fawcett and Monica Serrano (Basingstoke; New York: Palgrave Macmillan, 2005), 185–207.
91. For a critical assessment, see Ricardo Ffrench-Davis, *Reforming Latin America's Economies: After Market Fundamentalism* (Basingstoke; New York: Palgrave Macmillan, 2005).
92. Luiz Carlos Bresser Pereira and Yoshiaki Nakano, "The Missing Social Contract. Governability and Reform in Latin America," in *What Kind of Democracy? What Kind of Market? Latin America in the Age of Neoliberalism*, ed. Philip D. Oxhorn and Graciela Ducatenzeiler (University Park: The Pennsylvania State University Press, 1998), 21–41.
93. Hirschman, "Search for Paradigms," 329–343.

4 Lessons from Economic Cooperation in the Americas

1. Kenneth A. Oye, "Explaining Cooperation Under Anarchy: Hypotheses and Strategies," in *Cooperation Under Anarchy*, ed. author (Princeton, NJ: Princeton University Press, 1986), 9.
2. As Keohane and Nye argue, "whether the benefits of a relationship (of interdependence) will exceed the costs...will depend on the values of the actors as well as on the nature of the relationship," in Robert Keohane and Jospeh Nye, *Power and Interdependence*, 3rd ed. (New York; San Francisco: Longman, 2001 [1st ed. 1977]), 8.
3. In a 1958 article, Ernst Haas warned that "systematic research into the expectations entertained by Latin American elites with respect to the OAS might reveal an anti-United States mutual responsiveness pattern which at the same time would imply a number of non-integrative consequences for the work of the OAS" (458). In Ernst Haas, "The Challenge of Regionalism," *International Organization* 12.4 (Autumn 1958), 440–458.
4. G. Pope Atkins provides an informative compendium of the history of the inter-American system through 1996 in *Encyclopedia of the Inter-American System* (Westport, CT: Greenwood Press, 1997).
5. For a retrospective view on the different concepts of regionalism in Latin America, see Louise Fawcett, "The Origins and Development of Regional Ideas in the Americas," in *Regionalism and Governance in the Americas. Continental Drift*, ed. Louise Fawcett and Monica Serrano. (Basingstoke; New York: Palgrave Macmillan, 2005), 27–51.
6. David Shenin, ed., *Beyond The Ideal: Pan Americanism in Inter-American Affairs* (Westport, CT: Greenwood Press, 2000).
7. The argument of supremacy of U.S. values in comparison to Latin American values can be found in Lawrence E. Harrison, *The Pan-American Dream: do*

Latin America's Cultural Values Discourage True Partnership with the United States and Canada? (New York: Basic Books, 1997); Lawrence E. Harrison and Samuel P. Huntington, eds., *Culture Matters: How Values Shape Human Progress* (New York: Basic Books, 2000).

8. Richard Feinberg and Javier Corrales, "Why Did It Take 200 Years? The Intellectual Journey to the Summit of the Americas," in Richard E. Feinberg, *Summitry of the Americas. A Progress Report.* (Washington, DC: Institute for International Economics, 1997), 16.
9. Originally cited in Thomas L. Karnes, ed., *Readings in the Latin American Policy of the United States* (Tucson: The University of Arizona Press, 1972), 17. Reproduced in Feinberg and Corrales, "Why Did it Take 200 Years?," 16.
10. Robert Pastor, *Exiting the Whirlpool. US Foreign Policy toward Latin America and the Caribbean*, 2nd ed. (Boulder, CO: Westview Press, 2001).
11. Peter H. Smith, *The Talons of the Eagle. Latin America, the United States, and the World*, 3rd ed. (Oxford; New York: Oxford University Press, 2008), 29.
12. Letter from James G. Blaine, Formerly Secretary of State, to President Chester A. Arthur, February 3, 1882, in James W. Gantenbein, *The Evolution of our Latin-American Policy. A Documentary Record* (New York: Octagon Books, 1971), 49–52.
13. Joseph Smith, "The First Conference of American States (1889–1890) and the Early Pan American Policy of the United States," in Shenin, *Beyond the Ideal*, 19–32.
14. Letter from Thomas Bayard, Secretary of State, to the United States Diplomatic Representatives in the Other American Republics and the Empire of Brazil, July 13, 1888. In Gantenbein, *Evolution of our Latin-American Policy*, 52–54.
15. Bilateral trade agreements were signed with Brazil, Central American countries, Dominican Republic, Spain (for Cuba) and Great Britain, on behalf of the British West Indies. In 1894, the U.S. credibility was further eroded when the Wilson-Gorman Tariff Act repealed the reciprocity incorporated into the existing trade agreements. Smith, "First Conference," 26–29.
16. A detailed history of the formulation of the policy and its implications is provided in Bryce Wood, *The Making of the Good Neighbor Policy* (New York: Columbia University Press, 1961).
17. The Pan-American Operation was proposed in 1958 by Brazil's president, Juscelino Kubitschek. For the official document proosing the Pan-American Operation, see Alexandra de Mello e Silva, "A Política Externa Brasileira no Cenário da Guerra Fria," *Os Anos JK*, Centro de Pesquisa e Documentação de História Contemporânea do Brasil, Fundação Getúlio Vargas, Rio de Janeiro, http://www.cpdoc.fgv.br/nav_jk/htm/O_Brasil_de_JK/A_politica_externa_brasileira_no_cenario_da_Guerra_Fria.asp
18. Henry Raymont, *Troubled Neighbors. The Story of US-Latin American Relations, from FDR to the Present* (New York: Westview Press, 2005), 131–135.
19. For an analysis associating the modernization ideology to beliefs of U.S. cultural and moral supremacy, see Michael E. Latham, *Modernization as Ideology. American Social Science and "Nation Building" in the Kennedy Era* (Chapel Hill; London: The University of North Carolina Press, 2000). The

books offers a fascinating account of the rise of modernization theory and theorists and their influence in policymaking during the Kennedy administration, examining three policy initiatives implemented in the period: The Alliance for Progress, the Peace Corps, and the Strategic Hamlet Program in Vietnam.
20. Albert O. Hirschman's article, "Second Thoughts on the Alliance for Progress," was first published in *The Reporter* on May 25, 1961. Reprinted in Albert O. Hirschman, *A Bias for Hope. Essays on Development and Latin America* (New Haven: Yale University Press, 1971), 175–182.
21. Simon G. Hanson, *Dollar Diplomacy Modern Style: Chapters in the Failure of the Alliance for Progress* (Washington, DC: Inter-American Affairs Press, 1970). For a recent analysis of the implementation of the Alliance for Progress in individual Latin American countries, see Jeffrey F. Taffet, *Foreign Aid as Foreign Policy: the Alliance for Progress in Latin America* (New York: Routledge, 2007).
22. Ronald Reagan, Announcement for Presidential Candidacy, November 13, 1979, http://www.reagan.utexas.edu/archives/reference/11.13.79.html
23. Brian W. Tomlin, "The Stages of Pre-Negotiation: The Decision to Negotiate North American Free Trade," *International Journal* XLIV (1989), 255.
24. Tomlin, "Stages of Pre-Negotiation," 263; Murray Smith, "The North American Free Trade Agreement: A Canadian Perspective," in *The Enterprise for the Americas Initiative. Issues and Prospects for a Free Trade Agreement in the Western Hemisphere*, ed. Roy E. Green (Westport, CT: Praeger, 1993), 35–50.
25. A detailed account of the making of CUSFTA within Canada is offered by G. Bruce Doern and Brian W. Tomlin in *Faith and Fear: The Free Trade Story* (Toronto: Stoddart, 1991). For a commented collection of official documents and surveys conducted in Canada, related to the CUFSTA proposal, see Duncan Cameron, ed., *The Free Trade Papers* (Toronto: James Lorimer & Company, 1986).
26. Michael M. Hart, "Canadian Economic Development and the International Trading System: Constraints and Opportunities." Monograph commissioned by the Royal Commission on the Economic Union and Development Prospects of Canada (Toronto: University of Toronto Press, 1985), 38.
27. Paul Wonnacott summarized the key economic arguments raised in favor of the agreement in *The United States and Canada. The Quest for Free Trade* (Washington, DC: Institute for International Economics, 1987).
28. Tomlin, "Stages of Pre-Negotiation," 269.
29. Arlene E. Wilson, "A US Perspective on the Canada-US Free Trade Agreement," in Green, *Enterprise for the Americas*, 53.
30. Dryden, *Trade Warriors*, 340–343.
31. Commenting on the lack of technical support, Peter Murphy noted disappointedly, "Can you imagine?...This was a big negotiation, with (the prestige of) Reagan and Mulroney involved." Quote in Dryden, *Trade Warriors*, 341, note 27.
32. Allan Gotlieb, *"I'll Be with You in a Minute, Mr. Ambassador." The Education of a Canadian Diplomat in Washington* (Toronto: University of Toronto Press, 1991), 101–112.
33. Gotlieb, *I'll Be with You in a Minute*, 112.

34. Article 1906 of CUSFTA determines that "The provisions of this Chapter shall be in effect for five years pending the development of a substitute system of rules in both countries for antidumping and countervailing duties as applied to their bilateral trade. If no such system of rules is agreed and implemented at the end of five years, the provisions of this Chapter shall be extended for a further two years. Failure to agree to implement a new regime at the end of the two-year extension shall allow either Party to terminate the Agreement on six-month notice." Full text of the agreement available at http://wehner.tamu.edu/mgmt.www/NAFTA/index.htm
35. Carsten Kowalczyk and Ronald J. Wonnacott, "Hubs and Spokes, and Free Trade in the Americas," Working Paper No.4198, National Bureau of Economic Research, October 1992, http://www.nber.org/papers/w4198.pdf?new_window=1
36. Nora Lustig, *Mexico, the Remaking of an Economy*, 2nd ed. (Washington, DC: Brookings Institution Press, 1998), 136.
37. Data from Mexico's Instituto Nacional de Estadística, Geografia e Informática, cited in M. Angeles Villareal, *Mexico's Maquiladora Industry*, U.S. Congressional Research Service Report updated December 14, 1993 (Washington, DC: U.S. Library of Congress/CRS, 1993), 3–5. The Mexican government came to support the *maquiladora* production program when the *Bracero* Program, through which Mexicans were employed as seasonal farm workers in the United States, was terminated in 1964. Through the *maquiladora* program, foreign companies were allowed to install assembling plants in predetermined zones and export with reduced tariffs, mainly to the United States. In the United States, *maquiladora*-assembled imports benefited from reduced import duties through provision 9802.00.80 of the U.S. Harmonized Tariff Schedule and through the U.S. General System of Preferences.
38. Robert R. Kaufman, Carlos Bazdresch, and Blanca Heredia, "Mexico: Radical Reform in a Dominant Party System," in *Voting for Reform. Democracy, Political Liberalization, and Economic Adjustment*, ed. Stephan Haggard and Steven B. Webb (New York: Oxford University Press, 1994), 360–410; Manuel Pastor and Carol Wise, "The Origins and Sustainability of Mexico's Free Trade Policy," *International Organization* 48.3 (Summer 1994), 469.
39. Victor Bulmer-Thomas, Nikki Craske, and Mónica Serrano, "Who Will Benefit?," in *Mexico and the North American Free Trade*, ed. Victor Bulmer-Thomas, Nikki Craske, and Mónica Serrano (New York: St. Martin's Press, 1994), 203–232.
40. Salinas team included Pedro Aspe (PhD in Economics, MIT) as minister of finance, Jaime Serra Puche (PhD in Economics, Yale University) as minister of commerce, Miguel Mancera (PhD in economics, Yale University) as the head of the central bank, and Herminio Blanco (PhD in Economics, University of Chicago) as deputy minister of foreign trade. For a detailed study on the Mexican case, see Sarah Babb, *Managing Mexico. Economists from Nationalism to Neoliberalism* (Princeton, NJ: Princeton University Press, 2001).
41. On the ideological dimension of hegemony, see Robert W. Cox, "Gramsci: Hegemony and International Relations: An Essay on Method," *Millenium: Journal of International Studies* 12.2 (1983), 162–175.

42. Leah F. Vosko, "Fabric Friends and Clothing Foes: A Comparative Analysis of Textile and Apparel Industries under the NAFTA," *Review of Radical Political Economics* 25.4 (December 1993), 45–58.
43. See Gustavo Vega and Luz María de Mora, "Mexico's Trade Policy: Financial Crisis and Economic Recovery," in *Confronting Development. Assessing Mexico's Economic and Social Policy* Challenges, ed. Kevin J. Middlebrook and Eduardo Zepeda (Stanford, CA: Stanford University Press, 2003), 172.
44. Albert Hirschman, *National Power and the Structure of Foreign Trade* (Berkeley and Los Angeles: University of California Press, 1969), 17.
45. A Mexican negotiator recognized that despite the academic credentials, the negotiation team had little practical experience and was unable to capture the rationale behind protectionist arguments. See Maxwell A. Cameron and Brian W. Tomlin, *The Making of NAFTA: How the Deal was Done* (Ithaca, NY: Cornell University Press, 2000), 234.
46. The book by Gary C. Hufbauer, Jeffrey J. Schott, Robin Dunnigan, and Diana Clark, *NAFTA: An Assessment* (Washington, DC: Institute for International Economics, 1993), became the central reference for the pro-NAFTA group, who found in the estimations of job generation the numbers needed to contain critics arguing the risk of job losses in the United States. Among the U.S. voices of opposition was the think tank Economic Policy Institute. Thea Lee, who during her time at the Institute, wrote the polemic briefing paper "False Prophets. The Selling of NAFTA" (Washington, DC: Economic Policy Institute, 1995), later joined the Policy Department of the AFL-CIO.
47. Jaime Ros refers to a "lacunae" in the economic models in "Mexico and NAFTA: Economic Effects and the Bargaining Process," in Bulmer-Thomas, Craske, and Serrano, *Mexico and the North America Free Trade*, 11–28. On the NAFTA impact on the polarization of the Mexican economy, see Enrique Dussel Peters, "La Polarización de la Economía Mexicana: Aspectos Económicos y Regionales," in *Impactos del TLC en México y Estados Unidos. Efectos Subregionales del Comercio y la Integración Económica*, ed. John Bailey (Mexico, DF: Facultad Latinoamericana de Ciencias Sociales, México; Georgetown University, 2003), 41–68.
48. Jesus Velasco offers an account of the Mexican strategy with the think tanks in "Reading Mexico, Understanding the United States: American Transnational Intellectuals in the 1920s and 1990s," *The Journal of American History* 86.2 (September 1999), 641–667.
49. James M. Cypher, "The Ideology of Economic Science in the Selling of NAFTA: The Political Economy of Elite Decision-Making," *Review of Radical Political Economics* 25.4 (December 1993), 146–163.
50. Paul Krugman, "Book Review of NAFTA: An Assessment," *Journal of Economic Literature* 33.2 (June 1995), 850.
51. Barry Carr, "Crossing Borders: Labor Internationalism in the Era of NAFTA," in *Neoliberalism Revisited. Economic Restructuring and Mexico's Political Future*, ed. Gerardo Otero (Boulder, CO: Westview Press, 1996), 209–231. Carr points out that in past experiences during the 1930s and 1940s, labor internationalism was able to effectively exchange knowledge in a less asymmetrical pattern.
52. David Barkin, "A Constructive Labor Strategy for Free Trade," *Review of Radical Political Economics* 25.4 (December 1993), 133–145.

53. Compared to organized labor, environmental nongovernmental organizations were more successful in getting a side agreement closer to their pledges, and managed to advance cross-border interaction in the post-NAFTA context. However, the North-South asymmetry was also reproduced among environmental groups. Blanca Torres, "Transnational Actors and NAFTA: The Search for Coalitions on Labor and the Environment," in Fawcett and Serrano, *Regionalism and Governance*, 117–134.
54. Herman W. Konrad, "North American Continental Relationships: Historical Trends and Antecedents," in *NAFTA in Transition*, ed. Stephen Randall and Herman W. Konrad (Toronto: University of Calgary Press, 1995), 15–35. An interesting account of the development of fluid relations between U.S. and Mexican government elites is offered by Hermann von Bertrab, the Mexican head of the Washington office (from December 1990 to May 1994) in charge of coordinating operations for public and governmental relations, with regard to NAFTA. In Hermann von Bertrab, *Negotiating NAFTA. A Mexican Envoy's Account*, The Washington Papers 173 (Westport; London: Praeger and Center for Strategic and International Studies, 1997).

5 U.S. Foreign Trade Policy: Leadership in a Constrained System

1. For a discussion on the development of multilateralism and its principles of conduct, see John G. Ruggie, "Multilateralism: The Anatomy of an Institution," in *Multilateralism Matters. The Theory and Praxis of an Institutional Form* (New York: Columbia University Press, 1993), 3–47.
2. For a history of the USTR, see Steve Dryden, *Trade Warriors. USTR and the American Crusade for Free Trade* (New York, NY: Oxford University Press, 1995).
3. Marcus Noland, "Chasing Phantoms. The Political Economy of USTR," *International Organization* 51.3 (Summer 1997), 367.
4. Jon E. Huenemann, "On the Trade Policy-Making Process in the United States," *The Trade Policy-Making Process. Level One of the Two-Level Game: Country Studies in the Western Hemisphere*, ed. Inter-American Development Bank, Inter-American Dialogue and Munk Centre for International Studies (Buenos Aires: INTAL, ITD, STA, 2002), 67–73.
5. Michael Mastanduno, "The United States Political System and International Leadership: A 'Decidedly Inferior' Form of Government?," Paper presented at the Darmouth College-International House of Japan Conference, "The United States and Japan on the Eve of the 21st Century: Prospects for Joint Leadership," June 27–28, 1994. Reprinted in *American Foreign Policy. Theoretical Essays*, ed. G. John Ikenberry (London; Boston: Scott, Foreman and Co., 1989), 243.
6. See James M. McLindsay, *Congress and the Politics of US Foreign Policy* (London; Baltimore: The Johns Hopkins University Press, 1994).
7. Max Weber, "Parlamentarismo e Governo numa Alemanha Reconstruída," in *Ensaios de Sociologia e OutrosEscritos*, trans. Mauricio Tragtenberg (São Paulo: Abril Cultural, 1974), 32.
8. On the role of bureaucrats in advocating and creating policies in Europe, see Hugh Heclo, *Modern Social Politics in Britain and Sweden. From Relief to Income Maintenance* (New Haven; London: Yale University Press, 1974).

9. Joel Aberbach, Robert Putnam, and Bert Rockman, *Bureaucrats and Politicians in Western Democracies* (Cambridge, MA: Harvard University Press, 1981), 16–23. For a detailed historical comparative study on the evolution of bureaucratic structures, including France, Japan, the United States and Great Britain, see Bernard Silberman, *Cages of Reason: the Rise of the Rational State in France, Japan, the United States, and Great Britain* (Chicago: Chicago University Press, 1993).
10. Margareth Weir, "Ideas and the Politics of Bounded Innovation," in *Structuring Politics: Historical Institutionalism in Comparative Perspective*, ed. Sven Steinmo, Katheen Thelen, and Frank Longstreth (Cambridge: Cambridge University Press, 1992), 192–193; Silberman, *Cages of Reason*, 227–283.
11. For a study on the institutional development and structure of the White House, and the institutional leadership performance of various presidents in the United States, see John P. Burke, *The Institutional Presidency, Organizing and Managing the White House from FDR to Clinton*, 2nd ed. (Baltimore and London: The Johns Hopkins University Press, 2000).
12. Graham T. Allison, *Essence of Decision. Explaining the Cuban Missile Crisis* (Boston: Little Brown, 1971).
13. Stephen D. Krasner, "Are Bureaucracies Important? (Or Allison Wonderland)," *Foreign Policy* 7 (Summer 1971). Reprinted in G. John Ikenberry, *American Foreign Policy. Theoretical Essays* (London; Boston: Scott, Foreman and Co., 1989), 419–433.
14. Sharyn O"Halloran, *Politics, Process and American Trade Policy* (Ann Arbor: University of Michigan Press, 1994), 2.
15. Judith Goldstein, *Ideas, Interests, and American Trade Policy* (Ithaca; London: Cornell University Press, 1993).
16. For a classic study of the domestic interests and pressure politics leading to the Smoot-Hawley Act, see E.E. Schattschneider, *Politics, Pressure, and the Tariff: a Study of Free Private Enterprise in Pressure Politics, as Shown in the 1929–1930 Revision of the Tariff* (Hamnden: Archon Books, 1935).
17. Karen E. Schnietz, "The Institutional Foundation of U.S. Trade Policy: Revisiting Explanations for the 1934 Reciprocal Trade Agreements Act," *Journal of Policy History* 12.4 (2000), 418.
18. In 1936, the United States signed its first international agreement for monetary cooperation—the Tripartite Agreement—with Great Britain and France. See Jeff Frieden, "Sectoral Conflict and U.S. Foreign Economic Policy, 1914–1940," *International Organization* 42.1 (Winter 1988), 59–90.
19. W. Michael Weis, "Pan American Shift: Oswaldo Aranha and the Demise of the Brazilian-American Alliance," in *Beyond the Ideal. Pan-Americanism in Inter-American Affairs*, ed. David Shenin (Westport, CT: Greenwood Press, 2000), 138.
20. Various authors describe the RTAA as a congressional choice to diminish the burden of tariff legislation and the continuous political pressures from interest groups. Destler credits the change to the decision of Congress to get out of "the business of making product-specific trade law," in I.M. Destler, *American Trade Politics*, 4th ed. (Washington, DC: Institute for International Economics, 2005), 13. Others agree with the view of delegation as a rational choice, but emphasize that Congress continued to be an active player in trade policy. See Sharyn O"Halloran, *Politics, Process*; Robert A. Pastor,

Congress and the Politics of US Foreign Economic Policy 1929–1976 (Berkeley, Los Angeles, London: University of California Press, 1980); Robert A. Pastor and Rafael Fernandez de Castro, eds., *The Controversial Pivot: The US Congress and North America* (Washington, DC: The Brookings Institution, 1998).

21. Schnietz, "Institutional Foundation," 676.
22. Judith Goldstein, "Creating the GATT Rules: Politics, Institutions, and American Policy," in Ruggie, *Multilateralism Matters*, 208–211.
23. Ibid., 201–232.
24. George Myconos, *The Globalizaytions of Organized Labour: 1945–2005* (Basingstoke; New York: Palgrave Macmillan, 2005), 53.
25. Original article by Oscar Gass first published in *The New Republic*, March 19, 1962. Quoted in Dryden, *Trade Warriors*, 50.
26. See Robert A. Pastor, "Cry-and-Sigh Syndrome: Congress and Trade Policy," in *Making Economic Policy in Congress*, ed. Allen Schick (London; Washington, DC: American Enterprise Institute for Public Policy Research, 1983), 165–167.
27. Michael J. Hiscox, "The Magic Bullet? The RTAA, Institutional Reform, and Trade Liberalization," *International Organization* 53.4 (Autumn 1999), 669–698.
28. Pastor, "Cry-and-Sigh Syndrome," 166–167.
29. The system consisted of a customs evaluation based on an assessment of the cost of producing the imported commodity within the United States, frequently leading to the imposition of extremely high import duties.
30. Gilbert Winham, *International Trade and the Tokyo Round Negotiation* (Princeton, NJ: Princeton University Press, 1986), 131.
31. Nat Goldfinger, "A Labor View of Foreign Investment and Trade Issues," paper submitted to the Commission on International Trade and Investment Policy and published in conjunction with the Commission's Report to the President, *United States International Economic Policy in an Interdependent World*, vol. I (Washington, DC: G.P.O, 1971), 920.
32. In announcing his New Economic Policy, president Richard Nixon affirmed the concern of his administration with "the American workers, and with fair competition around the world." In Address to the Nation Outlining a New Economic Policy: The Challenge of Peace, August 15, 1971, http://www.presidency.ucsb.edu/ws/index.php?pid=3115#
33. Destler, *American Trade Politics*, 71–73.
34. Winham, *International Trade*, 308–310.
35. Dick K. Nanto and Thomas Lum, "US International Trade: Data and Forecasts," Congressional Research Service Report No.IB96038 (Washington, DC: U.S. Library of Congress/CRS, 2003).
36. John W. Sloan, *The Reagan Effect. Economics and Presidential Leadership* (Lawrence, KS: University Press of Kansas, 1999), 205.
37. Destler, *American Trade Politics*, 165–166.
38. Miguel Rodríguez Mendoza, "Latin America and the US Trade and Tariff Act," *Journal of World Trade Law* 20.1 (January-February 1986), 47–60.
39. For an analysis of the value placed in the ideal of multilateralism in the United States, see John Ruggie, "Third Try at World Order? America and Multilateralism after the Cold War," *Political Science Quarterly* 109.4 (1994), 553–570.

40. Charles S. Pearson, *Free Trade, Fair Trade? The Reagan Record, FPI Papers in International Affairs* (Washington, DC: Foreign Policy Institute, School of Advanced International Studies, Johns Hopkins University. Lanham, MD: Distributed by University Press of America, 1988), 72–76.
41. On the politics and motivations for the U.S.-Israel free trade agreement, see W. Charles Sawyer and Richard Sprinkle, "U.S.-Israel Free Trade Area. Trade Expansion Effects of the Agreement," *Journal of World Trade Law* 20.5 (September-October 1986), 526–539; Howard Rosen, "Free Trade Agreements as Foreign Policy Tools: The US-Israel and US-Jordan FTAs," in *Free Trade Agreements. U.S. Strategies and Priorities*, ed. Jeffrey J. Schott (Washington, DC: Institute for International Economics, 2004), 51–61.
42. Anne O. Krueger, *American Trade Policy. A Tragedy in the Making* (Washington, DC: The American Enterprise Institute, 1995), 87–92.
43. Hugh Heclo, "Ronald Reagan and the American Public Philosophy," in *The Reagan Presidency. Pragmatic Conservatism and Its Legacies*, ed. W. Elliot Brownlee and Hugh Davis Graham (Lawrence, KS: University Press of Kansas, 2003), 17–39.
44. President Reagan's "crusade for democracy" in Central America was a powerful example. See Thomas Carothers, *In The Name of Democracy: US Policy Toward Latin America in the Reagan Years* (Berkeley: University of California Press, 1991).
45. Judith Goldstein, "International Forces and Domestic Politics: Trade Policy and Institutional Building in the United States," in *Shaped by War and Trade*, ed. Ira Katznelson and Martin Shefter (Princeton and Oxford: Princeton University Press, 2002), 213.
46. Gary Hufbauer and Jeffrey Schott, *Western Hemisphere Economic Integration* (Washington, DC: Institute for International Economics, 1994), 17.
47. Ibid., 25–49.
48. In the United States, Sidney Weintraub explored the benefits of a U.S.-Mexico free trade agreement in a 1984 publication. See Sidney Weintraub, *Free Trade Between Mexico and the United States?* (Washington, DC: Brookings Institution, 1984).
49. Alan Zarembo, "Bush Family Ties: The Texas Clan Came to Mexico for Oil and Have Built a Complex Web of Friends and Partners," *Newsweek International*, 26 February 2001, 28.
50. U.S. Census Bureau, Foreign Trade Statistics, http://www.census.gov/foreign-trade/statistics/state/data/index.html
51. Personal interview with a national security adviser for the Clinton administration, Washington, DC, March 21, 2006.
52. See interview with Deputy USTR Jules Katz, cited in Dryden, *Trade Warriors*, 370.
53. Maxwell Cameron and Brian Tomlin, *The Making of NAFTA. How the Deal Was Done* (Ithaca, NY: Cornell University Press, 2000), 68–78.
54. Henry Raymont, *Troubled Neighbors. The Story of US-Latin American Relations, from FDR to the Present* (New York: Westview Press, 2005), 260.
55. Bill Clinton, Announcement Speech, Old State House, Little Rock, Arkansas, October 3, 1991. Reprinted in Bill Clinton and Al Gore, *Putting People First. How We Can All Change America*. (Toronto; New York: Times Books, 1992), 191.
56. Clinton and Gore, *Putting People First*, viii.

57. Ibid., 33; 93; 129–130; 155.
58. Al Gore, *A Vision for America*, speech given during the Democratic National Convention, New York City, July 16, 1992. Reprinted in Clinton and Gore, *Putting People First*, 212. A Senator for Tennessee, Al Gore had been the chairman of the U.S. Senate delegation to the Earth Summit of 1992, and was known for advocating environmental policies. In 1992, he published the *Earth in the Balance: Ecology and the Human Spirit* (Boston, MA: Houghton Mifflin, 1992).
59. According to Allan Metz, Clinton's disapproval by "both ends of the ideological spectrum" turned to be an asset, as he was able to appeal for the majority of the voters at the center. In Allan Metz, *Bill Clinton: A Bibliography* (Westport, CT: Greenwood Press, 2002), xi.
60. See accounts of the period in Elizabeth Drew, *On the Edge* (New York: Simon & Schuster, 1994), 107–113; Christopher J. Bailey, "Clintonomics," in *The Clinton Presidency. The First Term, 1992–1996*, ed. Paul S. Herrnson and Dilys M. Hill (Basingstoke: Macmillan Press, Ltd /New York: St. Martin Press, 1999), 85–103.
61. Michael Cox, *US Foreign Policy after the Cold War. Superpower without a Mission?* (London: The Royal Institute of International Affairs, 1995), 24–27.
62. Laura D"Andrea Tyson. *Who's Bashing Who? Trade Conflict in High-Technology Industries* (Washington, DC: Institute for International Economics, 1992).
63. Jeffrey E. Garten, *A Cold Peace: America, Japan, Germany and the Struggle for Supremacy* (New York: Times Books, 1992).
64. Doug Henwood, "Impeccable Logic: Trade, Development and Free Markets in the Clinton Era," *NACLA Report on the Americas* 26.5 (May 1993), 23–28.
65. Leonard Silk, "Head off a Trade War," *New York Times*, February 4, 1993, A23.
66. Michael Prowse, "A Prussian in the White House," *Financial Times*, February 21, 1994, 16.
67. Paul Krugman, "Competitiveness: A Dangerous Obsession," *Foreign Affairs* 73.2 (March–April 1994), 28–45.
68. Cox, *US Foreign Policy*, 23.
69. Rachel L. Holloway, "A Time for Change in American Politics: The Issue of the 1992 Presidential Election," in *The 1992 Presidential Campaign. A Communication Perspective*, ed. Robert E. Denton, Jr. (Westport, CT: Praeger Publishers, 1994), 129–167.
70. Steven E. Schier, "A Unique Presidency," in *The Postmodern Presidency. Bill Clinton's Legacy in US Politics* (Pittsburgh: University of Pittsburgh Press, 2000), 9.
71. On gaps between policymakers' perceptions and public opinion, see Steven Kull, I.M. Destler, and Clay Ramsay. *The Foreign Policy Gap. How Policymakers Misread the Public*. Report by the Center for International and Security Studies and its Program on International Policy Attitudes, University of Maryland, October 1997; Lawrence R. Jacobs and Robert Y. Shapiro, "Public Opinion in President Clinton's First Year: Leadership and Responsiveness," in *The Clinton Presidency. Campaigning, Governing & the Psychology of Leadership*, ed. Stanley A. Renshon (Boulder, CO: Westview Press, 1995), 195–211; Leonie G. Murray, *Clinton, Peacekeeping and*

Humanitarian Intervention. Rise and Fall of a Policy (Abingdon, Oxon; New York: Routledge, 2008).
72. Fred I. Greenstein, *The Presidential Difference. Leadership Style from FDR to Clinton* (New York: Martin Kessler Books/ Free Press, 2000), 174.
73. John P. Burke, *The Institutional Presidency, Organizing and Managing the White House from FDR to Clinton*, 2nd ed. (Baltimore; London: The Johns Hopkins University Press, 2000), 180; David Mitchell, *Making Foreign Policy. Presidential Management of the Decision-Making Process* (Aldershot; Burlington, VT: Ashgate, 2005), 141. For a multidisciplinary collection of articles on Clinton's leadership style, see Renshon, *Clinton Presidency.*
74. Mitchell, *Making Foreign Policy*, 141–173; Phillippe R. Girard, *Clinton in Haiti: the 1994 US Invasion of Haiti* (Houndmills, Basingstoke; New York: Palgrave Macmillan, 2004).
75. George A. MacLean, *Clinton's Foreign Policy in Russia. From Deterrence and Isolation to Democratization and Engagement* (Aldershot; Burlington, VT: Ashgate, 2006).
76. For a report published at that time on the free-fair trade debate, see Alfred Reifman and Craig Elwell, "US Trade Policy: Free Trade-Fair Trade and Their Discontents," Congressional Research Service Report No. 22 (Washington, DC: U.S. Library of Congress/CRS, 1992).
77. Sidney Weintraub, "The North American Free Trade Agreement as Negotiated: A US Perspective," in *Assessing NAFTA: A Trinational Analysis*, ed. Steven Globerman and Michael Walker (Vancouver: The Fraser Institute, 1992), 24–31.
78. Personal interview with a former member of U.S. State Department's NAFTA task force, Washington, DC, May 30, 2006.
79. For the full text of the North American Agreement on Labor Cooperation, see the website of NAFTA's Commission for Labor Cooperation at www.naalc.org. The North American Agreement on Environmental Cooperation is available at the website of the Commission for Environment Cooperation at www.cec.org
80. Quoted in Cameron and Tomlin, *Making of NAFTA*, 200.
81. In the House of Representatives, NAFTA was supported by 132 votes from the Republicans (against 43 "no" votes), and 102 votes from the Democrats (against 157 "no" votes). In the Senate, 34 Republican senators voted pro-agreement (against 10 who voted "no"), while 27 Democratic senators supported NAFTA (against 28 who voted "no"). In Bailey, "Clintonomics," 96.
82. Bob Woodward, *The Agenda. Inside the Clinton White House* (New York: Simon & Schuster, 1994), 317–319.
83. Ross Perot and Pat Choate, *Save your Job, Save your Country: Why NAFTA Must be Stopped-Now!* (New York: Hyperion Books, 1993).
84. Eric M. Uslaner, "Let the Chits Fall Where They May? Executive and Constituency Influences on Congressional Voting on NAFTA," *Legislative Studies Quarterly* 23.3 (August 1998), 347–371.
85. Robert A. Pastor, *Exiting the Whirlpool. U.S. Foreign Policy Toward Latin America and the Caribbean.* 2nd ed. (Boulder, CO: Westview Press, 2001), 114.
86. Personal interview with a former member of U.S. State Department's NAFTA task force, Washington, DC, May 30, 2006.

87. Weintraub, "The North American Free Trade Agreement," 31.
88. Council of the Americas Meeting on May 3–4, 1993, Washington, DC. Reported in *Inside U.S. Trade*, "Clinton officials trumpet NAFTA support, prod business to lobby Congress," May 7, 1993.
89. See analysis by Hufbauer and Schott, *Western Hemisphere Economic Integration*.
90. For an account on the Mexican domestic politics preceding the crisis, see Peter H. Smith, "The Mexican Peso Crisis," in *East Asia and Latin America. The Unlikely Alliance*, ed. Peter H. Smith, Kotaro Horisaka, and Shoji Nishijima (Lanham, MD: Rowman & Littlefield Publishers, Inc., 2003), 187–208.
91. John Bailey, "Deterioro del Apoyo de la Opinión Pública al TLC en Estados Unidos. Dinámica Regional y Partidista, 1994–1996," in *Impactos del TLC en México y Estados Unidos. Efectos Subregionales del Comercio y la Integración Económica* (Mexico, DF: Facultad Latinoamericana de Ciencias Sociales/Georgetown University, 2003), 271–299.
92. Robert A. Pastor and Rafael Fernandez de Castro, "Congress and Mexico," in Pastor and Fernandez, *Controversial Pivot*, 47.
93. Chile and Canada, faced with U.S. lack of interest in Chile's accession, signed a free trade agreement in 1996. Modeled in NAFTA, the Chile-Canada free trade agreement was seen as a preparation for Chile's entrance into NAFTA. The preamble of the Chile-Canada free trade agreement includes the resolution of the parties to "facilitate the accession of Chile to the *North American Free Trade Agreement*." The full text of the agreement is available at the OAS/SICE database of trade agreements, at http://www.sice.oas.org/trade/chican_e/chcatoc.asp
94. The descriptive part of this section was based substantially on I.M. Destler, "Congress and Foreign Trade," in Pastor and Fernandez, *Controversial Pivot*, 121–146.
95. Norman Ornstein, "The New Congress," in Pastor and Fernandez, *Controversial Pivot*, 103.
96. Marc Levinson, "Kantor's Cant. The Hole in Our Trade Policy," *Foreign Affairs* (March/April 1996), 7.
97. The report "The Failed Experience. NAFTA at Three Years," released on June 26, 1997, was a joint publication of the Economic Policy Institute, Institute for Policy Studies, International Labor Rights Fund, Public Citizen's Global Trade Watch, Sierra Club, and U.S. Business and Industrial Council Educational Foundation. The Executive Summary is available at http://www.epi.org/content.cfm/studies_failedexp
98. The results in the House of Representatives followed party lines: on the Republican side, there were 151 votes in favor against 71 rejecting ratification. Among Democrats, rejection votes reached 171 against 29 in favor of the agreement. For a review of the process in Congress, see Lenore Sek, "Trade Promotion Authority (Fast-Track Authority for Trade Agreements): Background and Developments in the 107th Congress," *CRS Issue Brief for Congress*, updated January 14, 2003 (Washington, DC: U.S. Library of Congress/CRS, 2003).
99. Allen Myerson, "In Texas, Labor is Feeling Trade Accord's Pinch," *The New York Times*, May 8, 1997, 1.
100. Manuel Pastor, Jr. and Carol Wise, "Trading Places: U.S. Latinos and Trade Liberalization in the Americas," in *Borderless Borders. U.S. Latinos, Latin*

Americans, and the Paradox of Interdependence, ed. Frank Bonilla et al. (Philadelphia: Temple University Press, 1998), 35–51.
101. On the Seattle battle, see Mary Kaldor, "'Civilising' Globalisation? The Implications of the 'Battle in Seattle,'" *Millennium: Journal of International Studies* 29.15 (2000), 105–114; Ronaldo Munck, "The Anti-Globalization Movement. From Seattle (1999) to the Future," in *Globalization and Contestation. The New Great Counter-Movement* (London; New York: Routledge, 2007), 57–74.
102. David E. Sanger, "The shipwreck of Seattle," *The New York Times*, December 5, 1999, 26.
103. Nancy Bernkopf Tucker, "The Clinton Years: The Problem of Coherence," in *Making China Policy: Lessons from the Bush and Clinton Administrations*, ed. Ramon Myers, Michel Oksenberg, and David Shambaugh (Lanham, MD: Rowman & Littlefield Publishers, Inc., 2001), 68–69.
104. For the tone of discussions between economists, see Jeffrey Frankel, "The Crusade for Free Trade: Evaluating Clinton's International Economic Policy," *Foreign Affairs* 80.2 (March-April 2001), http://www.foreignaffairs.org/20010301fareviewessay4270/jeffrey-frankel/the-crusade-for-free-trade-evaluating-clinton-s-international-economic-policy.html
105. William J. Clinton, *Address Before a Joint Session of the Congress on the State of the Union*, February 4, 1997, http://www.presidency.ucsb.edu/ws/index.php?pid=53358
106. On the shift in Clinton's foreign policy, see James M. McCormick, "Clinton and Foreign Policy. Some Legacies for a New Century," in Schier, *Postmodern President*, 60–83.
107. Clinton, *Address Before a Joint Session of the Congress*.
108. Alexander F. Watson, Assistant Secretary for Inter-American Affairs, *Key Issues in Inter-American Relations*, U.S. Department of State Dispatch 1994, vol. 5, no. 3, 26. In Cox, *US Foreign Policy*, 146, fn.34.
109. Palmer, David Scott Palmer, *US Relations with Latin America during the Clinton Years* (Gainesville, FL: University Press of Florida, 2006), 92–95.
110. Pastor, *Exiting the Whirlpool*, 109–134. Pastor was national security adviser to the Carter administration and senior adviser to the Clinton administration in the case of Haiti.
111. Personal interview with a national security adviser to the Clinton administration, Washington, DC, March 21, 2006.
112. Quoted in Raymont, *Troubled Neighbors*, 289.
113. In the U.S. foreign policy to the Caribbean, for instance, the lack of an articulated vision on foreign policy led to an increasing interference of domestic groups representing particular interests of individual nations in the region. Thomas Carothers, "Lessons for Policymakers," in *Haitian Frustrations. Dilemmas for US Policy. A Report of the CSIS Americas Program*, ed. George Fauriol (Washington, DC: Center for Strategic and International Studies, 1995), 121–122.
114. Economist Jeffrey E. Garten articulated the strategy at the beginning of the first Clinton administration, identifying as the ten emerging markets: China, India, Indonesia, South Korea, Mexico, Brazil, Argentina, Poland, Turkey, and South Africa. His ideas were later published in his book *The Big Ten: Big Emerging Markets and How They will Change our Lives* (New

York: Basic Books, 1997). A brief assessment of the strategy is offered by Richard A. Melanson, *American Foreign Policy since the Vietnam War. The Search for Consensus from Richard Nixon to George W. Bush*, 4th ed. (Armonk, NY: M.E. Sharpe, 2005), 270–280.
115. The advantages for U.S. national security interests of bilateral cooperation, in relation to Brazil's System for Surveillance of the Amazon (SIVAM), are addressed in E. Peter Wittkoff, "Amazon Surveillance System (SIVAM): US and Brazilian Cooperation." (Master's diss., Naval Postgraduate School, Monterey, California, December 1999).
116. Alexander F. Watson, Assistant Secretary for Inter-American Affairs, *The Americas in the 21st Century: the US-Brazilian Relationship*. U.S. Department of State Dispatch, December 12, 1994.
117. President Fernando Henrique Cardoso, in *The President's News Conference with President Fernando Cardoso of Brazil in Brasilia*, October 14, 1997. Administration of William J. Clinton, 1997, http://bulk.resource.org/gpo.gov/papers/1997/1997_vol2_1354.pdf
118. President Bill Clinton, in *The President's News Conference with President Fernando Cardoso of Brazil in Brasilia*, October 14, 1997. Administration of William J. Clinton, 1997, http://bulk.resource.org/gpo.gov/papers/1997/1997_vol2_1356.pdf
119. George W. Bush, *State of the Union Address Before a Joint Session of the Congress on Administration Goals*, February 27, 2001. Available at the "American President Project" website, at http://www.presidency.ucsb.edu/ws/print.php?pid=29643
120. Robert B. Zoellick, quoted in Melanson, *American Foreign Policy*, 213.
121. Robert B. Zoellick, "A Republican Foreign Policy," *Foreign Affairs* 79.1 (2000), 63–78.
122. Kenneth Kidd, "Baker Says Free Trade May Prod Other Nations. Pact Could Result in 'Market Liberalization Club'," *Toronto Star*, June 23, 1988, ME2.
123. Zoellick, "A Republican Foreign Policy," 72.
124. Project for the New American Century, "Statement of Principles," June 3, 1997, http://www.newamericancentury.org/statementofprinciples.htm
125. William Kristol and Robert Kagan, "Toward a Neo-Reaganite Foreign Policy," *Foreign Affairs* 75.4 (July/August 1996), 18–32.
126. On the Bush Doctrine, see Robert Jervis, "Understanding the Bush Doctrine," in *American Foreign Policy in a New Era* (Abingdon; New York: Routledge, 2005), 79–101.
127. George W. Bush's interview with Bob Woodward. Quoted in Bob Woodward, *Bush at War* (New York: Simon & Schuster, 2002), 96.
128. Ibid., 341.
129. Arthur Schlesinger, Jr., "Eyeless in Iraq: The Bush Doctrine and Its Consequences," in *War and the American Presidency* (New York: W.W. Norton & Company, 2004), 35; Peter Singer, *The President of Good & Evil. The Ethics of George W. Bush* (Melbourne: The Text Publishing Company, 2004).
130. Woodward, *Bush at War*, 131.
131. Robert B. Zoellick, Statement at the Fourth WTO Ministerial Conference, Doha, Qatar, November 9–13, 2001 (WT/MIN(01)/ST/3).
132. As president George W. Bush stated, "Together with friends and allies from Europe to Asia and Africa to Latin America, we will demonstrate that the

forces of terror cannot stop the momentum of freedom." Address Before a Joint Session of the Congress on the State of the Union, January 29, 2002, http://www.presidency.ucsb.edu/ws/print.php?pid=29644

133. George W. Bush, *Steel Products Proclamation to Facilitate Positive Adjustment to Competition from Imports of Certain Steel Products, by the President of the United States*. White House, Office of the Press Secretary, March 5, 2002, http://www.whitehouse.gov/news/releases/2002/03/20020305-7.html

134. Kevin K. Ho, "Trading Rights and Wrongs: The 2002 Bush Steel Tariffs," *Berkeley Journal of International Law* 21 (2003), 825–846.

135. The fall was even more pronounced when specific products categories of products were taken into account, reaching 74 percent for steel plates, 86 percent for cold rolled products, and almost 100 percent for galvanized products. Brazilian Embassy, *US Barriers to Brazilian Goods, Services and Investment*, Washington, DC, October 2002, 8.

136. Brazilian Embassy, *US Barriers to Brazilian Goods*, 84.

137. Lenore Sek, "Trade Promotion Authority (Fast-Track Authority for Trade Agreements): Background and Developments in the 107th Congress," *CRS Issue Brief for Congress*, Congressional Research Service, updated January 2002 (Washington, DC: U.S. Library of Congress/CRS, 2002), 6.

138. U.S. Public-Law, 107–210.

139. The potential beneficiaries of the Andean Trade Promotion and Drug Eradication Act, previously named the Andean Trade Preference Act are Bolivia, Colombia, Ecuador, and Peru. The Caribbean Basin Trade Partnership Act of 2000 provided NAFTA-parity in market access potentially to countries located in Central America and the Caribbean Basin. NAFTA-parity.

140. ASEAN currently includes 10 members: Brunei, Cambodia, Indonesia, Laos, Malaysia, Myanmar, Philippines, Singapore, Thailand, and Vietnam. On the initiative, see White House, *Expanding Opportunity. The Enterprise for ASEAN Initiative*, http://www.whitehouse.gov/infocus/international-trade/aseaninitiative.html

141. The full texts of the bilateral trade agreements can be accessed at the USTR website, at http://www.ustr.gov

142. Critical views of this politicization of trade pacts can be found in Jeffrey Schott, "Assessing US FTA Policy," in *Free Trade Agreements*, 359–381; Sidney Weintraub, "History Repeats Itself in Trade Policy," *CSIS Issues in International Political Economy* 34 (October 2002), http://www.csis.org/media/csis/pubs/issues200210.pdf

143. Office of the United States Trade Representative, *2003 Trade Policy Agenda and 2002 Annual Report on the Trade Agreements Program* (Washington, DC: U.S. Government Printing Office, 2003), 29.

144. According to Arturo Valenzuela, "in an era when the heads of state in the Americas meet frequently, scrutinized by ubiquitous media attention, the elements of foreign policy based on petty retributions became widely known." In "The United States and Latin America: The Road Ahead," LASA *Forum* XXXV.4 (Winter 2005), 9.

145. Griswold's analysis of the trade-related votes of the 107th Congress (2001–2002) shows that while Republicans are more willing to vote for tariff cuts, there was no substantial difference between parties in the issue of agricultural

subsidies. Daniel T. Griswold, "Free Trade, Free Markets. Rating the 107th Congress," Center for Trade Policy Studies, January 2003, http://www.freetrade.org/pubs/pas/tpa-022.pdf
146. Edmund E. Andrews, "How CAFTA Passed House by 2 Votes," *The New York Times*, July 29, 2005.
147. In 2002, the tariffs imposed on these products were: sugar (U.S.$338 per over-quota metric ton), tobacco (350 percent per over-quota), ethanol (2.5 percent ad valorem plus U.S.$0.52 per gallon), orange juice (U.S.$ 0.785 per liter), and textiles (38 percent ad valorem, plus U.S.$ 0.485 per kilo). In Brazilian Embassy, *US Barriers*, 9.
148. Data from the World Steel Association, http://www.worldsteel.org/?action=newsdetail&id=285
149. Lula da Silva then commented that he would not respond to "the deputy of the deputy of the American deputy secretary". Neil King and Jonathan Karp, "A Global Journal Report: US, Brazil Key to Trade Quest–Nations Need to Open their Markets in Hemisphere's Treaty Plan," *Wall Street Journal*, November 4, 2002, A13.
150. Howard Wiarda, *Dilemmas of Democracy in Latin America. Crises and Opportunity*. With the assistance of Esther M. Skelley (Lanham, MD: Rowman & Littlefield Publishers, Inc., 2005), 155.
151. John G. Ruggie, "International Regimes, Transactions, and Change: Embedded Liberalism in the Postwar Economic Order," *International Organization* 36.2 (Spring 1982), 379–415.
152. On the alignment of social forces, see Peter A. Gourevitch, "Reinventing the American State: Political Dynamics in the Post-Cold War Era," in Katznelson and Shefter, *Shaped by War and Trade*, 301–330; Hiscox, "The Magic Bullet?," 670.
153. For the concept of whirlpool in U.S. foreign policy to Latin America, see Robert Pastor, *Exiting the Whirlpool. U.S. Foreign Policy Toward Latin America and the Caribbean*, 2nd ed. (Boulder, CO: Westview Press, 2001).

6 Brazilian Foreign Trade Policy: Instrument for an Autonomous Nation

1. Ambassador João Augusto de Araújo Castro, "O Congelamento do Poder Mundial," *Revista Brasileira de Estudos Políticos* 33 (January 1972), 30. Original in Portuguese: "Nenhum país escapa a seu destino e, feliz ou infelizmente, o Brasil está condenado à grandeza...As soluções medíocres e pequenas não convém nem interessam ao Brasil....Ou aceitamos nosso destino como país grande, livre e generoso, sem ressentimentos e sem preconceitos, ou corremos o risco de permanecer à margem da História, como povo e como nacionalidade."
2. Justin Robertson presents six analytical categories of foreign policymaking in developing countries, consisting of: (i) conventional diplomacy; (ii) new state capacity, which focuses on the use of new techniques and technology to deal with increasing complexity of issues; (iii) capital-driven, highlighting the role of capitalist interests behind foreign policy; (iv) marginalization, in which the constraints imposed by international regimes and powerful states greatly diminish the scope for foreign policymaking in developing contexts;

(v) regime or elite survival, or foreign policy as a power dispute between self-interested regimes and/or elites; and (vi) privatization, which emphasizes the role of non-state actors as actors in foreign policy. In "Introduction: The Research Direction and Typology of Approaches," in *Diplomacy and Developing Nations. Post-Cold War Foreign-Policy Making Structures and Processes*, ed. Justin Robertson and Maurice A. East (Abington; New York: Routledge, 2005), 1–35.

3. For a classic study of Brazilian foreign policymaking, see Maria Regina Soares de Lima, "The Political Economy of Brazilian Foreign Policy. Nuclear Energy, Trade, and Itaipú" (PhD diss., Vanderbilt University, Nashville, August 1986).

4. According to Neack, the term "middle power" can be applied to describe "states that commit their relative affluence, managerial skills, and international prestige to the preservation of the international order and peace...serving as international mediators and 'go-betweens'" (224). She then lists among the middle powers Canada, Australia, the Netherlands, Norway, Sweden, Brazil, Mexico, Algeria, and India. See Laura Neack, "Linking State Type with Foreign Policy Behavior," in *Foreign Policy Analysis. Continuity and Change in its Second Generation*, ed. Laura Neack, Jeanne A. K. Hey, and Patrick J. Haney (Englewood Cliffs, NJ: Prentice Hall, 1995), 215–228. For the notion of Brazil as a middle power, see Ricardo Sennes, "Mudanças da Política Externa Brasileira na Década de 1980: uma Potência Média Recém-Industrializada." (Master's diss., Department of Political Science, University of Sao Paulo, 1996).

5. Joaquim Nabuco, "The Nationality Sentiment in the History of Brazil," address to the Hispanic Club of the Yale University, May 15, 1908. Quoted in Celso Lafer, "Brazilian International Identity and Foreign Policy: Past, Present, and Future," *Daedalus Journal of the American Academy of Arts and Sciences* 129.2 (Spring 2000), 207.

6. On the need to consider both economic and political variables in the assessment of states' goals, see Lawrence Krause and Joseph Nye, "Reflections on the Economics and Politics of International Economic Organizations," *International Organization* 29.1 (Winter 1975), 323–342.

7. An interdisciplinary study on the FTAA from a Brazilian perspective is offered in Tullo Vigevani and Marcelo Passini Mariano, *ALCA. O Gigante e os Anões* (Sao Paulo: Editora SENAC, 2001).

8. For economic evaluations of the impact conducted in Brazil, see Honorio Kume and Guida Piani, "Alca: Uma Estimativa do Impacto no Comércio Bilateral Brasil-Estados Unidos," IPEA *Texto para Discussão* No.1058, Rio de Janeiro, December 2004; João Alberto de Negri, Jorge S. Arbache e Maria L.F. Silva, "A Formação da Alca e seu Impacto no Potencial Exportador Brasileiro para os Mercados dos Estados Unidos e do Canadá," IPEA *Texto para Discussão* No.991, Brasíia, October 2003. For a recent estimate, which points to the FTAA potentially providing more trade benefits to Mercosur than a Mercosur-EU trade agreement, see G. Philippidis and A.I. Sanjuán, "An Analysis of Mercosur's Regional Trade Agreements," *The World Economy* 30.3 (2007), 504–531.

9. On the convergence of different interpretations of Brazil's role in South America toward the notion of the country's hegemony in the subcontinent, see Octávio Ianni, *Diplomacia e Imperialismo na América Latina*, Cadernos CEBRAP no.12, Sao Paulo, 1973.

10. In August 2009 Brazil signed cooperation agreements with Bolivia, and announced it would fund a highway in that country, with estimated investment of more than U.S.$ 300 million.
11. Annex I, Article I of Decree no.3959 of October 10, 2001.
12. CAMEX's attributions are defined by Decree n.4732, of June 10, 2003. A summary of its functions can be found at the Brazilian Ministry of Development, Industry and Foreign Trade website at http://www.mdic.gov.br/sitio/interna/interna.php?area=1&menu=433
13. Ben Ross Schneider, *Politics within the State. Elite, Bureaucrats and Industrial Policy in Authoritarian Brazil* (Pittsburgh, PA: University of Pittsburgh Press, 1991), 7.
14. Edson Nunes describes Brazil's "political grammar" as characterized by four main components, namely, clientelism, corporatism, bureaucratic insulation, and universalism of procedures. In *A Gramática Política do Brasil. Clientelismo e Insulamento Burocrático*, 3rd ed. (Rio de Janeiro: Jorge Zahar Editor, 2003).
15. On the insulation of federal regulatory agencies set up by the Cardoso administration in the 1990s, see Paulo T.L. Mattos, "A Formação do Estado Regulador," *Novos Estudos CEBRAP* 76 (November 2006), 152–154, http://www.cebrap.org.br/imagens/Arquivos/a_formacao_do_estado_regulador.pdf. For critical views of the insulation strategy, see Carlos R. Pio da Costa Filho, "Liberalização do Comércio: Padrões de Interação entre Elites Burocráticas e Atores Sociais," in *Reforma do Estado e Democracia no Brasil: Dilemas e Perspectivas*, ed. Eli Diniz and Sergio de Azevedo (Brasília: Universidade de Brasília, 1997), 174–184; David Stark and Laszlo Bruzt, "Enabling Constraints: Fontes Institucionais de Coerência nas Políticas Públicas no Pós-Socialismo," *Revista Brasileira de Ciências Sociais* 13.36 (1998), 13–40.
16. The term "efficiency islands" was commonly applied in Brazil to agencies with an outstanding performance in a predominantly inefficient bureaucratic structure, and which were usually "protected by the presidency through insulation." For a history of the institutional development of Itamaraty, see Zairo Borges Cheibub, "Diplomacia e Construção Institucional: O Itamaraty em uma Perspective Histórica," *Dados* 28.1 (1985), 113–31.
17. Former Itamaraty members have been invited to occupy high positions in various ministries. The military, in particular, much appreciated the institution, with a growing presence of diplomats in other ministries during the military regime. See Alexandre de S.C. Barros, "The Formulation and Implementation of Brazilian Foreign Policy: Itamaraty and the New Actors," in *Latin American Nations in World Politics*, ed. Heraldo Muñoz and Joseph Tulchin (Boulder, CO: Western Press, 1984), 33.
18. As Brazilian diplomat Paulo Roberto de Almeida remarks critically, "the 'excellence of Itamaraty' is certainly one of the most entrenched beliefs in our professional group, having obtained a reasonable level of public acceptance, both internally and externally." In Paulo Roberto de Almeida, *Relações Internacionais e Política Externa do Brasil. História e Sociologia da Diplomacia Brasileira*, 2nd ed. (Porto Alegre: Editora da UFRGS, 2004), 185. Original in Portuguese: "a 'excelência do Iamaraty' é certamente uma das crenças mais arraigadas em nosso estamento profissional, tendo obtido um grau razoável de aceitação pública, interna e externamente."

19. See, for instance, Maurice A. East, "Conclusion: The Narrowing Distinction and Cross-cutting Comparative Observations," in Robertson and East, *Diplomacy and Developing Nations*, 258. In the area of international trade negotiations, references to the high quality of the Brazilian diplomats are common and can be traced back to their activism in the multilateral trading system since the birth of the GATT in 1947.
20. In the words of Ambassador Luiz Felipe Lampréia, "Brazilian diplomacy does not invent interests, it identifies and projects them." See Luiz Felipe Lampréia, *Diplomacia Brasileira. Palavras, Contextos e Razões*, 2nd ed. (Rio de Janeiro: Editora Nova Aguilar, 1999), 314. Original in Portuguese: "a diplomacia brasileira não inventa interesses, ela os identifica e projeta." However, multiple interests and power sites exist in any society and the task of selecting what interests should count as national interests remains. See Leticia Pinheiro, "How Much Foreign Policy Teaching Can Be Foreign Policy Making?," Paper delivered at the 4th Annual APSA Conference on Teaching and Learning in Political Science, Charlotte, North Carolina, February 9–11, 2007.
21. Andrew Hurrell, "The Politics of Regional Integration in MERCOSUR," in *Regional Integration in Latin America and the Caribbean: The Political Economy of Open Regionalism*, ed. Victor Bulmer-Thomas (London: Institute of Latin American Studies, University of London., 2001), 195.
22. See Maria Regina Soares de Lima, "Ejes Analíticos y Conflicto de Paradigmas en la Política Externa Brasileña," *América Latina/Internacional* 1.2 (October 1994), 31–33; Letícia Pinheiro, "Unidades de Decisão e Processo de Formulação de Política Externa durante o Regime Militar," in *Sessenta Anos de Política Externa Brasileira (1930–1990). Prioridades, Atores e Políticas*, vol. IV, ed. José Augusto Guilhon Albuquerque (Sao Paulo: Anablume/NUPRI/USP, 2000), 449–474; Ronald M. Schneider, *Brazil. Foreign Policy of a Future World Power* (Boulder, CO: Westview Press, 1976), 101–107.
23. Former minister of foreign affairs Celso Lafer maintains that while many people can discuss national identity, for diplomats, their position in the debate has direct practical consequences. In Celso Lafer, "Preface" to *O Itamaraty na Cultura Brasileira*, ed. Carlos Leal (Rio de Janeiro: Livraria Francisco Alves Editora S.A., 2002), 10–11.
24. Afonso Arinos de Mello Franco, quoted in *Brazil Herald*, Rio de Janeiro, July 23 1962. Reproduced in E. Bradford Burns, *The Unwritten Alliance. Rio-Branco and Brazilian-American Relations* (New York: Columbia University Press, 1966).
25. In the period of the post-independence monarchy, many diplomats and foreign ministers came from the wealthy sugar-producing states in the northeast. Under the Republic, with the growing importance of coffee in the south-center, that area became the new source for young diplomats. E. Bradford Burns, "Tradition and Variation in Brazilian Foreign Policy," *Journal of Inter-American Studies* 9.2 (1967), 202.
26. Alberto da Costa e Silva, "Diplomacia e Cultura," in Leal, *O Itamaraty na Cultura Brasileira*, 22. Original in Portuguese: "não apenas o seu imperador fazia parte das grandes famílias reais européias, mas que suas elites se entroncavam nas nobrezas do Velho Continente." The claim was highly problematic as it neutralized the fact that Black slaves formed the base of Brazilian society.

27. For an analysis of the contributions of individual diplomats in the formation of the Brazilian culture, see Leal, *O Itamaraty na Cultura Brasileira*; Teresa Malatian, "Diplomacia e Letras na Correspondência Acadêmica: Machados de Assis e Oliveira Lima," *Estudos Históricos* 13.24 (1999), 377–392.
28. André Botelho, "Circulação de Idéias e Construção Nacional: Ronald de Carvalho no Itamaraty," *Estudos Históricos* 35 (2005), 1–32.
29. The Itamaraty palace was built in the capital city of Rio de Janeiro in the mid-1850s, and was purchased in 1889 to host the Republican Provisional Government. In 1897, the palace was ceded to the Ministry of Foreign Affairs. The edifice which had hosted presidents and military staff was transformed into the headquarters of the Brazilian diplomacy and remained so until 1974, when the ministry was transferred to the new capital, Brasilia. Brazilian Minister of Foreign Affairs, *Palácio Itamaraty. Resenha Histórica e Guia Descriptivo* (Rio de Janeiro: Imprensa Nacional, 1937).
30. For a detailed historical account of the Baron of Rio Branco's role in Brazilian diplomacy, see Burns, *Unwritten Alliance.*
31. Burns, "Tradition and Variation," 197.
32. Celso Lafer, *A Identidade Internacional do Brasil e a Política Externa Brasileira. Passado, Presente e Futuro* (Sao Paulo: Editora Perspectiva S.A., 2004), 47.
33. Burns argues that by avoiding partisan politics, Rio Branco succeeded in associating the idea of foreign policy with that of a "unified nationality," in *Unwritten Alliance*, 57.
34. Cheibub, "Diplomacia e Construção Institucional."
35. See Zairo Borges Cheibub, "A Carreira Diplomática no Brasil: O Processo de Burocratização do Itamarati," *Revista de Administração Pública* 23.2 (1989), 97–128.
36. The phrase is attributed to former minister of foreign affairs, Antonio Francisco Azevedo da Silveira. Original in Portuguese: "a melhor tradição do Itamaraty é saber renovar-se."
37. On the experience of reforms of diplomatic institutions in France and Germany in order to respond to demands on international trade issues, see Paul Gordon Lauren, *Diplomats and Bureaucrats* (Stanford: Hoover Institution Press, 1976), 154–177.
38. Ambassador Paulo Tarso Flecha de Lima, who worked on the development of foreign trade functions in Itamaraty in the 1970s, offers a detailed account of the reforms in "Diplomacia e Comércio: Notas sobre a Política Externa Brasileira nos Anos 70," in *Sessenta Anos de Política Externa 1930–1990. Diplomacia para o Desenvolvimento*, vol. 2, ed. José Augusto Gilhon de Albuquerque (Sao Paulo: Cultura/NUPRI-USP, 1996), 219–237.
39. Luiz Felipe Lampréia and Ademar Seabra da Cruz Jr., "Brazil: Copying with Structural Constraints," in Robertson and East, *Diplomacy and Developing Nations*, 97–113.
40. In 2001, the responsibilities of the Economic Department (under the General Sub-Secretariat of Integration, Economic and Foreign Trade Issues) were enhanced to include the proposal of guidelines in foreign trade negotiations, including market access, trade remedies and safeguards, services, investment, international flow of capital, and intellectual property, among others. See Article 18 of Decree N.3959, of October 10, 2001.

41. For a recent analysis of the relevance of studies of diplomatic culture, see Andrew Hurrell, "Working with Diplomatic Culture: Some Latin American and Brazilian Questions," Paper prepared for ISA Meeting, Montreal, March 2004.
42. On the inter-bureaucratic disputes of power during the 1970s, see Barros, "Formulation and Implementation," 35.
43. Alexandre de S.C. Barros, "A Formação das Elites e a Continuação da Construção do Estado Nacional Brasileiro," *Dados* no.15 (1977), 114–115.
44. See comparison in Barros, "A Formação das Elites," Zairo Borges Cheibub, "Diplomacia e Formação do Estado Nacional," *Política e Estratégia* 5.1 (1987), 56–68.
45. Lafer, *A Identidade Internacional do Brasil e a Política Externa Brasileira*, 21.
46. Norma Breda dos Santos, "História das Relações Internacionais no Brasil: Esboço de uma Avaliação sobre a Área," *História* 24.1 (2005), 11–39.
47. Pinheiro defines paradigm in diplomacy as the "the identification of theories of diplomatic action made up by a set of ideas which constitute a view of the nature of the international system on the part of the policymakers." See Leticia Pinheiro, "Traídos pelo Desejo: Um Ensaio sobre a Teoria e a Prática da Política Externa Brasileira Contemporânea," *Contexto Internacional* 22.2 (June–December 2000), 308. Original in Portuguese: "a identificação de teorias de ação diplomática formadas por um conjunto de idéias que constitui a visão da natureza do sistema internacional por parte dos formuladores de política."
48. For the political economy of trade liberalization in Brazil, see Marcelo de Paiva Abreu, "Trade Liberalization and the Political Economy of Protection in Brazil since 1987," *Working Paper* SITI-08b, IDB-INTAL, Buenos Aires, 2004.
49. Monica Hirst and Maria Regina Soares de Lima, "Contexto Internacional, Democracia e Política Externa," *Política Externa* 11.2 (2002), 78–98.
50. The role of the Brazilian state in economic development has been a central subject of research on the country. See, for instance, Peter Evans, *Dependent Development. The Alliance of Multinational, State, and Local Capital in Brazil* (Princeton, NJ: Princeton University Press, 1979); Kathryn Sikkink, *Ideas and Institutions. Developmentalism in Brazil and Argentina* (Ithaca and London: Cornell University Press, 1991). For comparative studies including Brazil, see Atul Kohli, *State-Directed Development. Political Power and Industrialization in the Global Periphery* (New York: Cambridge University Press, 2004), particularly chapters 4 and 5; Gilmar Masiero, "Pragmatism and Planning in East Asia and Brazil," in *East Asia and Latin America. The Unlikely Alliance*, ed. Peter H. Smith, Kotaro Horisaka, and Shoji Nishijima (Lanham, MD: Rowman & Littlefield Publishers, Inc., 2003), 109–129.
51. For an analysis of the relation between nationalism and economic policies in Latin America during the 1930s, see Eduardo Devés Valdés, "O Pensamento Nacionalista na América Latina e a Reivindicação da Identidade Econômica," *Estudos Históricos* 10. 20 (1997), 321–343.
52. A detailed review of the impact of the Second World War and its aftermath on Latin American economies is offered by Marcelo de Paiva Abreu, "Latin America: The External Context, 1928–1982," in *Cambridge Economic History*

of Latin America, Volume II. The Long 20th Century, ed. Victor Bulmer-Thomas, John H. Coatsworth, and Roberto Cortés-Conde (Cambridge;; New York: Cambridge University Press, 2006), 101–134.
53. Sikkink, *Ideas and Institutions*, 12.
54. Nathaniel H. Leff, *Economic Policy-Making and Development in Brazil, 1947–1964* (New York;; London; Sydney; Toronto: John Wiley & Sons, Inc., 1968), 4. Leff also highlights the role of economic policymakers in pushing the developmentalist project autonomously, even when different visions existed among the business groups in Brazil.
55. Ibid., 48.
56. Costa Filho, "Liberalização do Comércio," 189. See also Mario Marconini, "Trade Policy-Making Process in Brazil," Paper presented at the London School of Economics, May 25, 2005.
57. Sikkink, *Ideas and Institutions*, 24; 129–132.
58. On the synchronicity between Brazilian trade diplomacy and the interests of the "congressional-industrialist coalition," see Maria Regina Soares de Lima and Fabiano Santos, "Brazilian Congress and Foreign Trade Policy," Paper prepared for the 1998 meeting of the Latin American Studies Association, Chicago, Illinois, September 24–26, 1998, 11–12.
59. For reviews of the paradigms, see Lima, "Ejes Analíticos," 36–37; Pinheiro, "Traídos pelo Desejo," 308–312.
60. Maria Regina Soares de Lima and Mônica Hirst, "Brazil as Intermediate State and Regional Power: Action, Choice and Responsibilities," *International Affairs* 82.1 (2006), particularly 22–25.
61. On the relations between the two countries, from the late 1800s through the 1930s, see Joseph Smith, *Unequal Giants: Diplomatic Relations between the United States and Brazil, 1889–1930* (Pittsburgh, PA: University of Pittsburgh Press, 1991).
62. W. Michael Weis, "Pan American Shift: Oswaldo Aranha and the Demise of the Brazilian-American Alliance," in *Beyond the Ideal. Pan-Americanism in Inter-American Affairs,* ed. David Shenin (Westport, CT: Greenwood Press, 2000), 139–140.
63. In 1905, Brazil announced its decision to send an ambassador to Washington, DC. In an analysis of the decision at the time, a Chilean diplomat commented that the Brazilian alliance with the United States was advantageous to Brazil, which perceived itself as "destined to exercise in South America part of the hegemony which the United States...exercises over all America." Quoted in Burns, *Unwritten Alliance,* 192, fn. 68.
64. By 1902, about 94.5 percent of Brazilian exports to the United States entered free, despite the fact that there was no import duty exemption for U.S. products in Brazil. Burns, *Unwritten Alliance*, 63.
65. On the influence of U.S. military doctrines among the Brazilian military, see José Augusto Guilhon Albuquerque, "As Relações Brasil-EUA na Percepção dos Militares," in *A Política Externa Brasileira na Visão dos Seus Protagonistas,* ed. Henrique Altemani de Oliveira and José A. Guilhon Albuquerque (Rio de Janeiro: Editora Lumen Juris, 2005), 15–27.
66. In 1953, during the negotiations of the Brazilian debt with the Eximbank, Ambassador Oswaldo Aranha, then minister of finance, stated, "we welcome investments that will be governed here and not govern us. We need them badly, but we are not asking for them. You don't invite in your house people

who ask for guarantees to enter, guarantees to stay and guarantees to leave." Quoted in Weis, "Pan American Shift," 145.
67. Jânio Quadros, "Brazil's New Foreign Policy," *Foreign Affairs* 40 (1961), 19–27.
68. Ibid., 22.
69. On the ideological consistency between the political orientation of the new government and the foreign policy changes, see Keith Larry Storrs, "Brazil's Independent Foreign Policy, 1961–1964. Background, Tenets, Linkage to Domestic Politics, and Aftermath" (PhD diss., Cornell University, Ithaca, NY, 1973).
70. Quadros, "Brazil's New Foreign Policy," 27.
71. See Fernando Henrique Cardoso, "O Modelo Político Brasileiro," in *O Modelo Político Brasileiro e Outros Ensaios*, 2nd ed. (Sao Paulo: Corpo e Alma do Brasil, 1973), 50–82.
72. For a comparison of the two doctrines, see Ambassador Gelson Fonseca Jr., "Mundos Diversos, Argumentos Afins: Notas sobre Aspectos Doutrinários da Política Externa Independente e do Pragmatismo Responsável," in *Sessenta Anos de Política Externa. Crescimento, Modernização e Política Externa*, vol.1, ed. José Augusto Guilhon Albuquerque (Sao Paulo: Cultura Editores Associados/NUPRI, 1996), 299–336.
73. In conversations with former U.S. secretary of state and national security adviser, Henry Kissinger, Brazil's minister of foreign affairs Antonio Francisco Azeredo da Silveira argued that Brazil could assist the United States in the development of "a more constructive dialogue with other countries," particularly in South America. He also clarified that Brazil's recognition of Angola's independence was less a manifestation of Third Worldism than a result of Brazil's interests in Africa. Henry Kissinger, *Years of Renewal* (New York: Simon and Schuster, 1999), 741–742.
74. See Araújo Castro, "O Congelamento do Poder," 18–19.
75. Brazil's rejection of the nonproliferation treaty on nuclear armaments during the military regime exemplifies the diplomatic ability to combine the pursuit of national autonomy with the anti-asymmetries discourse in the international system.
76. During the elaboration of the ITO Charter, Brazil and Australia defended the right to differentiated treatment of products with the purpose of fostering national industrialization. For a detailed review of the Brazilian position in multilateral trade negotiations through 1990, see Marcelo de Paiva Abreu, "O Brasil e o GATT: 1947–1990," in Albuquerque, *Diplomacia para o Desenvolvimento*, 201–218.
77. A system for nonreciprocal concession of trade preferences to developing countries—the Generalized System of Preferences—had been adopted under the UNCTAD II, in 1968. Since the system violated the most favored nation principle, it was necessary to obtain a derogation to make it compatible with the GATT. Such derogation was granted in 1971 for an initial period of a decade. In 1979, at the end of the Tokyo Round, the GATT members agreed on the "Enabling Clause," which in practice consolidated the GSP as a legal exception.
78. Abreu, "O Brasil e o GATT," 204–207.
79. Paulo Cabral de Mello, "O Brasil e os Problemas Econômicos Mundiais," *Revista Brasileira de Estudos Políticos* 42 (January 1976), 155–156. Quoted in Schneider, *Brazil*, 34.

80. Mônica Hirst, "Pesos y Medidas de la Política Exterior Brasileña," in *América Latina: Políticas Exteriores Comparadas,* vol.1, ed. Juan Carlos Puig (Buenos Aires: Editor Latinoamericano, 1984), 181.
81. Mônica Hirst, *The United States and Brazil. A Long Road of Unmet Expectations.* Contemporary Inter-American Relations Series (New York: Routledge, 2005), 8.
82. Lima, "Diplomacia e Comércio," 235–236.
83. In 1971, the United States accounted for 38 percent of the foreign direct investment and reinvestment in Brazil. In 1978, the U.S. share had decreased to 28 percent, while West Germany's had risen from 11 to 15 percent, Japan's from 4 to 10 percent and Switzerland's from 6 to 12 percent. Wayne A. Selcher, "Brazil in the World: Multipolarity as Seen by a Peripheral ADC Middle Power," in *Latin American Foreign Policies. Global and Regional Dimensions,* ed. Elizabeth G. Ferris and Jennie K. Lincoln (Boulder, CO: Westview Press, 1981), 89.
84. Schneider, *Brazil,* xiii.
85. Kissinger, *Years of Renewal,* 744.
86. Ambassador Gelson Fonseca Jr., "O Pensamento Brasileiro em Relações Internacionais: o Tema da Identidade Nacional (1950–1995)," in *A Legitimidade e Outras Questões Internacionais* (Sao Paulo: Paz e Terra, 1998), 272–273.
87. In an empirical study on national role conceptions, six out of ten foreign policy officials interviewed in Brazil during 1967 and 1968 identified internal development as a priority, with the second most cited national role (2) being that of independent or nonaligned nation. K.J. Holsti, "National Role Conceptions in the Study of Foreign Policy," *International Studies Quarterly* 14 (1970), 274, Table 2.
88. Alexandre S.C. Barros notes that at the early stages of the military regime, in contrast to the reshuffle of staff observed in other state agencies, Itamaraty was preserved from military intervention, and rather than being divested from their positions, diplomats were invited to exercise state functions outside the diplomatic sphere. In "The Formulation and Implementation,"32–33.
89. On the differences of perspectives on foreign policy among the military, and the domestic politics that led to the dominance of the visions of the Responsible Pragmatism policy, see Pinheiro "Unidades de Decisão," 449–474; Mônica Hirst, "Democratic Transition and Foreign Policy: The Experience of Brazil," in Munoz and Tulchin, *Latin American Nations,* 218–219.
90. Lima, *Political Economy;* Pinheiro, "Traídos pelo Desejo."
91. Selcher, "Brazil in the World," 91.
92. An in-depth and up-to-date analysis of the postmilitary Brazilian foreign policy from the mid-1980s to the Lula administration is offered by Tulllo Vigevani and Gabriel Cepaluni in *Brazilian Foreign Policy in Changing Times: The Quest for Autonomy from Sarney to Lula.* Translated by Leandro Moura (Lanham: Lexington Books, 2009).
93. Expressions of the globalist paradigm in the postmilitary government included the move to full political recognition of Cuba and Vietnam, and the resumption of closer diplomatic relations with China and the former Soviet Union.
94. For a historical overview of the politics behind Mercosur's formation, see Janina Onuki, "Brasil-Argentina: Do Conflito à Cooperação," in Oliveira and Albuquerque, *Política Externa Brasileira,* 29–44.

95. For the politics of the Latin American Free Trade Association, from the 1960s through 1990, see Rubens Barbosa, "O Brasil e a Integração Regional: A ALALC e a ALADI (1960–1990)," in Albuquerque, *Sessenta Anos de Política Externa*, vol. 2, 135–168.
96. As Ambassador Gelson Fonseca Jr. describes it, autonomy involves both a doctrinaire and a concrete dimension. Thus, "one thing is, for instance, the wish to expand exchange with developing countries, another is to have the concrete means to allow that to happen." Fonseca Jr., "Mundos Diversos," 305. Original in Portuguese: "uma coisa é, por exemplo, a vontade de ampliar o intercâmbio com os países em desenvolvimento, outra é dispor de meios concretos que permitam que tal aconteça."
97. For a detailed analysis of the transformations in Brazil's foreign trade policymaking in the last two decades, see Pedro da Motta Veiga, "Política Comercial no Brasil: Características, Condicionantes Domésticos e Policy-Making," in *Políticas Comerciais Comparadas. Desempenho e Modelos Organizacionais*, ICONE, FIPE, and DFID (Sao Paulo: Editora Singular, 2007), 71–162.
98. Regis Bonelli, Pedro da Motta Veiga, and Adriana Fernandes de Brito, "As Políticas Industrial e de Comércio Exterior no Brasil: Rumos e Indefinições," IPEA *Texto para Discussão* No.527, Rio de Janeiro, November 1997.
99. For an analysis of the foreign policy under President de Mello, see Ademar Seabra da Cruz Junior, Antonio Ricardo F. Cavalcante, and Luiz Pedone, "Brazil's Foreign Policy Under Collor," *Journal of Interamerican Studies and World Affairs* 35.1 (1993), 119–144; Mario Antonio M. de Carvalho Vieira, "Idéias e Instituições: Uma Reflexão sobre Política Externa Brasileira do Início da Década de 90," *Contexto Internacional* 23.2 (2001), particularly 249–255.
100. On the use of the "past" as a reference to think the present, see Vieira, "Idéias e Instituições," 267–273; and Pinheiro, "Traídos pelo Desejo," 312.
101. Ambassador Roberto Abdenur, "A Política Externa Brasileira e o 'Sentimento de Exclusão'," in Fonseca Jr. and Castro, *Temas da Política Externa Brasileira II*, 32.
102. As former minister of foreign affairs Rubens Ferreira de Mello stated in 1948, "the diplomatic art does not belong to the domain of sentiments; it is, at first, realist, and it is characterized by the interests which is upon itself to defend, almost always of a permanent nature," in *Gênese e Evolução da Diplomacia*, Master Lecture, Instituto Católico de Direito Comparado da Pontifícia Universidade Católica do Rio de Janeiro (Rio de Janeiro: Ministry of Foreign Affairs, 1948), 18. Original in Portuguese: "a arte diplomática não pertence ao domínio do sentimento; ela é, antes de tudo, realista, e se caracteriza pelos interesses que lhe incumbe defender, quase sempre de natureza permanente."
103. Former minister of foreign affairs Lafer defends the notion of Brazil's soft power, based on what he describes as credibility deriving from the country's capacity to act as an international consensus-builder. In Lafer, *A Identidade Internacional do Brasil e a Política Externa Brasileira*, 76–78.
104. Gelson Fonseca Jr., "Alguns Aspectos da Política Externa Brasileira Contemporânea," in *A Legitimidade e Outras Questões*, 358–359. Original in Portuguese: "suas idéias ou, mais precisamente, as bases conceituais de suas ações internacionais."

105. José Maria Arbilla, "Arranjos Institucionais e Mudança Conceitual na Política Externa Argentina e Brasileira (1989–1994)," *Contexto Internacional* 22.2 (July–December. 2000), 359.
106. During the 1970s, Ambassador Castro used the term 3 "Ds" to refer to the three main issues that should orient the UN's activities. In 1993, Ambassador Celso Amorim, as minister of foreign affairs, adapted the term to the new world context, changing the emphasis on decolonization to democracy. See speech given during the opening of the 48th Session of the United Nations General Assembly, New York, September 27, 1993. Reproduced in Celso Luiz Nunes Amorim, "Uma Diplomacia Voltada para o Desenvolvimento e a Democracia," in Gelson Fonseca Jr. and Castro, *Temas da Política Externa Brasileira* II, 19–29.
107. For the notion of "autonomy through distance" and "autonomy through participation," see Fonseca Jr., "Alguns Aspectos da Política Externa," 359–367. A similar comparison is developed through the notions of "autonomy through detachment" and "autonomy through integration," in Tullo Vigevani, Marcelo F. de Oliveira, and Rodrigo Cintra, "Política Externa do Governo FHC: A Busca da Autonomia pela Integração," *Tempo Social* 15.2 (November 2003), 31–61.
108. For a Brazilian diplomatic perspective on the EAI, signaling the priority for Mercosur of the multilateral negotiations, see Celso Amorim and Renata Pimentel, "Iniciativa para as Américas: 'O Acordo do Jardim das Rosas'," in Albuquerque, *Sessenta Anos de Política Externa*, vol.2, 103–133.
109. Ambassador Rubens A. Barbosa and Luís Fernando Panelli César, "A Integração Sub-Regional, Regional e Hemisférica: O Esforço Brasileiro," in Fonseca Jr. and Castro, *Temas de Política Externa Brasileira II*, 285–303.
110. For a summary of Cardoso's intellectual path, see Mauricio A. Font, "Introduction" to *Charting a New Course. The Politics of Globalization and Social Transformation*, by Fernando Henrique Cardoso. Edited by Mauricio A. Font (Oxford; Lanham, MD: Rowman & Littlefield Publishers, Inc., 2001), 1–34.
111. For his autobiography, see Fernando Henrique Cardoso, *A Arte da Política. A História que Vivi* (Rio de Janeiro: Editora Civilização Brasileira, 2006). For an adapted and shorter version of his memoirs published in English, see *The Accidental President of Brazil: A Memoir* (Cambridge, MA: Public Affairs, 2006).
112. Werner Baer and Claudio Paiva, "Brazil's Drifting Economy. Stagnation and Inflation During 1987–1996," in *What Kind of Democracy? What Kind of Market? Latin America in the Age of Neoliberalism*, ed. Phillip D. Oxhorn and Graciela Ducatenzeiler (University Park, PA: The Pennsylvania State University Press, 1998), 89–126.
113. Rosemary Thorp, *Progress, Poverty and Exclusion: An Economic History of Latin America in the 20th century* (Washington, DC: Inter-American Development Bank, 1998), 255.
114. Marcelo de Paiva Abreu, "O Brasil e o GATT: 1947–1990," in Albuquerque, *Sessenta Anos de Política Externa*, vol.2, 213.
115. See Carlos Pio, "A Estabilização Heterodoxa no Brasil: Idéias e Redes Políticas," *Revista Brasileira de Ciências Sociais* 16.46 (June 2001), 29–54; Federico Neiburg, "Economistas e Culturas Econômicas no Brasil e na Argentina. Notas para uma Comparação a Propósito das Heterodoxias,"

Tempo Socia Revista de Sociologia da USP 16.2 (November 2004), 177–202. The political empowerment of economists in Brazil is analyzed by Maria Rita Loureiro in *Os Economistas no Poder* (Sao Paulo: Editora da Fundação Getúlio Vargas, 1997).

116. Pérsio Arida and Andé Lara Resende became known for their work on ways to address the phenomenon of inertial inflation. On their association with neostructrualism, see Nora Lustig, "From Structuralism to Neostructuralism: The Search for a Heterodox Paradigm," in *The Latin American Development Debate. Neostructuralism, Neomonetarism, and Adjustment Processes*, ed. Patricio Meller (Boulder, CO: Westview Press, 1991), 38.

117. As President Cardoso once declared, "Brazil is so large and so diverse it is possible to be radical." Interview with Rosemary Thorp, April1 997. Quoted in Thorp, *Economic History*, 256.

118. Pedro da Motta Veiga, "Brazil in Mercosur: Reciprocal Influence," in Riordan Roett, ed., *Mercosur. Regional Integration, World Markets* (Boulder, CO: Lynne Rienner Publishers, 1999), 28.

119. Paulo Totti, "Definido prazo de integração das Américas," *Gazeta Mercantil*, December 12, 1994.

120. Amado Luiz Cervo, "Neoliberalism and the Historiography of International Relations: Influences in Argentina and Brazil," Paper prepared for the 20th International Conference of Historical Sciences, Sydney, July 3–9, 2005.

121. Pinheiro, "Traídos pelo Desejo," particularly 318–328.

122. Vigevani, Oliveira, and Cintra, "Política Externa do Governo FHC."

123. Paulo Fagundes Vizentini, "From FHC to Lula (1995–2004): Brazil's Foreign Policy and Regional Integration," Paper prepared for the 20th International Conference of Historical Sciences, Sydney, July 3–9, 2005.

124. On pragmatic institutionalism, see Pinheiro, "Traídos pelo Desejo." For the development and application of the notion of "autonomy through integration" during the Cardoso government, see Vigevani, Oliveira, and Cintra, "Política Externa do Governo FHC."

125. On Mercosur's persistent institutional deficit, see Mario Carranza, "Clinging Together: Mercosur's Ambitious External Agenda, Its Internal Crisis, and the Future of Regional Economic Integration in South America," *Review of International Political Economy* 13.5 (December 2006), 802–829.

126. As president, Cardoso used to refer to Machiavelli's *The Prince* as fundamental to understanding politics.

127. See for instance, Vizentini, "From FHC to Lula," 2.

128. Fernando Henrique Cardoso, "Globalization and Politics," in *Charting a New Course. The Politics of Globalization and Social Transformation*. Edited and introduced by Mauricio A. Font (Oxford; Lanham, MD: Rowman & Littlefield Publishers, Inc., 2001), 244–250.

129. Cardoso, "Viable Utopia," in *Charting a New Course*, 282–283.

130. Quoted in João Resende-Santos, "Fernando Henrique Cardoso. Social and Institutional Rebuilding in Brazil," in *Technopols. Freeing Politics and Markets in Latin America in the 1990si*, Jorge Domínguez (University Park, PA: The Pennsylvania State University Press, 1997), 180.

131. Fernando Henrique Cardoso, "'Teoria da Dependência' ou Análises Concretas de Situações de Dependência?" in *O Modelo Político Brasileiro*, 2nd ed. (Sao Paulo: Difusão Européia do Livro, 1973), 124.

132. Cardoso, "O Modelo Político Brasileiro," in *O Modelo Político*, 71. Original in Portuguese: "Eu não penso, entretanto, que a burguesia local, fruto de um capitalismo dependente, possa realizar uma revolução econômica no sentido forte do conceito. A sua 'revolução' consiste em integrar-se no capitalismo internacional como associada e dependente. Lutando, naturalmente, para obter o máximo de proveito possível. Mas limitada por um processo objetivo: a acumulação capitalista nas economias dependentes não se completa."
133. Cardoso, "Viable Utopia."
134. For a commented collection of Ambassador Lampréia's speeches during his time as minister, see Luiz Felipe Lampréia, *Diplomacia Brasileira. Palavras, Contextos e Razões*, 2nd ed. (Rio de Janeiro: Editora Nova Aguilar, 1999).
135. Lafer was chief of the Brazilian mission to the WTO and to the United Nations. He was president of the WTO Dispute Settlement Body in 1996 and president of the WTO General Council in 1997. From 1999 to 2001, he headed the Ministry of Development, Industry and Trade.
136. For a detailed institutionalist analysis of the reconceptualization of foreign policy under Cardoso, see Flavia de Campos Mello, "Regionalismo e Inserção Internacional: Continuidade e Transformação da Política Externa Brasileira nos Anos 90" (PhD diss., Department of Political Science, University of Sao Paulo, September 2000).
137. Vieira, "Idéias e Instituições," 268; and Sergio Danese, *Diplomacia Presidencial* (Rio de Janeiro: Topbooks, 1999).
138. In the words of Cardoso, "there are things which, for their very nature, presuppose a vocation of tradition, of contact with the past. Diplomacy, for reasons of content and form, is certainly one of them." Preface to Luiz Felipe Lampréia, *Diplomacia Brasileira. Palavras, contextos e razões*, 2nd ed. (Rio de Janeiro: Editora Nova Aguilar, 1999), 7. Original in Portuguese: "há coisas que, por sua própria natureza, possuem uma vocação de tradição, de contato com o passado. A diplomacia, por razão de fundo e forma, é certamente uma delas."
139. See views of former minister of foreign affairs Luiz Felipe Lampréa, in Lampréia and Cruz Jr., "Brazil."
140. For Brazil's commitments in the security area and its implications for the Western Hemisphere, see Mônica Herz, "Brazilian Foreign Policy since 1990 and the Pax Americana," in *Between Compliance and Conflict: East Asia, Latin America, and the "New" Pax Americana*, ed. Jorge Domínguez and Byung-Kook Kim (New York: Routledge, 2005), 165–192.
141. Sylvia Ferreira Marques, "A Imagem Internacional do Brasil no Governo Cardoso (1995–2002). Uma Leitura Construtivista do Conceito de Potência Média" (Master's diss., Pontifícia Universidade Católica do Rio de Janeiro, Rio de Janeiro, 2005).
142. In the words of Celso Lafer, "the search for development and of the possible autonomy, in our day requires integration to the world economy which in turn presupposes the expansion of our exports." In "O Brasil e sua Inserção no Mundo," in Lafer, *Mudam-se os Tempos. Diplomacia Brasileira, 2001–2002* (Brasília: Fundação Alexandre de Gusmão/Instituto de Pesquisa de Relações Internacionais, 2002), 173. Original in Portuguese: "A busca do desenvolvimento e da autonomia possível, nos dias de hoje, requer a integração na economia mundial, a qual, por sua vez, pressupõe a expansão de nossas exportações."

143. The Brazilian initiative raised concerns from the Mexican government, which saw it as clear manifestation of Brazil's hegemonic ambitions in South America. O Estado de S. Paulo, "Cúpula Sul-Americana preocupa mexicanos," June 11, 2000, A8.
144. Veiga, "Brazil in Mercosur"; Carranza, "Clinging Together."
145. Ricardo A. Markwald describes three structural limitations of Mercosur: the asymmetries of size of the economies involved, differences in the productive structures of each member, and conflictive monetary and exchange rate policies. Ricardo A. Markwald, "2003: Novo Mercosul?," in *Governo Lula. Novas Prioridades e Desenvolvimento Sustentado*, ed. João Paulo dos Reis Velloso (Rio de Janeiro: Editora José Olympio, 2003), 373–388.
146. Veiga, "Brazil in Mercosur," 30.
147. For the data used in this section and a detailed analysis of Brazil's agricultural profile, see Mario Jales et al., "Agriculture in Brazil and China. Challenges and Opportunities," Occasional Paper No.44, Intal/ITD, Buenos Aires, October 2006, http://www.iadb.org/INTAL/aplicaciones/uploads/publicaciones/i_INTALITD_OP_44_2006_Jank_Jales_Yao_Carter_.pdf
148. Brazilian minister of development, industry and foreign trade, "Estados Unidos terminam o ano como principal parceiro commercial do Brasil," posted January 4, 2010, http://www.siscomex.com.br/topic/10231-mdic-estados-unidos-terminam-o-ano-como-principal-parceiro-comercial-do-brasil/
149. Negri, Arbache, and Silva, "A Formação da Alca," 8–9.
150. Andre M. Nassar, Zuleika Arashiro, and Marcos S. Jank, "Tariff Spikes and Tariff Escalation," in *Handbook on International Trade Policy*, ed. William A. Kerr and James D. Gaisford (Cheltenham; Northampton, MA: Edward Elgar, 2006), 236.
151. Kume and Piani, "Alca."
152. On the impact on Brazil of an erosion of preferences within the ALADI system, see the study by Rubens Barbosa & Associados, FIESP, and ICONE. *A Erosão das Preferências Comerciais Brasileiras na América Latina*. Sao Paulo, November 2004:
http://www.fiesp.com.br/publicacoes/pdf/relacoes/estudo_erosao.pdf
153. See speech by minister of foreign affairs, Luiz Felipe Lampréia, at the opening ceremony of the III FTAA Trade Ministerial Meeting, Belo Horizonte, May 18, 1997. Reprinted in Lampréia, *Diplomacia Brasileira*, 316–317.
154. Brazil, unlike the United States, did not chair any of the working groups established from 1995 through 1998, which seems to indicate cautious participation in the initial phase of the FTAA process.
155. Cardoso, *A Arte da Política*, 626–627.
156. An explanation of Brazil's foreign policy rationale is provided by the Brazilian ambassador to the United States, 1999–2004, Rubens A. Barbosa, in "A View from Brazil," *The Washington Quarterly* 24.2 (2001), 149–157.
157. Tullo Vigevani, "Brazilian Foreign Policy at the End of the Twentieth Century: An Exercise in Autonomy through Integration." Paper prepared for the 20th Conference of Historical Sciences, Sydney, July 3–9, 2005.
158. Celso Lafer, "A Importância da Alca para o Brasil," in *Mudam-se os Tempos*, 203.
159. Ibid., 210. Original in Portuguese: "se a Alca nos puder assegurar condições melhores e mais previsíveis de acesso aos mercados do Hemisfério, em troca

da consolidação de reformas que de qualquer maneira teriam que ser feitas de forma autônoma, haveria a possibilidade de ganhos consideráveis para o País."
160. Regis Bonelli, Pedro da Motta Veiga, and Adriana Fernandes de Brito, "As Políticas Industrial e de Comércio," *IPEA Texto para discusssão* 527, Rio de Janeiro, November 1997.
161. Eli Diniz and Renato Boschi, "Globalização, Herança Corporativa e a Representação dos Interesses Empresariais: Novas Configurações no Cenário Pós-Reformas," in *Elites Políticas e Econômicas no Brasil Contemporâneo*, ed. Renato Boschi, Eli Diniz, and Fabiano Santos. Série Pesquisas n.18 (Sao Paulo: Fundação Konrad Adenauer, 2000), 16–17.
162. Personal interview with Sandra Rios, consultant to the *Confederação Nacional das Indústrias* (CNI).
163. Wagner Praton Mancuso and Amâncio Jorge de Oliveira, "Abertura Econômica, Empresariado e Política: os Planos Doméstico e Internacional," *Lua Nova* 69 (2006), 147–172.
164. Various associations in the agribusiness, together with the Federation of Industries of the State of Sao Paulo, funded the establishment of the Institute for International Trade Negotiations (Icone) in 2003. Icone was Brazil's first research institute created with the specific purpose of expanding knowledge of and influencing international trade negotiations.
165. While CUT defended the inclusion of a social clause in the FTAA, it rejected the same proposal in the multilateral trade negotiations. See Marconini, "Trade Policy-Making," 9.
166. For the list of members and official positions, see REBRIP's webpage, www.rebrip.org.br
167. The model was later reproduced to the Mercosur-EU negotiations, with the establishment of SENEUROPA.
168. Participants include the CNI, the CUT, and the General Confederation of Workers (CGT).
169. Veiga, "Política Comercial."
170. See Hirst and Lima, "Contexto Internacional," 92.
171. Celso Ming, "O plebiscito da Alca," *Jornal da Tarde*, September 12 , 2002.
172. Luiza Damé, "Plebiscito contabiliza cerca de 10 milhões contra a Alca," *Folha de São Paulo*, September 18 , 2002.
173. In early 2003, Workers' Party's Senator, Eduardo Suplicy, submitted a legal project for the creation of a Brazilian version of the U.S. trade promotion authority, based on which congressional assessment would precede any decision to sign free trade agreements.
174. Emir Sader and Ken Silverstein, *Without Fear of Being Happy. Lula, the Workers Party and Brazil* (London; New York: Verso, 1991), 3.
175. Ibid., 104.
176. On the Workers' Party experience at the municipal level, see Gianpaolo Baiocchi, *Radicals in Power. The Workers' Party (PT) and Experiments in Urban Democracy in Brazil* (London; New York: Zed Books, 2003); Brian Wempler, *Participatory Budgeting in Brazil: Contestation, Cooperation, and Accountability* (University Park, PA: The Pennsylvania State University Press, 2007).
177. Alan Touraine, "A Volta da Esperança," *Folha de São Paulo*, October 4, 2002.

178. Boaventura de Sousa Santos, "A Importância de ser Brasileiro," *Correio Sindical Mercosul*, October 2002.
179. Alistair Scrutton, "Brazil's Lula Says War-Focused Bush Ignores Latam," Reuters, September 18, 2002.
180. Celso Ming, "O PT e o projeto da Alca," O Estado de S. Paulo, July 10, 2002, B2.
181. Folha de São Paulo, "PT não participará da organização do plebiscito," August 11, 2002. Reprinted in *Correio Sindical Mercosul* no.124, August 11–17, 2002.
182. Interview transcribed in Sader and Siverstein, *Without Fear*, 164.
183. Wendy Hunter, "The Normalization of an Anomaly. The Workers' Party in Brazil," *World Politics* 59 (April 2007), 440–475.
184. As the 2010 presidential elections approached, ideological conflicts among key figures of the party once again reinforced the sense of abandonment of a more radical agenda.
185. Keith Larry Storrs developed a similar argument for the case of 'president Quadros' Independent Foreign Policy. In "Brazil's Independent Foreign Policy."
186. Anthony Jarvis, "Societies, States and Geopolitics: Challenges from Historical Sociology," *Review of International Studies* 15 (1989), 283.
187. Arbilla, "Arranjos Institucionais."
188. Ambassador Amorim's speech during the opening of the 48th Session of the United Nations General Assembly, New York, September 27, 1993. Reprinted in Celso Luiz Nunes Amorim, "Uma Diplomacia Voltada para o Desenvolvimento e a Democracia." In Fonseca Jr. and Castro, *Temas da Política Externa Brasileira II*, 19–29.
189. Celso Amorim, "A Inserção Global do Brasil," in Velloso, *Governo Lula*, p.353. Original in Portuguese: "Ao voltarmos os olhos para o mercado internacional de bens, serviços, tecnologia, temos que nos perguntar se devemos nos resignar a tentativas de integração sem qualificações no contexto vigente, ou se nossa inserção global pressupõe um esforço—em coordenação com outros parceiros governamentais e não governamentais—pela promoção de condições mais equânimes de competição e distribuição de frutos."
190. Interview with Ambassador Samuel Pinheiro Guimarães, former director of Itamaraty's Research Institute on International Relations. Correio Braziliense, "O Inimigo Número 1 da Alca," April 19, 2001.
191. Ibid.
192. Ambassador Samuel Pinheiro Guimarães, "A Alca e o Fim do Mercosul," in *Quinhentos Anos de Periferia. Uma Contribuição ao Estudo da Política Internacional*, 3rd ed. (Porto Alegre: Contraponto, 2001), 133. Original in Portuguese: "pois (o Brasil) veria reduzida drasticamente, com a ALCA e o acordo com a União Européia, a possibilidade legal de utilizar os mecanismos de política indusrtial, tecnológica e comercial para acelerar a acumulacao interna de capital, necessária ao aumento da produtividade, da producao e da renda de sua poulacao crescente." For an updated compilation of his reflections, see Samuel Pinheiro Guimarães, *Desafios Brasileiros na Era dos Gigantes* (Rio de Janeiro: Contraponto, 2005).
193. Ambassador Samuel Pinheiro Guimarães. Speech delivered during his inauguration ceremony as Secretary General of External Relations, Brasília, January 9, 2003. Original in Portuguese: "são os três únicos países que

aparecem simultaneamente, nas relações dos dez países de maior território, de maior população, de maior produto." http://www.mre.gov.br/index.php?Itemid=64&id=19&option=com_content&task=view

194. Lima and Hirst, "Brazil as Intermediate State," 30, fn.22.
195. Decree N.4759, of June 21, 2003, particularly Articles 14 through 19. For the current organizational structure, including a new department for negotiations with Mexico, Central America, and the Caribbean under the Sub-Secretariat of South America—see Decree N.5979, of December 6, 2006.
196. Paulo Sotero, "Tropeço isola país nas negociações da Alca," *O Estado de S. Paulo*, October 5, 2003.
197. Amauri Arrais, "Para ex-embaixador, mudança prejudica serviço diplomático," *Folha de São Paulo*, January 13, 2005; Luciana Brafman e Carolina Brígido, "Mudança na prova do Rio Branco é criticada," *O Globo*, January 12, 2005; Luiz Orlando Carneiro, "Itamaraty rebate críticas sobre prova de inglês," *JB Online*, January 15, 2005: http://jbonline.terra.com.br/jb/papel/brasil/2005/01/14/jorbra20050114004.html
198. Ambassador Roberto Abdenur, interview with Otávio Cabral."A Marcha da Insensatez," *Veja*, February 5, 2007. Original in Portuguese: "Há um sentimento generalizado de que os diplomatas hoje são promovidos de acordo com sua afinidade política e ideológica, e não por competência."
199. O Estado de S. Paulo, "Itamaraty discute posição brasileira com ministérios," November 6, 2003, B10.
200. Arbilla, "Arranjos Institucionais," 347.
201. Miriam Gomes Saraiva, "As Estratégias de Cooperação Sul-Sul nos Marcos da Política Externa Brasileira de 1993 a 2007," *Revista Brasileira de Política Internacional* 50.2 (2007), 45–46.
202. Veiga, "Política Comercial," 116–126.
203. For a reflection on the relevance of the World Social Forum, see Boaventura de Sousa Santos, *The Rise of the Global Left. The World Social Forum and Beyond* (New York: Zed Books, 2006).
204. Nicholas Winning, "Thousands march against FTAA at Brazil's Forum," *Reuters*, January 27, 2003.
205. For coverage of the reactions in Brazil, see O Estado de S. Paulo, "Especialista ve armadilhas para o Brasil," February 12, 2003; "Alca: proposta americana é discriminatória," February 14, 2003.
206. In May 2006, I conducted a brief search for the term "Alca" in the database of O Estado, which contains articles published in *O Estado de S. Paulo* and *Jornal da Tarde*. Between 01/01/1998 and 12/31/2001, only 134 entries for the term were located. Between 01/01/2003 and 03/01/2004, the number of entries rose to 336. After the stagnation of negotiations in 2004, it declined again, with only 88 entries registered between 07/01/2004 and 05/10/2006.
207. Through the *à la carte* FTAA approach, once a minimum common framework was agreed, the parties would be allowed to negotiate market access and rules, bilaterally or plurilaterally Marcos S. Jank and Zuleika Arashiro, "Free Trade Area of the Americas: Where are we? Where could we be headed?," in *Free Trade in the Americas: Getting There from Here*, ed. The Inter-American Dialogue (Washington, DC: The Inter-American Dialogue, 2004), 27–34.

208. This low enthusiasm was cited by all Brazilian representatives of the business sector, media and think tanks during personal interviews.
209. An example of the asymmetrical concession is the schedule for tariff elimination between Brazil and Venezuela. While Brazil committed to eliminate the tariffs on approximately 91 percent of the negotiated products within five years, Venezuela's commitment in the same period covered only 16 percent of its products. CNI, "Mercosul-CAN: Fracos Resultados em Termos do Acesso a Mercados para o Brasil," *Comércio Exterior em Perspectiva* 14.1/2 (October–November 2004), 1–9.
210. These preferential agreements covered a small list of products and are not expected to have a significant trade impact. See CNI, "As Relações Comerciais do Brasil com a India e a África do Sul," *Comércio Exterior em Perspectivca* 14.8/9 (May–June 2005), 1–8.
211. The declaration was signed between Mercosur and Saudi Arabia, Qatar, Bahrain, the United Arab Emirates, Kuwait, and Oman. David Fleischer, *Brazil Focus*, Weekly Report January 6–19, 2007.
212. For an analysis of the G20, see Amrita Narlikar and Diana Tussie, "The G20 at the Cancún Ministerial: Developing Countries and their Evolving Coalitions in the WTO," *The World Economy* 27.7 (2004), 947–966.
213. On the importance of developing markets for Brazilian agricultural exports, see Mario Queiroz de Monteiro Jales, "Inserção do Brasil no Comércio Inernacional Agrícola e Expansão dos Fluxos Comerciais Sul-Sul," Instituto de Estudos do Comércio e Negociações Internacionais, Sao Paulo, September 2005, http://www.iconebrasil.org.br/arquivos/noticia/10.pdf
214. Mecosur abc, "Brasil quiere retomar negociaciones con Europa," July 19, 2006. Reprinted in *Correo Sindical Latinoamericano* no.28, July 1–25, 2006.
215. O Estado de S. Paulo, "EUA querem impor suas condições para negociar a Alca," February 14–15, 2005.
216. Miami Herald, "Lula: El Alca no está en la agenda de Brasil," April 24, 2005.
217. Minister of Foreign Affairs Celso Amorim, quoted in Folha de São Paulo, "Alca nao sai antes de 2009, diz Amorim," May 20, 2005.
218. ABC Digital, "Amorim cree más viable un acuerdo Mercosur-EE.UU. que salvar el ALCA," February 12, 2007. Original in Spanish: "Intentar resucitar el ALCA exige un esfuerzo muy grande...Creo que es mucho mejor que pensemos en asociaciones bilaterales," http://www.abc.com.py/articulos.php?fec=2007-02-12&pid=310346&sec=12
219. It appears, therefore, that both the PSDB and the Workers' Party saw selective participation as instrumental in legitimizing previously defined foreign policy options.
220. Cardoso, *A Arte da Política*, 629. Original in Portuguese: "Posteriormente, já no governo Lula, substituiu-se a dificuldade crescente em dar passos à frente por uma mudança de postura fundamental: tanto o governo americano como o brasileiro resolveram colocar de lado o princípio do *single undertaking*."
221. See Inter-American Dialogue, "A Second Chance. US Policy in the Americas," March 2009, http://www.thedialogue.org/PublicationFiles/A%20Second%20Chance,%20FINAL%20to%20post.pdf

Conclusion

1. Karl Polanyi, *The Great Transformation* (Boston: Beacon Press, 1957), 254.

Appendices

1. Document retrieved from the FTAA official website: http://www.ftaa-alca.org.
2. Document retrieved from the FTAA official website: www.ftaa-alca.org.

References

Abdenur, Roberto. "A Política Externa Brasileira e o 'Sentimento de Exclusão'." In *Temas de Política Externa Brasileira II*, edited by Gelson Fonseca Jr. and Sergio Henrique Nabuco de Castro. Sao Paulo: Paz e Terra, 1994.

Aberbach, Joel, Robert Putnam, and Bert Rockman. *Bureaucrats and Politicians in Western Democracies.* Cambridge, MA: Harvard University Press, 1981.

Abreu, Marcelo de Paiva. "Latin America: The External Context, 1928–1982." In *The Cambridge Economic History of Latin America, Volume II. The Long 20th Century*, edited by Victor Bulmer-Thomas, John H. Coatsworth, and Roberto Cortés-Conde. Cambridge; New York: Cambridge University Press, 2006.

———. "O Brasil e o GATT: 1947–1990." In *Sessenta Anos de Política Externa Brasileira (1930–1990). Diplomacia para o Desenvolvimento*, vol. 2, edited by José A. Guilhon Albuquerque. Sao Paulo: Cultura/NUPRI-USP, 1996.

———. "Trade Liberalization and the Political Economy of Protection in Brazil since 1987." Working Paper SITI-08b, IDB-INTAL, Buenos Aires, 2004.

Adler, Emanuel. *The Power of Ideology. The Quest for Technological Autonomy in Argentina and Brazil.* Berkeley: University of California Press, 1987.

Aggarwal, Vinod and Kun-Chin Lin. "Strategy without Vision: The U.S. and Asia-Pacific Economic Cooperation." In *APEC: The First Decade*, edited by Jürgen Rüland, Eva Manske, and Werner Draguhn. London: Curzon Press, 2002.

Aggestam, Lisbeth. "Role Theory and European Foreign Policy. A Framework of Analysis." In *The European Union's Roles in International Politics. Concepts and Analysis*, edited by Ole Elgström and Michael Smith. London: Routledge, 2006.

Agosin, Manuel R. and Ricardo Ffrench-Davis. "Trade Liberalization in Latin America." *CEPAL Review 50* (August 1993), 41–62.

Ahearn, Raymond J. and Alfred Reifman. *U.S. Interest in Western Hemisphere Free Trade.* US Congressional Research Service Report, November 12, 1993. Washington, DC: U.S. Library of Congress/CRS, 1993.

Albuquerque, José Augusto Gilhon de, ed. *Sessenta Anos de Política Externa 1930–1990. Diplomacia para o Desenvolvimento*, vol. 2. Sao Paulo: Cultura/NUPRI-USP, 1996.

———. "As Relações Brasil-EUA na Percepção dos Militares." In *A Política Externa Brasileira na Visão dos Seus Protagonistas*, edited by Henrique Altemani de Oliveira and José A. Guilhon Albuquerque Rio de Janeiro: Editora Lumen Juris, 2005.

Allison, Graham T. *Essence of Decision. Explaining the Cuban Missile Crisis.* Boston: Little Brown, 1971.

Almeida, Paulo Roberto de. *Relações Internacionais e Política Externa do Brasil. História e Sociologia da Diplomacia Brasileira.* 2nd ed. Porto Alegre: Editora da UFRGS, 2004.
Amorim, Celso. "A Inserção Global do Brasil." In *Governo Lula. Novas Prioridades e Desenvolvimento Sustentado,* edited by João Paulo dos Reis Velloso. Rio de Janeiro: Editora José Olympio, 2003.
———. Speech during the opening of the 48th Session of the United Nations General Assembly, New York, September 27, 1993. Reprinted in *Temas da Política Externa Brasileira II,* edited by Gelson Fonseca Jr. and Sergio Henrique Nabuco de Castro. Sao Paulo: Paz e Terra, 1994.
——— and Renata Pimentel. "Iniciativa para as Américas: 'O Acordo do Jardim das Rosas'." In *Sessenta Anos de Política Externa Brasileira (1930–1990). Diplomacia para o Desenvolvimento,* vol. 2, edited by José A. Guilhon Albuquerque. Sao Paulo: Cultura/NUPRI-USP, 1996.
Arashiro, Zuleika. "Preferências Comerciais Unilaterais: Cooperação ou Coerção? O Caso do Programa de Preferências Comerciais para os Andes." Master's dissertation, Fundação Getúlio Vargas/EAESP, São Paulo, 2004.
Arbilla, José Maria. "Arranjos Institucionais e Mudança Conceitual na Política Externa Argentina e Brasileira (1989–1994)." *Contexto Internacional* 22.2 (July-December 2000), 337–385.
Arriagada, Genaro. *Pinochet. The Politics of Power.* Boston, MA: Allen & Unwin, 1988.
Atkins, G. Pope. *Encyclopedia of the Inter-American System.* Westport, CT: Greenwood Press, 1997.
Axelrod, Robert and Robert O. Keohane. "Achieving Cooperation under Anarchy: Strategies and Institutions." *World Politics* 38.1 (October 1985), 226–254.
Babb, Sarah. *Managing Mexico. Economists from Nationalism to Neoliberalism.* Princeton, NJ: Princeton University Press, 2001.
Baer, Werner and Claudio Paiva. "Brazil's Drifting Economy. Stagnation and Inflation During 1987–1996." In *What Kind of Democracy? What Kind of Market? Latin America in the Age of Neoliberalism,* edited by Phillip D. Oxhorn and Graciela Ducatenzeiler. University Park, PA: The Pennsylvania State University Press, 1998.
Bailey, Christopher J. "Clintonomics." In *The Clinton Presidency. The First Term, 1992–1996,* edited by Paul S. Herrnson and Dilys M. Hill. Basingstoke: Macmillan Press Ltd/New York: St. Martin Press, 1999.
Bailey, John. "Deterioro del Apoyo de la Opinión Pública al TLC en Estados Unidos. Dinámica Regional y Partidista, 1994–1996." In *Impactos del TLC en México y Estados Unidos. Efectos Subregionales del Comercio y la Integración Económica.* Mexico, DF: Facultad Latinoamericana de Ciencias Sociales/Georgetown University, 2003.
Baiocchi, Gianpaolo. *Radicals in Power. The Workers' Party (PT) and Experiments in Urban Democracy in Brazil.* London; New York: Zed Books, 2003.
Baldwin, David A. "Neoliberalism, Neorealism, and World Politics." In *Neorealism and Neoliberalism. The Contemporary Debate,* edited by David A. Baldwin. New York: Columbia University Press, 1993.
Baldwin, Robert E. "Openness and Growth: What's the Empirical Evidence?." NBER Working Paper No. 9578, National Bureau of Economics Research, Cambridge, March 2003.
Barbosa, Rubens A. "A View from Brazil." *The Washington Quarterly* 24.2 (2001), 149–157.

———. "O Brasil e a Integração Regional: a ALALC e a ALADI (1960–1990)." In *Sessenta Anos de Política Externa Brasileira (1930–1990). Diplomacia para o Desenvolvimento*, vol. 2, edited by José A. Guilhon Albuquerque. Sao Paulo: Cultura/NUPRI-USP, 1996.

——— and Luís Fernando Panelli César. "A Integração Sub-Regional, Regional e Hemisférica: O Esforço Brasileiro." In *Temas da Política Externa Brasileira II*, edited by Gelson Fonseca Jr. and Sergio Henrique Nabuco de Castro. Sao Paulo: Paz e Terra, 1994.

Barkin, David. "A Constructive Labor Strategy for Free Trade." *Review of Radical Political Economics* 25.4 (December 1993), 133–145.

Barros, Alexandre de S.C. "A Formação das Elites e a Continuação da Construção do Estado Nacional Brasileiro." *Dados* no.15 (1977).

———. "The Formulation and Implementation of Brazilian Foreign Policy: Itamaraty and the New Actors." In *Latin American Nations in World Politics*, edited by Heraldo Muñoz and Joseph Tulchin. Boulder, CO: Western Press, 1984.

Barton, John H., Judith L. Goldstein, Timothy E. Josling, and Richard H. Steinberg. *The Evolution of the Trade Regime. Politics, Law and Economics of the GATT and the WTO.* Princeton and Oxford: Princeton University Press, 2006.

Bergsten, C. Fred. "A Renaissance for U.S. Trade Policy?." *Foreign Affairs* 81.6 (November/December 2002), 86–98.

———. "Open Regionalism." Working Paper 97–3, Peterson Institute for International Economics, Washington, DC, 1997. http://www.petersoninstitute.org/publications/wp/wp.cfm?ResearchID=152

———. "Globalizing Free Trade." *Foreign Affairs* 75.3 (May/June 1996), 105–120.

Bernal, Richard. "CARICOM: Externally Vulnerable Regional Economic Integration." In *Economic Integration in the Western Hemisphere*, edited by Roberto Bouzas and Jaime Ros. Notre Dame, IN; London: University of Notre Dame Press, 1994.

Bertrab, Hermann von. *Negotiating NAFTA. A Mexican Envoy's Account*. The Washington Papers 173. Westport; London: Praeger and Center for Strategic and International Studies, 1997.

———. *The World Trading System at Risk*. Princeton, NJ: Princeton University Press, 1991.

——— and Arving Panagaryia, eds. *Free Trade Areas or Free Trade? The Economics of Preferential Trade Arrangements*. Washington, DC: AEI Press, 1995.

Bielschowsky, Ricardo. "Evolución de las Ideas de la CEPAL." Revista de la CEPAL, Número Extraordinario, *CEPAL. Cincuenta Años. Reflexiones sobre América Latina y el Caribe*. Santiago: United Nations, 1998.

Biglaiser, Glen. *Guardians of the Nation? Economists, Generals, and Economic Reform in Latin America*. Notre Dame, IN: University of Notre Dame Press, 2002.

Birdsall, Nancy, Augusto de la Torre, and Rachel Menezes. *Washington Contentious: Economic Policies for Social Equity in Latin America*. Washington, DC: Carnegie Endowment for International Peace and Inter-American Dialogue, 2001.

Bisley, Nick. "East Asia's Changing Regional Architecture: Toward an East Asian Economic Community." *Pacific Affairs* 80.4 (2007), 603–625.

Bizzozero, Lincoln. "Uruguayan Foreign Policies in the 1990s: Continuities and Changes with a View to Recent Regionalisms." In *National Perspectives on the New Regionalism in the South*, edited by Björn Hettne, András Inotai, and Osvaldo Sunkel. Basingstoke; New York: Palgrave Macmillan, 2000.

Blyth, Mark. *Great Transformations. Economic Ideas and Institutional Change in the Twentieth Century.* Cambridge: Cambridge University Press, 2002.

———. "Any More Bright Ideas? The Ideational Turn of Comparative Political Economy." *Comparative Politics* 29.2 (January 1997), 229–250.

Bøas, Morten, Marianne H. Marchand, and Timothy M. Shaw. "The Weave-World: The Regional Interweaving of Economies, Ideas and Identities." In *Theories of New Regionalism. A Palgrave Reader*, edited by Fredrik Söderbaum and Timothy M. Shaw. Basingstoke; New York: Palgrave Macmillan, 2003.

Bonelli, Regis, Pedro da Motta Veiga, and Adriana Fernandes de Brito. "As Políticas Industrial e de Comércio Exterior no Brasil:Rumos e Indefinições." IPEA *Texto para Discussão* No.527, Rio de Janeiro, November 1997.

Botelho, André. "Circulação de Idéias e Construção Nacional: Ronald de Carvalho no Itamaraty." *Estudos Históricos* 35 (2005), 1–32.

Bouzas, Roberto and Jaime Ros, eds. *Economic Integration in the Western Hemisphere.* Notre Dame, IN; London: University of Notre Dame Press, 1994.

Brazilian Embassy. *US Barriers to Brazilian Goods, Services and Investment.* Washington, DC, October 2002, 8.

Brazilian Minister of Foreign Affairs. *Palácio Itamaraty. Resenha Histórica e Guia Descriptivo.* Rio de Janeiro: Imprensa Nacional, 1937.

Brown, M. Leann. *Developing Countries and Regional Economic Cooperation.* Westport, CT: Praeger Publishers, 1994.

Bryant-Tokalau, Jenny and Ian Frazer, eds. *Redefining the Pacific?: Regionalism. Past, Present and Future.* Aldershot; Burlington, VT: Ashgate, 2006.

Bulmer-Thomas, Victor. *The Economic History of Latin America since Independence.* 2nd ed. Cambridge: Cambridge University Press, 2003.

———, ed. *Regional Integration in Latin America and the Caribbean: The Political Economy of Open Regionalism.* London: Institute of Latin American Studies, University of London, 2001.

———, Nikki Craske, and Mónica Serrano, eds. *Mexico and the North American Free Trade.* New York: St. Martin's Press, 1994.

———, Nikki Craske, and Mónica Serrano. "Who Will Benefit?." In *Mexico and the North American Free Trade.* New York: St. Martin's Press, 1994.

Burke, John P. *The Institutional Presidency, Organizing and Managing the White House from FDR to Clinton.* 2nd ed. Baltimore and London: The Johns Hopkins University Press, 2000.

Burns, E. Bradford. "Tradition and Variation in Brazilian Foreign Policy." *Journal of Inter-American Studies* 9.2 (1967), 195–212.

———. *The Unwritten Alliance. Rio-Branco and Brazilian-American Relations.* New York: Columbia University Press, 1966.

Bush, George W. *Steel Products Proclamation to Facilitate Positive Adjustment to Competition from Imports of Certain Steel Products, by the President of the United States.* White House, Office of the Press Secretary, March 5, 2002. http://www.whitehouse.gov/news/releases/2002/03/20020305-7.html

———. Address before a Joint Session of the Congress on the State of the Union, January 29, 2002. http://www.presidency.ucsb.edu/ws/print.php?pid=29644

———. Speech delivered at the Third Summit of the Americas, Quebec City, April 21, 2001. Reprinted in *The George W. Bush Foreign Policy Reader. Presidential Speeches with Commentary*, edited by John W. Dietrich. New York: M.E. Shapiro, 2005.

———. *State of the Union Address Before a Joint Session of the Congress on Administration Goals*, February 27, 2001. http://www.presidency.ucsb.edu/ws/print.php?pid=29643

---. *Century of the Americas*, Florida International University, Miami, Florida, August 25, 2000. Reprinted in *The George W. Bush Foreign Policy Reader. Presidential Speeches with Commentary*, edited by John W. Dietrich. New York: M.E. Shapiro, 2005.
Bustillo, Inés and José Antonio Ocampo. "Asymmetries and Cooperation in the FTAA." In *Integrating the Americas. FTAA and Beyond*, edited by Antoni Estevadeordal, Dani Rodrik, Alan M. Taylor, and Andrés Velasco. Cambridge, MA: Harvard University Press, 2004.
Caldentey, Esteban Pérez, and Matías Vernengo. "Ideas, Policies and Economic Development in the Americas." In *Ideas, Policies and Economic Development in the Americas*. Abingdon; New York: Routledge, 2007.
Cameron, Angus and Ronen Palan. "The National Economy in the Contemporary Global System." In *Politics and Globalisation. Knowledge, Ethics and Agency*, edited by Martin Shaw. London: Routledge, 1999.
Cameron, Duncan, ed. *The Free Trade Papers*. Toronto: James Lorimer & Company, 1986.
Cameron, Maxwell A. and Brian W. Tomlin. *The Making of NAFTA: How the Deal was Done*. Ithaca, NY: Cornell University Press, 2000.
Capling, Ann. *All the Way with the USA: Australia, the US and Free Trade*. Sydney: University of NSW, 2005.
Cárdenas, Juan-Camilo and Elinor Ostrom. "What Do People Bring into the Game: Experiments in the Field about Cooperation in the Commons." CAPRI Working Paper No.32, International Food Policy Research Institute, Washington, DC, June 2004. http://www.capri.cgiar.org/pdf/capriwp32.pdf
Cardoso, Fernando Henrique. *A Arte da Política. A História que Vivi*. Rio de Janeiro: Editora Civilização Brasileira, 2006.
---. *Charting a New Course: The Politics of Globalization and Social Transformation*. Edited by Mauricio A. Font. Oxford; Lanham, MD: Rowman & Littlefield Publishers, Inc., 2001.
---. "Preface" to *Diplomacia Brasileira. Palavras, Contextos e Razões*, by Luiz Felipe Lampréia. 2nd ed. Rio de Janeiro: Editora Nova Aguilar, 1999.
---. *The President's News Conference with President Fernando Cardoso of Brazil in Brasilia*, Administration of William J. Clinton, October 14, 1997. http://bulk.resource.org/gpo.gov/papers/1997/1997_vol2_1354.pdf
---. *O Modelo Político Brasileiro e Outros Ensaios*. 2nd ed. Sao Paulo: Corpo e Alma do Brasil, 1973.
--- and Enzo Faletto. *Dependencia y Desarrollo en América Latina: Ensayos de Interpretación Sociológica*. Mexico, DF: Siglo XXI, 1969.
Carlos Leal, ed. *O Itamaraty na Cultura Brasileira*. Rio de Janeiro: Livraria Francisco Alves Editora S.A., 2002.
Carothers, Thomas. "Lessons for Policymakers." In *Haitian Frustrations. Dilemmas for US Policy. A Report of the CSIS Americas Progam*, edited by George Fauriol. Washington, DC: Center for Strategic and International Studies, 1995.
---. *In The Name of Democracy: US Policy Toward Latin America in the Reagan Years*. Berkeley: University of California Press, 1991.
Carr, Barry. "Crossing Borders: Labor Internationalism in the Era of NAFTA." In *Neoliberalism Revisited. Economic Restructuring and Mexico's Political Future*, edited by Gerardo Otero. Boulder, CO: Westview Press, 1996.
Carranza, Mario. "Clinging Together: Mercosur's Ambitious External Agenda, Its Internal Crisis, and the Future of Regional Economic Integration in South America." *Review of International Political Economy* 13.5 (December 2006), 802–829.

Castro, João Augusto de Araújo. "O Congelamento do Poder Mundial." *Revista Brasileira de Estudos Políticos* 33 (January 1972), 7–30.

Centeno, Miguel A. *Democracy Within Reason: Technocratic Revolution in Mexico*. University Park, PA: Pennsylvania State University Press, 1994.

Cervo, Amado Luiz. "Neoliberalism and the Historiography of International Relations: Influences in Argentina and Brazil." Paper prepared for the 20th International Conference of Historical Sciences, Sydney, Australia, July 3–9, 2005.

Cheibub, Zairo Borges. "A Carreira Diplomática no Brasil: O Processo de Burocratização do Itamarati." *Revista de Administração Pública* 23.2 (1989), 97–128.

———. "Diplomacia e Formação do Estado Nacional." *Política e Estratégia* 5.1 (1987), 56–68.

———. "Diplomacia e Construção Institucional: O Itamaraty em uma Perspective Histórica." *Dados* 28.1 (1985), 113–131.

Clinton, William J. *The President's News Conference with President Fernando Cardoso of Brazil in Brasilia*, Administration of William J. Clinton, October 14, 1997. http://bulk.resource.org/gpo.gov/papers/1997/1997_vol2_1356.pdf

———. *Address Before a Joint Session of the Congress on the State of the Union*, February 4, 1997. http://www.presidency.ucsb.edu/ws/index.php?pid=53358

———. *Address to the Nation on Haiti*, September 15, 1994. http://www.presidency.ucsb.edu/ws/index.php?pid=49093

———. *Remarks to the Executive Committee of the Summit of the Americas in Miami*, Florida, July 18, 1994. http://www.presidency.ucsb.edu/ws/index.php?pid=50504&st=Remarks+to+the+Executive+Committee+of+the+Summit+of+the+Americas&st1=

———. Announcement Speech, Old State House, Little Rock, Arkansas, October 3, 1991. Reprinted in Bill Clinton and Al Gore, *Putting People First. How We Can All Change America*. Toronto; New York: Times Books, 1992.

Coatsworth, John. "Structures, Endowments, and Institutions in the Economic History of Latin America." *Latin American Research Review* 40.3 (2005), 126.

——— and Jeffrey G. Williamson. "Always Protectionist? Latin American Tariffs from Independence to Great Depression." *Journal of Latin American Studies* 36 (2004), 205–232.

Confederação Nacional das Indústrias (CNI). "As Relações Comerciais do Brasil com a India e a África do Sul." *Comércio Exterior em Perspectivca* 14.8/9 (May-June 2005), 1–8.

———. "Mercosul-CAN: Fracos Resultados em Termos do Acesso a Mercados para o Brasil." *Comércio Exterior em Perspectiva* 14.1/2 (October-November 2004), 1–9.

Connell, Raewyn. "Dependency, Autonomy and Culture." In *Southern Theory. The Global Dynamics of Knowledge in Social Science*. Crows Nest, NSW: Allen & Unwin, 2007.

Cooper, Andrew F. and Thomas Legler. "The OAS Democratic Solidarity Paradigm: Questions of Collective and National Leadership." *Latin American Politics and Society* 43.1 (Spring 2001), 103–126.

Cox, Michael. "Wilsonianism Resurgent? The Clinton Administration and the Promotion of Democracy." In *American Democracy Promotion. Impulses, Strategies and Impacts*, edited by Michael Cox, G. John Ikenberry, and Takashi Inoguchi. New York: Oxford University Press, 2000.

———. *US Foreign Policy after the Cold War. Superpower without a Mission?*. London: The Royal Institute of International Affairs, 1995.
———, G. John Ikenberry, and Takashi Inoguchi, eds. *American Democracy Promotion. Impulses, Strategies and Impacts.* New York: Oxford University Press, 2000.
Cox, Robert W. "Beyond Empire and Terror: Critical Reflections on the Political Economy of World Order." *New Political Economy* 9.3 (2004), 307–323.
———. "Critical Political Economy." In *International Political Economy Understanding Global Disorder*, edited by Björn Hettne. London; New Jersey: Zed Books, 1995.
———. "Gramsci: Hegemony and International Relations: An Essay on Method." *Millenium: Journal of International Studies* 12.2 (1983), 162–175.
———. "Social Forces, States and World Orders: Beyond International Relations Theory." *Millenium: Journal of International Studies* 10.2 (1981), 126–155.
Crawford, Neta C. "The Passion of World Politics: Propositions on Emotion and Emotional Relationships." *International Security* 24 (Spring 2000), 116–156.
Cruz Junior, Ademar Seabra, Antonio Ricardo F. Cavalcante, and Luiz Pedone. "Brazil's Foreign Policy Under Collor." *Journal of Interamerican Studies and World Affairs* 35.1 (1993), 1.
Cypher, James M. "The Ideology of Economic Science in the Selling of NAFTA: The Political Economy of Elite Decision-Making." *Review of Radical Political Economics* 25.4 (December 1993), 146–163.
Danese, Sergio. *Diplomacia Presidencial.* Rio de Janeiro: Topbooks, 1999.
Das, Dilip K. *Regionalism in Global Trade.* Cheltenham, UK; Northampton, MA: Edward Elgar, 2004.
Denzau, Arthur T. and Douglass G. North. "Shared Mental Models: Ideologies and Institutions." *Kyklos* 47 (1994), 3–31.
——— and Ravi K. Roy. "Shared Mental Models: A *Postcript.*" In *Neoliberalism. National and Regional Experiments with Global Ideas*, edited by Ravi K.Roy, Arthur T. Denzau, and Thomas D. Willett. Abingdon; New York: Routledge, 2007.
Destler, I.M. *American Trade Politics.* 4th ed. Washington, DC: Institute for International Economics, 2005.
———. "The United States and a Free Trade Area of the America. Notes Toward a Political-Economic Analysis." Notes of presentation delivered on June 1, 2002.
———. "Congress and Foreign Trade." In *The Controversial Pivot: The US Congress and North America*, edited by Robert A. Pastor and Rafael Fernandez de Castro. Washington, DC: The Brookings Institution, 1998.
Devlin, Robert and Paolo Giordano. "The Old and New Regionalism: Benefits, Costs, and Implications for the FTAA." In *Integrating the Americas. FTAA and Beyond*, edited by Antoni Estevadeordal, Dani Rodrik, Alan M. Taylor, and Andrés Velasco. Cambridge, MA: Harvard University Press, 2004.
——— and Ricardo Ffrench-Davis. "Toward an Evaluation of Regional Integration in Latin America in the 1990s." Working Paper 2, Institute for the Integration of Latin America and the Caribbean, and Integration, Trade and Hemispheric Issues Division, Buenos Aires, December 1998. http://www.iadb.org/intal/aplicaciones/uploads/publicaciones/i_intalitd_wp_02_1998_devlin.pdf
Diniz, Eli and Renato Boschi. "Globalização, Herança Corporativa e a Representação dos Interesses Empresariais: Novas Configurações no Cenário Pós-Reformas." In

Elites Políticas e Econômicas no Brasil Contemporâneo, edited by Renato Boschi, Eli Diniz, and Fabiano Santos. Série Pesquisas n.18. Sao Paulo: Fundação Konrad Adenauer, 2000.

Doern, G. Bruce and Brian W. Tomlin. *Faith and Fear: The Free Trade Story.* Toronto: Stoddart, 1991.

Domínguez, Jorge, ed. *Technopols. Freeing Politics and Markets in Latin America in the 1990s.* University Park, PA: The Pennsylvania State University Press, 1997.

Dosch, Jörn. "The Post Cold-War Development of Regionalism in East Asia." In *Regionalism in East Asia. Paradigm Shifting?*, edited by Fu-Kuo Liu and Philippe Régnier. London; New York: Routledge Curzon, 2003.

Drake, William J. and Kalypso Nicolaidis. "Ideas, Interests, and Institutionalization: Trade in Services and the Uruguay Round." *International Organization* 46.1 (Winter 1992), 37–100.

Drew, Elizabeth. *On the Edge.* New York: Simon & Schuster, 1994.

Dryden, Steve. *Trade Warriors. USTR and the American Crusade for Free Trade.* New York: Oxford University Press, 1995.

East, Maurice A. "Conclusion: The Narrowing Distinction and Cross-cutting Comparative Observations." In *Diplomacy and Developing Nations. Post-Cold War Foreign-Policymaking Structures and Processes*, edited by Justin Robertson and Maurice A. East. Abington; New York: Routledge, 2005.

Economic Commission for Latin America and the Caribbean. *Una Década de Luces y Sombras: América Latina y el Caribe en los Años Noventa.* Bogotá: ECLAC and Alfaomega, 2001.

———. *Open Regionalism in Latin America and the Caribbean.* Santiago, Chile: United Nations, 1994.

———. *Relaciones Económicas Internacionales y Cooperación Regional de América Latina y el Caribe.* Estudios e Informes de la CEPAL 63. Santiago, Chile: United Nations, 1987.

Edwards, Sebastian. *Crisis and Reform in Latin America. From Despair to Hope.* New York: Oxford University Press, 1995.

———. "The United and Foreign Competition in Latin America." In *The United States in the World Economy*, edited by Martin Feldstein. Chicago; London: The University of Chicago Press, 1988.

Elliot, Lorraine, John Ravenhill, Helen E.S. Nesadurai, and Nick Bisley. *APEC and the Search for Relevance: 2007 and Beyond.* Canberra: The Australian National University/RSPAS, 2006. http://rspas.anu.edu.au/ir/pubs/keynotes/documents/Keynotes-7.pdf

Estevadeordal, Antoni, Dani Rodrik, Alan M. Taylor, and Andrés Velasco, eds. *Integrating the Americas. FTAA and Beyond.* Cambridge, MA: Harvard University Press, 2004.

Evans, Mark and Jonathan Davies. "Understanding Policy Transfer: A Multi-Level, Multi-Disciplinary Perspective." *Public Administration* 77.2 (1999), 361–385.

Evans, Peter. *Dependent Development. The Alliance of Multinational, State, and Local Capital in Brazil.* Princeton, NJ: Princeton University Press, 1979.

———, Harold K. Jacobson, and Robert D. Putnam, eds. *Double-Edged Diplomacy. International Bargaining and Domestic Politics.* London; Berkeley and Los Angeles: University of California Press, Ltd., 1993.

Fajnzylber, Fernando. "Technical Progress, Competitiveness and Institutional Change." In *Strategic Options for Latin America in the 1990s*, edited by Colin I. Bradford Jr. Paris: Organization for Economic Co-operation and Development, 1992.

——. *Industrialización en América Latina: de la "Caja Negra" al "Casillero Vacío": Comparación de Patrones Contemporáneos de Industrialización.* Santiago: ECLAC, 1989.
Fauriol, Georges. "The Shadows of Latin America Affairs." *Foreign Affairs* 69.1 (1989/1990), 116–134.
Fawcett, Louise. "The Origins and Development of Regional Ideas in the Americas." In *Regionalism and Governance in the Americas. Continental Drift*, edited by Louise Fawcett and Monica Serrano. Basingstoke; New York: Palgrave Macmillan, 2005.
—— and Monica Serrano, eds. *Regionalism and Governance in the Americas Continental Drift.* Basingstoke; New York: Palgrave Macmillan, 2005.
Feinberg, Richard E. *Summitry of the Americas. A Progress Report.* Washington, DC: Institute for International Economics, 1997.
—— and Javier Corrales. "Why Did It Take 200 Years? The Intellectual Journey to the Summit of the Americas." In *Summitry of the Americas. A Progress Report*, edited by Richard E. Feinberg. Washington, DC: Institute for International Economics, 1997.
Ffrench-Davis, Ricardo. *Reforming Latin America's Economies: After Market Fundamentalism.* Basingstoke; New York: Palgrave Macmillan, 2005.
——. *Reforming Latin America's Economies: After Market Fundamentalism.* Basingstoke; New York: Palgrave Macmillan, 2005.
Filho, Carlos R. Pio da Costa. "Liberalização do Comércio: Padrões de Interação entre Elites Burocráticas e Atores Sociais." In *Reforma do Estado e Democracia no Brasil: Dilemas e Perspectivas*, edited by Eli Diniz and Sergio de Azevedo. Brasília: Universidade de Brasília, 1997.
Fonseca Jr., Gelson. "Alguns Aspectos da Política Externa Brasileira Contemporânea." In *A Legitimidade e Outras Questões*. Sao Paulo: Paz e Terra, 1998.
——. "O Pensamento Brasileiro em Relações Internacionais: O Tema da Identidade Nacional (!950–1995)." In *A Legitimidade e Outras Questões Internacionais*. Sao Paulo: Paz e Terra, 1998.
——. "Mundos Diversos, Argumentos Afins: Notas sobre Aspectos Doutrinários da Política Externa Independente e do Pragmatismo Responsável." In *Sessenta Anos de Política Externa. Crescimento, Modernização e Política Externa*, vol. 1, edited by José Augusto Guilhon Albuquerque. Sao Paulo: Cultura Editores Associados/NUPRI, 1996.Font, Mauricio A. "Introduction" to *Charting a New Course. The Politics of Globalization and Social Transformation*, by Fernando Henrique Cardoso. Edited by Mauricio A. Font. Oxford; Lanham, MD: Rowman & Littlefield Publishers, Inc., 2001.
Fontaine, Roger W. *The Andean Pact: A Political Analysis.* The Washington Papers Vol. 5, No.45, Beverly Hills and London: Sage Publications, 1977.
Foxley, Alejandro. *Latin American Experiments in Neoconservative Economics.* Berkeley and Los Angeles; London: University of California Press, 1983.
Fraga, Arminio. "A Fork in the Road." *Finance and Development* 42.4 (December 2005). http://www.imf.org/external/pubs/ft/fandd/2005/12/fraga.htm
Frankel, Jeffrey. The Crusade for Free Trade: Evaluating Clinton's International Economic Policy." *Foreign Affairs* 80.2 (March-April 2001). http://www.foreignaffairs.org/20010301fareviewessay4270/jeffrey-frankel/the-crusade-for-free-trade-evaluating-clinton-s-international-economic-policy.html
Frieden, Jeff. "sectoral Conflict and U.S. Foreign Economic Policy, 1914–1940." *International Organization* 42.1 (Winter 1988), 59–90.

Fritsch, Winston and Alexandre A. Tombini. "The Mercosul: An Overview." In *Economic Integration in the Western Hemisphere*, edited by Roberto Bouzas and Jaime Ros. Notre Dame, IN; London: University of Notre Dame Press, 1994.

Frohmann, Alicia. "Regional Initiatives for Peace and Democracy: The Collective Diplomacy of the Rio Group." In *Responses to Regional Problems: The Case of Latin America and the Caribbean*, edited by Carl Kaysen, Robert A. Pastor, and Laura W. Reed. Cambridge: American Academy of Arts and Sciences, 1994.

Furtado, Celso. *Teoria e Política do Desenvolvimento Econômico*. 4th ed. Sao Paulo: Editora Nacional, 1971.

———. *Economic Development of Latin America. A Survey from Colonial Times to the Cuban Revolution*. New York: Cambridge University Press, 1970.

Gamble, Andrew. "Regional Blocs, World Order and the New Medievalism." In *European Union and New Regionalism: Regional Actors and Global Governance in a Post-hegemonic Era*, edited by Mario Telò. Aldershot: Ashgate, 2001.

——— and Anthony Payne. "The World Order Approach." In *Theories of New Regionalism. A Palgrave Reader*, edited by Fredrik Söderbaum and Timothy M. Shaw. Basingstoke; New York: Palgrave Macmillan, 2003.

——— and Anthony Payne, eds. *Regionalism & World Order*. Basingstoke: Macmillan, 1996.

Gantenbein, James W. *The Evolution of our Latin-American Policy. A Documentary Record*. New York: Octagon Books, 1971.

Garnaut, Ross. "Australian Security and Free Trade with America." In *Balancing Act: Law, Policy and Politics in Globalisation and Global Trade*, edited by Jianfu Chen and Gordon Walker. Leichhardt, NSW: The Federation Press, 2004.

———. *Open Regionalism and Trade Liberalization. An Asia-Pacific Contribution to the World Trade System*. Singapore: Institute of South Asian Studies; Sydney, NSW: Allen & Unwin, 1996.

Garten, Jeffrey E. *A Cold Peace: America, Japan, Germany and the Struggle for Supremacy*. New York: Times Books, 1992.

———. *The Big Ten: Big Emerging Markets and How They will Change our Lives*. New York: Basic Books, 1997.

Gavin, Brigid and Luk Van Langenhove. "Trade in a World of Regions." In *Regionalism, Multilateralism, and Economic Integration: The Recent Experience*, edited by Gary Sampson and Stephen Woolcock. New York: United Nations University Press, 2003.

Gereffi, Gary and Donald L. Wyman, eds. *Manufacturing Miracles. Paths of Industrialization in Latin America and East Asia*. Princeton, NJ: Princeton University Press, 1990.

——— and Peter Evans. "Transnational Corporations, Dependent Development, and State Policy in the Semi-Periphery: A Comparison of Brazil and Mexico." *Latin American Research Review* 16.3 (1981), 31–64.

Gilpin, Robert. *War and Change in World Politics*. Cambridge, MA: Cambridge University Press, 1981.

Goldfinch, Shaun. *Remaking New Zealand and Australian Economic Policy: Ideas, Institutions and Policy Communities*. Wellington, NZ: Victoria University Press, 2000.

Goldfinger, Nat. "A Labor View of Foreign Investment and Trade Issues," paper submitted to the Commission on International Trade and Investment Policy and published in conjunction with the Commission's Report to the President,

United States International Economic Policy in an Interdependent World, vol. I. Washington, DC: G.P.O, 1971.
Goldstein, Judith. "International Forces and Domestic Politics: Trade Policy and Institutional Building in the United States." In *Shaped by War and Trade*, edited by Ira Katznelson and Martin Shefter. Princeton and Oxford: Princeton University Press, 2002.
———. "Creating the GATT Rules: Politics, Institutions, and American Policy." In *Multilateralism Matters. The Theory and Praxis of an Institutional Form*, edited by John Ruggie. New York: Columbia University Press, 1993.
———. *Ideas, Interests, and American Trade Policy*. Ithaca, NY: Cornell University Press, 1993.
——— and Robert Keohane. "Ideas and Foreign Policy. An Analytical Framework." In *Ideas and Foreign Policy. Beliefs, Institutions, and Political Change*. Ithaca, NY: Cornell University Press, 1993.
Gore, Albert. *Earth in the Balance: Ecology and the Human Spirit*. Boston, MA: Houghton Mifflin, 1992.
———. *A Vision for America*. Speech given during the Democratic National Convention, New York City, July 16, 1992. Reprinted in Bill Clinton and Al Gore, *Putting People First. How We Can All Change America*. Toronto; New York: Times Books, 1992.
Gotlieb, Allan. *"I'll Be with You in a Minute, Mr. Ambassador." The Education of a Canadian Diplomat in Washington*. Toronto: University of Toronto Press, 1991.
Gourevitch, Peter A. "Reinventing the American State: Political Dynamics in the Post-Cold War Era." In *Shaped by War and Trade*, edited by Ira Katznelson and Martin Shefter. Princeton and Oxford: Princeton University Press, 2002.
Green, Roy E. *The Enterprise for the Americas Initiative. Issues and Prospects for a Free Trade Agreement in the Western Hemisphere*. Westport, CT: Praeger, 1993.
Greenstein, Fred I. *The Presidential Difference. Leadership Style from FDR to Clinton*. New York: Martin Kessler Books/ Free Press, 2000.
Grieco, Joseph M. *Cooperation Among Nations: Europe, America, and Non-Tariff Barriers to Trade*. Ithaca, NY: Cornell University Press, 1990.
———. "Anarchy and the Limits of Cooperation: A Realist Critique of the Newest Liberal Institutionalism." *International Organization* 42.3 (Summer 1988), 485–507.
Griswold, Daniel T. "Free Trade, Free Markets. Rating the 107th Congress." Center for Trade Policy Studies, January 2003. http://www.freetrade.org/pubs/pas/tpa-022.pdf
Grugel, Jean. "Democratization and the Realm of Politics in International Political Economy." In *Globalizing International Political Economy*, edited by Nicola Phillips. Basingstoke; New York: Palgrave Macmillan, 2005.
———. "The Chilean State and New Regionalism: Strategic Alliances and Pragmatic Integration." In *Regionalism across the North-South Divide: State Strategies and Globalization*, edited by Jean Grugel and Wil Hout. London: Routledge, 1999.
———. "Latin America and the Remaking of the Americas." In *Regionalism and World Order*, edited by Andrew Gamble and Anthony Payne. Basingstoke: Macmillan, 1996.
——— and Wil Hout. "Regions, Regionalism and the South." In *Regionalism across the North-South Divide: State Strategies and Globalization*. London; New York: Routledge, 1999.

Guimarães, Samuel Pinheiro. *Desafios Brasileiros na Era dos Gigantes*. Rio de Janeiro: Contraponto, 2005.

———. Speech delivered during his inauguration ceremony as Secretary General of External Relations, Brasília, January 9, 2003. Original in Portuguese: "são os três únicos países que aparecem simultaneamente, nas relações dos dez países de maior território, de maior população, de maior produto." http://www.mre.gov.br/index.php?Itemid=64&id=19&option=com_content&task=view

———. *Quinhentos Anos de Periferia. Uma Contribuição ao Estudo da Política Internacional*. 3rd ed. Porto Alegre: Contraponto, 2001.

Haas, Ernst. "Turbulent Fields and the Theory of Regional Integration." *International Organization* 30.2 (Spring 1976), 173–178.

———. "The Challenge of Regionalism." *International Organization* 12.4 (Autumn 1958), 440–458.

——— and Philippe C. Schmitter. "Economics and Differential Patterns of Political Integration: Projections about Unity in Latin America." *International Organization* 18.4 (Autumn 1964), 705–737.

Haas, Peter. "Introduction: Epistemic Communities and International Policy Coordination." *International Organization* 46.1 (1992), 1–35.

Haas, Richard. *The Reluctant Sheriff: The United States After the Cold War*. New York: Council on Foreign Relations Press, 1997.

Haggard, Stephan. "The Political Economy of Regionalism in Asia and the Americas." In *The Political Economy of Regionalism*, edited by Edward D. Mansfield and Helen V. Milner. New York: Columbia University Press, 1997.

Hall, Peter, ed. *The Political Power of Economic Ideas*. Princeton: Princeton University Press, 1989.

———. "Conclusion" to *The Political Power of Economic Ideas*, edited by Peter A. Hall. Princeton: Princeton University Press, 1989.

———. "Policy Paradigms, Social Learning, and the State: The Case of Economic Policymaking in Britain." *Comparative Politics* 25.3 (1993), 275–296.

——— and Rosemary C.R. Taylor. "Political Science and the Three New Institutionalisms." *Political Studies* XLIV (1996), 936–957.

Hamwey, Robert M. "Expanding National Policy Space for Development: Why the Multilateral Trading System Must Change." Working Paper 25, South Centre, September 2005. http://www.southcentre.org/publications/workingpapers/wp25.pdf

Hanson, Simon G. *Dollar Diplomacy Modern Style: Chapters in the Failure of the Alliance for Progress*. Washington, DC: Inter-American Affairs Press, 1970.

Harrison, Lawrence E. *The Pan-American Dream: do Latin America's Cultural Values Discourage True Partnership with the United States and Canada?*. New York: Basic Books, 1997.

——— and Samuel P. Huntington, eds. *Culture Matters: How Values Shape Human Progress*. New York: Basic Books, 2000.

Hart, Michael M. "Canadian Economic Development and the International Trading System: Constraints and Opportunities." Monograph commissioned by the Royal Commission on the Economic Union and Development Prospects of Canada. Toronto: University of Toronto Press, 1985.

Hartlyn, Jonathan, Lars Schoultz, and Augusto Varas, eds. *The United States and Latin America in the 1990s: Beyond the Cold War*. Chapel Hill: University of North Carolina Press, 1992.

Harvie, Charles, Fukunari Kimuar, and Hyun-Hoon Lee, eds. *New East Asian Regionalism. Causes, Progress and Country Perspectives*. Cheltenham, UK; Northampton, MA: Edwar Elgar, 2005.

Hay, Colin. "The Genealogy of Neoliberalism." In *Neoliberalism. National and Regional Experiments with Global Ideas*, edited by Ravi K.Roy, Arthur T. Denzau, and Thomas D. Willett. Abingdon; New York: Routledge, 2007.

Hay, Peter. "Contemporary Capitalism, Globalization, Regionalization and the Persistence of National Variation." *Review of International Studies* 26 (2000), 509–531.

Heclo, Hugh. "Ronald Reagan and the American Public Philosophy." In *The Reagan Presidency. Pragmatic Conservatism and Its Legacies*, edited by W. Elliot Brownlee and Hugh Davis Graham. Lawrence, KS: University Press of Kansas, 2003.

———. "Issue Networks and the Executive Establishment." In *The New American Political System*, edited by Anthony King. Washington, DC: American Enterprise Institute, 1990.

———. *Modern Social Politics in Britain and Sweden. From Relief to Income Maintenance*. New Haven; London: Yale University Press, 1974.

Helleiner, Eric. "Preface" to *Neoliberalism. National and Regional Experiments with Global Ideas*. Edited by Ravi K.Roy, Arthur T. Denzau, and Thomas D. Willett. Abingdon; New York: Routledge, 2007.

———. *States and the Re-emergence of Global Finance: From Bretton Woods to the 1990s*. Ithaca, NY: Cornell University Press, 1994.

Henwood, Doug. "Impeccable Logic: Trade, Development and Free Markets in the Clinton Era." *NACLA Report on the Americas* 26.5 (May 1993), 23–28.

Herz, Mônica. "Brazilian Foreign Policy since 1990 and the Pax Americana." In *Between Compliance and Conflict: East Asia, Latin America, and the "New" Pax Americana*, edited by Jorge Domínguez and Byung-Kook Kim. New York: Routledge, 2005.

Hettne, Björn. "Beyond the 'New' Regionalism." In *Key Debates n New Political Economy*, edited by Anthony Payne. London: Routledge, 2006.

———. "The New Regionalism Revisited." In *Theories of New Regionalism. A Palgrave Reader*, edited by Fredrik Söderbaum and Timothy M. Shaw. Basingstoke; New York: Palgrave Macmillan, 2003.

———. "Regionalism, Security and Development: A Comparative Perspective." In *Comparing Regionalisms: Implications for Global Development*, edited by Björn Hettne, András Inotai, and Osvaldo Sunkel. Basingstoke; New York: Palgrave Macmillan, 2001.

Hettne, Björn, András Inotai, and Osvaldo Sunkel, eds. *Comparing Regionalisms: Implications for Global Development*. Basingstoke; New York: Palgrave Macmillan, 2001.

———, eds. *National Perspectives on the New Regionalism in the North*. Basingstoke; New York: Palgrave Macmillan, 2000.

———, eds. *National Perspectives on the New Regionalism in the South*. Basingstoke; New York: Palgrave Macmillan, 2000.

———. eds. *The New Regionalism and the Future of Security and Development*. Basingstoke; New York: Palgrave Macmillan, 2000.

———, eds. *Globalism and the New Regionalism*. Basingstoke; New York: Palgrave Macmillan, 1999.

Hey, Jeane A.K. "Foreign Policy in Dependent States." In *Foreign Policy Analysis. Continuity and Change in Its Second Generation*, edited by Laura Neack, Jeanne A.K. Hey, and Patrick J. Haney. Englewood Cliffs, NJ: Prentice Hall, 1995.

Hirschman, Albert O. "Second Thoughts on the Alliance for Progress," 1961. Reprinted in Albert O. Hirschman, *A Bias for Hope. Essays on Development and Latin America*. New Haven: Yale University Press, 1971.

———. "The Search for Paradigms as a Hindrance to Understanding." *World Politics* 22.3 (April 1970), 329–343.

———. *National Power and the Structure of Foreign Trade*. Berkeley and Los Angeles: University of California Press, 1969.

Hirst, Mônica. *The United States and Brazil. A Long Road of Unmet Expectations*. Contemporary Inter-American Relations Series. New York: Routledge, 2005.

———. "Democratic Transition and Foreign Policy: The Experience of Brazil." In *Latin American Nations in World Politics*, edited by Heraldo Muñoz and Joseph Tulchin. Boulder, CO: Western Press, 1984.

———. "Mercosur's Complex Political Agenda." In *Mercosur: Regional Integration, World Markets*, edited by Riordan Roett. Boulder, CO: Lynne Rienner Publishers, Inc., 1999.

———. "Pesos y Medidas de la Política Exterior Brasileña." In *América Latina: Políticas Exteriores Comparadas*, vol. 1, edited by Juan Carlos Puig. Buenos Aires: Editor Latinoamericano, 1984.

——— and Maria Regina Soares de Lima. "Contexto Internacional, Democracia e Política Externa." *Política Externa* 11.2 (2002), 78–98.

Hiscox, Michael J. "The Magic Bullet? The RTAA, Institutional Reform, and Trade Liberalization." *International Organization* 53.4 (Autumn 1999), 669–698.

Ho, Kevin K. "Trading Rights and Wrongs: The 2002 Bush Steel Tariffs." *Berkeley Journal of International Law* 21 (2003), 825–846.

Holloway, Rachel L. "A Time for Change in American Politics: The Issue of the 1992 Presidential Election." In *The 1992 Presidential Campaign. A Communication Perspective*, edited by Robert E. Denton, Jr. Westport, CT: Praeger Publishers, 1994.

Holsti, K.J. "National Role Conceptions in the Study of Foreign Policy." *International Studies Quarterly* 14 (1970), 232–309.

Hout, Wil. "Theories of International Relations and the New Regionalism." In *Regionalism across the North-South Divide: State Strategies and Globalization*, edited by Jean Grugel and Wil Hout. London; New York: Routledge, 1999.

Huenemann, Jon E. "On the trade policy-making process in the United States." In *The Trade Policy-Making Process. Level One of the Two-Level Game: Country Studies in the Western Hemisphere*, edited by Inter-American Development Bank, Inter-American Dialogue, and Munk Centre for International Studies. Buenos Aires: INTAL, ITD, STA, 2002.

Hufbauer, Gary C. and Jeffrey J. Schott. *Western Hemisphere Economic Integration*. Washington, DC: Institute of International Economics, 1994.

——— and Barbara Kotschwar. "US Interests in Free Trade in the Americas." In *The United States and the Americas: A Twenty-First Century View*, edited by Albert Fishlow and James Jones. New York: W.W. Norton & Co., 1999.

———, Robin Dunnigan, and Diana Clark. *NAFTA: An Assessment*. Washington, DC: Institute for International Economics, 1993.

Hunter, Wendy. "The Normalization of an Anomaly. The Workers' Party in Brazil." *World Politics* 59 (April 2007), 440–475.

Hurrell, Andrew. "Hegemony and Regional Governance in the Americas." In *Regionalism and Governance in the Americas Continental Drift*, edited by Louise Fawcett and Monica Serrano. Basingstoke; New York: Palgrave Macmillan, 2005.

———. "Working with Diplomatic Culture: Some Latin American and Brazilian Questions." Paper prepared for ISA Meeting, Montreal, March 2004.

———. "The Politics of Regional Integration in MERCOSUR." In *Regional Integration in Latin America and the Caribbean: The Political Economy of Open Regionalism*, edited by Victor Bulmer-Thomas. London: Institute of Latin American Studies, University of London, 2001.

Ianni, Octávio. *Diplomacia e Imperialismo na América Latina*. Cadernos CEBRAP no.12, Sao Paulo, 1973.

Ikenberry, G. John. "America's Liberal Grand Strategy: Democracy and National Security in the Post-war Era." In *American Democracy Promotion. Impulses, Strategies and Impacts*, edited by Michael Cox, G. John Ikenberry, and Takashi Inoguchi. New York: Oxford University Press, 2000.

Insanally, S.R. "Multilateralism in International Relations: Past Practice and Future Promise." In *Caribbean Imperatives. Regional Governance and Integrated Development*, edited by Kenneth Hall and Denis Benn. Kingston, Jamaica: Ian Randle Publishers, 2005.

Inter-American Development Bank. *Mas Allá de las Fronteras. El Nuevo Regionalismo en América Latina*. Washington, DC: Inter-American Development Bank, 2002.

Inter-American Dialogue. "A Second Chance. US Policy in the Americas." March 2009.http://www.thedialogue.org/PublicationFiles/A%20Second%20 Chance,%20FINAL%20to%20post.pdf

——— and Munk Centre for International Studies, eds. *The Trade Policy-Making Process. Level One of the Two-Level Game: Country Studies in the Western Hemisphere*. Buenos Aires: INTAL, ITD, STA, 2002.

Jacobs, Lawrence R. and Robert Y. Shapiro. "Public Opinion in President Clinton's First Year: Leadership and Responsiveness." In *The Clinton Presidency. Campaigning, Governing & the Psychology of Leadership*, edited by Stanley A. Renshon. Boulder, CO: Westview Press, 1995.

Jaguaribe, Helio. "A View from the Southern Cone." In *Latin America in a New World*, edited by Abraham Lowenthal and G.Treverton. Boulder, CO: Westview Press, 1994.

Jales, Mario Queiroz de Monteiro. "Inserção do Brasil no Comércio Inernacional Agrícola e Expansão dos Fluxos Comerciais Sul-Sul." Instituto de Estudos do Comércio e Negociações Internacionais, Sao Paulo, September 2005. http://www.iconebrasil.org.br/arquivos/noticia/10.pdf

———, Marcos S. Jank, Shunli Yao, and Colin A. Carter. "Agriculture in Brazil and China. Challenges and Opportunities." Occasional Paper No.44, Intal/ITD, Buenos Aires, October 2006. http://www.iadb.org/INTAL/aplicaciones/uploads/publicaciones/i_INTALITD_OP_44_2006_Jank_Jales_Yao_Carter_.pdf

Jank, Marcos S. and Zuleika Arashiro. "Free Trade Area of the Americas: Where Are We? Where Could We Be headed?." In *Free Trade in the Americas: Getting There from Here*, edited by The Inter-American Dialogue. Washington, DC: The Inter-American Dialogue, 2004.

Jarvis, Anthony. "Societies, States and Geopolitics: Challenges from Historical Sociology." *Review of International Studies* 15 (1989), 281–293.

Jervis, Robert. "Understanding the Bush Doctrine." In *American Foreign Policy in a New Era*. Abingdon; New York: Routledge, 2005.
———. *Perception and Misperception in International Politics*. Princeton: Princeton University Press, 1976.
———. *The Logic of Images in International Relations*. Princeton: Princeton University Press, 1970.
———, Richard N. Lebow, and Janice Gross Stein, eds. *Psychology and Deterrence*. Baltimore; London: The Johns Hopkins University Press, 1985.
Kahler, Miles. "Rationality in International Relations." *International Organization* 52.4 (Autumn 1988), 929–932.
Kaldor, Mary. " 'Civilising' Globalisation? The Implications of the 'Battle in Seattle'." *Millennium: Journal of International Studies* 29.15 (2000), 105–114.
Karnes, Thomas L., ed. *Readings in the Latin American Policy of the United States*. Tucson: The University of Arizona Press, 1972.
Katzenstein, Peter. "Regionalism and Asia." In *New Regionalisms in the Global Political Economy*, edited by Shaun Breslin, Christopher W. Hughes, Nicola Phillips, and Ben Rosamond. London; New York: Routledge, 2002.
———, ed. *The Culture of National Security: Norms and Identity in World Politics*. New York: Columbia University Press, 1996.
Kaufman, Robert R., Carlos Bazdresch, and Blanca Heredia. "Mexico: Radical Reform in a Dominant Party System." In *Voting for Reform. Democracy, Political Liberalization, and Economic Adjustment*, edited by Stephan Haggard and Steven B. Webb. New York: Oxford University Press, 1994.
Kay, Cristóbal. "Relevance of Structuralist and Dependency Theories in the Neoliberal Period: A Latin American Perspective." Working Paper Series No.281, Institute of Social Sciences, The Hague, Netherlands, October 1998.
Kelly, Paul. *The End of Certainty. Power, Politics and Business in Australia*. Sydney, NSW: Allen & Unwin Pty Ltd., 1994.
Keohane, Robert O. "Institutional Theory and the Realist Challenge After the Cold War." In *Neorealism and Neoliberalism. The Contemporary Debate*, edited by David A. Baldwin. New York: Columbia University Press, 1993.
———. *After Hegemony: Cooperation and Discord in the World Political Economy*. Princeton, NJ: Princeton University Press, 1984.
——— and Joseph S. Nye. *Power and Interdependence*. 3rd ed. New York; San Francisco: Longman, 2001.
Kerner, Daniel. "La CEPAL, las Empresas Transnacionales y la Búsqueda de una Estrategia de Desarrollo Latinoamericano." *Revista de la CEPAL* 79 (2003), 85–99.
Khun, Thomas S. *The Road since Structure*. Chicago: University of Chicago Press, 2000.
———. *The Structure of Scientific Revolution*. Chicago: The University of Chicago Press, 1970.
Kingdon, John. *Agendas, Alternatives, and Public Policies*. Boston: Little Brown, 1984.
Kissinger, Henry. *Years of Renewal*. New York: Simon and Schuster, 1999.
Klaveren, Alberto van. "Chile: The Search for Open Regionalism." In *National Perspectives on the New Regionalism in the South*, edited by Björn Hettne, András Inotai, and Osvaldo Sunkel. Basingstoke; New York: Palgrave Macmillan, 2000.

———. "The Analysis of Latin American Foreign Policies. Theoretical Perspectives." In *Latin American Nations in World Politics*, edited by Heraldo Muñoz and Joseph S. Tulchin. Boulder, CO: Westview Press, 1984.
Kohli, Atul. *State-Directed Development. Political Power and Industrialization in the Global Periphery.* New York: Cambridge University Press, 2004.
Konrad, Herman W. "North American Continental Relationships: Historical Trends and Antecedents." In *NAFTA in Transition*, edited by Stephen Randall, and Herman W. Konrad. Toronto: University of Calgary Press, 1995.
Kowalczyk, Carsten and Ronald J. Wonnacott. "Hubs and Spokes, and Free Trade in the Americas." Working Paper No.4198, National Bureau of Economic Research, October 1992. http://www.nber.org/papers/w4198.pdf?new_window=1
Krasner, Stephen D. "Are Bureaucracies Important? (Or Allison Wonderland)," *Foreign Policy* 7, Summer 1971. Reprinted in *American Foreign Policy. Theoretical Essays*, edited by G. John Ikenberry. London; Boston: Scott, Foresman and Co., 1989.
Krause, Lawrence and Joseph Nye. "Reflections on the Economics and Politics of International Economic Organizations." *International Organization* 29.1 (Winter 1975), 323–342.
Kristol, William and Robert Kagan. "Toward a Neo-Reaganite Foreign Policy." *Foreign Affairs* 75.4 (July/August 1996), 18–32.
Krueger, Anne O. *American Trade Policy. A Tragedy in the Making.* Washington, DC: The American Enterprise Institute, 1995.
Krugman, Paul. "Book Review of NAFTA: An Assessment." *Journal of Economic Literature* 33.2 (June 1995), 849–851.
———. "Competitiveness: A Dangerous Obsession." *Foreign Affairs* 73.2 (March-April 1994), 28–45.
Kull, Steven, I.M. Destler, and Clay Ramsay. *The Foreign Policy Gap. How Policymakers Misread the Public.* Report by the Center for International and Security Studies, Program on International Policy Attitudes, University of Maryland, October 1997.
Kume, Honorio and Guida Piani. "Alca: Uma Estimativa do Impacto no Comércio Bilateral Brasil-Estados Unidos." IPEA *Texto para Discussão* No.1058 (2004), Rio de Janeiro, December 2004.
Lafer, Celso. *A Identidade Internacional do Brasil e a Política Externa Brasileira. Passado, Presente e Futuro.* Sao Paulo: Editora Perspectiva S.A., 2004.
———. *Mudam-se os Tempos. Diplomacia Brasileira, 2001–2002.* Brasília: Fundação Alexandre de Gusmão/ Instituto de Pesquisa de Relações Internacionais, 2002.
———. *Novos Cenários de Negociação.* Address delivered during the Seminar "Doha e o Pós-Doha: Novos Desafios da Negociação Comercial Internacional," São Paulo, January 24, 2002. Reprinted in Celso Lafer, *Mudam-se os Tempos. Diplomacia Brasileira, 2001–2002.* Brasília: Fundação Alexandre de Gusmão/ Instituto de Pesquisa de Relações Internacionais, 2002.
———. "Preface" to *O Itamaraty na Cultura Brasileira*, edited by Carlos Leal. Rio de Janeiro: Livraria Francisco Alves Editora S.A., 2002.
———. "Brazilian International Identity and Foreign Policy: Past, Present, and Future." *Daedalus Journal of the American Academy of Arts and Sciences* 129.2 (Spring 2000), 207–238.
Lampréia, Luiz Felipe. *Diplomacia Brasileira. Palavras, Contextos e Razões.* 2nd ed. Rio de Janeiro: Editora Nova Aguilar, 1999.
——— and Ademar Seabra da Cruz Jr. "Brazil: Copying with Structural Constraints." In *Diplomacy and Developing Nations. Post-Cold War Foreign-Policymaking*

Structures and Processes, edited by Justin Robertson and Maurice A. East. Abington; New York: Routledge, 2005.

Latham, Michael E. *Modernization as Ideology. American Social Science and "Nation Building" in the Kennedy Era*. Chapel Hill; London: The University of North Carolina Press, 2000.

Lauren, Paul Gordon. *Diplomats and Bureaucrats*. Stanford: Hoover Institution Press, 1976.

Lavagna, Roberto. *Argentina, Brasil, Mercosur. Una Decisión Estratégica, 1986–2001*. Buenos Aires: Ciudad Argentina, 1998.

Lawrence, Robert Z. *Regionalism, Multilateralism, and Deeper Integration*. Washington, DC: The Brookings Institution, 1996.

Leadership Council for Inter-American Summitry. *An Evaluation of the Santiago Summit of the Americas and Its Aftermath*. Policy Report II, North South Center, University of Miami, Florida, March 1999.

Lebow, Richard N. "Reason, Emotion and Cooperation." *International Politics* 42 (2005), 283–313.

Lee, Thea. "False Prophets. The Selling of NAFTA." Economic Policy Institute, Washington, DC, 1995.

Leff, Nathaniel H. *Economic Policy-Making and Development in Brazil, 1947–1964*. New York; London; Sydney; Toronto: John Wiley & Sons, Inc., 1968.

Leiva, Fernando Ignacio. *Latin American Neostructuralism. The Contradictions of Post-Neoliberal Development*. Mnneapolis; MN: University of Minnesota Press, 2008.

Levinson, Marc. "Kantor's Cant. The Hole in Our Trade Policy." *Foreign Affairs* (March/April 1996), 2–7.

Lima, Maria Regina Soares de. "Ejes Analíticos y Conflicto de Paradigmas en la Política Externa Brasileña." *América Latina/Internacional* 1.2 (October 1994), 27–47.

———. "The Political Economy of Brazilian Foreign Policy. Nuclear Energy, Trade, and Itaipú." PhD dissertation, Vanderbilt University, Nashville, August 1986.

———and Mônica Hirst. "Brazil as Intermediate State and Regional Power: Action, Choice and Responsibilities." *International Affairs* 82.1 (2006), 21–40.

——— and Fabiano Santos. "Brazilian Congress and Foreign Trade Policy." Paper prepared for delivery at the 1998 meeting of the Latin American Studies Association, Chicago, Illinois, 24–26 September 1998.

Lima, Paulo Tarso Flecha de. "Diplomacia e Comércio: Notas sobre a Política Externa Brasileira nos Anos 70." In *Sessenta Anos de Política Externa 1930–1990. Diplomacia para o Desenvolvimento*, vol. 2, edited by José Augusto Gilhon de Albuquerque. Sao Paulo: Cultura/NUPRI-USP, 1996.

Lima-Campos, Aluisio de, and Adriana Vito. "The Impact of Anti-dumping and Countervailing Duty Proceedings on Brazilian Exports to the United States." *Journal of World Trade* 38.1 (2004), 37–68.

Lipson, Charles. "International Cooperation in Economic and Security Affairs." *World Politics* 37 (October 1984), 1–23.

Liu, Fu-Kuo and Philippe Régnier, eds. *Regionalism in East Asia: Paradigm Shifting?*. London; New York: Routledge Curzon, 2003.

Loureiro, Maria Rita. *Os Economistas no Poder*. Sao Paulo: Editora da Fundação Getúlio Vargas, 1997.

Love, Joseph. "structuralism and Dependency in Peripheral Europe: Latin American Ideas in Spain and Portugal." *Latin American Research Review* 39.2 (2004), 114–140.

———. "The Rise and Decline of Economic Structuralism in Latin America: New Dimensions." *Latin American Research Review* 40.3 (2005), 100–125.

——— and Nils Jacobsen. "Preface" to *Guiding the Invisible Hand. Economic Liberalism and the State in Latin American History*, by Joseph Love and Nils Jacobsen. New York: Praeger Publishers, 1988.

Lowenthal, Abraham. "Latin America: Ready for Partnership?" *Foreign Affairs* 72.1 (1993), 74–92.

Lustig, Nora. "From Structuralism to Neostructuralism: The Search for a Heterodox Paradigm." In *The Latin American Development Debate. Neostructuralism, Neomonetarism, and Adjustment Processes*, edited by Patricio Meller. Boulder, CO: Westview Press, 1991.

———. *Mexico, the Remaking of an Economy*. 2nd ed. Washington, DC: Brookings Institution Press, 1998.

Mackay, Donald R. "Challenges Confronting the Free Trade Area of the Americas." *FOCAL Policy Papers* 02–7 (June 2002).

MacLean, George A. *Clinton's Foreign Policy in Russia. From Deterrence and Isolation to Democratization and Engagement*. Aldershot; Burlington, VT: Ashgate, 2006. Gerard, Phillippe R. *Clinton in Haiti: The 1994 US Invasion of Haiti*. Basingstoke; New York: Palgrave Macmillan, 2004.

MacLean, John. "Toward a Political Economy of Agency in Contemporary International Relations." In *Politics and Globalisation. Knowledge, Ethics and Agency*, edited by Martin Shaw. London; New York: Routledge, 1999.

Malatian, Teresa. "Diplomacia e Letras na Correspondência Acadêmica: Machados de Assis e Oliveira Lima." *Estudos Históricos* 13.24 (1999), 377–392.

Manger, Mark S. "Competition and Bilateralism in Trade Policy: The Case of Japan's Free Trade Agreements." *Review of International Political Economy* 15.5 (December 2005), 804–828.

———, Mark A. Pickup, and Tom Snijders. "When Country Interdependence is not a Nuisance: The Longitudinal Network Approach." Working paper in progress, 2008.

Mancuso, Wagner Praton and Amâncio Jorge de Oliveira. "Abertura Econômica, Empresariado e Política: os Planos Doméstico e Internacional." *Lua Nova* 69 (2006), 147–172.

Marconini, Mario. "Trade Policy-Making Process in Brazil." Paper presented at the London School of Economics, May 25, 2005.

Markwald, Ricardo A. "2003: Novo Mercosul?." In *Governo Lula. Novas Prioridades e Desenvolvimento Sustentado*, edited by João Paulo dos Reis Velloso. Rio de Janeiro: Editora José Olympio, 2003.

Marques, Sylvia Ferreira. "A Imagem Internacional do Brasil no Governo Cardoso (1995–2002). Uma Leitura Construtivista do Conceito de Potência Média." Master's dissertation, Pontifícia Universidade Católica do Rio de Janeiro, Rio de Janeiro, 2005.

Masiero, Gilmar. "Pragmatism and Planning in East Asia and Brazil." In *East Asia and Latin America. The Unlikely Alliance*, edited by Peter H. Smith, Kotaro Horisaka, and Shoji Nishijima. Lanham, Maryland: Rowman & Littlefield Publishers, Inc., 2003.

Mastanduno, Michael. "The United States Political System and International Leadership: A 'Decidedly Inferior' Form of Government?." Paper presented at the Darmouth College-International House of Japan Conference. "The United States and Japan on the Eve of the 21st Century: Prospects for Joint Leadership," June 27-28, 1994. Reprinted in *American Foreign Policy. Theoretical Essays,* edited by G. John Ikenberry. London; Boston: Scott, Foreman and Co., 1989.

Mattos, Paulo T.L. "A Formação do Estado Regulador." *Novos Estudos CEBRAP* 76 (November 2006), 152–154. http://www.cebrap.org.br/imagens/Arquivos/a_formacao_do_estado_regulador.pdf

McCormick, James M. "Clinton and Foreign Policy. Some Legacies for a New Century." In *The Postmodern Presidency. Bill Clinton's Legacy in US Politics,* edited by Steven E. Schier. Pittsburgh: University of Pittsburgh Press, 2000.

McLindsay, James M. *Congress and the Politics of US Foreign Policy.* London; Baltimore: The Johns Hopkins University Press, 1994.

McNamara, Kathleen R. *The Currency of Ideas: Monetary Politics and the European Union.* Ithaca, NY: Cornell University Press, 1998.

Melanson, Richard A. *American Foreign Policy since the Vietnam War. The Search for Consensus from Richard Nixon to George W. Bush.* 4th ed. Armonk, NY: M.E. Sharpe, 2005.

Mello, Flavia de Campos. "Regionalismo e Inserção Internacional: Continuidade e Transformação da Política Externa Brasileira nos Anos 90." PhD dissertation, Department of Political Science, University of Sao Paulo, September 2000.

Melo, Jaime de and Arvind Panagaryia, eds. *New Dimension in Regional Integration.* Cambridge: Cambridge University Press, 1993.

———. *New Dimensions in Regional Integration.* Cambridge: Cambridge University Press, 1993.

Mello, Rubens Ferreira de. *Gênese e Evolução da Diplomacia.* Master Lecture, Instituto Católico de Direito Comparado da Pontifícia Universidade Católica do Rio de Janeiro. Rio de Janeiro: Ministry of Foreign Affairs, 1948.

Mendoza, Miguel Rodríguez. "Latin America and the US Trade and Tariff Act." *Journal of World Trade Law* 20.1 (January-February 1986), 47–60.

Metz, Allan. *Bill Clinton: A Bibliography.* Westport, CT: Greenwood Press, 2002.

Milner, Helen. *Interests, Institutions and Information.* Princeton, NJ: Princeton University Press, 1997.

Minns, John. *The Politics of Developmentalism. The Midas States of Mexico, South Korea, and Taiwan.* Basingstoke; New York: Palgrave Macmillan, 2006.

Mitchell, David. *Making Foreign Policy. Presidential Management of the Decision-Making Process.* Aldershot; Burlington, VT: Ashgate, 2005.

Montecinos, Veronica and John Markoff. "From the Power of Economic Ideas to the Power of Economists." In *The Other Mirror. Grand Theory through the Lens of Latin America,* edited by Miguel A. Centeno and Fernando Lopez-Alves. Princeton, NJ; Oxford: Princeton University Press, 2001.

Montero, Alfredo P. "Macroeconomic Deeds, Not Reform Words: The Determinants of Foreign Direct Investment in Latin America." *Latin American Research Review* 43.1 (2008), 55–77.

Montero, Jerónimo. "Cumbre de las Américas en Mar del Plata: Victorias, Debates y Limitaciones de la Oposición." *ACME: An International E-Journal for Critical Geographies* 6.1 (2007), 124–130. http://www.acme-journal.org/vol6/JM_s.pdf

Moravcsik, Andrew. "Preferences and Power in the European Community: A Liberal Intergovernmentalist Approach." *Journal of Common Market Studies* 31.4 (December 1993), 473–524.

———. "Introduction" in *Double-Edged Diplomacy. International Bargaining and Domestic Politics*, edited by Peter B. Evans, Harold K. Jacobson, and Robert D. Putnam. London; Berkeley and Los Angeles: University of California Press Ltd., 1993.
Mortimore, Michael. "Flying Geese or Sitting Ducks? Transnational and Industry in Developing Countries." *CEPAL Review* 51 (December 1993), 15–34.
Munck, Ronaldo. "The anti-Globalization Movement. From Seattle (1999) to the Future." In *Globalization and Contestation. The New Great Counter-Movement*. London; New York: Routledge, 2007.
Murray, Leonie G. *Clinton, Peacekeeping and Humanitarian Intervention. Rise and Fall of a Policy*. Abingdon, Oxon; New York: Routledge, 2008.
Myconos, George. *The Globalizations of Organized Labour: 1945–2005*. Basingstoke; New York: Palgrave Macmillan, 2005.
Nanto, Dick K. and Thomas Lum. "US International Trade: Data and Forecasts." Congressional Research Service Report No.IB96038. Washington, DC: US Library of Congress/CRS, 2003.
Narine, Shaun. *Explaining ASEAN: Regionalism in the Southeast Asia*. Boulder, CO: Lynne Rienner, 2002.
Narlikar, Amrita and Diana Tussie. "The G20 at the Cancún Ministerial: Developing Countries and their Evolving Coalitions in the WTO." *The World Economy* 27.7 (2004), 947–966.
Nassar, Andre M., Zuleika Arashiro, and Marcos S. Jank. "Tariff Spikes and Tariff Escalation." In *Handbook on International Trade Policy*, edited by William A. Kerr and James D. Gaisford. Cheltenham; Northampton, MA: Edward Elgar, 2006.
Neack, Laura. "Linking State Type with Foreign Policy Behavior." In *Foreign Policy Analysis. Continuity and Change in its Second Generation*, edited by Laura Neack, Jeanne A.K. Hey, and Patrick J. Haney. Englewood Cliffs, NJ: Prentice Hall, 1995.
Negri, João Alberto de, Jorge S. Arbache, and Maria L.F. Silva. "A Formação da Alca e seu Impacto no Potencial Exportador Brasileiro para os Mercados dos Estados Unidos e do Canadá." IPEA *Texto para Discussão* No.991, Brasília, October 2003.
Neiburg, Federico. "Economistas e Culturas Econômicas no Brasil e na Argentina. Notas para uma Comparação a Propósito das Heterodoxias." *Tempo Socia Revista de Sociologia da USP* 16.2 (November 2004), 177–202.
Newumann, Iver. "A Region-Building Approach." In *Theories of New Regionalism. A Palgrave Reader*, edited by Fredrik Söderbaum and Timothy M. Shaw. Basingstoke; New York: Palgrave Macmillan, 2003.
Nicholls, Shelton, Garnett Samuel, Philip Colthrust, and Earl Boodoo. "Open Regionalism and Institutional Development among the Smaller Integration Schemes of CARICOM, the Andean Community and the Central American Common Market." In *Regional Integration in Latin America and the Caribbean: The Political Economy of Open Regionalism*, edited by Victor Bulmer-Thomas. London: Institute of Latin American Studies, University of London, 2001.
Nixon, Richard. *"Address to the Nation Outlining a New Economic Policy: The Challenge of Peace."* August 15, 1971. http://www.presidency.ucsb.edu/ws/index.php?pid=3115#
Nogués, Julio J., Andrzej Olechowski, and L. Alan Winters. "The Extent of Nontariff Barriers to Industrial Countries' Imports." *The World Bank Economic Review* 1.1 (1986), 181–199.

Noland, Marcus. "Chasing Phantoms. The Political Economy of USTR." *International Organization* 51.3 (Summer 1997), 367.
Nölke, Andreas. "The Relevance of Transnational Policy Networks: Some Examples from the European Commission and the Bretton Woods Institutions." *Journal of International Relations and Development* 6.3 (2003), 276–298.
Nunes, Edson. *A Gramática Política do Brasil. Clientelismo e Insulamento Burocrático*. 3rd ed. Rio de Janeiro: Jorge Zahar Editor, 2003.
O"Donnell, Guillermo A. *Bureaucratic Authoritarianism. Argentina, 1966–1973, in Comparative Perspective*. Berkeley, CA: University of California Press, 1986.
O"Halloran, Sharyn. *Politics, Process and American Trade Policy*. Ann Arbor: University of Michigan Press, 1994.
Ocampo, José Antonio. "Lights and Shadows in Latin American Structural Reforms." In *Economic Reforms, Growth and Inequality in Latin America. Essays in Honor of Albert Berry*, edited by Gustavo Indart. Aldershot; Burlington: Ashgate, 2004.
——— and Pilar Esguerra. "The Andean Group and Latin American Integration." In *Economic Integration in the Western Hemisphere*, edited by Roberto Bouzas and Jaime Ros. Notre Dame, IN; London: University of Notre Dame Press, 1994.
Odell, John S. "Introduction" to *Negotiating Trade. Developing Countries in the WTO and NAFTA*. Cambridge, UK: Cambridge University Press, 2006.
——— and Susan K. Sell. "Reframing the Issue: The WTO Coalition on Intellectual Property and Public Health, 2001." In *Negotiating Trade. Developing Countries in the WTO and NAFTA*, edited by John S. Odell. Cambridge; New York: Cambridge University Press, 2006.
Office of the United States Trade Representative. *2003 Trade Policy Agenda and 2002 Annual Report on the Trade Agreements Program*. Washington, DC: U.S. Government Printing Office, 2003.
Oliveira, Henrique Altemani de. "Apresentação" to *A Política Externa Brasileira na Visão dos Seus Protagonistas*, edited by Henrique Altemani de Oliveira and José A. Guilhon Albuquerque. Rio de Janeiro: Editora Lumen Juris, 2005.
Onuf, Nicholas G. *World of our Making: Rules and Rule in Social Theory and International Relations*. Columbia, SC: University of South Carolina Press, 1989.
Onuki, Janina. "Brasil-Argentina: Do Conflito à Cooperação." In *A Política Externa Brasileira na Visão dos Seus Protagonistas*, edited by Henrique Altemani de Oliveira and José A. Guilhon Albuquerque. Rio de Janeiro: Editora Lumen Juris, 2005.
———. "As Mudanças da Política Externa Argentina no Governo Menem." PhD dissertation, Political Science Department, Universidade de São Paulo, 2002.
Ornstein, Norman. "The New Congress." In *The Controversial Pivot: The US Congress and North America*, edited by Robert A. Pastor and Rafael Fernandez de Castro. Washington, DC: The Brookings Institution, 1998.
Overbeek, Henk, ed. *Restructuring Hegemony in the Global Political Economy. The Rise of Transnational Liberalism in the 1980s*. London; New York: Routledge, 1993.
Oxfam. "Running into Sand. Why Failure at the Cancún Trade Talks Threatens the World's Poorest People." *Briefing Paper* 53, August 2003.
Oye, Kenneth A. "Explaining Cooperation Under Anarchy: Hypotheses and Strategies." In *Cooperation under Anarchy*. Princeton, NJ: Princeton University Press, 1986.

Page, Sheila. "Regional Integration and the Investment Effect." In *Regional Integration in Latin America and the Caribbean: The Political Economy of Open Regionalism*, edited by Victor-Bulmer Thomas. London: Institute of Latin American Studies, University of Lodnon, 2001.

Palmer, David Scott. *US Relations with Latin America during the Clinton Years.* Gainesville, FL: University Press of Florida, 2006.

Pastor, Jr., Manuel and Carol Wise. "Trading Places: U.S. Latinos and Trade Liberalization in the Americas." In *Borderless Borders. U.S. Latinos, Latin Americans, and the Paradox of Interdependence*, edited by Frank Bonilla, Edwin Melendez, Rebecca Morales, and Maria de los Angeles Torres. Philadelphia: Temple University Press, 1998.

———. "The Origins and Sustainability of Mexico's Free Trade Policy." *International Organization* 48.3 (Summer 1994), 459–489.

Pastor, Robert A. *Exiting the Whirlpool. U.S. Foreign Policy Toward Latin America and the Caribbean.* 2nd ed. Boulder, CO: Westview Press, 2001.

———. "The Bush Administration and Latin America: The Pragmatic Style and the Regionalist Option." *Journal of Interamerican Studies and World Affairs* 33.3 (1991), 1–34.

———. "Cry-and-Sigh Syndrome: Congress and Trade Policy." In *Making Economic Policy in Congress*, edited by Allen Schick. London; Washington, DC: American Enterprise Institute for Public Policy Research, 1983.

———. *Congress and the Politics of US Foreign Economic Policy 1929–1976.* Berkeley, Los Angeles; London: University of California Press, 1980.

———and Rafael Fernandez de Castro, eds. *The Controversial Pivot: The US Congress and North America*. Washington, DC: The Brookings Institution, 1998.

Patel, Chandrakant. "single Undertaking: A Straitjacket or a Variable Geometry?." *Trade-Related Agenda, Development and Equity (T.R.A.D.E) Working Papers* no.15, South Centre, May 2003. http://www.southcentre.org/index.php?option=com_content&task=view&id=363&Itemid=67

Pearson, Charles S. *Free Trade, Fair Trade? The Reagan Record.* Washington, DC: Foreign Policy Institute, School of Advanced International Studies, Johns Hopkins University/Lanham, MD: Distributed by University Press of America, 1988.

Peloso, Vincent C. and Barbara A. Tenenbaum, eds. *Liberals, Politics and Power. State Formation in Nineteenth-Century Latin America*. Athens, Georgia: The University of Georgia Press, 1996.

Pereira, Luiz Carlos Bresser and Yoshiaki Nakano. "The Missing Social Contract. Governability and Reform in Latin America." In *What Kind of Democracy? What Kind of Market? Latin America in the Age of Neoliberalism*, edited by Philip D. Oxhorn and Graciela Ducatenzeiler. University Park, PA: The Pennsylvania State University Press, 1998.

Perot, Ross and Pat Choate. *Save your Job, Save your Country: Why NAFTA Must be Stopped-Now!*. New York, NY: Hyperion Books, 1993.

Peters, B. Guy, Jon Pierre, and Desmond S. King. "The Politics of Path Dependence: Political Conflict in Historical Institutionalism." *The Journal of Politics* 67.4 (November 2005), 1275–1300.

Peters, Enrique Dussel. "La Polarización de la Economía Mexicana: Aspectos Económicos y Regionales."In *Impactos del TLC en México y Estados Unidos. Efectos Subregionales del Comercio y la Integración Económica*, edited by John

Bailey. Mexico, DF: Facultad Latinoamericana de Ciencias Sociales; México: Georgetown University, 2003.

Petras, James. "The Metamorphosis of Latin America's Intellectuals." *Latin American Perspectives* 17.2 (Spring 1990), 102–112.

Philippidis, G. and A.I. Sanjuán. "An Analysis of Mercosur's Regional Trade Agreements." *The World Economy* 30.3 (2007), 504–531.

Phillips, Lynne. "Introduction: Neoliberalism in Latin America." In *The Third Wave of Modernization in Latin America: Cultural Perspectives on Neoliberalism.* Wilimington, DE: Scholarly Resources, Inc., 1998.

Phillips, Nicola. "Whither IPE?." In *Globalizing International Political Economy.* Basingstoke; New York: Palgrave Macmillan, 2005.

———. "The Rise and Fall of Open Regionalism? Comparative Reflections on Regional Governance in the Southern Cone of Latin America." *Third World Quarterly* 24.2 (2003), 217–234.

Pinheiro, Leticia. "How Much Foreign Policy Teaching Can Be Foreign Policymaking?." Paper delivered at the 4th Annual APSA Conference on Teaching and Learning in Political Science, Charlotte, North Carolina, February 9–11, 2007.

———. "Traídos pelo Desejo: Um Ensaio sobre a Teoria e a Prática da Política Externa Brasileira Contemporânea." *Contexto Internacional* 22.2 (June-December 2000), 305–335.

———. "Unidades de Decisão e Processo de Formulação de Política Externa durante o Regime Militar." In *Sessenta Anos de Política Externa Brasileira (1930–1990). Prioridades, Atores e Políticas*, vol. 4, edited by José Augusto Guilhon Albuquerque. Sao Paulo: Anablume/NUPRI/USP, 2000.

Pio, Carlos. "A Estabilização Heterodoxa no Brasil: Idéias e Redes Políticas." *Revista Brasileira de Ciências Sociais* 16.46 (June 2001), 29–54.

Pizarro, Ramiro. *Comparative Analysis of Regionalism in Latin America and Asia-Pacific.* CEPAL Serie Comercio Internacional No. 6. Santiago, Chile: United Nations, 1999. http://www.eclac.cl/publicaciones/xml/5/4285/lcl1307i.pdf

Polanyi, Karl. *The Great Transformation.* Boston: Beacon Press, 1957.

Porter, Roger. "The Enterprise of the Americas Initiative: A New Approach to Economic Growth." *Journal of Interamerican Studies and World Affairs* 32.4 (Winter 1990), 1–12.

Prebisch, Raúl. "Five Stages in my Thinking on Development." In *Pioneers of Development*, edited by Gerald M. Meier and Dudley Seers. Oxford: Oxford University Press, 1984.

———. "statement at the Second Session of the Special Committee to Study the Formulation of New Measures for Economic Co-operation, of the Organization of American States," Buenos Aires, 28 April 1959. Reproduced in ECLA, *The Latin American Common Market.* s.l.: United Nations Department of Economic and Social Affairs, 1959.

———. *The Economic Development of Latin America and Its Principal Problems.* Lake Success, NY: United Nations Department of Economic Affairs, 1950.

Pusey, Michael. *Economic Rationalism in Canberra: A Nation-building State Changes its Mind.* Cambridge, UK: Cambridge University Press, 1991.

Putnam, Robert. "Diplomacy and Domestic Politics: The Logic of Two-level Games." *International Organization* 42.3 (Summer 1988), 427–460.

Quadros, Jânio. "Brazil's New Foreign Policy." *Foreign Affairs* 40 (1961), 19–27.

Quiggin, John. "'Economic Liberalism' Fall, Revival and Resistance." In *Ideas and Influence. Social Science and Public Policy in Australia*, edited by Peter Sandlers and James Walter. Sydney, NSW: UNSW Press, 2005.

Raymont, Henry. *Troubled Neighbors. The Story of US-Latin American Relations, from FDR to the Present*. New York: Westview Press, 2005.

Reagan, Ronald. *Announcement for Presidential Candidacy*, November 13, 1979. http://www.reagan.utexas.edu/archives/reference/11.13.79.html

Reifman, Alfred and Craig Elwell. "US Trade Policy: Free Trade-Fair Trade and Their Discontents." Congressional Research Service Report No.22. Washington, DC: US Library of Congress/CRS, 1992.

Reina, Mauricio and Gladys Cristina Barrera. "An Analysis of Colombian Reactions to the EAI: Prospects for Success." In *The Enterprise for the Americas Initiative. Issues and Prospects for a Free Trade Agreement in the Western Hemisphere*, edited by Roy E. Green. Westport, CT: Praeger, 1993.

Renshon, Stanley A., ed. *The Clinton Presidency. Campaigning, Governing & the Psychology of Leadership*. Boulder, CO: Westview Press, 1995.

Resende-Santos, João. "Fernando Henrique Cardoso. Social and Institutional Rebuilding in Brazil." In *Technopols. Freeing Politics and Markets in Latin America in the 1990si*, Jorge Domínguez. University Park, PA: The Pennsylvania State University Press, 1997.

Rippy, James F. *Latin America. A Modern History*. Ann Arbor: The University of Michigan Press, 1968.

Risse-Kappen, Thomas. "Ideas Do not Float Freely: Transnational Coalitions, Domestic Structures and the End of the Cold War." *International Organization* 48.2 (Spring 1994), 185–214.

Robertson, Justin. "Introduction: The Research Direction and Typology of Approaches." In *Diplomacy and Developing Nations. Post-Cold War Foreign-Policymaking Structures and Processes*, edited by Justin Robertson and Maurice A. East. Abington; New York: Routledge, 2005.

——— and Maurice A. East, eds. *Diplomacy and Developing Nations. Post-Cold War Foreign-Policymaking Structures and Processes*. Abington, New York: Routledge, 2005.

Rodas-Martini, Pablo. "Central America: Toward Open Regionalism or Toward an Opening without Regionalism?." In *Regional Integration in Latin America and the Caribbean: The Political Economy of Open Regionalism*, edited by Victor-Bulmer Thomas. London: Institute of Latin American Studies, University of London, 2001.

Rodríguez, Francisco and Dani Rodrik. "Trade Policy and Economic Growth: A Skeptic's Guide to the Cross-National Evidence." In *NBER Macroeconomics Annual 2000*, edited by Ben Bernanke and Kenneth S. Rogoff. Cambridge, MA: MIT Press for National Bureau of Economic Research, 2001.

Rodrik, Dani. "The Rush to Free Trade in the Developing World: Why So Late? Why Now? Will it Last?" In *Voting for Reform. Democracy, Political Liberalization, and Economic Adjustment*, edited by Stephan Haggard and Steven B. Webb. New York: Oxford University Press, 1994.

Roett, Riordan. *Mercosur: Regional Integration, World Markets*. Boulder, CO: Lynne Rienner Publishers, Inc., 1999.

Ros, Jaime. "Mexico and NAFTA: Economic Effects and the Bargaining Process." In *Mexico and the North American Free Trade*, edited by Victor Bulmer-Thomas, Nikki Craske, and Mónica Serrano. New York: St. Martin's Press, 1994.

Rosati, Jerel A. "A Cognitive Approach to the Study of Foreign Policy." In *Foreign Policy Analysis. Continuity and Change in its Second Generation*, edited by Jeanne A.K.Hey and Patrick J. Haney. Englewood Cliffs, NJ: Prentice Hall, 1995.

Rosen, Howard. "Free Trade Agreements as Foreign Policy Tools: The US-Israel and US-Jordan FTAs." In *Free Trade Agreements. U.S. Strategies and Priorities*, edited by Jeffrey J. Schott. Washington, DC: Institute for International Economics, 2004.

Rowat, Malcolm D. "Future Accession to NAFTA: The Case of Chile and the Mercosur." In *Beyond NAFTA: An Economic, Political and Sociological Perspective*, edited by A.R. Riggs and Tom Velk. Vancouver, BC: The Fraser Institute, 1993.

Rubens Barbosa & Associados, FIESP, and ICONE. *A Erosão das Preferências Comerciais Brasileiras na América Latina*. Sao Paulo, November 2004. http://www.fiesp.com.br/publicacoes/pdf/relacoes/estudo_erosao.pdf

Ruggie, John G. "What Makes the World Hang Together? Neo-Utilitarianism and the Social Constructivist Challenge." *International Organization* 52.4 (Autumn 1998), 855–885.

———. "Third Try at World Order? America and Multilateralism after the Cold War." *Political Science Quarterly* 109.4 (1994), 553–570.

———. "Multilateralism: The Anatomy of an Institution." In *Multilateralism Matters. The Theory and Praxis of an Institutional Form*. New York: Columbia University Press, 1993.

———. "International Regimes, Transactions, and Change: Embedded Liberalism in the Postwar Economic Order." *International Organization* 36.2 (Spring 1982), 379–415.

Sabatier, Paul A. and Hank C. Jenkins-Smith. *Policy Change and Learning: An Advocacy Coalition Approach*. Boulder, CO: Westview Press, 1993.

Sader, Emir and Ken Silverstein. *Without Fear of Being Happy. Lula, the Workers Party and Brazil*. London; New York: Verso, 1991.

Sáez, Sebastián. *Trade Policymaking in Latin America: A Compared Analysis*. CEPAL Serie Comercio Internacional No. 55. Santiago, United Nations, 2005. http://www.eclac.org/publicaciones/xml/8/23238/lcl2410i.pdf

Salazar-Xirinachs, José Manuel. "The Integrationist Revival: A Return to Prebisch's Policy Prescription." *CEPAL Review* 50 (1998), 21–40.

Sampson, Gary and Stephen Woolcock, eds. *Regionalism, Multilateralism, and Economic Integration: The Recent Experience*. New York: United Nations University Press, 2003.

Santos, Boaventura de Sousa. *The Rise of the Global Left. The World Social Forum and Beyond*. New York: Zed Books, 2006.

Santos, Norma Breda. "História das Relações Internacionais no Brasil: Esboço de uma Avaliação sobre a Área." *História* 24.1 (2005), 11–39.

Saraiva, Miriam Gomes. "As Estratégias de Cooperação Sul-Sul nos Marcos da Política Externa Brasileira de 1993 a 2007." *Revista Brasileira de Política Internacional* 50.2 (2007), 42–59.

Saul, John Ralston. *On Equilibrium*. Toronto: Penguin Books, 2001.

Sawyer, W. Charles and Richard Sprinkle. "U.S.-Israel Free Trade Area. Trade Expansion Effects of the Agreement." *Journal of World Trade Law* 20.5 (September-October 1986), 526–539.

Schattschneider, E.E. *Politics, Pressure, and the Tariff: A Study of Free Private Enterprise in Pressure Politics, as Shown in the 1929–1930 Revision of the Tariff*. Hamnden: Archon Books, 1935.

Schelling, Thomas C. *The Strategy of Conflict*. Cambridge: Harvard University Press, 1960.
Schier, Steven E. "A Unique Presidency." In *The Postmodern Presidency. Bill Clinton's Legacy in US Politics*. Pittsburgh: University of Pittsburgh Press, 2000.
Schirm, Stefan. *Globalization and the New Regionalism. Global Markets, Domestic Politics and Regional Cooperation*. Cambridge: Polity Press, 2002.
Schlesinger, Jr., Arthur. "Eyeless in Iraq: The Bush Doctrine and Its Consequences." In *War and the American Presidency*. New York: W.W. Norton & Company, 2004.
Schneider, Anne and Helen Ingram. "Systematically Pinching Ideas: A Comparative Approach to Policy Design." *Journal of Public Policy* 8.1 (1988), 61–80.
Schneider, Ben Ross. *Politics Within the State. Elite, Bureaucrats and Industrial Policy in Authoritarian Brazil*. Pittsburgh, PA: University of Pittsburgh Press, 1991.
Schneider, Ronald M. *Brazil. Foreign Policy of a Future World Power*. Boulder, CO: Westview Press, 1976.
Schnietz, Karen E. "The Institutional Foundation of U.S. Trade Policy: Revisiting Explanations for the 1934 Reciprocal Trade Agreements Act." *Journal of Policy History* 12.4 (2000), 417–444.
Schott, Jeffrey J., ed. *Free Trade Agreements. U.S. Strategies and Priorities*. Washington, DC: Institute for International Economics, 2004.
———. "Assessing US FTA Policy." *Free Trade Agreements. U.S. Strategies and Priorities*. Washington, DC: Institute for International Economics, 2004.
Schultz, Michael, Fredrik Söderbaum, and Joakim Öjendal. "Key Issues in the New Regionalism: Comparisons from Asia, Africa and the Middle East." In *Comparing Regionalisms: Implications for Global Development*, edited by Björn Hettne, András Inotai, and Osvaldo Sunkel. Basingstoke; New York: Palgrave Macmillan, 2001.
Sek, Lenore. "Trade Promotion Authority (Fast-Track Authority for Trade Agreements): Background and Developments in the 107th Congress." *Issue Brief for Congress*, updated January 14, 2003. Washington, DC: US Library of Congress/CRS, 2003.
Selcher, Wayne A. "Brazil in the World: Multipolarity as Seen by a Peripheral ADC Middle Power." In *Latin American Foreign Policies. Global and Regional Dimensions*, edited by Elizabeth G. Ferris and Jennie K. Lincoln. Boulder, CO: Westview Press, 1981.
Sennes, Ricardo. "Mudanças da Política Externa Brasileira na Década de 1980: uma Potência Média Recém-Industrializada." Master's dissertation, Department of Political Science, University of Sao Paulo, 1996.
Sheehan, Peter J. "Reason, Values and Public Policy." Working Paper No.3, Centre for Strategic Economic Studies, Victoria University of Technology, Melbourne, March 1995. http://www.cfses.com/documents/wp3cses.pdf
Shenin, David, ed. *Beyond The Ideal: Pan Americanism in Inter-American Affairs*. Westport, CT: Greenwood Press, 2000.
Sikkink, Kathryn. *Ideas and Institutions. Developmentalism in Brazil and Argentina*. Ithaca, NY: Cornell University Press, 1991.
Silberman, Bernard. *Cages of Reason: The Rise of the Rational State in France, Japan, the United States, and Great Britain*. Chicago: Chicago University Press, 1993.
Silva, Alberto da Costa. "Diplomacia e Cultura." In *O Itamaraty na Cultura Brasileira*, edited by Carlos Leal. Rio de Janeiro: Livraria Francisco Alves Editora S.A., 2002.

Silva, Alexandra de Mello. "A Política Externa Brasileira no Cenário da Guerra Fria." *Os Anos JK*. Centro de Pesquisa e Documentação de História Contemporânea do Brasil, Fundação Getúlio Vargas, Rio de Janeiro. http://www.cpdoc.fgv.br/nav_jk/htm/O_Brasil_de_JK/A_politica_externa_brasileira_no_cenario_da_Guerra_Fria.asp

Simmons, Beth A. and Zachary Elkins. "The Globalization of Liberalization: Policy Diffusion in the International Political Economy." *American Political Science Review* 98.1 (February 2004), 171–189.

Simon, Herbert A. "Rationality as Process and as Product of Thought." *The American Economic Review* 68.2 (May 1978), 1–16.

Singer, Hans W. "The Distribution of Gains between Investing and Borrowing Countries." *American Economic Review* XL (May 1950), 433–485.

Singer, Peter. *The President of Good & Evil. The Ethics of George W. Bush*. Melbourne: The Text Publishing Company, 2004.

Sloan, John W. *The Reagan Effect. Economics and Presidential Leadership*. Lawrence, KS: University Press of Kansas, 1999.

Smith, Joseph. *Unequal Giants: Diplomatic Relations between the United States and Brazil, 1889–1930*. Pittsburgh: University of Pittsburgh Press, 1991.

———. "The First Conference of American States (1889–1890) and the Early Pan American Policy of the United States." In *Beyond The Ideal: Pan Americanism in Inter-American Affairs*, edited by David Shenin. Westport, CT: Greenwood Press, 2000.

Smith, Murray. "The North American Free Trade Agreement: A Canadian Perspective." In *The Enterprise for the Americas Initiative. Issues and Prospects for a Free Trade Agreement in the Western Hemisphere*, edited by Roy E. Green. Westport, CT: Praeger, 1993.

Smith, Peter H. *The Talons of the Eagle. Latin America, the United States, and the World*. 3rd ed. Oxford; New York: Oxford University Press, 2008.

———. "The Mexican Peso Crisis." In *East Asia and Latin America. The Unlikely Alliance*, edited by Peter H. Smith, Kotaro Horisaka, and Shoji Nishijima. Lanham, Maryland: Rowman & Littlefield Publishers, Inc, 2003.

Snidal, Duncan. "Relative Gains and the Pattern of International Cooperation." *American Political Science Review* 85.3 (1991), 701–726.

Snyder, Richard, H.W. Bruck, and Burton Sapin. "Decision-Making as an Approach to the Study of International Politics," Foreign Policy Analysis Project no.3 (1954). Reprinted in Richard Snyder, H.W. Bruck and Burton Sapin, *Foreign Policy Decision-Making (Revisited)*. Basingstoke; New York: Palgrave Macmillan, 2002.

Söderbaum, Fredrik and Timothy M. Shaw, eds. *Theories of New Regionalism. A Palgrave Reader*. Basingstoke; New York: Palgrave Macmillan, 2003.

Stark, David and Laszlo Bruzt. "Enabling Constraints: Fontes Institucionais de Coerência nas Políticas Públicas no Pós-Socialismo." *Revista Brasileira de Ciências Sociais* 13.36 (1998), 13–40.

Steinmo, Sven, Katheen Thelen, and Frank Longstreth, eds. *Structuring Politics: Historical Institutionalism in Comparative Perspective*. Cambridge: Cambridge University Press, 1992.

Storrs, Keith Larry. "Brazil's Independent Foreign Policy, 1961–1964. Background, Tenets, Linkage to Domestic Politics, and Aftermath." PhD dissertation, Cornell University, Ithaca, NY, 1973.

Strange, Susan. *States and Markets*. 2nd ed. London; New York: Pinter Publishers, 1988.

Sunkel, Osvaldo and Michael Mortimore. "Transnational Integration and National Disentegration Revisited." In *Comparing Regionalisms: Implications for Global Development*, edited by Björn Hettne, András Inotai, and Osvaldo Sunkel. Basingstoke; New York: Palgrave Macmillan, 2001.

―――― and Pedro Paz. *El Subdesarrollo Latinoamericano y la Teoría del Desarrollo.* Mexico, DF: Siglo XXI Editores, 1970.

Taffet, Jeffrey F. *Foreign Aid as Foreign Policy: The Alliance for Progress in Latin America.* New York: Routledge, 2007.

Teichman, Judith. *The Politics of Freeing the Markets in Latin America. Chile, Argentina, and Mexico.* London; Chapel Hill: The University of North Carolina, 2001.

Terada, Takashi. "Constructing an 'East Asian' Concept and Growing Regional Identity: From EAEC to ASEAN+3." *The Pacific Review* 16.2 (2003), 251–277.

Thelen, Kathleen. "Historical Institutionalism in Comparative Politics." *Annual Review of Political Science* 2 (1999), 369–404.

Thorp, Rosemary. *Progress, Poverty and Exclusion: An Economic History of Latin America in the 20th century.* Washington, DC: Inter-American Development Bank, 1998.

Tomlin, Brian W. "The Stages of Pre-Negotiation: The Decision to Negotiate North American Free Trade." *International Journal* XLIV (1989), 254–279.

Torres, Blanca. "Transnational Actors and NAFTA: The Search for Coalitions on Labor and the Environment." In *Regionalism and Governance in the Americas Continental Drift*, edited by Louise Fawcett and Monica Serrano. Basingstoke; New York: Palgrave Macmillan, 2005.

Trentmann, Frank. "Political Culture and Political Economy: Interest, Ideology, and Free Trade." *Review of International Political Economy* 5.2 (Summer 1998), 217–251.

Tucker, Nancy Bernkopf. "The Clinton Years: The Problem of Coherence." In *Making China Policy: Lessons from the Bush and Clinton Administrations*, edited by Ramon Myers, Michel Oksenberg, and David Shambaugh. Lanham, Maryland: Rowman & Littlefield Publishers, Inc., 2001.

Tussie, Diana. "Regionalism: Providing a Substance to Multilateralism?." In *Theories of New Regionalism. A Palgrave Reader*, edited by Fredrik Söderbaum and Timothy M. Shaw. Basingstoke; New York: Palgrave Macmillan, 2003.

―――― and Ignacio Labaqui. "The Free Trade Area of the Americas: The Hunt for the Hemispheric Grand Bargain." In *Regionalism and Governance in the Americas Continental Drift*, edited by Louise Fawcett and Monica Serrano. Basingstoke; New York: Palgrave Macmillan, 2005.

Tyson, Laura D"Andrea. *Who's Bashing Who? Trade Conflict in High-Technology Industries.* Washington, DC: Institute for International Economics, 1992.

Uslaner, Eric M. "Let the Chits Fall Where They May? Executive and Constituency Influences on Congressional Voting on NAFTA." *Legislative Studies Quarterly* 23.3 (August 1998), 347–371.

Vaitsos, Constantino V. *Crisis en la Cooperación Económica Regional. La Integración entre Países Subdesarrollados.* Mexico, D.F.: Instituto Latinoamericano de Estudios Transnacionales, 1978.

Valdés, Eduardo D. "O Pensamento Nacionalista na América Latina e a Reivindicação da Identidade Econômica (1920–1940)." *Estudos Históricos* 20 (1997), 1–19.

Valdés, Juan Gabriel. *Pinochet's Economists. The Chicago School in Chile.* Cambridge; New York: Cambridge University Press, 1995.

Valenzuela, Arturo. "The United States and Latin America: The Road Ahead." *LASA Forum* XXXV.4 (Winter 2005), 9.

Vega, Gustavo and Luz María de Mora. "Mexico's Trade Policy: Financial Crisis and Economic Recovery." In *Confronting Development. Assessing Mexico's Economic and Social Policy* Challenges, edited by Kevin J. Middlebrook and Eduardo Zepeda. Stanford, CA: Stanford University Press, 2003.

Veiga, Pedro da Motta. "Política Comercial no Brasil: Características, Condicionantes Domésticos e Policy-Making." In *Políticas Comerciais Comparadas. Desempenho e Modelos Organizacionais*, ICONE, FIPE, and DFID. Sao Paulo: Editora Singular, 2007.

———. "Brazil in Mercosur: Reciprocal Influence." In *Mercosur: Regional Integration, World Markets*, edited by Riordan Roett. Boulder, CO: Lynne Rienner Publishers, Inc., 1999.

———. "El Mercosur y el proceso de construcción del ALCA." *Revista Integración & Comercio* 3 (September-December 1997), 3–31.

Velasco, Jesus. "Reading Mexico, Understanding the United States: American Transnational Intellectuals in the 1920s and 1990s." *The Journal of American History* 86.2 (September 1999), 641–667.

Vieira, Mario Antonio M. de Carvalho. "Idéias e Instituições: Uma Reflexão sobre Política Externa Brasileira do Início da Década de 90." *Contexto Internacional* 23.2 (2001), 245–293.

Vigevani, Tullo. "Brazilian Foreign Policy at the End of the Twentieth Century: An Exercise in Autonomy through Integration." Paper prepared for the 20th Conference of Historical Sciences, Sydney, Australia, July 3–9, 2005.

——— and Gabriel Cepaluni. *Brazilian Foreign Policy in Changing Times: The Quest for Autonomy From Sarney to Lula*. Translated by Leandro Moura. Lanham: Lexington Books, 2009.

———, Marcelo F. de Oliveira, and Rodrigo Cintra. "Política Externa do Governo FHC: A Busca da Autonomia pela Integração." *Tempo Socia* 15.2 (November 2003), 31–61.

——— and Marcelo Passini Mariano. *ALCA. O Gigante e os Anões*. Sao Paulo: Editora SENAC, 2001.

Villareal, M. Angeles. *Mexico's Maquiladora Industry*. US Congressional Research Service Report updated 14 December 1993. Washington, DC: US Library of Congress/CRS, 1993.

Viner, Jacob. "Conflicts of Principle in Drafting a Trade Charter." *Foreign Affairs* 25.4 (July 1947), 612–628.

Vizentini, Paulo Fagundes. "From FHC to Lula (1995–2004): Brazil's Foreign Policy and Regional Integration." Paper prepared for the 20th International Conference of Historical Sciences, Sydney, Australia, July 3–9, 2005.

Vosko, Leah F. "Fabric Friends and Clothing Foes: A Comparative Analysis of Textile and Apparel Industries under the NAFTA." *Review of Radical Political Economics* 25.4 (December 1993), 45–58.

Walt, Stephen M. "Two Cheers for Clinton's Foreign Policy." *Foreign Affairs* 79.3 (2000), 63–79.

Walter, James, ed. *Ideas and Influence. Social Science and Public Policy in Australia*. Sydney, NSW: UNSW Press, 2005.

Waltz, Kenneth N. Theory of International Politics. Reading, MA: Addison-Wesley, 1979.

Warleigh-Lack, Alex. "Toward a Conceptual Framework of Regionalisation: Bridging 'New Regionalism' and 'Integration Theory'." *Review of International Political Economy* 13.5 (December 2006), 750–771.

Watson, Alexander F. *The Americas in the 21st Century: The US-Brazilian Relationship*. US Department of State Dispatch, December 12, 1994.

Watson, Matthew. *Foundations of International Political Economy*. Basingstoke; New York: Palgrave Macmillan, 2005.

Weber, Max. "Parlamentarismo e Governo numa Alemanha Reconstruída." In *Ensaios de Sociologia e OutrosEscritos*, translated by Mauricio Tragtenberg. São Paulo: Abril Cultural, 1974.

Weintraub, Sidney. "History Repeats Itself in Trade Policy." *CSIS Issues in International Political Economy* 34 (October 2002). http://www.csis.org/media/csis/pubs/issues200210.pdf

———. "The North American Free Trade Agreement as Negotiated: A US Perspective." In *Assessing NAFTA: A Trinational Analysis*, edited by Steven Globerman and Michael Walker. Vancouver: The Fraser Institute, 1992.

———. *Free Trade Between Mexico and the United States?*. Washington, DC: Brookings Institution, 1984.

Weir, Margareth. "Ideas and the Politics of Bounded Innovation." In *Structuring Politics: Historical Institutionalism in Comparative Perspective*, edited by Sven Steinmo, Katheen Thelen, and Frank Longstreth. Cambridge: Cambridge University Press, 1992.

———. "Ideas and Politics: The Acceptance of Keynesianism in Britain and the United States." In *The Political Power of Economic Ideas*, edited by Peter Hall. Princeton: Princeton University Press, 1989.

Weis, W. Michael. "Pan American Shift: Oswaldo Aranha and the Demise of the Brazilian-American Alliance." In *Beyond The Ideal: Pan Americanism in Inter-American Affairs*, edited by David Shenin. Westport, CT: Greenwood Press, 2000.

Wendt, Alexander. "Anarchy is what States Make of it: The Social Construction of Power Politics." *International Organization* 46.2 (1992), 391–425.

———. *Social Theory of International Politics*. Cambridge: Cambridge University Press, 1999.

Whitwell, Greg. *The Treasury Line*. Sydney, NSW: George Allen & Unwin, 1986.

Wiarda, Howard. *Dilemmas of Democracy in Latin America. Crises and Opportunity*. With the assistance of Esther M. Skelley. Lanham, Maryland: Rowman & Littlefield Publishers, Inc., 2005.

———. "After Miami: The Summit, the Peso Crisis, and the Future of US-Latin American Relations." *Journal of Interamerican Studies and World Affairs* 37.1(1995), 43–68.

Williamson, John. "In Search of a Manual for Technopols." In *The Political Economy of Policy Reform*. Washington, DC: Institute for International Economics, 1994.

———. *Latin American Adjustment: How Much Has Happened?*. Washington, DC: Institute for International Economics, 1990.

———. *The Progress of Policy Reform in Latin America*. Washington, DC: Institute for International Economics, 1990.

Wilson, Arlene E. "A US Perspective on the Canada-US Free Trade Agreement." In *The Enterprise for the Americas Initiative. Issues and Prospects for a Free Trade Agreement in the Western Hemisphere*, edited by Roy E. Green. Westport, CT: Praeger, 1993.

Winham, Gilbert. *International Trade and the Tokyo Round Negotiation.* Princeton, New Jersey: Princeton University Press, 1986.

Winters, Alan L. "Regionalism vs. Multilateralism." In *Market Integration, Regionalism and the Global Economy,* edited by Richard Baldwin, Daniel Cohen, Andre Sapir, and Anthony Venables. Cambridge: Cambridge University Press, 1999.

Wittkoff, E. Peter. "Amazon Surveillance System (SIVAM): US and Brazilian Cooperation." Master's dissertation, Naval Postgraduate School, Monterey, California, December 1999.

Wonnacott, Paul. *The United States and Canada. The Quest for Free Trade.* Washington, DC: Institute for International Economics, 1987.

Wood, Bryce. *The Making of the Good Neighbor Policy.* New York: Columbia University Press, 1961.

Woods, Ngaire. "Economic Ideas and International Relations: Beyond Rational Neglect." *International Studies Quarterly* 39.2 (June 1995), 161–180.

Woodward, Bob. *Bush at War.* New York: Simon & Schuster, 2002.

———. *The Agenda. Inside the Clinton White House.* New York: Simon & Schuster, 1994.

World Bank. "swimming against the Tide: How Developing Countries are Coping with the Global Crisis." Background paper prepared by World Bank staff for the 20 Finance Ministers and Central Bank Governors Meeting, Horshmam, United Kingdom, March 13–14, 2009.

World Trade Organization (WTO). *Regionalism and the World Trading System.* Geneva: World Trade Organization, 1995.

Yee, Albert S. "Thick Rationality and the Missing 'Brute Fact': The Limits of Rationalist Incorporation of Norms and Ideas." *The Journal of Politics* 59.4 (1997), 1001–1039.

Zoellick, Robert B. *Statement at the Fourth WTO Ministerial Conference.* Doha, Qatar, November 9–13, 2001 (WT/MIN(01)/ST/3).

———. "A Republican Foreign Policy." *Foreign Affairs* 79.1 (January/February 2000), 63–78.

Index

Page numbers in bold face denote tables.

accession, NAFTA, 29, 30, 33, 36, 46, 144
Adams, John Quincy, 66
agency and developing countries, 4, 9, 109, 137
agency and structure, 12–13, 17, 52, 144, 149
agriculture
   liberalization, 40, 84, 88–9, 130
   negotiations, 4, 40, 42, 71, 73, 83, 84, 94, 103–6, 137
   sensitive products, 41, 73
   subsidies, 40, 41, 42, 43, 73, 104, 106
ALADI. *See* Latin American Integration Association
Albright, Madeleine, 98, 128
Alliance for Progress, 34, 67–8, 74–5
Americas Business Forum, 37
Amorim, Celso Luiz Nunes, 132–3, 138
Andean Community, **25**, **29**, 30, 39, 110, 136
Andean Pact, 55, 56. *See also* Andean Community
Andean Trade Preference Act, 87, 89
annexation, U.S.-Latin America, 67, 106, 131, 139
antidumping, 36, 38, 40, 42, 43, 71, 73, 84–5, 91, 103, 106, 127
anti-free trade movement, 40, 99
anti-NAFTA movement, 88, 92, 93, 94
APEC (Asia-Pacific Economic Cooperation), 8, 24, 61, 94, 97, 98
Argentina, **25**, 28–9, 33, 34, 44, 45, 55, 56, 59, 60, 62, 116, 120, 126, 136, 137

ASEAN (Association of Southeast Asian Nations), 104
asymmetrical interdependence, 12, 72, 73, 75, 120, 133, 138
asymmetry
   economic, 28, 55, 56, 66, 92, 126, 136, 137, 147
   power, 12, 14, 44, 46, 63, 66, 73, 119, 129, 140, 146, 147
   technical, 35, 130
Australia, 46, **105**, 147

Babb, Sarah, 60
Baker, James, 42, 71, 88, 100, 101, 145
bargaining power, 7, 8, 25, 28, 46, 126
behind the border issues, 6
Bentsen, Lloyd, 88, 90, 94
bilateral trade agreements, United States, 105. *See also individual names*
bilateralism, 3, 45, 47, 72, 144, 146
Brazil
   congress and the FTAA, 130–1
   democratization, 115, 129, 135
   economic liberalization, 115, 123, 129, 135, 143
   exports, 29–30, 40, 42, 106, 116, 118, 120, 126, 127, 136
   foreign policy and autonomy, 18, 29, 46, 110, 115–21, 123–8, 135, 138, 140, 145–7
   foreign policy paradigms, 116–19
   foreign trade policy system, 111–15
   industrialization, 115–17
   international identity, 110, 139

INDEX

Brazil—*Continued*
  market-based reforms, 120, 122–3, 144
  middle power, 27, 109, 115–19
  military regime, 28, 56, 112, 113, 116–19, 125
  Ministry of Development, Industry and Foreign Trade Ministry, 111
  Ministry of Foreign Affairs. *See* Itamaraty
  modernization, 68, 115–18
  national identity, 110, 113–14
Brazil-Argentina relations, 29, 44, 116, 120, 126, 136
Brazilian Business Coalition (CEB), 129
Brazilian Social Democratic Party (PSDB), 122
Brazil-U.S. bilateral cooperation, 116
  ethanol agreement, 138
  FTAA meetings, 37
Bretton Woods, 79, 83
BRIC (Brazil, Russia, India, and China) summit, 137
Bruck, H.W., 13
bureaucracy
  autonomy, Brazil, 111–15
  insulation, 59, 74, 112
  politicization, 71, 81–2, 84, 112
  United States, 80–2
Bush (George H.W.) administration, 51, 80–1, 86–7, 89, 91, 100, 104, 108
Bush (George W.) administration, 40, 100–8, 146–7
business sector, 14, 37, 46, 57, 83, 88, 94, 96, 99, 112, 120, 122, 129–30

CACM (Central American Common Market), **25**, 27, **29**, 55, 56, 62
CAFTA-DR (Central America and Dominican Republic Free Trade Agreement), **105**, 106
Canada, 27, 33, 37, 39, 42, 44, 46–8
  Conservative Party, 71
  Liberal Party, 70
Cancún WTO Ministerial Conference, 43
Cardoso (Fernando Henrique) administration, 122–31, 132, 133, 135, 138, 139, 140

CARICOM (Caribbean Community), 25, 27–8, 37, 43, 55, 62
Castro, João Augusto de Araújo, 109, 118
CEPAL (Economic Commission for Latin America and the Caribbean), 33, 34, 53–4, 56, 61
Chamber of Foreign Trade (Brazil), 111
Chavez, Hugo, 42, 45
checks and balances, 81
Cheney, Dick, 101
Chile, 13, **25**, 30–1, 33, 35, 37, 38, 39, 44, 46, 55, 56, 59, 60, 95, 97, 99, 104, **105**
China, 40, 97, 98, 119, 127, 133, 134, 137
Christopher, Warren, 98
civil society and the FTAA, 37, 38, 41, 97, 130, 135, 138
clientelism, 112. *See also* corporatism
Clinton (William Jefferson) administration, 31–5, 36, 38–9, 89–100, 101, 108
commodity dependence, 53, 54, 57, **58**
competitive liberalization, 42, 46, 100, 101, 106, 145
cooperation
  coercion, 13
  concept, 11–12
  policy idea, 11–18
corporatism, 57, 74, 92, 112, 115, 122, 127, 129
Cox, Robert W., 12
Cuba, 34, 45, 68, 74, 82
CUSFTA (Canada-U.S. Free Trade Agreement), 6, 42, 68–71
CUT (United Central Workers Federation), 129–30

da Silva (Luiz Inácio Lula) administration, 42, 106–7, 110–11, 131–8, 139
de Castro, Rafael Fernandez, 95
de Mello, Fernando Collor, 120, 123
debt crisis, 58, 60–1, 62, 87, 119–20, 144–5
decision-making, ideas and beliefs, 5, 10, 13, 16–19, 51, 62, 72, 75, 83, 101

delegation mechanism, U.S. *See* fast-track authority
democracy promotion, 26–7, 31–3, 41, 59, 62, 66, 87, 98, 99, 107
Denzau, Arthur T., 15
dependency theory, 122
dependent development, 56
developing countries, 4, 6, 9, 35, 39, 43, 58, 72, 97, 109, 125, 137
development ideas in Latin America, 51–7
Doha Round, 4, 5, 43, 102, 103, 136, 137–8, 143
drugs and security, 30, 98, 99, 103

East Asia, 8, 9, 57, 58, 79, 86, 100
ECLAC. *See* CEPAL
economic cooperation, 8, 26, 28, 46, 51, 62, 63, 65–75, 120, 145
economic integration, ideology, 12–13, 26–7, 61, 62, 65–75, 121, 123, 125, 128–9, 133
Economic Policy Council (U.S.), 81
economists, role in policymaking, 56, 59, 90, 122
embedded liberalism, 5, 107
emerging markets, 99
Enterprise for the Americas Initiative (EAI), 23–4, 26, 29, 30, 62, 80, 87, 89, 104, 108
Environmental issues, 33, 34, 36, 41, 74, 88, 89–90, 92–7, 100, 102, 103, 104, 128, 140
European, Community, 84, 86
single market, 61, 91, 119
exports, intra-Western Hemisphere, 25, 29, 39, 53, 56, 61, 118

fair trade, 84, 86, 89, 92, 95–8
Farm Bill (U.S., 2002), 41, 103, 106, 130
fast-track authority, 35, 41, 70, 84–5, 88, 95–9. *See also* trade promotion authority
Feinberg, Richard, 32
financial crisis, 57, 94, 119, 123, 140
First International Conference of American States, 67, 74–5, 148
Fisher, Richard, 40
Fonseca, Gelson, Jr., 121

foreign debt, 58
foreign direct investment, 7, 39, 58, 87, 115
Fox, Vicente, 104
Franco, Itamar, 121–3
free market democracies, 3, 26, 27, 31, 59, 63, 66, 79, 107, 144
freer trade, 82–6
FTAA
  anti-FTAA movement, 45, 131, 135
  fragmentation, 18, 25, 46, 47, 104, 108, 110, 136, 139, 146–7
  lite, 42, 43
  negotiation groups, 38
  plebiscite, 130–1, 132
  policy idea, 3–4, 31–5
  politicization, Brazil, 112, 129–30, 139
  trade ministerial meetings, 36–7, 44, 45

G20, 43, 137
Gamble, Andrew, 9
Garten, Jeffrey E., 90
Gass, Oscar, 84
GATT (General Agreement on Tariffs and Trade), 5, 35, 71, 72, 73, 83, 86, 143
Geisel, Ernesto, 117
General System of Preferences (GSP), 80
Gillespie, Charles, Jr., 33
Ginrich, Newt, 97
globalization and regionalism, 7–8, 61, 143, 146–7
Goldfinger, Nat, 84
Goldstein, Judith, 16, 83
Good Neighbor Policy, 67
Gore, Al, 32, 89–90, 93, 94
Gotlieb, Allan, 71
gradualism, Brazil, 29, 34, 38–9, 128
Great Depression, 52, 53, 82
Greenspan, Alan, 90
Guimarães, Samuel Pinheiro, 133–4

hegemony, 12, 57, 143, 146–7
hemispheric cooperation, 26, 32, 37, 45, 67, 87
Hemispheric Social Alliance, 38
heterodox economic plans, 59, 122

Hills, Carla, 88
Hirschman, Albert, 63, 68
hub-and-spoke, 27, 30, 44, 71
Hull, Cordell, 82

IBSA (India, Brazil and South Africa), 137
ideas, role in policymaking, 16–18
import substitution industrialization (ISI), 25, 56, 57, 117
Independent Foreign Policy, Brazil, 116–17, 118
industrialization, Latin America, 25, 53–7
Institutionalism, Political Science, 16–18
intellectual property negotiations, 33, 35, 36, 40, 42, 43, 67, 72
intellectuals, role, 31, 53, 75, 101, 113, 122, 135
Inter-American Development Bank (IDB), 33, 34, 137
interdependence, 12, 61, 72–3, 75, 118, 120, 125, 133, 137, 138, 140, 147
interest groups, 8, 18, 83, 85, 94, 111, 112, 115, 122
International Monetary Fund (IMF), 58, 83
international political economy and regionalism, 6–9
inward-looking model, 6, 8, 61
Israel, 79, 86, **105**
Itamaraty, 112–15, 120, 124, 125, 130, 132, 134, 139–40

Jaguaribe, Helio, 26
Japan, 6, 30, 53, 58, 67, 69, 70, 72, 90, 91,100, 107, 118
Jordan, 97, 99, **105**

Kantor, Mickey, 37, 90, 95, 96
Kennedy, John, 68, 84, 96
Kennedy Round, 84
Keohane, Robert, 11–12
Kissinger, Henry, 119
Krasner, Stephen, 82
Kubitschek, Juscelino, 68

Labaqui, Ignacio, 26–7
labor, organized, 37–8, 70, 74, 83, 88, 92–3, 129, 130, 131, 135, 138

Lafer, Celso, 42, 114, 125, 129, 133, 134
LAFTA (Latin American Free Trade Area), 55–6, 61
Lampréia, Luiz Felipe, 37, 125
Latin American Integration Association, 24, 29, 57, 118, 120, 128
liberal economic order, 5, 8, 9, 79, 84, 124, 143
Lula administration. *See* da Silva (Luiz Inácio Lula) administration

maquiladoras, 71
Mastanduno, Michael, 81
McLarty, Thomas, 90
Menem, Carlos, 29
Mercosur (Southern Common Market), **25**, 28–30, 37, 39, 121, 126, 128–9, 133
  democracy clause, 33, 125; US offer, 43, 99–100, 121
  EU trade relations, 28, 39, 43, 129–30, 136
  U.S. relations, **25**, 28–9, 43, 99–100, 128, 135–8, 144
Mexico, 23, 24, **25**, 44, 45, 46, 55, 56, 58, 60, 62, 68–9, 104, **105**, 147. *See also* NAFTA
Middle East, 89, 97, 104, **105**, 118, 127
middle power, 27, 109, 115–19
modernization, 54, 56, 62, 68, 115–18
Monroe Doctrine, 66
moral crusade, 101
Morgenthau, Henry, 84
Mosbacher, Robert, 88
most-favored nation, 83, 97
Mulroney, Brian, 69
multilateral trading system, 5, 35, 46, 72, 104, 118
multilateralism, 5–7, 41, 43, 79, 83–6, 91, 101, 102, 107, 108, 118, 121, 123, 139, 145
Murphy, Peter, 70

Nabuco, Joaquim, 109–10
NAFTA (North American Free Trade Agreement), 26–7, 71–5, 88–9, 92–7

National Confederation of Industry (CNI), 129
National Economic Council, 80–1
neoconservatives, 101, 145
neoliberal ideas, empowerment, 57–60
neoliberal institutionalism, 11–12
neorealistm, 11–12
neostructuralism, 122
new regionalism, 7–9
New Regionalism Approach, 8–9
new trade regionalism, 9, 12, 24, 61
New Zealand, 105
Nixon, Richard, 84
nontariff barriers, 58, 84, 86, 127
North, Douglass G., 15
North-South relations, 7–9, 14, 26, 66, 73, 119, 124, 135–6
nuclear cooperation, Brazil-Germany, 118
Nye, Joseph, 12

Obama, Barack, 45, 92
open regionalism, 24, 60–3
Organization of American States (OAS), 33, 67

Padilla, Chris, 43
Panama invasion, Bush administration, 87
Pan-Americanism, 66
Pastor, Robert, 95
Payne, Anthony, 9
Perot, Ross, 93
Polanyi, Karl, 17, 148
policy communities, 16, 17, 59, 60, 62, 74, 94, 97
policy crisis, 17
policy innovation, 17, 18
political leadership, 38, 80, 98, 120, 147
Porter, Roger, 24
pragmatic institutionalism, 123
pragmatism, 31, 43, 63, 87
Prebisch, Raúl, 54
presidential attention, 82, 87, **105**, 108
presidential diplomacy, 124
Project for the New American Century, 101
Putnam, Robert, 14

Quadros, Jânio, 116–17

rationality, 12–16, 83, 146
Reagan, Ronald, 68, 71, 80, 84–6, 87, 100, 107
Real Plan, 122
realism, 11, 12, 98, 138
reciprocity, trade agreements, 67, 73, 82, 83, 85, 103, 136
regionalism concept, 6–9
regulatory policies and trade, 6, 8, 15, 25, 35, 38, 72, 73, 89, 94, 110, 136
Reich, Robert, 90
Reisman, Simon, 70
responsible pragmatism, 117–18, 132
Rio Branco, Baron of, 113–14, 116, 125
Roosevelt, Franklin D., 67, 82
Rostenkowski, Dan, 88
Rostow, Walt, 68
Rumsfeld, Donald, 101

SAFTA (South American Free Trade Area), 30, 39, 121
Salinas de Gortari, Carlos, 60, 72, 88
Sapin, Burton, 13
Schirm, Stefan, 7–8
Seattle WTO meeting, 40, 97
SENALCA (National Secretariat for the Coordination of FTAA-related issues), 130, 134
September 11, 2001, 41, 101–5
Services negotiations, 29, 35, 40, 42, 43, 62, 72, 73, 110, 127, 129, 120, 133, 136
Sikkink, Kathryn, 17, 115
Singapore, 97, 99, 104, **105**
single undertaking, 36, 38, 44, 128, 139
small economies, 27–8, 37, 40, 146
Smoot-Hawley Tariff Act, 82
Snyder, Richard, 13
special and differential treatment, 118
state intervention, economy, 41–3, 139
steel industry, 41, 91, 102, 103, 106, 127
Structural adjustments, 58, 59, 60, 87
structuralism, 52–5, 57, 122
Summers, Lawrence, 90

Summit of the Americas
  Mar del Plata (2005), 45
  Miami (1994), 32–4
  Quebec (2001), 41–2
  Santiago (1998), 38–9
Super 301, 89–90

tariff law, U.S. (1789), 82
technopols, 59
terms of trade, 54
three-track approach, 43
Tokyo Round, 84
Trade Acts, 85, 103
trade and aid, 24, 98, 102
trade as carrot, 26, 104
trade dependence, 23, 27, 28, 30, 54, 57, 61, 69, 71, 73, 145
trade promotion authority, 102–3, 105
trade regionalism, 5–7, 11–12, 24, 27, 51–63, 66, 101, 119, 120, 123, 143–7
transnational corporations, 56, 57, 84, 122
Treaty of Tlatelolco, 125
Treaty on the Non-Proliferation of Nuclear Weapons, 125
Truman, Henry S., 95
Tussie, Diana, 26–7
two-level game, 14
Tyson, Laura D'Andrea, 90

UN Security Council, 104, 137
UNASUL (Union of South American Nations), 110
uncertainty and international negotiations, 11, 13, 15, 35, 62, 65, 86, 128
UNCTAD (United Nations Trade and Development Conference), 54, 118
unilateral trade liberalization, 24, 60, 87, 120
unilateral trade preferences, 27, 103
unilateralism, 42, 67, 80, 86, 91, 99, 101–2, 108, 111, 130, 145

United States
  Brazil relations. *See* Brazil-U.S. bilateral cooperation
  Congress and trade, 40, 41, 67, 70, 74–5, 80–5, 91–2, 95–106
  Democrats, 40, 82–4, 95–7, 101–2
  exports to Latin America, 25, 39, 46, 69–70, 71, 87, 98
  foreign policy, Latin America, 66, 67
  foreign trade policy system, 80–2
  free trade agreements, **105**. *See also individual names*
  House Ways and Means Committee, 81, 88
  opinion polls, 91, 95
  Republicans, 82–4, 95, 96, 102, 106
  Senate Finance Committee, 81
Universalism, 117, 124
Uruguay, **25**, 28, 44, 51, 62, 126
Uruguay Round, 24, 33, 35, 39, 61, 70, 72, 85, 87, 88, 91, 93, 95, 97, 123
USTR (Office of the United States Trade Representative), 33, 40, 80–2, 85, 88, 96, 103, 104

Venezuela, 12, **25**, 42, 46, 134
Vigevani, Tullo, 128–9
Viner, Jacob, 54

war against terror, 41, 103, 105
Washington Consensus, 45, 52, 59
Watson, Alexander, 99
Western democracies, 4, 14
Western Hemisphere idea, 66
Wolfowitz, Paul, 101
Workers' Party (Brazil), ideology, 131, 139–40, 146
World Bank, 57, 72, 83
WTO-plus, 35, 36, 42, 94

Zoellick, Robert, 41, 43
  effects on the FTAA, 104, 106, 107
  Republican foreign policy agenda, 100–2

GPSR Compliance

The European Union's (EU) General Product Safety Regulation (GPSR) is a set of rules that requires consumer products to be safe and our obligations to ensure this.

If you have any concerns about our products, you can contact us on

ProductSafety@springernature.com

In case Publisher is established outside the EU, the EU authorized representative is:

Springer Nature Customer Service Center GmbH
Europaplatz 3
69115 Heidelberg, Germany